The easy success of National Social "coordination" of German lawyers in private practice in 1933 has puzzled historians. Within five months, a profession that had been considered a bulwark of civil society bowed to the demands of a party whose leader viewed lawyers with contempt and valued race over right. In this volume, Kenneth F. Ledford argues that the quiet surrender of the German bar can be understood only in the context of the history of the German *Bürgertum,* of German liberalism and the doctrine of the *Rechsstaat,* and of the private legal profession. He concludes that exaggerated expectations for the legal profession in public life exposed the limitations of procedural liberalism, with tragic consequences for Germany.

From General Estate to Special Interest

From General Estate to Special Interest
German Lawyers 1878–1933

Kenneth F. Ledford
Case Western Reserve University

CAMBRIDGE
UNIVERSITY PRESS

Published by the Press Syndicate of the University of Cambridge
The Pitt Building, Trumpington Street, Cambridge CB2 1RP
40 West 20th Street, New York, NY 10011–4211, USA
10 Stamford Road, Oakleigh, Melbourne 3166, Australia

First published 1996

Printed in the United States of America

Library of Congress Cataloging-in-Publication Data

Ledford, Kenneth F.
  From general estate to special interest : German lawyers 1878–1933
/ Kenneth F. Ledford.
     p.   cm.
  Includes bibliographical references.
  ISBN 0-521-56031-4 (hc)
  1. Practice of law – Germany – History.   2. Practice of law –
Political aspects – Germany – History.   3. Practice of law – Social
aspects – Germany – History.   4. Lawyers – Germany – History.
KK3789.A65L43   1996
340′.115′0943 – dc20   95-44521
                                                                      CIP

A catalog record for this book is available from the British Library

ISBN   0-521-56031-4 Hardback

For Susan

Contents

Illustrations

Hierarchy of Courts
District of the Court of Appeal at Celle

SUPERIOR COURT AURICH
9 District Courts

Aurich
Berum
Emden
Esens
Leer
Norden
Weener
Wilhelmshaven
Wittmund

SUPERIOR COURT GÖTTINGEN
12 District Courts

Duderstadt
Einbeck
Gieboldehausen
Göttingen
Herzberg am Harz
Moringen
Münden (Hannoversch-Münden)
Northeim
Osterode am Harz
Reinhausen
Uslar
Zellerfeld

SUPERIOR COURT HANNOVER
16 District Courts

Burgwedel
Calenburg
Coppenbrügge

Hameln
Hannover
Lauenstein
Münder
Neustadt am Rübenberg
Obernkirchen
Hessisch-Oldendorf
Polle
Rinteln
Rodenberg
Springe
Wennigsen
Bad Pyrmont

SUPERIOR COURT HILDESHEIM
11 District Courts

Alfeld
Bockenem
Burgdorf
Elze
Fallersleben
Gifhorn
Goslar
Hildesheim
Liebenburg
Meinersen
Peine

SUPERIOR COURT LÜNEBURG
12 District Courts

Bergen bei Celle
Bleckede

Celle	Freiburg an der Elbe
Dannenberg	Harburg
Isenhagen	Jork
Lüchow	Neuhaus
Lüneburg	Osten
Medingen	Otterndorf
Neuhaus	Stade
Soltau	Tostedt
Ülzen	Zeven
Winsen	

SUPERIOR COURT OSNABRÜCK	COURT OF APPEAL VERDEN
16 District Courts	*21 District Courts*

Bentheim	
Bersenbrück	Achim
Diepholz	Ahlden
Freren	Bassum
Fürstenau	Blumenthal
Iburg	Bruchhausen
Lingen	Dorum
Malgarten	Geestemünde
Melle	Hagen
Meppen	Hoya
Neu enhaus	Lehe
Osnabrück	Lesum
Papenburg	Lilenthal
Quakenbrück	Nienburg
Sögel	Osterholz
Wittlage	Rotenburg
	Stolzenau

SUPERIOR COURT STADE	Sulingen
11 District Courts	Syke
	Uchte
Bremervörde	Verden
Buxtehude	Walsrode

Glossary of Legal and Other Terms

Advokatur (*Advokat*, *-en*): "Advocates"; after the reception of the Roman law, the "higher branch" of the private legal profession, usually *not* appointed to a particular court, unlimited in number, and usually requiring university legal training.

Anwaltskammer: "Lawyers' chamber"; the institution of self-government and self-discipline sought by reform-minded lawyers from the 1830s and incorporated into the Lawyers' Statute (*Rechtsanwaltsordnung*) of 1878.

Anwaltstag: "Lawyers' convention"; the national convention of the *Deutscher Anwaltverein*, generally held biennially.

Anwaltsverein: "Lawyers' association"; a voluntary bar association.

Anwaltszwang: "Mandatory representation by a lawyer"; the requirement under the code of civil procedure that a party to a civil case *must* be represented by a lawyer. This rule pertained only before collegial (higher) courts under the reforms of 1877–9.

Arbeitsgericht: "Labor court," with jurisdiction over all employer-employee disputes in employment matters, enacted in 1926. The law excluded lawyers from representing parties before these courts. These courts, and the exclusion of lawyers, had been presaged by the trade courts (*Gewerbegerichte*) of 1890 and the commercial employment courts (*Kaufmannsgerichte*) of 1904.

Assessor: "Judicial candidate"; one who has passed the second state bar examination but not yet entered the judiciary or the private bar.

Assistenzrat: "Assistance counsellor"; the judicial office created by the reform of Frederick II in Prussia in 1781 to replace private lawyers in the representation of parties.

Bagatellsachen: Petty civil cases, involving small claims.

Beamter: "State official"; a civil servant with an academic, often university, education, who possessed tenure in his position. A status that conferred high prestige.

Deutscher Anwaltverein: "German Bar Association"; the national, voluntary bar association for German lawyers in private practice, founded in 1871.

Deutscher Juristentag: "German Jurists' Convention"; a national voluntary association for all persons trained in the law, founded in 1860.

Ehrengericht: "Disciplinary panel"; literally "court of honor." Elected by the executive board of each lawyers' chamber to hear and decide disciplinary cases.

Ehrengerichtshof: "Supreme disciplinary court"; the supreme disciplinary panel, seated at Leipzig and composed of judges and lawyers from the Imperial supreme court there. The court of last resort for lawyers' disciplinary cases.

Erste Staatsprüfung: First state bar examination. Also called *Referendarprüfung*. Taken by candidates immediately after completion of university studies. Successful candidates then entered the period of practical legal training, the *Referendariat*.

Freie Advokatur: The principle of free entry into the bar for all candidates who proved themselves qualified by passing both bar examinations.

Gebührenordnung für Rechtsanwälte: "Fees Statute for Lawyers"; the law of 1879 that regulated the remuneration of lawyers for courtroom representation.

Gerichtsverfassungsgesetz: "Constitution of the Courts"; the law of 1877 that created the unified imperial system of courts and set out the qualifications for service as a judge.

Gewerbefreiheit: "Freedom of occupation"; the principle whereby ancient guild privileges were abolished in the 1860s.

Großdeutsch: "Big German"; the solution to the question of German unification which would have *included* the German, or even all, the lands of the Habsburgs. Always an anti-Prussian, often a pro-Austrian, sentiment.

Große Staatsprüfung: "Great state bar examination"; the second state bar examination, taken after completion of the period of practical legal training (*Referendariat*). Successful candidates became *Assessoren* and were qualified to serve as judges, for appointment to permanent judicial positions, and to enter the private bar.

Gutachten: "Advisory opinion."

Juristen: "Jurists"; the broadest conception of lawyer in German, including all persons trained in the law, including judges, academics, all state officials with legal degrees, and lawyers in private practice.

Justizkommissar: "Justice commissar"; the civil-servant-like position created in 1793 to provide representation to parties in court cases in Prussia after the failure of the abolition of the bar in 1781. The title for all lawyers in private practice in Prussia until 1847.

Kleindeutsch: "Small German"; the solution to the question of German unification which would have excluded all possessions of the Habsburgs. A pro-Prussian sentiment.

Mündlichkeit: "Oral civil procedure"; a legal reform, based upon French procedure, which transferred the emphasis given by civil procedure from the written pleadings to oral argument. It allowed for more liberality in amending arguments and raised in importance the forensic skills of eloquence and quick thinking on the part of the lawyer.

Numerus clausus: A maximum, a cap, on the number of persons who could pursue a trade or profession.

Öffentlichkeit: "Publicity"; a principle of civil procedure reform, based upon the French model, which established the openness of court hearings to the public. A concomitant of *Mündlichkeit*, it had the effect of placing the forensic skills of the lawyer in the public spotlight.

Prokuratur (Prokurator, -en): "Procurators"; after the reception of the Roman law, the "lower branch" of the private legal profession, appointed to a particular court, limited in number, and often without any university legal training.

Prorogation: "Agreed-upon jurisdiction"; a device whereby district court lawyers could retain representation in cases that exceeded the jurisdictional limit of district courts.

Rechtsanwalt (Rechtsanwälte, Rechtsanwaltschaft, Rechtsanwaltstand): "Lawyer in private practice"; "bar in private practice"; "practicing bar." A *Jurist* who, upon passing the second bar examination and becoming an *Assessor*, decided to leave the judicial service and enter the free profession of the private practice of law. Combined the functions both of *Advokat* and *Prokurator*.

Rechtsanwaltsordnung: "Lawyers' Statute"; adopted in 1878, one of the four imperial justice laws of 1877–9 that determined the framework for the private practice of law until 1933.

Rechtskonsulenten (Winkelkonsulenten, Prozeßagenten): "Lay practitioners"; nonacademically trained practitioners who could, when the courts permitted, represent parties for a fee before district courts.

Referendar: "Legal trainee"; a person who had passed the first state bar examination and was in the period of unpaid practical legal training (*Referendariat*) before he could sit for the second bar examination.

Stand: "Estate"; a social group identification based upon ascribed characteristics and status rather than wealth. A member of a *Stand* possessed, or was expected to possess, corporate (*ständisch*) values, those peculiar to his group and which set it off from other social groups. Members of a *Stand* expected themselves and other members of the group to conduct themselves in a *standesgemäß* fashion, in accordance with the dignity of their estate.

Syndikus: "Salaried lawyer"; a lawyer in a salaried employment relationship with a municipality, association, or private business company.

Vereinigung der Vorstände der Deutschen Anwaltskammern: "Association of Executive Boards of German Lawyers' Chambers"; an umbrella organization of the various lawyers' chambers founded in 1907.

Vertreter- (Abgeordeneten-)versammlung: "Representatives' assembly"; an organ of the German Bar Association (DAV), created in 1909 to provide for representation of the membership between lawyers' conventions.

Vorstand: "Executive board"; the organ of lawyers' chambers which conducted the business of the institution between plenary meetings of the membership.

Zivilprozeßordnung: "Code of Civil Procedure"; the law of 1877 which created a uniform civil procedure in the empire and adopted the principles of *Mündlichkeit* and *Öffentlichkeit*.

Zweigvereine: "Branch associations."

Abbreviations

AcP	*Archiv für die civilistische Praxis*
AG	Amtsgericht
DAV	Deutscher Anwaltverein
DJZ	*Deutsche Juristen-Zeitung*
ES	Max Weber, *Economy and Society*
GOfRA	Gebührenordnung für Rechtsanwälte
G.St.A.	Geheimes Staatsarchiv, Preußischer Kulturbesitz, Berlin-Dahlem
GVG	Gerichtsverfassungsgesetz
JW	*Juristische Wochenschrift*
LG	Landgericht
N.H.St.A.	Niedersächsisches Hauptstaatsarchiv
OLG	Oberlandesgericht
OLGP	Oberlandesgerichtspräsident
PJM	Preußisches Justizministerium
RAO	Rechtsanwaltsordnung
RJM	Reichsjustizministerium
StPO	Strafprozeßordnung
ZPO	Zivilprozeßordnung

Preface

This is a book about German lawyers in private practice, but it is also an effort to address larger questions about the social and political history of Germany between the middle of the nineteenth century and the National Socialist seizure of power in 1933. It traces the history of German lawyers from the heady days of legal and professional reform in 1878 to their abject defeat in a quiet and swift "coordination" in the spring of 1933. In the 1870s, lawyers could bask in the widespread liberal assessment of their profession as a sort of Hegelian "general estate," representing the general interest and the common good and entitled to respect, deference, and leadership. Opinion leaders believed that reform of the legal profession formed the touchstone of success in the project of the liberal *Bürgertum* to bring into existence its chief goal of the *Rechtsstaat*, the state ruled by law. Lawyers and liberals achieved almost all of their aims for the legal profession in 1878, carving out space for the bar to create its own institutions, to govern its internal affairs, and to assume the important public role that theory ascribed to it.

But developments between 1878 and 1933 did not turn out the way that either the liberal reformers, most of whom were legally trained and many of whom were private practitioners, or professional leaders of the bar expected. Reform of the structure of the profession upset the old balance by attracting new social groups to the practice of law and by creating inchoate cleavages that emerged as the bar expanded. Professional institutions, structured along lines typical for the *Bürgertum*, for liberalism, and for the "bourgeois public sphere," predicated upon deference and unity, became the terrain of intra-professional power struggles. Lawyers also suffered the same fate as the liberal parties, as the growth of the mass electorate eliminated their leading role in national politics and threatened to erode it as well at the local level. By the 1920s, the argument was no longer tenable that lawyers were the "general estate," entitled to deference and respect. The organized bar was merely one of many special interests in a society and state that to increasing numbers of Germans appeared dangerously fragmented. Indeed, the bar no longer represented even a single special interest but was rather itself riven into multiple special interests that struggled to control its institutions. By 1933, at least in the minds of lawyers, the practicing bar had completed the decline, real or imagined, from "general estate" to special interest.

This book originated in the mid-1980s out of my dissatisfaction with the comparative neglect of both the *Bürgertum* and the law in the historiography of modern Germany. Despite repeated characterizations of the nineteenth century as the "bourgeois century" in Europe, social historians of Germany have not carefully investigated the *Bürgertum* until quite recently.[1] Moreover, despite Franz Schnabel's injunction that the nineteenth century was the "century of the formal *Rechtsstaat*," and despite the emphasis that social theory has placed on the centrality of law and lawyers for social analysis, historians of the German *Kaiserreich* have paid surprisingly little attention to law and lawyers.[2]

Neglect of the social history of the *Bürgertum* seemed particularly glaring because of the important role ascribed to its "failure" to fulfill its historic mission by the *Sonderweg* ("special path") thesis of German history. Briefly stated, the *Sonderweg* thesis holds that Germany followed a special path that culminated in the crimes of the National Socialist era because the *Bürgertum* failed to assume the leading role in politics and society that it should have. It failed to appropriate, inter-

1   "As much as the nineteenth century is characterized as the '*bürgerlich*' century, the *Bürgertum* of the nineteenth century must be counted among the lesser-researched social groups"; Werner Conze and Jürgen Kocka, "Einleitung," in idem, eds., *Bildungsbürgertum im 19. Jahrhundert. Teil I: Bildungssystem und Professionalisierung im internationalen Vergleich* (Stuttgart, 1985), 9–26, 9, and Charles E. McClelland, "Zur Professionalisierung der akademischen Berufe in Deutschland," ibid., 233–47, 233. An older attempt at continental synthesis is Charles Morazé, *The Triumph of the Middle Classes. A Study of European Values in the Nineteenth Century* (Cleveland and New York, 1967).

2   Franz Schnabel, *Deutsche Geschichte im neunzehnten Jahrhundert*, 4 vols. (Freiburg i. Br., 1929–37; repr. ed. Frankfurt, 1988), III:v. Michael John recently detailed the shortcomings of the standard textbooks on German history; Michael John, *Politics and the Law in Late Nineteenth-Century Germany: The Origins of the Civil Code* (Oxford, 1989), 2. More recent texts move toward rectifying prior neglect; impressive treatments of substantive law, especially the background to the *Bürgerliches Gesetzbuch* and the growth of legal positivism, are found in Thomas Nipperdey, *Deutsche Geschichte 1866-1918*, vol. 1, *Arbeitswelt und Bürgergeist* (Munich, 1990), 655–65, and vol. 2, *Machtstaat vor der Demokratie* (Munich, 1992), 193–201.

nalize, and realize liberal ideas of parliamentary democracy and the market economy. Instead, it lacked self-assurance and depth of commitment to individual rights and splintered into conflicting interest groups when it was confronted on the one hand by a tough and authoritarian imperial government, dedicated to the preservation of the traditional hegemony of the east-Elbian *Junkertum*, and on the other by an apparently dynamic working-class Social Democratic Party.[3]

The *Sonderweg* thesis came under sharp criticism in the 1980s as a "new orthodoxy" that was based upon an inaccurate theoretical model of development of the English constitution, middle class, and liberalism. David Blackbourn and Geoff Eley suggested that the German legal system after 1871 provided evidence of the success of the German *Bürgertum* in establishing its ideology of the *Rechtsstaat* as part of the fundamental character of the *Kaiserreich*, in accomplishing a "bourgeois revolution from above," in which it achieved the political and economic system needed to sustain capitalist development in Germany.[4] The thrust of the criticism also was to draw the attention of scholars to forms of *bürgerlich* expression other than the pursuit of parliamentary power and to refocus attention upon law, the legal order, and legal practitioners.[5]

---

3   Perhaps the most forceful formulation of the *Sonderweg* thesis is the synthetic textbook, Hans-Ulrich Wehler, *Das deutsche Kaiserreich 1871–1918* (Göttingen, 1973). Wehler of course did not originate the thesis, which sought the roots of National Socialism in the structures of society, economy, and politics during the *Kaiserreich*; he was strongly influenced by Hans Rosenberg, *Bureaucracy, Aristocracy and Autocracy: The Prussian Experience 1660–1815* (Cambridge, Mass., 1958), idem, *Große Depression und Bismarckzeit. Wirtschaftsablauf, Gesellschaft und Politik in Mitteleuropa* (Berlin, 1967), and Ralf Dahrendorf, *Society and Democracy in Germany* (New York, 1967; originally published in German as *Gesellschaft und Demokratie in Deutschland* [Munich, 1965]). The theme of the continued political power and social dominance of aristocratic preindustrial elites over the emergent middle class was generalized to all of Europe in Arno J. Mayer, *The Persistence of the Old Regime: Europe to the Great War* (New York, 1981), esp. ch. 2, "The Ruling Classes: The Bourgeoisie Defers," 79–127.

4   David Blackbourn, "The Discreet Charm of the Bourgeoisie: Reappraising German History in the Nineteenth Century," in David Blackbourn and Geoff Eley, *The Peculiarities of German History: Bourgeois Society and Politics in Nineteenth Century Germany* (Oxford, 1984), 157–292, 190–5.

5   Thoughtful review articles that detail the history of the debate include: Konrad H. Jarausch, "Illiberalism and Beyond: German History in Search of a Paradigm," *Journal of Modern History* 55 (1983): 268–84; James N. Retallack, "Social History with a Vengeance? Some Reactions to H.-U. Wehler's 'Das Deutsche Kaiserreich," *German Studies Review* 7 (1984): 423–50; Roger Fletcher, "Recent Developments in West German Historiography: The Bielefeld School and Its Critics," *German Studies Review* 7 (1984): 451–80; Robert G. Moeller, "The Kaiserreich Recast? Continuity and Change in Modern German Historiography," *Journal of Social History* 17 (1984): 655–83; Jürgen Kocka, "German History before Hitler: The Debate about the German *Sonderweg*," *Journal of Contemporary History* 23 (1988): 3–16. See more recently William W. Hagan, "Descent of the *Sonderweg*: Hans Rosenberg's

The contours of the *Sonderweg* debate revealed two shortcomings in the existing historical literature that treated the German *Bürgertum*. First, most historians treated the *Bürgertum* as an abstract category with ascribed behaviors and roles. Whether they drew their inspiration from Marxist or modernization theories, prior investigators believed that there was a way the German *Bürgertum ought* to have acted, and they interpreted failure so to act as failure to fulfill the historical social and political mission of that social group. This methodological certainty led, with few exceptions, to the second shortcoming: namely that there were few empirical studies of the development of the German *Bürgertum* or of any of its most important components over the course of the nineteenth and early twentieth centuries. The second half of the 1980s thus saw the emergence of a new research focus upon the *Bürgertum* as researchers found the existing literature inadequate.[6] Beginning with a massive research project inaugurated in 1984 at Bielefeld, this new focus has begun to bear fruit.[7]

History of Old-Regime Prussia," *Central European History* 24 (1991): 24–50. An insightful and persuasive essay that also points to a way out of the *Sonderweg* debate is Konrad H. Jarausch and Larry Eugene Jones, "German Liberalism Reconsidered: Inevitable Decline, Bourgeois Hegemony, or Partial Achievement," in idem, eds., *In Search of a Liberal Germany. Studies in the History of German Liberalism from 1789 to the Present* (New York, Oxford, and Munich, 1990), 1–23, which reviews the historiography of German liberalism and calls for a focus upon specific tensions within the German liberal tradition instead of a formulaic opposition of success or failure.

Theodore S. Hamerow provides a wide-ranging interpretation of the modern historiography of Germany in "Guilt, Redemption, and Writing German History," *American Historical Review* 88 (1983): 53–72. Finally, the most comprehensive account of the complex history of the conception of a German *Sonderweg* apart from the historical path of western Europe is Helga Grebing, ed., *Der "deutsche Sonderweg" in Europa 1806–1945. Eine Kritik* (Stuttgart, 1986), especially 11–22 and 76–137. For a short description of this two-sided *Sonderweg* tradition, see Jürgen Kocka, "Bürgertum und Bürgerlichkeit als Probleme der neueren Geschichte," in idem, ed., *Bürger und Bürgerlichkeit im 19. Jahrhundert* (Göttingen, 1987), 21–63.

6 Much of the existing scholarship was limited to the *Bildungsbürgertum,* or educated middle class, was quite old, and was often based upon secondary, anecdotal, or literary evidence; see for example Hans H. Gerth, *Bürgerliche Intelligenz um 1800: Zur Soziologie des deutschen Frühliberalismus* (Göttingen, 1976; originally published as an *Habilitationsschrift* under the title *Die sozialgeschichtliche Lage der bürgerlichen Intelligenz um die Wende des 18. Jahrhunderts* in 1935); W. H. Bruford, *Germany in the Eighteenth Century: The Social Background of the Literary Revival* (Cambridge, 1935); and Ernest K. Bramsted, *Aristocracy and the Middle Classes in Germany: Social Types in German Literature 1830–1900* (Chicago, 1964; originally published in 1937). Some exemplary works and suggestive collections existed in isolation: Hansjoachim Henning, *Das westdeutsche Bürgertum in der Epoche der Hochindustrialisierung 1860–1914. Soziales Verhalten und soziale Strukturen. Teil I: Das Bildungsbürgertum in den preußischen Westprovinzen* (Wiesbaden, 1972); and Klaus Vondung, ed., *Das wilhelminische Bildungsbürgertum. Zur Sozialgeschichte seiner Ideen* (Göttingen, 1976).

7 The Center for Interdisciplinary Research at the University of Bielefeld inaugurated the project "Social History of the Modern *Bürgertum*: Germany in International Comparison,"

Secondly, scholars from the Bielefeld project, and also scholars in the United States, have pursued another approach to the study of the German *Bürgertum* that has produced a number of important works in the last half-decade: the history of professions and professionalization. These studies have gone some distance toward remedying laments about the neglect of the social history of the learned professions and in adding the handiwork of the social historian to that of the sociologist.[8] In doing so, these historical studies have had to carve out space within the discourse of professionalization to permit examination of the professions in the circumstances of central Europe during the nineteenth century.[9]

One problem with most older sociological models of professionalization was the overwhelming preponderance of Anglo-American professions as the sample cases for formulating the theory.[10] The necessary result of the focus upon the organic development of the professions in England and the United States, especially the "classic" free professions of law, medicine, and the clergy, was an emphasis upon the autonomy and independence of professional development from guidance or interference by or dependence upon the state. Some sociologists therefore dismissed the process of professionalization on the continent *because* of the larger role there of

in 1984. Thus far, it has produced a number of useful volumes including Conze and Kocka, eds., *Bildungsbürgertum im 19. Jahrhundert;* Jürgen Kocka, ed., *Bürger und Bürgerlichkeit;* idem, *Bildungsbügertum im 19. Jahrhundert. Teil IV: Politischer Einfluß und gesellschaftliche Formation* (Stuttgart, 1989), and idem, ed., *Bürgertum im 19. Jahrhundert. Deutschland im europäischen Vergleich*, 3 vols. (Munich, 1988). Some of the essays in this latter work have been translated in Jürgen Kocka and Allan Mitchell, eds., *Bourgeois Society in Nineteenth-Century Europe* (Oxford and Providence, 1993).

8 Wilfred R. Prest, "Preface," and "Introduction: The Professions and Society in Early Modern England," in idem, ed., *The Professions in Early Modern England* (London, 1987), 1–24, 2, 4.

9 Geoffrey Cocks and Konrad H. Jarausch, eds., *German Professions, 1800–1950* (New York and Oxford, 1990); Konrad H. Jarausch, *The Unfree Professions. German Lawyers, Teachers, and Engineers, 1900–1950* (Oxford, 1990); and Charles E. McClelland, *The German Experience of Professionalization. Modern Learned Professions and their Organizations from the Early Nineteenth Century to the Hitler Era* (Cambridge, 1991). The Bielefeld project has not neglected the study of the professions; see the issue of *Geschichte und Gesellschaft* 6 (1980) devoted to "*Professionalisierung,*" and especially Hannes Siegrist, ed., *Bürgerliche Berufe. Zur Sozialgeschichte der freien und akademischen Berufe im internationalen Vergleich* (Göttingen, 1988).

10 From the very beginning of the functionalist analysis of the professionals, the background and evidence upon which the theorists drew was Anglo-American. A. M. Carr-Saunders and P. A. Wilson, *The Professions* (Oxford, 1933); Talcott Parsons, "The Professions and Social Structure," in idem, *Essays in Sociological Theory*, rev. ed. (New York, 1954), 34–49. For a criticism of this "parochialism," see Dietrich Rueschemeyer, *Lawyers and their Society: A Comparative Study of the Legal Profession in Germany and the United States* (Cambridge, Mass., 1973), 14–15.

the state. One of the leading theorists in the field argued that the legal profession in Prussia conformed more to the civil service model than to the market-oriented free professions of England and the United States and declined to examine it further.[11] Another scholar, however, after a well-grounded historical analysis of the legal profession in Germany, concluded that the "professionalization from above" of lawyers in Germany, in the sense of the strong and continued role of the state even after the establishment of a "modern" footing for the profession in 1879, resulted in a mixture of the civil servant model with both the traditional and the modern independent forms of professions.[12]

Yet the theory puzzled out in the Anglo-American context has provided vital tools for analysis of the professions in Germany.[13] The older functionalist sociological approach stressed the "silent contract" between the profession and the consumers of the professional service, whereby the latter traded trust, high income, and high prestige to the members of the profession in return for high ethical standards, trustworthiness, qualification, and diligence, guaranteed by a long and rigorous education and by a strict system of self-discipline and self-government. The newer structuralist approach views the "professional project" as a process in which the profession establishes market control, thereby securing high income and social status, safe from the vagaries of the marketplace. Although minimizing the development of the professions on the continent because of the more

11 Magali Sarfatti Larson, *The Rise of Professionalism: A Sociological Analysis* (Berkeley and Los Angeles, 1977), xvii–xviii, excluded German lawyers from her analysis because "[T]he Prussian legal profession was reformed by direct and repeated state intervention and remains to this day closely supervised and regulated by the state; . . . The model of professions should be closer in these cases to that of the civil service than it is to professions in England or, especially, in the United States."

12 Hannes Siegrist, "Gebremste Professionalisierung – Das Beispiel der Schweizer Rechtsanwaltschaft im Vergleich zu Frankreich und Deutschland im 19. und frühen 20. Jahrhundert," in Conze and Kocka, eds., *Bildungsbürgertum im 19. Jahrhundert*, 301–31, 312, 329 (in English as idem, "Professionalization with the Brakes On: The Legal Profession in Switzerland, France and Germany in the Nineteenth and Early Twentieth Centuries," *Comparative Social Research* 9 [1986]: 267–98). For a discussion of the traditional and modern patterns of professionalization, see Albert L. Mok, "Alte und neue Professionen," *Kölner Zeitschrift für Soziologie und Sozialpsychologie* 21 (1969): 770–82. Konrad H. Jarausch argued that lawyers are the free profession in Germany that comes closest to the Anglo-American pattern of professionalization. Konrad H. Jarausch, "The Crisis of German Professions 1918–33," *Journal of Contemporary History* 20 (1985): 379–98, 380.

13 A helpful summary of the theoretical literature of professionalization is contained in Richard L. Abel, *American Lawyers* (New York and Oxford, 1989), 14–39. This study questions how "professionalized" the American bar, often held out as the paradigmatic profession, ever was.

salient role of the state, this emphasis upon the professions' use of state sanctions to enforce their claims to market control actually *advances* the examination of professions in Germany. It brings the state back into the analysis.[14] It shows that professions strove for hegemony in their markets, invoking state power to help secure their goals for themselves. By bringing the state back in, the theory can be applied with greater ease to the German context.[15] The recent examination of the professions in Germany has led to the conclusion that the state official model was in fact the central paradigm for professions in central Europe, and that involvement with the state in no way contradicts the professional project.[16]

The recent professionalization studies help to provide a framework for the investigation of lawyers in private practice. By accepting a central European ethos of profession, "the German concept of profession" as *Berufsstand* with its inner vocation, they move beyond earlier limitations that stressed complete autonomy from the state and turn the researcher's attention to the inner workings of professional institutions in Germany. They direct attention to the importance of professional unity to the success of the group in working its corporate will upon members and upon the market for its services.[17] Finally, they point to the interactions between professional politics and the politics of professionals. Thus they serve as a jumping-off point for an in-depth examination of the inner working of the bar in private practice that seeks the links between the professional project and the middle class project.

The third consequence of the reexamination of the German *Bürgertum* prompted by the *Sonderweg* debate has been a reawakened awareness of the importance of Schnabel's emphasis upon the role of law in the history of Germany in the nineteenth century. A number of

---

14 The central work here is Peter B. Evans, Dietrich Rueschemeyer, and Theda Skocpol, eds., *Bringing the State Back In* (Cambridge, 1985).

15 Larson, *The Rise of Professionalism*, 14–15, 53. See Dietrich Rueschemeyer, "Professionalisierung. Theoretische Probleme für die vergleichende Geschichtsforschung," *Geschichte und Gesellschaft* 6 (1980): 311–25, 317; Conze and Kocka, "Einleitung," 20; and McClelland, "Zur Professionalisierung," 241–2. McClelland also develops this argument explicitly in *German Experience of Professionalization*, 7.

16 McClelland, *German Experience of Professionalization*, 33, 109, 127; this point is also made in Jane Caplan, "Profession as Vocation: The German Civil Service," in Cocks and Jarausch, eds., *German Professions, 1800–1950*, 163–82.

17 For an account of a German profession that failed to attain organizational unity, see Kees Gispen, *New Profession, Old Order: Engineers and German Society, 1815–1914* (Cambridge, 1989), as well as Jarausch, *The Unfree Professions*, 22, and McClelland, *German Experience of Professionalization*, 91–4.

reasons exist to explain why social historians had neglected law as an historical artifact. Legal history in Germany has long been the almost exclusive domain of the legal faculties, and legal historians have directed their inquiry toward narrow technical examinations of legal doctrine and institutions, producing few contributions to social history more broadly defined.[18] The complexity of legal issues makes it a daunting task for the social or political historian to place legal reform in context. The study of legal procedure can be as dry as dust, and its rewards are not always obvious. Thus, institutional separation and intellectual arcaneness have reinforced one another with the result that historians have neglected law as a source for their analysis of the social history of the *Bürgertum*.

Recent work has used a focus on law to transcend the sterile polarities of the *Sonderweg* debate and to focus attention upon the power of law, legal thought, and the legal profession to frame the discourse surrounding social and political options in nineteenth-century Germany. Michael John has examined the debates surrounding the great codification of substantive civil law between 1873 and 1896 to argue convincingly that there are limits to the claim that the *Bürgertum* established its hegemony and politics through legal reform. He concludes that the Civil Law Code did not so much establish a comprehensive, bourgeois, capitalist system of law as defer leadership to the narrow and technical vision of professional lawyers and legal scholars and postpone debate and decision in legal areas of ideological or economic-interest contention. Thus, this long sought-after victory of the liberal *Bürgertum* contained within it evidence of the limits of German liberalism.[19]

Similarly, James Q. Whitman has shown how the vocabulary of Roman law, which had supported the emergence of the absolutist state since the reception in the fifteenth and sixteenth centuries, after the Napoleonic Wars coincided with the values of liberalism both to advance the political cause of the *Rechtsstaat* and the social cause of the *Bürgertum*.[20] Serving as a means both of obtaining certainty and pre-

18 For a comment upon the narrow nature of German legal history periodicals, see Michael John, "The Peculiarities of the German State: Bourgeois Law and Society in the Imperial Era," *Past and Present* 119 (May 1988): 105–31, 106.

19 John, *Politics and the Law*, 241–57; the essentials of John's argument are also found in idem, "The Politics of Legal Unity in Germany, 1870–1897," *Historical Journal* 28 (1985): 341–55, and idem, "The Peculiarities of the German State."

20 James Q. Whitman, *The Legacy of Roman Law in the German Romantic Era* (Princeton, N.J., 1990). See also the thoughtful review essay discussing both John and Whitman, David J.

dictability and of justifying and securing power, Roman law benefited university-trained legal graduates, especially university law professors, but increasingly other legally-trained persons as well.

The past decade, therefore, has seen an efflorescence of creative work from the direction of studies of the *Bürgertum*, of professions, and of legal reforms and legal idea-systems. I seek in this book to contribute to all of those developing literatures. But lawyers are more than simply a constituent part of the *Bürgertum* or a model profession. Lawyers in private practice stood on the cusp or at the convergence of uniquely important trends of social development and thought in the middle of the nineteenth century. First, training as lawyers instilled in them a reverence for procedure, for values of uniformity, regularity, and certainty in decision making, values that form the basis both of the "rule of law" and of the German conception of the *Rechtsstaat*. These were values too that were central both to political liberalism and to capitalism.[21] So lawyers in Germany were drawn, seemingly irresistibly, to liberalism. Second, liberals in mid-nineteenth-century Germany viewed lawyers in private practice as the crucial social bearers of change toward a liberal polity and society in Germany. Referring explicitly to the English model, but drawing also on the native German model of the Hegelian "general estate," liberal theorists came to view lawyers, proudly independent, dispassionate, and nonpartisan, as representing the general interest, the common good, and hence as qualified to lead and instruct other citizens. Lawyers, already inclined toward the *Rechtsstaat* goals of liberalism, quite naturally embraced this notion of their high calling both before and after winning rights of professional self-governance and self-discipline in 1878.

But lawyers brought with them to this role of "general estate" inherent limitations of conceptual vision, professional structure, and social flexibility. The belief in the efficacy and primacy of procedures that their legal education imprinted upon them linked them with liberal theory but constrained their imagination and vocabulary of discourse as they faced the massive changes of 1878 to 1933. Lawyers built for themselves professional organizations that reflected liberal practice but which were elite institutions, grounded upon deference

Gerber, "Idea-Systems in Law: Images of Nineteenth-Century Germany," *Law and History Review* 10 (1992): 153–67.

21 Max Weber, *Economy and Society. An Outline of Interpretive Sociology*, ed. by Guenther Roth and Claus Wittich, 2 vols. (Berkeley and Los Angeles, 1978), II:883.

on the part of most practitioners toward elites who practiced before higher courts. These institutions also proved unable to cope with change. Finally, the influx of new social elements and new patterns of professional practice created social and economic tensions and frictions that eventually paralyzed professional institutions, rendering them unable to represent professional interests or even to maintain the claim that a unitary professional interest existed in the face of a less-friendly state between 1919 and 1933. Lawyers never became the general estate that some hoped; rather, they suffered from limits of conceptual vocabulary, institutional vision, and economic confidence. As a result, they increasingly conceived of themselves as an interest group in society, but they resented this conception for its disjunction with their original vision of a more central role. This trajectory, from general estate to special interest, explains their paralysis and inaction in 1933 more than any putative betrayal of liberalism or of professional ideals.

My book has three goals. First, it presents a detailed empirical study of the development of the practicing bar in Germany, both on the national level of legislative debate and reform and bar association politics, and through a case study of lawyers who practiced in the Prussian province (until 1866 the Kingdom) of Hannover between 1878 and 1933. This level of analysis provides new evidence about the behavior of a group of professionals whom most liberals thought to be crucial to the project of the *Bürgertum* and depicts the differential experience of lawyers as they coped with the tumultuous experience of economic and political change. The case study also explains with new insight the strategies pursued by lawyers within their own professional institutions.

Second, my study recaptures law and legal thinking as an historical artifact, as a suitable object of study for the social historian. This does not mean a return to dry and arcane study of legal doctrine. Rather, it recognizes that in modern societies law is so integral to the cultural workings of society and polity that a grasp of its meaning and of the behavior of its practitioners can help provide the key to decoding the social thought and goals of social actors. "It seems much more probable that the specific legal practices of a culture are simply dialects of a parent social speech and that studying that speech helps you to understand the dialect and vice-versa."[22] Understanding legal discourse

22   Robert W. Gordon, "Critical Legal Histories," *Stanford Law Review* 36 (1984): 57–125, 90.

helps historians understand broader social discourse, and understanding legal practitioners helps historians understand the behavior of the broader social group of the *Bürgertum*.

Third, my work uses these insights, the importance of law and its mediators and interpreters to social discourse in modern society and the importance of lawyers to the project of the *Bürgertum*, to expand the intersection of older and newer historiography on German liberalism with the newer focus on the *Bürgertum*.[23] Lawyers were critical to the project of the liberal *Bürgertum* as nineteenth-century theorists defined it; they and their methods and idea-systems are critical to liberal procedural emphasis upon the *Rechtsstaat*; and the proceduralism of liberal thought continues to frame debate in twentieth-century political philosophy.[24] Thus, a study of lawyers is uniquely well situated to interweave the histories of liberalism and the *Bürgertum* with insights gained more recently into the procedural character of liberalism. My goal is to show how lawyers' adaptations to their social, economic, political, and professional context within German society between 1878 and 1933 interwove their professional project with the larger project of the liberal *Bürgertum* and to show how legal forms, vocabularies, and idea-systems structured and shaped their spectrum of responses to changes around them.

The conclusion that this study reaches is that the very conceptual and organizational basis of the liberal expectations of lawyers contained the contradictions that led to the "failure" of lawyers in 1933. The proceduralism of both liberalism and legal thinking and the elite expectations and institutions of a "general estate" contributed to paralysis in the face of rival claimants of power who had clear substantive claims of "justice." Residual idealism about the high calling and the elevated ethical standards of professions, left over from functionalist

---

23 The standard work on the divergence of German liberal thought from that of western Europe is still Leonard Krieger, *The German Idea of Freedom: History of a Political Tradition* (Chicago, 1957); the newer and more liberated works on liberalism include James J. Sheehan, *German Liberalism in the Nineteenth Century* (Chicago, 1978); Dieter Langewiesche, *Liberalismus in Deutschland* (Frankfurt, 1988); and especially the essays contained in Jarausch and Jones, eds., *In Search of German Liberalism*.

24 The central work in renewing debate on a procedurally focused, deontological liberalism is John Rawls, *A Theory of Justice* (Oxford, 1971). For criticism of the proceduralism of this approach to liberal theory, see Michael J. Sandel, *Liberalism and the Limits of Justice* (Cambridge, 1982), 113–22; and idem, "The Procedural Republic and the Unencumbered Self," *Political Theory* 12 (1984): 81–96, reprinted in Shlomo Avineri and Avner de-Shalit, eds., *Communitarianism and Individualism* (Oxford, 1992), 12–28. See also the additional essays in the Avineri and de-Shalit volume and Michael J. Sandel, ed., *Liberalism and Its Critics* (New York, 1984).

sociological notions about the "silent contract" between professions and society, simply replicates in new form the normative expectations of nineteenth-century liberals. But it is not enough simply to conclude that German lawyers (and professions) were no worse than those of any other country. What historians must grasp is that lawyers in private practice were the wrong horse to bet on. Their organizational structure lacked imagination and representativeness; the power of the professional doctrine of independence atomized lawyers and blocked efforts at collective action; the statutory framework attained in 1879 and the changes in professional structure created by its interaction with economic transformation caused rifts within the bar that also blocked solidarity. Most importantly, the proceduralism of legal thought and training blocked lawyers from ever coalescing to protect any notion of substantive justice. Therein lies a greater message, not only for Germany but also for western society as a whole, about the efficacy of procedurally focused liberalism in time of crisis.

No comprehensive treatment of lawyers in their professional, political, economic, and social context during the Second Empire and Weimar Republic exists.[25] In addition to the perceptive analyses of

25 The historical literature on lawyers in other European countries is also sparse, but it is growing. Work on English lawyers in the modern period includes: Robert Robson, *The Attorney in Eighteenth Century England* (Cambridge, 1959); W. J. Reader, *Professional Men: The Rise of the Professional Classes in Nineteenth Century England* (London, 1966); Brian Abel-Smith and Robert Stevens, *Lawyers and the Courts: A Sociological Study of the English Legal System 1750–1965* (Cambridge, Mass., 1967); Raymond Cocks, *Foundations of the Modern Bar* (London, 1983); and Daniel Duman, *The English and Colonial Bars in the Nineteenth Century* (London, 1983). The early modern era for lawyers in England has begun to be explored in depth; in addition to the essays contained in the two volumes edited by Prest, see C. W. Brooks, *Pettyfoggers and Vipers of the Commonwealth: The "Lower Branch" of the Legal Profession in Early Modern England* (Cambridge, 1986), Wilfred R. Prest, *The Rise of the Barristers: A Social History of the English Bar 1590–1640* (Oxford, 1986), and idem, ed., *The Professions in Early Modern England* (London, 1987).
  Interestingly, no study of French lawyers during the nineteenth and twentieth centuries exists in English. The work that exists focuses upon the eighteenth century, the Revolution, and its immediate aftermath. See Philip Dawson, "The Bourgeoisie de Robe in 1789," *French Historical Studies* 4 (1965): 1–21; Lenard R. Berlanstein, *The Barristers of Toulouse in the Eighteenth Century (1740–1793)* (Baltimore, 1975); Michael P. Fitzsimmons, *The Parisian Order of Barristers and the French Revolution* (Cambridge, Mass., 1987); and Isser Woloch, "The Fall and Resurrection of the Civil Bar, 1789–1820s," *French Historical Studies* 15 (1987): 241–62. Most recently, see the perceptive book by David A. Bell, *Lawyers and Citizens: The Making of a Political Elite in Old Regime France* (Oxford, 1994), and idem, "Barristers, Politics, and the Failure of Civil Society in Old Régime France," in Terence Halliday and Lucien Karpik, eds., *Politics Matter: Lawyers and the Rise of Western Political Liberalism* (Oxford, forthcoming 1996). For a brief essay that describes the recent history of the French legal profession, see Anne Boigeol, "The French Bar: The Difficulties of Unifying a Divided Profession," in Richard L. Abel and Philip S. C. Lewis, eds.,

the professionalization of lawyers in the recent books by Konrad
Jarausch and Charles McClelland, the most important existing work
is an institutional history of the German legal profession by Fritz
Ostler, published in 1971 on the occasion of the one-hundredth anni-
versary of the founding of the German Bar Association (*Deutscher
Anwaltverein*, "DAV").[26] Ostler traced the institutional development
of the DAV, together with tensions within the bar caused by structural fissures created by that legal framework. His work provides a
clear and comprehensive account of the institutional development of
the bar, but he did little to place lawyers in the context of German
society as a whole. He built upon an older tradition of institutional
history of the bar, especially Adolf Weißler's sometimes quirky history of lawyers in Germany, published in 1905, which described at
length their primeval origins and the roles that they played under
both Germanic and received Roman law.[27]

Beginning in the 1960s, sociologists turned their attention to the
"personality" of lawyers in modern Germany. Taking a lead from
Ralf Dahrendorf's treatment of lawyers in *Society and Democracy*,
Wolfgang Kaupen and Dietrich Rueschemeyer attempted to understand the roles and attitudes of lawyers in contemporary German
society.[28] Both recounted the institutional history of lawyers in Germany, especially as it bore upon lawyers' attitudes in the Federal
Republic, but a social-historical exploration was not the focus of
either.[29] Finally, the recent reexamination of the *Bürgertum* and of the

Lawyers in Society, 3 vols. (Berkeley and Los Angeles, 1988), vol. 2: *The Civil Law World*, 258–94, and Lucien Karpik, "Lawyers and Politics in France, 1814–1950: The State, the Market, and the Public," *Law and Social Inquiry* 13 (1988): 707–36.

26 Fritz Ostler, *Die deutschen Rechtsanwälte 1871–1971*, 2d ed. (Essen, 1982). Ostler previously had published a much shorter work concerning lawyers, which served as a preliminary study for his expanded book; Fritz Ostler, *Der deutsche Rechtsanwalt. Das Werden des Standes seit der Reichsgründung* (Karlsruhe, 1963).

27 Adolf Weißler, *Geschichte der Rechtsanwaltschaft* (Leipzig, 1905). General works on the administration of justice, the constitution of the courts, and civil procedure often contain overviews of the history of the bar and many acute insights into the social prestige of lawyers; see, e.g., Erich Döhring, *Geschichte der deutschen Rechtspflege seit 1500* (Berlin, 1953), especially ch. 3, 111–77.

28 Dahrendorf, *Society and Democracy in Germany*, ch. 15, "Lawyers of the Monopoly," 221–36. Wolfgang Kaupen, *Die Hüter von Recht und Ordnung. Die soziale Herkunft, Erziehung und Ausbildung der deutschen Juristen. Eine soziologische Analyse* (Neuwied and Berlin, 1969) and Rueschemeyer, *Lawyers and their Society*, esp. ch. 5, 146–84.

29 A final and fundamentally unsatisfactory, approach to the analysis of the role of lawyers in German society is a sociopsychological one. Using interviews based upon free association in conversation, Walter Weyrauch attempted to describe the attitudinal makeup of German lawyers around 1960; Walter O. Weyrauch, *The Personality of Lawyers* (New Haven, 1964). See the strong criticism by Max Rheinstein in his review of Weyrauch's book in *Yale Law Journal* 74 (1965): 1331–4.

professions has produced a number of studies of German lawyers, often in their comparative context.[30] Thus, a social history of lawyers in Germany between 1879 and 1933 that weaves together the literatures of the history of the *Bürgertum*, of the professions, and of the importance of law to German liberalism remains unwritten.

Any project such as a book carries with it its own set of milestones, which measure its progress and record the debts that the author owes for help received along the way. All of the persons and institutions who have helped me with this project deserve my thanks and recognition; space and custom permit expression of gratitude toward only a few.

Whatever merit this work may have is owed to the intellectual challenge, support, and encouragement of teachers and colleagues. My particular thanks go to my teachers, Vernon L. Lidtke and Mack Walker, and to my colleagues as graduate students, William D. Bowman and Kathleen Canning. The Department of History at The Johns Hopkins University provided a supportive community in which this work began and for which I am grateful. Douglas Klusmeyer has contributed acute intellectual insight, a clear and critical editor's eye, and warm friendship and support ever since we met that August morning in Freiburg in 1985.

A position as Research Fellow at the German Historical Institute in Washington, D.C., supported me as I began to revise from dissertation to book, and I am grateful especially to the intellectual stimulation and collegiality offered to me there by then-Director Hartmut Lehmann, now Director of the Max-Planck-Institut für Geschichte at Göttingen. I also owe much to the encouragement and friendship of my fellow *wissenschaftliche Mitarbeiter* there, especially Stig Förster and Hanna Schissler. My colleagues at the Department of History of Case Western Reserve University also patiently bore with me through draft

30 Hannes Siegrist has contributed a number of insightful essays to the history of the German legal profession: besides "Gebremste Professionalisierung," see idem, "Die Rechtsanwälte und das Bürgertum. Deutschland, die Schweiz und Italien im 19. Jahrhundert," in Kocka, ed., *Bürgertum im 19. Jahrhundert*, II:92–123; and "Public Office or Free Profession? German Attorneys in the Nineteenth and Early Twentieth Centuries," in Cocks and Jarausch, eds., *German Professions*, 46–65. Siegrist has completed a *Habilitationsschrift* comparing lawyers in Germany, Italy, and Switzerland, entitled *Advokaten und Bürger*, which is forthcoming. See also Michael John, "Between Estate and Profession: Lawyers and the Development of the Legal Profession in Nineteenth-Century Germany," in David Blackbourn and Richard J. Evans, eds., *The German Bourgeoisie. Essays on the Social History of the German Middle Class from the Late Eighteenth to the Early Twentieth Century* (New York, 1991), 162–97.

after draft, and I am especially grateful to Michael Altschul, Michael Grossberg, Catherine Kelly, Alan Rocke, Jonathan Sadowsky, and Angela Woollacott. Frank Smith at Cambridge University Press, in his typically reserved and efficient way, showed interest in the book when my own spirits flagged, and I thank him. All the errors and infelicities that remain belong solely to me. Finally, the law firm of Mays, Valentine, Davenport & Moore in Richmond, Virginia (now Mays & Valentine), taught me much about thinking and writing, but even more about lawyers and the legal world, gifts from which I constantly benefit.

This work would not have been possible without the professional assistance of the Milton S. Eisenhower Library at The Johns Hopkins University, especially the Inter-Library Loan Department, and the Law Library of the Library of Congress and Ms. Marie-Louise Bernal of the European Law Division. In addition, I wish to thank the helpful archivists and staff at the *Niedersächsiches Hauptstaatsarchiv* in Hannover, especially Dr. Gieschen; the *Universitätsarchiv* at the University of Göttingen and the president of the university for permission to use it; the staffs of the *Niedersächsische Landes- und Universitätsbibliothek* in Göttingen and of the library of the *Juristisches Fakultät* there; and the *Geheimes Staatsarchiv, Preußischer Kulturbesitz* in Berlin-Dahlem. Finally, I would like to acknowledge the financial generosity of the following institutions: the Mellon Foundation, the Department of History of The Johns Hopkins University, the *Deutscher Akademischer Austauschdienst*, and the German Historical Institute. The W. P. Jones Presidential Faculty Development Fund at Case Western Reserve University provided support that helped make publication possible.

Academic life can be notoriously hard on family life, and I owe an irrecompensable debt to my family. My children, Peter and Sarah, have lived with these lawyers all their lives, and I can only hope that they will some day see why. Most importantly, I am grateful to my wife, Susan Holderness, for her ever-present and uncomplaining love and support; for her unequivocal support for the seemingly irrational decision to leave the practice of law for the uncertain world of graduate school in the humanities; for her willingness to seek a leave of absence from her church so that our family could be together in Germany; for her cheerful bearing of a disproportionate share of responsibility for the care of our children, and for her remarkable patience with the ups and downs of bringing this work to fruition.

She has always supported me with love and acceptance, and I cannot thank her enough.

Parts of this book have appeared in different form elsewhere, and I wish to thank the following journals and presses for allowing me to use the material here: Oxford University Press for "Conflict Within the Legal Profession: Simultaneous Admission and the German Bar 1903–1927," in Geoffrey Cocks and Konrad H. Jarausch, eds., *German Professions, 1800–1950* (Oxford, 1990), 252–69; Humanities Press International, Inc., for "Lawyers, Liberalism, and Procedure: The Imperial Justice Laws of 1877–79," *Central European History* 26 (1993): 165–93; and the University of Illinois Press for "German Lawyers and the State in the Weimar Republic," *Law and History Review* 13 (1995): 317–49.

Two notes on translation and usage of German terms are necessary before beginning the substance of the story to be told.

First, I have chosen to translate the German words *Advokat* and *Rechtsanwalt* as "private practitioner," "lawyer in private practice," or simply as "lawyer"; the collective nouns for all *Advokaten* and *Rechtsanwälte* are *Advokatur, Rechtsanwaltschaft,* or *Rechtsanwaltstand,* which I translate variously as "practicing bar," "lawyers in private practice," "private practitioners," or "lawyers." Whenever it is necessary to preserve a linguistic distinction, I have used the German terms.

There is no single word in American English that captures the exact meaning of *Rechtsanwalt* or *Rechtsanwaltschaft.* The words mean those lawyers who counsel private parties and who represent them in litigation. They are a subset of the entire universe of *Juristen,* those persons with university training in the law, which would include all judges, state prosecutors, most higher state officials, and lawyers in the full-time employ of businesses, associations, or local governments (*Syndiken*).

I have consciously avoided the use of the word "attorney," which some authors such as Konrad Jarausch prefer, because of its technical meaning in the organization and history of the English legal profession. Although commonly employed in late twentieth-century American usage to denote all lawyers in private practice, "attorney" is a term of art for nonuniversity-trained practitioners regulated by nineteenth-century English courts of common law, dealing with clients but not pleading cases before the court in most instances. The term was abolished in English usage by the Judicature Act of 1873 and replaced by the title "solicitor," which formerly applied only to practitioners regulated by the courts of chancery.[31]

Second, the double meaning of the German words *Bürger*, *Bürgertum*, and *bürgerlich* are axiomatic. Emerging from a simply descriptive term for those persons who lived in towns and possessed the right to vote and hold office, the words in modern German encompass both the group identity of the middle class and the generalized notion of citizenship. They thus can be translated either as "middle class" or as "citizen[ry]"; "pertaining to the middle class" or "civic, civil." Legal definition and theoretical construct often lacked congruence; the *Bürger* of the Prussian General Code of 1794 did not precisely match Hegel's *bürgerliche Gesellschaft* or "civil society." Finally, the meaning of the concept changed over time.[32] Complicating the picture are compound forms such as *Bürgerstand*, seemingly combining class and corporate characteristics, and collective forms such as *Bürgerschaft*. Rather than adopting murky and imprecise translations such as "middle class" or ideologically loaded and equally imprecise ones such as "bourgeoisie," wherever possible this study will simply use the actual German word employed by the author.

31 On the history of English attorneys and the Judicature Act of 1873, see Robson, *The Attorney in Eighteenth Century England,* and Reader, *Professional Men.*
32 For a detailed discussion of the secular plasticity of the concept "Bürger," see Manfred Riedel, "Bürger, Staatsbürger, Bürgertum," in Otto Brunner, Werner Conze, Reinhart Koselleck, eds., *Geschichtliche Grundbegriffe. Historisches Lexikon zur politisch-sozialen Sprache in Deutschland,* 7 vols. (Stuttgart, 1972–89), I:672–725. See also Kocka, "Bürgertum und Bürgerlichkeit," 21–63, for the terminological murkiness of the field. For the special peculiarities of the term "Bildungsbürgertum," see Ulrich Engelhardt, *Bildungsbürgertum. Begriffs- und Dogmengeschichte eines Etiketts* (Stuttgart, 1986), esp. 115–80.

From General Estate to Special Interest

1

The Archimedean Point: Lawyers, Liberalism, and the Middle-Class Project

In 1867, Rudolf von Gneist, professor of law at the University of Berlin, a founder of the Social Policy Association, member of the Reichstag for the National Liberal Party, and one of the leading moderate liberals in Germany, published a clarion call for the reform of the Prussian judicial and legal system in a slim volume entitled *The Free Legal Profession: The First Requirement for any Reform of the Justice System in Prussia*. After recounting and analyzing myriad shortcomings in the judicial and legal structures of the Kingdom of Prussia, Gneist reached the seemingly remarkable conclusion that "the correct organization of the private legal profession will prove to be the Archimedean point from which these relations are to be guided back into the right course."[1]

Gneist contended that the importance of the modernization of the German judicial and legal system transcended mere technical improvement of the conduct of trials; indeed, he viewed reform of the judicial and legal system as the very key to the success of the middle-class project of German liberalism. Voicing the goals of German liberals since the Prussian reform era, Gneist proclaimed:

We aspire to a self-reliance of the citizenry, which is flowing like an irresistible force through central European society. In modern political life, this self-reliance can only mean the free movement of the *Bürger* within legal bounds. . . . Political and personal freedom in Germany will be established upon the statutory regulation of the right of state sovereignty rather than upon sovereign majority decisions of state, county, city, and village assemblies. . . . [T]he personal rights of the individual will be protected against the arbitrariness of the administration with the existing laws.[2]

---

1 Rudolf Gneist, *Freie Advocatur. Die erste Forderung aller Justizreform in Preußen* (Berlin, 1867), 49.
2 Ibid., 70–1.

The goal of the *Bürgertum*, the middle-class project, thus was to promote self-reliance and self-confidence by creating a realm of freedom of action for the citizen within the bounds prescribed by law.[3]

Despite the disappointments of 1848 and the Prussian constitutional crisis, Gneist shared a widespread belief that the triumph of the middle-class project was inevitable, and he was neither alone in this belief nor the first to hold it. After 1848, even the conservative social thinker Wilhelm Heinrich Riehl had conceded defeat for what he termed "the powers of persistence," the nobility and the peasantry. He wrote:

> [T]he *Bürgerstand* is the supreme bearer of legitimate social movement, of social reform. . . . The *Bürgertum* is indisputably in our time in possession of the preponderant material and moral authority. Our whole time bears a *bürgerlich* character. . . . Many accept the *Bürgertum* and modern society as meaning the same thing. They regard the *Bürgerstand* as the rule and the other estates as only exceptions, as the debris of the old society which is caught up incidentally in modern society.[4]

Most specifically, the *Bürgertum* embodied the interests of the whole of the civic community, certainly of the whole of civil society. Riehl conceded that this universality distinguished the *Bürgertum* from other social groups:

> Since olden days, the *Bürgerstand* is the supreme bearer of legitimate social movement, of social reform. It is therefore – especially in its modern form – the opposite of the peasantry. The *Bürgertum* strives for the general, the peasantry for the particular. But particularities are the things in society which have been on hand for a long time; the generality is only now being created.[5]

Driven by its "commercial sense of legality," the *Bürgertum* sought to attain independence of the individual from the political and economic restrictions of estate society and to establish a general, reliable, predictable legal order, protecting itself and the rights that it valued highly from interference by other individuals and groups and by the state.[6] Gneist argued that lawyers in private practice would and should lead in this struggle. Judicial reform in Prussia, and hence the reform of the private legal profession that Gneist identified as its

---

3   The term "middle-class project" is an extension of the concept of the "professional project," coined by Larson, *The Rise of Professionalism*, 49–52, 104.
4   Wilhelm Heinrich Riehl, *Die bürgerliche Gesellschaft*, ed. and intr. by Peter Steinbach (originally published 1851; repr. ed. Frankfurt, 1976), 153.
5   Ibid.
6   The quoted phrase is Riehl's, and the German term is *kaufmännische Rechtlichkeitsgefühl*; ibid., 192–3.

precondition and the necessary first step, would create a sphere of secure and predictable independence from state interference for the individual citizen; it would bring about a right relationship between citizen and state.

Gneist reasoned that any system that provided the citizen with legal protection from the arbitrariness of the state must be based upon an independent court system. The latter was at least as important as a political constitution, for "courts and judges exist precisely to become inconvenient to the government when it deviates from the laws."[7] It followed that for the public to have effective recourse to the courts and judges, they had to have legal advice and counsel from, and vigorous representation by, practitioners equal in dignity and learning to the judges. Gneist believed that this public role justified his expansive claim for the importance of the bar in private practice.

Of the constituent groups of the *Bürgertum*, Gneist argued that lawyers in private practice, both in their representation of clients and in their personal civic and political activity, bore a vital historic political mission. The assignment of lawyers in modern society was to school the *Bürgertum* in the art of citizenship, in resistance to the arbitrary exercise of governmental authority. Gneist looked to the role played by lawyers, especially barristers, in England, as watchdogs against government overreaching, as local unpaid government administrative and judicial officials such as justices of the peace, and as members of Parliament and concluded:

In addition to the needs of the justice-seeking public is the political consideration, just as important for the future, according to which the free practicing bar means nothing less than the precondition for all independence of communal life, of self-government, of constitutional life on the largest scale.[8]

The first step, according to Gneist, toward a realization of the use of existing laws to protect the personal rights of the individual against the arbitrariness of the administration was to make available to private persons the advice of legally trained counsel independent from the circles of the bureaucracy. In other words, an independent profes-

7 Gneist, *Freie Advocatur*, 47.
8 Ibid., 70. Much of Gneist's scholarly work involved studies of English government, especially local government; see Rudolf von Gneist, *Das heutige englische Verfassungs- und Verwaltungsrecht*, 2 vols. (Berlin, 1857–60); *Das englische Verwaltungsrecht, mit Einschluß des Heeres, der Gerichte und der Kirche, geschichtlich und systematisch*, 2d ed., 2 vols. (Berlin, 1867); and *Selfgovernment. Communalverfassung und Verwaltungsgerichte in England*, 3rd ed. (Berlin, 1871).

sion of legal practitioners was indispensable in order for citizens to
use existing laws as effective guarantees of individual rights. Such an
independent legal profession was also the foundation of local self-
administration and even for parliamentary government itself, as the
English example clearly showed.[9] Lawyers, then, were to be the
educators, guides, and spokesmen of the *Bürgertum*, awakening it to
its legal rights of protection against governmental arbitrariness, representing it before the courts in its struggles for certainty and regularity
in private law, and serving as its tutor and representative, first at the
local level and eventually at the national, as the *Bürgertum* grew in
political maturity to achieve self-government modeled after the English example.

But, Gneist believed, lawyers in the largest and arguably most
important German state, the Kingdom of Prussia, had been prevented from fulfilling their ascribed role because the state held them
in tutelage. Since the eighteenth century, the Prussian state had
viewed private practitioners with suspicion, as instigators of litigation and contention among the people. State regulation had kept the
number of lawyers low by means of a *numerus clausus*, a fixed number
of lawyers admitted before any court. The state determined the
numerus clausus and appointed lawyers to their positions, keeping the
total numbers very low. Since an attempt to abolish the private legal
profession altogether in the late eighteenth century, lawyers had been
subject to the same state disciplinary control as state officials, so that
the law and the public viewed them either as state officials or as state-
official-like (*beamtenähnlich*). Gneist demanded an end to the *numerus
clausus* and to the state-official-like status of lawyers. How could the
citizen, he reasoned, rely upon an advocate to represent his or her
interests aggressively and truly if that same advocate was closely
connected to the state? Gneist insisted that the legal profession be
restructured on the basis of the free private practice of law (*freie*

9 Gneist, *Freie Advocatur*, 73, 74–7. For a short review of Gneist's conception of the importance of local self-government for parliamentary government in England and his application of the lessons learned to Germany, see Charles E. McClelland, *The German Historians
   and England: A Study in Nineteenth-Century Views* (Cambridge, 1971), 135–44. McClelland
   points out that the English remedies that Gneist prescribed for Prussian ailments were often
   based upon a picture of English constitutional and communal life *before* the Reform Act of
   1832, and thus Gneist's prescriptions failed to take into account changes in the constitution
   necessitated by the effects of the growth of capitalism; ibid., 141–2, 144. Erich J. C. Hahn,
   "Rudolf von Gneist (1816–1895): The Political Ideas and Political Activity of a Prussian
   Liberal in the Bismarck Period" (Ph.D. diss., Yale University, 1971), also discusses Gneist's
   many misperceptions of English developments; see also idem, "Rudolf Gneist and the
   Prussian *Rechtsstaat*: 1862–1878," *Journal of Modern History* 49 (December 1977): D1361–81.

Advokatur): freedom from appointment by the state, freedom from the limitations upon their freedom of action caused by their state-official-like status, freedom from the disciplinary authority of judges or the justice bureaucracy, and freedom from judicial determination of lawyers' fees.[10] Only *freie Advokatur* could permit the private bar to invent itself and to fulfill the great expectations that Gneist placed upon its shoulders.

Gneist's call combined with existing currents of thought among German liberals and within the German bar in private practice to energize a legislative program for reform of the organization of courts, of codes of trial procedure, and of the governance of the private legal profession. Receiving new impetus from the unification of the German Empire in 1871, these strivings of lawyers and liberals culminated in the passage of the Imperial Justice Laws of 1877–9.[11] These laws, which became effective together on 1 October 1879, consisted of a constitution of the courts, governing court organization throughout Germany; codes of civil and criminal procedure; a lawyers' statute reshaping the private legal profession; and a fees statute for lawyers, governing and regulating their remuneration.[12]

10 This definition of *freie Advokatur* comes from Helga Huffmann, *Kampf um freie Advokatur* (Essen, 1967), 23–4. Regarding the protean character of the concept of the "free practicing bar," see Lothar Müller, "Die Freiheit der Advokatur. Ihre geschichtliche Entwicklung in Deutschland während der Neuzeit und ihre rechtliche Bedeutung in der Bundesrepublik Deutschland" (Dr. jur. diss., Würzburg, 1972), 1, 117–64.

11 Textbooks on German history contain only brief mention of the enactment of these important legal reforms in the first decade of the *Kaiserreich*, either naming them without comment or subsuming them under administrative initiatives of the National Liberal party; see John, *Politics and the Law*, 2. Nipperdey, *Deutsche Geschichte 1866–1918*, 2:188–91, calls the Imperial Justice Laws "completely decisive for legal life and the legal order" and discusses their interconnectedness. Even standard surveys of German liberalism devote only brief paragraphs to these reforms; Sheehan, *German Liberalism*, 138–9, and Langewiesche, *Liberalismus in Deutschland*, 167–8; see, however, the fuller treatments in Otto Pflanze, *Bismarck and the Development of Germany*, 3 vols. (Princeton, 1990), vol. 2, *The Period of Consolidation, 1871–1880*, 149–53, 347–50, and James F. Harris, *A Study in the Theory and Practice of German Liberalism. Eduard Lasker, 1829–1884* (Lanham, Maryland, 1984), 45–60.

The fullest discussions of the background to the Imperial Justice Laws are Kenneth F. Ledford, "Lawyers, Liberalism, and Procedure: The German Imperial Justice Laws of 1877–79," *Central European History* 26 (1993): 165–93, Peter Landau, "Die Reichsjustizgesetze von 1879 und die deutsche Rechtseinheit," in Bundesministerium der Justiz, ed., *Vom Reichsjustizamt zum Bundesministerium der Justiz. Festschrift zum 100jährigen Gründungstag des Reichsjustizamtes am 1. Januar 1877* (Cologne, 1977), 161–211, Heinrich Getz, *Die deutsche Rechtseinheit im 19. Jahrhundert als rechtspolitisches Problem* (Bonn, 1966), and Franz Laufke, "Der deutsche Bund und die Zivilgesetzgebung," in Paul Mikat, ed., *Festschrift der Rechts-und Staatswissenschaftlichen Fakultät der Julius-Maximilians-Universität Würzburg zum 75. Geburtstag von Hermann Nottarp* (Karlsruhe, 1961), 1–57.

12 The constitution of the courts (*Gerichtsverfassungsgesetz*, "GVG") was promulgated on 27 January 1877, in the *Reichsgesetzblatt* (hereafter cited as "*RGB*") (1877): 41 ff.; the code of

Viewed together, the Imperial Justice Laws established the German legal profession on an entirely new and substantially liberal footing, and they created a system that persisted "without essential systematic revision" until 1933 and under which German lawyers in private practice ordered their profession and their lives.[13]

Gneist's book represents the culmination of a strand of liberal thought that elevated lawyers in private practice to a role of crucial importance for the social and political agenda of the German liberal *Bürgertum* between 1871 and 1933. Moreover, it directs the historian's view to the multilayered affinity between lawyers and liberalism, between the professional project of private practitioners and the middle-class project of social, civic, and political leadership. Liberals were searching for a social bearer of their ideological program, for a "general estate" to advance the middle-class project. By 1867 the middle-class project had moved beyond the state-focused model of the Hegelian general estate to emphasize the central ideal of the independence of the individual and sought to secure the independence of the individual from the political and economic restrictions of estate society.[14] Lawyers in private practice provided an archetype for the truly free individual within this civil society. Dependent upon the market to earn their livings, possessed only of the capital of their education and intelligence, lawyers needed only to be freed from the remaining leading-strings of the bureaucratic state to become the social group dedicated to advancing the common good and leaders for other groups within the *Bürgertum*, models worthy of emulation.

Moreover, liberalism in Germany, as elsewhere in the emergence of modern Western society, articulated much of its emancipatory project in the vocabulary of law. It focused greatly upon the creation of a legal order, a *Rechtsstaat*, which secured for the citizen, principally through private law, as broad a sphere of uninhibited autonomy as possible. Further, in public law, but also in order to make private law meaningfully enforceable, the legal order of the middle-class project was legitimated and expressed primarily in terms of legal

---

civil procedure (*Zivilprozeßordnung*, "ZPO") promulgated on 30 January 1877, at *RGB* (1877): 83 ff.; the code of criminal procedure (*Strafprozeßordnung*, "StPO") of 1 February 1877, at *RGB* (1877): 253 ff.; the lawyers' statute (*Rechtsanwaltsordnung*, "RAO") of 1 July 1878, at *RGB* (1878): 177 ff.; and the fees statute for lawyers (*Gebührenordnung für Rechtsanwälte*, "GOfRA") of 17 June 1879, at *RGB* (1879): 176 ff.

13 Franz Wieacker, *Privatrechtsgeschichte der Neuzeit*, 2d ed. (Göttingen, 1967), 466.

14 For the centrality of the ideal of independence, *Selbständigkeit*, to the formation and cohesion of the German *Bürgertum*, see Lothar Gall, *Bürgertum in Deutschland* (Berlin, 1989), esp. 74–80.

procedure, the creation of the procedural *Rechtsstaat*. Finally, the legal order was structured, guided, and mediated to the civic community by a class of specialists trained in law at the universities. Of these jurists, those most independent from the state were lawyers in private practice. Thus, the middle-class project of the mid-nineteenth century had fixed upon the private bar as the key to reforms that would realize its aims.

Concomitantly, the private bar sought a means to raise its own status, to escape existing tutelage to the state that many felt demeaning, to open the profession to talent as a means of escaping political interference, and to attain such standard goals of the professional project as self-discipline and self-government. Quite naturally, lawyers responded by melding their professional project to the middle-class project. This mutuality of interest attracted lawyers to liberalism, to liberal legal reform projects, and especially to the call for reform of the private legal profession.

What also united the two projects and helped them appear as one, what structured the affinity of lawyers for liberalism and of liberalism for lawyers, was a common focus on procedure. A principal goal of liberal theory and the middle-class project consisted of the establishment of a general, reliable, predictable legal order, what A. V. Dicey called the rule of law, subsumed in German under the rubric *Rechtsstaat*.[15] In order to secure with certainty and

---

15 Albert Venn Dicey, *Introduction to the Study of the Law of the Constitution*, 3rd ed. (London, 1889), 184–9; Judith Shklar points out that procedure in criminal cases was what Montesquieu's Rule of Law was all about and that Dicey hollowed the inquiry out even further, to look only at the forms of juridical rigor rather than its structure or purposes; Judith Shklar, "Political Theory and the Rule of Law," in Allan C. Hutchinson and Patrick Monahan, eds., *The Rule of Law. Ideal or Ideology* (Toronto, 1987), 1–16, 5, 6.

Ernst-Wolfgang Böckenförde distinguishes the German concept of *Rechtsstaat* from the rule of law, indicating that, especially in its earlier manifestations, it was expressed more in political than juridical terms. It encompassed the rule of law, however, including elements such as an independent judiciary, the reliable administration of justice, and the supremacy of the rule of law in the form of statutes, and as its definition became narrower and more formal in the course of the nineteenth century the concept of the *Rechtsstaat* came more and more to resemble the rule of law; idem, "The Origin and Development of the Concept of the *Rechtsstaat*," in *State, Society and Liberty. Studies in Political Theory and Constitutional Law*, trans. by J. A. Underwood (New York and Oxford, 1991), 47–70; 48, n.3; 49–50. For the importance of this distinction, see also Harold J. Berman, "The Rule of Law and the Law-Based State with Special Reference to the Soviet Union," in Donald D. Barry, ed., *Toward the "Rule of Law" in Russia? Political and Legal Reform in the Transition Period* (Armonk, N.Y., and London, 1992), 43–60.

For the classic work on the equivocal nature of the German liberal conception of the *Rechtsstaat*, see Krieger, *The German Idea of Freedom*, esp. 252–61. See also Franz L. Neumann, *The Rule of Law. Political Theory and the Legal System in Modern Society* (Leamington

predictability a sphere in which the citizen could act free from the interference of the state, *Rechtsstaat* doctrine sought to replace both unwritten customary law and arbitrary bureaucratic law with a system of law that was general and autonomous, public and positive, aiming at generality in legislation and uniformity in adjudication, relying heavily upon the separation of the functions of legislation, administration, and adjudication.[16] Especially important to the German conception of the *Rechtsstaat*, and hence to the way that lawyers in private practice were to fit into it, were predictable frameworks for procedure.[17] Lawyers were to be the guardians and monitors of these frameworks for judicial and, by implication, political procedure.

Accepting the invitation extended by Gneist's short book, this chapter will begin the examination of the history of German lawyers by exploring first the steps by which the mantle of the Hegelian general estate passed from state officials to private practitioners. Then it will consider the central role ascribed to law and legal reform by the middle-class project in modern society, the particular emphasis placed upon procedure, and the ways in which both elements elevate the role of lawyers in private practice. Together, these lines of inquiry will help illuminate the etiology of the mutual affinity between lawyers and liberalism and set the stage for a more detailed exploration of the history of the Prussian bar and the reform effort of the first half of the nineteenth century.

The Search for the "General Estate"

An important part of understanding how Gneist arrived at his conclusion that private practitioners had so important a role to play in reforming Prussia lies in the history of the search for a social group whose purpose included representation of the general interest. Despite Riehl's assessment that the *Bürgertum* as a whole represented the general, a strong tradition in German, especially Prussian, political theory lodged responsibility for the common good in a smaller

Spa, 1986), 11–46, 179–265, the long-delayed publication of Neumann's 1936 dissertation at the London School of Economics.
16 Roberto Mangabeira Unger, *Law in Modern Society: Toward a Criticism of Social Theory* (New York, 1976), 66–86.
17 Wieacker, *Privatrechtsgeschichte der Neuzeit*, 464: "Court organization and procedure belong to the most important guarantees of the *Rechtsstaat*, so that this realm was of particular importance to the politically-rising liberal *Bürgertum*."

group. This general estate was to be the guardian of the legal order, guarantors of the functioning of a legal system that provided universality, certainty, predictability, and regularity of legal relationships for all members of the state. In 1821 Hegel published the *Philosophy of Right*, in which he postulated a group that fulfilled this function, a group established both within the "system of needs" that he defined as civil society *and* with a leading role in the superior ethical community, the state.[18] Hegel called that group, which represented the general interest of all members of society but which also represented the interests of the state, the general estate, and it consisted of higher state officials.[19] State officials, selected by merit and training, committed to selfless and ethical administration in service of the general good, and secure and stable in their income and status thus appeared as a "constitution substitute" guaranteeing government in the interests of all.[20] But the social basis of the general

18 Particularly helpful to this discussion of Hegel's conception of the general estate in the *Philosophy of Right* have been Andrew Arato, "A Reconstruction of Hegel's Theory of Civil Society," in Drucilla Cornell, Michel Rosenfeld, and David Gray Carlson, eds., *Hegel and Legal Theory* (New York, 1991), 301–20, and Jean L. Cohen and Andrew Arato, *Civil Society and Political Theory* (Cambridge, Mass., 1992), 102–4; Steven B. Smith, *Hegel's Critique of Liberalism. Rights in Context* (Chicago, 1989), ch. 5, "The Hegelian *Rechtsstaat*," 132–64, esp. 149–52 on "The Universal Class"; and Kenneth Westphal, "The basic context and structure of Hegel's *Philosophy of Right*," in Frederick C. Beiser, ed., *The Cambridge Companion to Hegel* (Cambridge, 1993), 234–69. I wish to thank my colleague in the Department of Philosophy at Case Western Reserve University, Prof. Barbara Krasner, for her insightful comments and helpful bibliographical suggestions.

19 According to Hegel, higher state officials represented not only the universal in civil society ("The universal estate has the universal interests of society as its business," ¶205), but also in that embodiment of universal interest, the state ("It is integral to the definition of the universal estate – or more precisely, the estate which devotes itself to the service of the government – that the universal is the end of its essential activity," ¶303); G. W. F. Hegel, *Elements of the Philosophy of Right*, ed. by Allen W. Wood and trans. by H. B. Nisbet (Cambridge, 1991), 237, 343–4. Although translators of the *Philosophy of Right* tend to use the terms "universal estate" or "universal class" to translate Hegel's *allgemeiner Stand*, and political philosophers tend to follow this convention, I prefer to render the term as "general estate," following the pattern set by Mack Walker, *German Home Towns. Community, State, and General Estate, 1648–1871* (Ithaca, N.Y., 1971), 197. For the German original, see *Georg Wilhelm Friedrich Hegel's Werke. Vollständige Ausgabe durch einen Verein von Freunden des Verewigten*, 18 vols. in 20 (Berlin, 1832–45), vol. 8, *Grundlinien der Philosophie des Rechts, oder Naturrecht und Staatswissenschaft im Grundrisse*, ed. by Eduard Gans, 3rd ed. (Berlin, 1854), ¶205 ("Der allgemeine Stand hat die allgemeinen Interessen des gesellschaftlichen Zustandes zu seinem Geschäfte") on 260, and ¶303 ("Der allgemeine, näher dem Dienst der Regierung sich widmende Stand hat unmittelbar in seiner Bestimmung, das Allgemeine zum Zwecke seiner wesentlichen Thätigkeit zu haben") on 389.

20 For the role of state officials as a *Verfassungsersatz*, see Fritz Hartung, "Studien zur Geschichte der preußischen Verwaltung," in idem, *Staatsbildenden Kräfte der Neuzeit. Gesammelte Aufsätze von Fritz Hartung* (Berlin, 1961), 178, 237, cited in Harro-Jürgen Rejewski, *Die Pflicht zur politischen Treue im preußischen Beamtenrecht (1850–1918). Eine rechtshistorische Untersuchung anhand von Ministerialakten aus dem Geheimen Staatsarchiv der*

estate, the locus of the constitution substitute, almost immediately came under challenge.

Although Hegel had introduced the concept of the general estate in his lectures at Berlin beginning in 1806, the *Philosophy of Right* was published only in 1821. From 1817 onward, all candidates for higher administrative positions in the Prussian bureaucracy had to complete at least three years' study of law at a German university.[21] But the retreat from state-initiated reform begun both in Prussia and more generally in Germany after the Karlsbad Decrees in 1819 led to political scrutiny of candidates for state service, so that only suitably conservative aspirants could hope for success.[22] Reform-minded state officials already in state service encountered political supervision and reduced chances for advancement, leading to discouragement and disillusionment. The era of reaction thus sent liberals looking for another social bearer of the general interest, one more independent from political control and tutelage.

Many fastened initially upon the judiciary as the new general estate, building upon separation-of-powers arguments in favor of judicial independence. Judges, secure in Prussia with lifetime appointments, fixed salaries, and independence guaranteed by the Prussian General Law Code of 1794, possessed sufficient distance and independence from the will of the sovereign to insulate them from political interference and permit them to represent the common interest.[23] Independent judges were the key to a just society:

Stiftung Preußischer Kulturbesitz (Berlin, 1973), 29, n. 97. For a discussion of "*Beamtenliberalismus*" in Germany as a whole, see Bernd Wunder, *Geschichte der Bürokratie in Deutschland* (Frankfurt, 1986), 60–6; for Prussia see Reinhart Koselleck, *Preußen zwischen Reform und Revolution. Allgemeines Landrecht, Verwaltung und soziale Bewegung vom 1791 bis 1848* (Stuttgart, 1967), 337–97.

21 See Koselleck, *Preußen*, esp. 87–115. For the history of the requirement that state officials be trained as lawyers, see Wilhelm Bleek, *Von der Kameralausbildung zum Juristenprivileg* (Berlin, 1972), 104, 262–85, and Carl J. Friedrich, "The Continental Tradition of Training Administrators in Law and Jurisprudence," *Journal of Modern History* 11 (1939): 133–42. See more generally John R. Gillis, *The Prussian Bureaucracy in Crisis 1840–1860: Origins of an Administrative Ethos* (Stanford, 1971).

22 For a history of political scrutiny of Prussian state officials and candidates for state service, see Hans Hattenhauer, *Geschichte des deutschen Beamtentums*, 2d ed. (Cologne, 1993), and Rejewski, *Die Pflicht zur politischen Treue*. For the condition of state officials by the 1840s, see Hans-Ulrich Wehler, *Deutsche Gesellschaftsgeschichte*, 4 vols. (Munich, 1987–), II:210–26.

23 *Das Allgemeine Landrecht für die Preußischen Staaten*, Theil II, 17. Titel:

§98. Every lower court judge is subject in his official duties solely to the direction of the State.

§99. Whoever occupies a judicial office can only be prosecuted, investigated, punished, or dismissed from office on account of his conduct of his office by the superior court or *Landeskollegium*.

[I]f the independence of the courts and the secure position of the judge ever ceases, . . . then it would be better that society dissolved itself and that its members sought in the rights of self-defense that exist in the state of nature substitutes for the guaranties of rights that the state has failed to give.[24]

By 1864, under the harsh conditions of neo-absolutism in Electoral Hesse, Otto Bähr abandoned hope in constitutional government as protector of the rights of the citizen and contended that reliable judicial procedures protected individual rights more effectively than political participation, for government ministers and constitutions, as well as state officials, were subject to change at the whim of the sovereign. Bähr argued that the law was "the stable element of the life of the state" and, when enforced by independent judges, a more effective check upon the personal rule of the sovereign than a constitution or ministers.[25]

By 1848 judges had become active political participants, using the security of their life tenure to permit them to agitate in public for reform. Judges were the largest single group in the Prussian National Assembly of 1848, with seventy-eight (19.5 percent of the total).[26] A similar percentage of the delegates to the German National Assembly in Frankfurt were judges.[27] The Prussian *Landtag* with which Bis-

See also Rejewski, *Die Pflicht zur politischen Treue*, 11–18, and Günther Plathner, *Der Kampf um die richterliche Unabhängigkeit bis zum Jahre 1848 unter besonderer Berücksichtigung Preußens. Eine dogmengeschichtliche Untersuchung* (Breslau, 1935), 50–68.

24 Carl von Rotteck, "Justiz," in Carl von Rotteck and Carl Welcker, *Staats-Lexikon oder Encyklopädie der Staatswissenschaften*, 15 vols. (Altona, 1834–43), 8 (1839): 720–56, 756. See more generally Albrecht Wagner, *Der Kampf der Justiz gegen die Verwaltung in Preußen. Dargelegt an der rechtsgeschichtlichen Entwicklung des Konfliktsgesetzes von 1854* (Hamburg, 1936).

25 Bähr, *Der Rechtsstaat*, 70: "[T]he minister . . . can offer no guarantees of the principles that he represents. . . . If the ruler of a state changes his minister today, tomorrow the whole public law may assume a completely different physiognomy. This phenomenon truly casts scorn upon the essence of the law . . . the stable element of the life of the state." For discussions of an independent judiciary and reformed court system as a *Verfassungsersatz*, see also Werner Schubert, ed., *Die deutsche Gerichtsverfassung (1869–1877). Entstehung und Quellen* (Frankfurt, 1981), 25, 111, and Eduard Kern, *Geschichte des Gerichtsverfassungsrechts* (Munich, 1954), 73, who cites Bähr.

26 Louis Rosenbaum, *Beruf und Herkunft der Abgeordneten zu den deutschen und preußischen Parlamenten 1847 bis 1919. Ein Beitrag zur Geschichte des deutschen Parlaments* (Frankfurt, 1923), 58–9.

27 The figures cited are calculated from Wolfram Siemann, *Die Frankfurter Nationalversammlung 1848/49 zwischen demokratischem Liberalismus und konservativer Reform. Die Bedeutung der Juristendominanz in den Verfassungsverhandlungen des Paulskirchenparlaments* (Bern and Frankfurt, 1976), "Abgeordnetenverzeichnis," 308–27. The largest number of *Juristen* (54) belonged to the moderate-conservative "Casino-Party" faction. Although 445 of the 812 delegates to the German National Assembly were *Volljuristen*, only 139 were judges or state

marck came into sharpest conflict, the one elected in 1862, has been called the "District Judges' Parliament" for the role that lower-court judges played in the leadership of the liberal parties and in defense of the prerogatives of the legislature.[28] Liberal judges so vexed Bismarck that he referred contemptuously to the rural district judge as the "constitutional house doctor."[29] But the harsh persecution of liberal-minded judges during the Prussian constitutional conflict of 1862–6 convinced many liberals that the general estate needed to be yet more independent of the state than were judges, and the focus of the search for the general estate shifted to private practitioners.[30] By the time that Gneist wrote in 1867, then, it was clear to him that *freie Advokatur* was the only way to create sufficient independence from the state for lawyers to serve as the general estate. Thus, the search for a viable general estate was one vector for Gneist's conclusion that private practitioners were the key to reform.

Liberalism, Procedure, the Rechtsstaat, and Lawyers

In order to understand how lawyers came to be so important to observers such as Gneist, historians must also pay attention to the conceptual vocabulary of law itself. Law and legal systems are a crucial analytical entry point into any understanding of modern society, and legal and social systems are inextricably intertwined so that neither can be understood without a grasp of the other, not least

prosecutors; ibid., 33–4 and 341, n. 7. By another count, 136 of the 808 delegates to the German National Assembly (16.8 percent) were judges; Heinrich Best, *Die Männer von Bildung und Besitz. Struktur und Handeln parlamentarischer Führungsgruppen in Deutschland und Frankreich 1848/49* (Düsseldorf, 1990), tabelle 1, 59.

28 Adalbert Hess, *Das Parlament das Bismarck widerstrebte. Zur Politik und sozialen Zusammensetzung des preußischen Abgeordnetenhauses der Konfliktszeit (1862–1866)* (Cologne and Opladen, 1964), esp. 61–3; the contemporary German phrase was *Kreisrichter-Parlament*. For the "doctrinaire" liberalism of lower court judges, see Eugene N. Anderson, *The Social and Political Conflict in Prussia 1858–1864* (Lincoln, Neb., 1954), 290.

29 Bismarck made this comment, calling the district judge the *konstitutionelle[r] Hausarzt*, in the course of a debate on the floor of the North German Reichstag on 22 April 1868; Otto von Bismarck, *Die gesammelten Werke*, 15 vols. in 19 (Berlin, 1924–35), vol. 10, *Reden: 1847 bis 1869*, ed. by Dr. Wilhelm Schüßler (1928), 456–62, 458. For a broader discussion of Bismarck's antipathy toward judges, replete with many examples of antijudge epithets, see Bartolomäus, "Fürst Bismarck und der preußische Richterstand," *Preußischer Jahrbücher* 99 (1900): 177–81.

30 For a survey of the persecution of liberal activists among the judiciary between 1848 and 1871, see Uwe Lorenz Kötschau, "Richterdisziplinierung in der preußischen Reaktionszeit. Verfahren gegen Waldeck und Temme" (Dr. jur. diss, Kiel, 1976), which focuses primarily upon the cases of Benedikt Waldeck and Ludwig Temme.

because legal modes of thought may shape or even limit broader social imagination.[31]

Following pathbreaking work in the sociology of law by Max Weber, social theorists have generally agreed that a fundamental characteristic of modern, western, liberal society has been the emergence of the *Rechtsstaat*, the rule of law, the "legal order."[32] In its rise to power, the *Bürgertum* adopted both as its means and as one of its ends the creation of a rational, predictable system of legal guarantees to protect itself and the rights that it valued highly from interference by other individuals and groups and by the state. In doing so, it created two fundamentally important binary pairs of categories: public and private law, and substantive and procedural law.[33] Public law orders and constrains relations between citizens and the state, while private law orders relations among citizens. Substantive law defines the rights and duties of citizens toward each other and toward the state and prescribes the rules of conduct that promote the welfare and security of society, while procedural law provides the means by which substantive law is enforced; it does not define rights or duties, but merely specifies the procedures to implement them.[34] Legal thought thus separates law into substance, material precepts of law related in some manner to external norms such as justice, and procedure, formal precepts of law that are content-neutral, that provide rules for the resolution of dispute and conduct of cases, and that are related to concepts such as predictability and regularity. Of course, the two kinds of law are not hermetically

31 Gordon, "Critical Legal Histories," 111.
32 Max Weber, *Economy and Society*, II:641–900, 883; hereafter cited as *ES*. The translation of the section on the "Sociology of Law" (*Rechtssoziologie*) in *ES* is drawn from Max Weber, *Max Weber on Law in Economy and Society*, ed. and trans. by Max Rheinstein and Edward Shils (Cambridge, Mass., 1954). Wherever possible, dual citations will be provided. Max Rheinstein's introduction to this latter volume is an excellent introduction to Weber's legal thought, although it must now be supplemented by Anthony T. Kronman, *Max Weber* (Stanford, 1983). The term "legal order" is drawn from Unger, *Law in Modern Society*, 52–4.
33 For a discussion of the distinct pairs of legal categories in which lawyers think, focusing upon civil law countries, see John Henry Merryman, *The Civil Law Tradition*, 2d ed. (Stanford, 1985), 97–8; for the importance of procedure to legal reforms after the Enlightenment, see R. C. van Caenegem, *An Historical Introduction to Private Law* (Cambridge, 1992), 128–34.
34 Milton D. Green, *Basic Civil Procedure*, 2d ed. (Mineola, N.Y., 1979), 5–6. In German, the distinction is framed in the opposition of *materielles Recht*, material law, the norms that order the law as such, and *formelles Recht*, formal law, the norms that serve to carry out the material law; the former corresponds to substantive law and the latter to procedural law. See the entry "Recht," in Carl Creifelds, *Rechtswörterbuch*, 8th ed., (Munich, 1986), 897–8, 898.

separate. Although procedural regularity and procedural justice generally encompass rules for the conduct of litigation, they indeed can have a substantive and material impact upon the rights of individuals within the state.[35]

Although most observers typically assume that the legitimacy of the legal order derives from substantive norms, in modern systems of formally rational law, the regularity, uniformity, and generality of procedure is the means of legitimation of the entire legal order.[36] As Niklas Luhmann argues, procedure serves the same role in the public sphere of the state that contract serves in the private sphere of society: that of the magic formula that assures the greatest measure of security and freedom.[37] Liberalism itself enshrines procedural right over substantive determination of good as the chief goal of the state, increasing the affinity between legal forms of thinking and liberal doctrine.[38] Both in the realm of public law and the political system and in that of private law and individual behavior, the importance of procedure in the legal thought in which lawyers are trained and in the legal order in which they are socialized combines with the procedural nature of liberalism to shape their approach to legal reform.

As legal specialists, private practitioners are particularly closely imbricated with proceduralism. Legal training inculcates in them the

35 Böckenförde, "The Origin and Development of the Concept of the *Rechtsstaat*," 67–8: "However this call for the material *Rechtsstaat* overlooks the special significance – at the material level – of formal legal guarantees and organized procedure. It is formal guarantees and procedures that shield and protect individual and social liberty by preventing, in the name of absolute established or accepted material meanings or 'values,' any discrimination against individuals or social groups. In this they show themselves to be institutions of liberty, having little to do with formalism and even less with positivism."
36 See the criticism of Weber for his overly formal conception of the modern legal order in Jürgen Habermas, *Theory of Communicative Action*, 2 vols., trans. Thomas by McCarthy (Boston, 1984), vol. 2, *Reason and the Rationalization of Society*, 254–71, esp. 264–5. Habermas's own reading of Weber's sociology of law is subject to challenge; Sally Ewing, "Formal Justice and the Spirit of Capitalism: Max Weber's Sociology of Law," *Law and Social Inquiry* 21 (1987): 487–512, 506–11.
37 Niklas Luhmann, *Legitimation durch Verfahren* (Neuwied, 1969), 7, and esp. 55–135 on "Gerichtsverfahren."
38 Sandel, "The Procedural Republic and the Unencumbered Self," 81–96. In fact, a workable definition of liberalism is as the political doctrine that stresses the creation of a set of more or less fair but uniform, known and certain procedures to constrain the state and within which many competing notions of justice or the good life can compete; John Breuilly, "State-Building, Modernization, and Liberalism from the Late Eighteenth Century to Unification: German Peculiarities," *European History Quarterly* 22 (1992): 257–84, 277. For recent restatements that confirm the formalism of rule of law theory, see Jeremy Waldron, "The Rule of Law in Contemporary Liberal Theory," *Ratio Juris* 2 (1989): 79–96, and Robert S. Summers, "A Formal Theory of the Rule of Law," *Ratio Juris* 6 (1993): 127–42.

distinction between substance and procedure, and the culture of practice reinforces the primacy of procedure.[39] Lawyers whose principal activity is the litigation of cases in court (and the vast preponderance of German private practitioners devote most of their practice to litigation, as will be seen later) are taught to accept substantive law as a given in all but the most exceptional cases, properly within the realm of the legislature or, in a common-law system, the courts. Their job as lawyers is first to find the law that most favors their client's interest through a search of legislation and jurisprudence and then most importantly to maneuver their client's case, through skillful manipulation of procedural rules, into the posture that presents it in the best light and offers the greatest chance of success. Thus, their inquiry does not address issues of justice or even fairness, but rather those of process: uniformity, regularity, and predictability.

Weber contended that the unique evolution of the western legal system constituted an essential element of the emergence of capitalism in western Europe. The hallmark of the western legal system's uniqueness was that it was logical, formal, and rational. This logical, formal rationality, particularly highly developed in continental European legal systems and especially so in Germany, provided the calculability and predictability that was conducive to the emergence of the capitalist economy.[40]

Weber differentiated legal thought into four types: substantively irrational, formally irrational, substantively rational, and formally rational. Despite his putative detachment and neutrality as a social scientist, Weber clearly viewed these types as a hierarchy or even an evolutionary progression, in which the final one, formally rational legal thought, was most conducive to capitalism.[41] Formally rational legal thought is profoundly procedural. Its uniqueness, and its affinity for capitalism, "lay not so much in the content of substantive

---

39 Despite the historical focus and abstract rationality of German legal education, a main purpose remained preparing graduates to find and apply the law to practical cases that they faced in their careers; see, for example, the discussion of German legal education in Friedrich Paulsen, *The German Universities and University Study* (New York, 1906), 391–5 (published in German in 1902).

40 Particularly clear expositions of Weber's arguments on the sociology of law are provided by David M. Trubek, "Max Weber on Law and the Rise of Capitalism," *Wisconsin Law Review* 1972: 720–53, and idem, "Reconstructing Max Weber's Sociology of Law," *Stanford Law Review* 37 (1985): 919–36, an extended review of Kronman, *Max Weber*.

41 *ES* II:882; *Weber on Law*, 303.

provisions as in the forms of legal organization and the resulting formal characteristics of the legal process."[42] This procedure-focused formally rational legal thought constitutes the legal framework of modern, western liberal society.

Law thus lay at the heart of the middle-class project of nineteenth-century liberalism. This manifested itself in two ways. First, while the liberal agenda encompassed some goal of constitutional reform to widen political representation and guarantee individual rights, it always stressed the crucial importance of reform of private law. Dieter Grimm argues:

> *Bürgerlich* society therefore can well forsake fundamental rights, but not private law. Constitutional law confers upon private autonomy only supplementary protection against intervention by the state. Its formal superiority [superordination] to private law thus has its basis in the substantive priority of the latter. The constitution of *bürgerlich* society was accessory to private law [*privatrechtsakzessorisch*].[43]

Accordingly, the primary protection of the rights of the citizen against interference by the state was *not* a constitution but rather general, regular, and predictable private law guaranteeing private individual autonomy. Second, as the *Bürgertum* sought to free itself from the tutelage of estate society and to maximize the playing field for individual choice, it sought to remove the state from the business of setting substantive goals for human behavior.[44] The role of the state was to provide a procedural framework, predictable and secure, for the resolution of disputes; substantive values were to be determined by voluntary contracts between formally equal individuals. Law was "unburdened"; what remained were negative and organizational functions.

It was precisely in this limitation to the solution of formal problems that law displayed its specific rationality. In this regard it did not merely contribute to the solution of problems. With only mild exaggeration it may be claimed

---

42   Trubek, "Weber on Law and Capitalism," 724. Formally rational legal thought requires the separation of adjudication from either political administration or the sacred rules of religion; it requires that law be seen as a body of human-made rules rather than a received tradition; general rules must govern judicial decision making rather than ad hoc conceptions of substantive justice; and law must apply uniformly across the whole of society rather than consist of a patchwork of special laws for particular status groups. Ibid.

43   Dieter Grimm, "Bürgerlichkeit im Recht," in Kocka, ed., *Bürger und Bürgerlichkeit*, 149–88, 166; this essay also appears in Dieter Grimm, *Recht und Staat der bürgerlichen Gesellschaft* (Frankfurt, 1987), 11–50.

44   Ibid., 159.

that the solution of problems lay in law itself. Thus *bürgerlich* society constituted itself in law as had no other. It is in specific ways a legally-stamped society.[45]

Bürgerlich society, then, was uniquely shaped by its conception of legal procedure.

The German conception of the *Rechtsstaat* shares this pronounced emphasis upon procedure.[46] Emerging in German political and constitutional theory after 1815, the concept of the *Rechtsstaat* evolved as an attempt to rationalize the combination of individualism in state purpose with traditionalism in state structure, and it consisted at first of both material (substantive) and formal (procedural) limitations upon state action. After the middle of the nineteenth century, however, the doctrine of the *Rechtsstaat* diverged from the prescription of the purposes of the state to the prescription of the outer forms of state action.[47] Liberals as well as conservatives embraced the distinctly procedural formulation of Friedrich Julius Stahl: "[The *Rechtsstaat*] signifies above all not the aim and content of the State, but only the method and nature of their realization."[48] Leonard Krieger contends that by the 1870s theorists, among them Gneist, had so emptied the *Rechtsstaat* of its substantive meaning that it now meant "simply the kind of state whose power was articulated in legal modes of action – that is, in measures which conformed to general rules."[49] *Rechtsstaat*

---

45 Ibid., 160–1. A similar argument is made in Dirk Blasius, "Bürgerliches Recht und bürgerliche Identität. Zu einem Problemzusammenhang in der deutschen Geschichte des 19. Jahrhunderts," in Helmut Berding, et al., *Vom Staat des Ancien Regimes zum modernen Parteienstaat. Festschrift für Theodor Schieder* (Munich, 1978), 213–24, 216.

46 The most accessible brief history of German *Rechtsstaat* doctrine is Böckenförde, "The Origin and Development of the Concept of the *Rechtsstaat*." See also the cautionary discussion in Whitman, *The Legacy of Roman Law*, 93–9.

47 Krieger, *The German Idea of Freedom*, 252–3; see also Neumann, *The Rule of Law*, 179–82, 180.

48 Friedrich Julius Stahl, *Die Philosophie des Rechts*, 3rd ed., 3 vols. in 2 (Heidelberg, 1856), vol. 2, *Rechts- und Staatslehre auf der Grundlage christlicher Weltanschauung*, 137, quoted in Neumann, *The Rule of Law*, 180, n. 6. The translation is that of the Neumann volume. The same quotation can be found in Krieger, *German Idea of Freedom*, 256, n. 103, as well as in two important post-1850 treatises: Bähr, *Der Rechtsstaat*, 1, and Rudolf von Gneist, *Der Rechtsstaat und die Verwaltungsgerichte in Deutschland*, 2d ed. (Berlin, 1879; repr. ed., Darmstadt, 1967), 33.

49 Krieger, *German Idea of Freedom*, 459–60, quotation from 460. Others share this view of Gneist's narrow conception; see particularly Hahn, "Rudolf Gneist and the Prussian *Rechtsstaat*," D1361–81, and at greater length, idem, "Rudolf von Gneist." Gneist's primary prescription for realization of the *Rechtsstaat* was creation of a system of administrative courts, which came into being in Prussia as a whole in 1883 but which were not as independent from the regime as courts of ordinary jurisdiction; see Gneist, *Der Rechtsstaat*. Gneist himself served for many years as a member of the Supreme Administrative Court, the *Oberverwaltungsgericht*.

doctrine, then, particularly after the end of the Prussian constitutional crisis in 1866, stressed the primacy of procedure in establishing
a rule of law.[50]

In his sociology of law, Weber argued further that the formally
rational legal system, the *Rechtsstaat*, both produced and was produced by a specific class of legal specialists:

> As the administration of justice requires more and more experience and,
> ultimately, specialized knowledge, we find as a further category private
> counselors and attorneys, whose influence in the formation of the law
> through "legal invention" has often been considerable. . . . The increased
> need for specialized legal knowledge created the professional lawyer.[51]

On the European continent, especially in Germany after the reception
of the Roman law, the absence of a guild-organized and powerful
group of lawyers who controlled education through the apprentice
system, such as the barristers of England, led to the establishment of
legal training in the universities, which emphasized legal theory and
"science" and the rational and systematic treatment of legal phenom-
ena.[52] The jurists who emerged from this university training were a
phenomenon unique to the west, with decisive consequences for the
political structure of continental Europe.[53] The typical products of this
form of formally rational legal education, the typical continental "legal *honoratiores* [notables]," were the judge, the notary, and the
university-trained advocate or lawyer in private practice.[54] Central

50 Other scholars have analyzed the difference in terms of a juridical rather than a political
    conception of the *Rechtsstaat*: Otto Pflanze, "Juridical and Political Responsibility in
    Nineteenth-Century Germany," in Leonard Krieger and Fritz Stern, eds., *The Responsibil-
    ity of Power. Historical Essays in Honor of Hajo Holborn* (Garden City, N.Y., 1967), 162–82,
    167, 180; and Guido de Ruggiero, *The History of European Liberalism*, trans. by R. G.
    Collingwood (Oxford, 1927; repr. ed. Gloucester, Mass., 1981), 251–64.
51 *ES* II:775; *Weber on Law*, 96.
52 *ES* II:785, 788–9; *Weber on Law*, 198, 204. For an example of the power of German law
    professors to shape debate on issues of constitutionalism and legal reform, with inevitable
    political consequences, see Whitman, *The Legacy of Roman Law*, ch. iv, "Imperial Tradition
    and the New Professoriate after 1814," 92–150, and ch. v, "High Cultural Tradition as an
    Instrument of Reform: The Professoriate and the *Agrarfrage*," 151–99. For an insightful
    discussion of the complexity that lay within the seemingly monolithic edifice of German
    legal science, see Mathias Reimann, "Nineteenth-Century German Legal Science," *Boston
    College Law Review* 31 (1990): 837–97.
53 Max Weber, "Politics as a Vocation," in Hans H. Gerth and C. Wright Mills, eds. and
    trans. *From Max Weber: Essays in Sociology* (Oxford, 1946), 77–128, 93–4, cited in Wilfred
    R. Prest, ed., *Lawyers in Early Modern Europe and America* (New York, 1981), 11.
54 *ES* II:855; *Weber on Law*, 278. Unger considers occupational autonomy of the law to be
    an indispensable element of the legal order, meaning that "a special group, the legal
    profession, defined by its activities, prerogatives, and training, manipulates the rules,
    staffs the legal institutions, and engages in the practice of legal argument"; *Law in Modern
    Society*, 53.

then to the procedure-focused, abstract system of formally rational legal thought were the specialists initiated into its mysteries and trained in its folkways, university-trained jurists. Thus, lawyers, including private practitioners, were decisively responsible for the emergence of capitalism and the "legal-rational" state in the West, functioning as standard bearers for the ideals and values of the middle class, advancing its goals, and enabling it to achieve social as well as political hegemony.

Weber also recognized a convergence of interests between the *Bürgertum* and the centralizing monarchies of Germany in the eighteenth century regarding legal training, legal certainty, the legal system, and hence the legal profession.[55] The centralizing monarchies sought to overcome the political power and particularist rights of the "intermediate bodies" of the estates and cities by favoring the *Bürgertum* because it served their fiscal and political power interests.[56] What the *Bürgertum* received in return was employment in service of the state as officials and progress toward the certainty of fixed objective norms of law. Wherever European society evolved from the aristocratic *Ständestaat* to modern liberal society, from a system of bureaucratic law to a truly generalized legal order, trained lawyers directed the process.[57]

The role of lawyers was particularly important in Germany, especially Prussia.[58] Crucial to the struggle of the Hohenzollern monarchs against the nobility and privileged intermediary bodies in the congeries of Prussian states was the creation of a royal bureaucratic counterweight composed, especially under Friedrich Wilhelm I in the first part of the eighteenth century, of men of *bürgerlich* origins, whose claim to office was one of ability as established by patents of university education, at first in cameralism but increasingly as the century progressed in law.[59] A protracted legal, quasi-constitutional, reform ef-

55 *ES* II:846–8; *Weber on Law*, 267–8.

56 For treatments of the points of view that opposed the efforts of the centralizing monarchs to impose their power through the actions of their bureaucratic "movers and doers," see Mack Walker, *German Home Towns*, and idem, *Johann Jakob Moser and the Holy Roman Empire of the German Nation* (Chapel Hill, N.C., 1981).

57 Unger, *Law in Modern Society*, 155–92.

58 For Unger's analysis of the German example, see *Law in Modern Society*, 181–92, 216–20.

59 See especially Rosenberg, *Bureaucracy, Aristocracy, Autocracy*. The reforms of Frederick William I and the social basis of his bureaucrats are set out in Reinhold A. Dorwart, *The Administrative Reforms of Frederick William I of Prussia* (Cambridge, Mass., 1953). Subsequent shifts in policy by Frederick the Great toward reservation of the highest posts for candidates of noble birth are treated in Hubert C. Johnson, *Frederick the Great and His Officials* (New Haven, 1975). For the supplanting of education in *Kameralistik* by education

fort begun by Friedrich II culminated in the Prussian General Law
Code of 1794, which restructured and reformed the *Ständestaat* to
create a clear "occupational estate" (*Berufsstand*) of "exempt" bureaucrats, whose membership was determined by education, achievement, and position of service to the state rather than by birth.[60] Their
training in law committed them to the improvement of the state, and
their belief in reason opened them to the questioning and innovation of
the Enlightenment. But, as has been discussed previously, during the
restoration years of 1815–48, the reactionary era of 1850–8, and the
continual constitutional crisis and turmoil of 1862–71, first state officials and then judges came under great stress, suffering from an oversupply of candidates as well as political supervision and repression.
With state officials and judges subject to discipline and political loyalty
testing at the hands of a monarchical state no longer committed to
reform, the final group of university-trained lawyers available to continue the project of creating a truly generalized legal order was the bar
in private practice. Thus, by 1867 Gneist could well argue that the
mantle of leadership had passed and that private practitioners were the
heirs of the Roman-law and bureaucratic traditions of juristic leadership in the modern legal order.

Conclusion

In 1871 liberal reformers and lawyers in the newly created German
empire believed that the opportunity was at hand to attain their long-
sought goal of the legal unification of Germany and the establishment of a legal order based upon liberal principles. They began their
campaign immediately, and it reached a first climax in the Imperial
Justice Laws of 1877–9.[61] By 1 October 1879, liberals could congratu-
late themselves upon a hard-fought legislative achievement that they
believed had created the conditions that Gneist and others had

in law and its implications for the methods and values of the Prussian bureaucracy, see
Walter L. Dorn, "The Prussian Bureaucracy in the Eighteenth Century," *Political Science
Quarterly* 46 (1931): 403–23, 47 (1932): 75–94, 259–73, in addition to the sources cited in
note 21.

60 Koselleck, *Preußen*, 87–115. For a general discussion of eighteenth-century developments
in judicial administration, and especially for the prolonged legislative project of Frederick
the Great, see Adolf Stölzel, *Brandenburg-Preußens Rechtsverwaltung und Rechtsverfassung,
dargestellt im Wirken seiner Landesfürsten und obersten Justizbeamten*, 2 vols. (Berlin, 1888;
repr. ed., Vaduz, 1989), II:141–309.

61 This first spate of legal reform also addressed some areas of substantive law, notably
criminal law and bankruptcy law. While both of these areas were of great import to liberal
values, they will remain outside the scope of this social history of lawyers.

thought necessary for the private bar to serve as the general estate. The path had been freed from government control and opened to talent and the forces of the marketplace. The private bar could now shoulder its historical burden and serve as the educators and leaders of the German people in the virtues of self-reliance, self-assurance, and political responsibility. But the private legal profession did not do so, and the historical question is: Why not?

The following chapters will examine the internal history of the private legal profession between 1878 and 1933 in order to advance five reasons why the German bar did not fulfill the high expectations that Gneist held for it. First, the reforms of 1877–9 widened opportunities for ambitious young men to become private practitioners and led, slowly at first and then more rapidly, to profound growth in the number of lawyers and a diversification of membership that changed the nature of the bar. New social groups were drawn to the study of law by the unrestricted opportunity to pursue a legal career provided by *freie Advokatur*. Growth in numbers of lawyers led to new career strategies and saw lawyers open practices in new settings, responding to demand in part but also responding to an increase in the supply of lawyers. After the turn of the century, and especially in the 1920s, new economic pressures increased the pace of diversification and change among the membership of the bar. Diversity of origin and of conditions of practice led to increased diversity of interest within the bar and to increased conflict among lawyers.

Second, when lawyers were freed in 1879 to structure their own professional institutions and to govern and administer themselves, they borrowed institutional models central to nineteenth-century German liberalism. The institutions of the private bar, like those of the National Liberal Party, were organizations of notables, in which local worthies expected and had traditionally received deference from the rank-and-file.[62] As time passed and the private bar became more diverse, the national system of voluntary bar associations and manda-

---

62 The concept of the organization of notables, *Honoratiorenorganisation*, crucial to Black-bourn and Eley's view that political liberalism suffered defeat because of its inability to respond to stirrings "from below," is defined in Thomas Nipperdey, *Die Organisation der deutschen Parteien vor 1918* (Düsseldorf, 1961), 86–109. For the limitations of *Honoratioren-politik* after 1890 and its effect upon the National Liberal Party, see Sheehan, *German Liberalism*, 221–38; Geoff Eley, *Reshaping the German Right: Radical Nationalism and Political Change after Bismarck* (New Haven, 1980), 19–40; Blackbourn and Eley, *The Peculiarities of German History*, 251–76; and Geoff Eley, "Notable Politics, the Crisis of German Liberalism, and the Electoral Transition of the 1890s," in Jarausch and Jones, eds., *In Search of a Liberal Germany*, 187–216.

tory lawyers' chambers, dominated by lawyers-notables who practiced before higher courts, proved inadequate either to the task of representing the interests of the bar as a whole as against other social and political groups or to that of containing conflict within the legal profession itself. The organization of notables proved unable to maintain the bar's comfortable and esteemed pose of standing above interest, of discharging its momentous civic functions, of serving as the general estate.

Third, the proceduralism of liberal and legal thought made mediation of substantive disputes within the bar most difficult. This book will examine two case studies, the long struggle between district-court and superior-court lawyers over simultaneous admission, and the equally long debate about the meaning of *freie Advokatur*, which resolved itself into the issue of whether to call for a limit to the number of lawyers, a *numerus clausus*. In both cases, the lawyer-notables who controlled the institutions of the bar discovered to their dismay that all of their efforts to provide procedural outlets for debate of the issues failed to satisfy parties convinced of the substantive rightness of their claims. The leaders of the organizations of notables then simply ran out of solutions, in one case permitting resolution of the conflict by an outside agency, the Reichstag, and in the other simply throwing up their hands in December 1932. Both case studies foreshadow the inadequacy of a procedural notion of justice that revealed itself in the bar's response to the seizure of power in the spring of 1933 by a party with a clear substantive plan for the ordering of society.

Fourth, if these difficulties were not enough, the German bar during the Weimar Republic endured a series of specific crises and political defeats that further weakened the credibility of the lawyer-notable leaders of the bar to represent either the general interests of society or even the general interests of lawyers. The experience of defeat upon defeat enervated and paralyzed the leadership of the bar, further fragmenting efforts to withstand the assault of illiberalism in 1933.

Overarching all of these reasons for the "failure" of the private legal profession to fulfill Gneist's expectations is the illusoriness of its self-conception as the general estate. As early as 1843, Marx had unmasked Hegel's claim for the impartiality and disinterest of the original general estate, state officials, although in the process of "standing Hegel on his head" Marx merely nominated his own candi-

date for the general estate, namely the proletariat.[63] Theories such as
that of Gneist provided reinforcement and higher ethical justification
for lawyers in their pursuit of their professional project, but their
embrace of the middle-class project, their posture as the general estate, was always subject to challenge as a mask for self-interest, either
of the bar as a whole or of the lawyer-notables who led its institutions. But lawyers so intermingled the two projects, so embraced the
role as general estate as part of their professional identity and self-
image, that when increased professional diversity and external challenge unmasked the pretentions of the bar, the disillusionment and
paralysis was all the greater.[64] Lawyers thus did not so much abandon
their commitment to liberalism as they embraced it too well; the
structural deficiencies of liberal procedural notions of justice and of
the general estate simply proved inadequate to German conditions in
the 1920s and 1930s.

63 Marx argues that "As for the individual bureaucrat, the purpose of the state becomes his
    private purpose, *a hunt for promotion, careerism,*" in his comment upon ¶297 of the *Philoso-
    phy of Right* in "Critique of Hegel's Doctrine of the State," in Karl Marx, *Early Writings*,
    intr. by Lucio Colletti and trans. by Rodney Livingstone and Gregor Benton (Har-
    mondsworth, 1992), 57–198, 108; for the proletariat as the true general estate, see "Cri-
    tique of Hegel's *Philosophy of Right*: Introduction," ibid., 243–57, 256. See also the discus-
    sion of Marx's critique in Cohen and Arato, *Civil Society*, 102–4, and Arato, "Hegel's
    Theory of Civil Society," 308–9.
64 The experience of the institutions of the private bar confirmed the observation that while
    professionalization strategies often functioned to promote the middle-class project, the
    border between the professional and middle-class strategies was porous; for lawyers in
    private practice the two strategies became *alternatives.* See Hannes Siegrist, "Bürgerliche
    Berufe. Die Professionen und das Bürgertum," in idem, ed., *Bürgerliche Berufe*, 11–48, 12,
    27, and also Jürgen Kocka, "'Bürgertum' and Professions in the Nineteenth Century: Two
    Alternative Approaches," Michael Burrage and Rolf Torstendahl, eds., *Professions in
    Theory and History. Rethinking the Study of the Professions* (London, 1990), 62–74.

2

Freie Advokatur: *The Blending of the Middle-Class and Professional Projects*

Gneist's publication of *The Free Legal Profession* in 1867 provided impetus and momentum to the movement to reform the legal profession that carried over beyond German unification in 1871 and culminated in the adoption of the Imperial Justice Laws in 1877–9. But its very importance and dramatic success also raise two questions. First, why were the reforms necessary in the first place; that is, how did the subjection of lawyers in private practice to the state, which Gneist saw as the obstacle to their fulfilling the normative role that he prescribed for them, come about? Second, a single call for reform could not have had such dramatic success unless it built upon previous reform efforts and fell upon fertile ground for change. What was the background upon which Gneist's prescriptions must be considered; what were the reasons that they were so quickly legislated into law?

Lawyers in private practice, especially in Prussia, had never attained the position of primacy within the larger legal profession that they had in France or especially in England. In fact, they had suffered over the course of the eighteenth century from a consistent pattern of royal and governmental hostility, in which they saw their numbers, incomes, and privileges reduced and ultimately the legitimacy and the very existence of their profession challenged. Thus, the first two-thirds of the nineteenth century saw lawyers engaged in a slow process of winning public opinion and legislative recognition of the legitimacy and importance of their role in the administration of justice and in civic life. In this regard, they found support in liberal writings and allies in liberal theorists. Gneist was not the first liberal who looked abroad to France and England and concluded that lawyers served as reformers and unifiers of civic and political life. German liberals from early in the nineteenth century had argued that reform of the legal profession was central to a larger project, attaining national legal unity and reform of the court system and trial procedure. The multifarious nature of the German polity under the German Confederation, seemingly confirmed in 1849, with multiple systems of courts, procedure, and governance of the private legal profession, blocked national unification and hindered rational reform of the legal system and legal profession. In the writings of lawyers and liberal theorists, the middle-class project of legal reform and the professional project of emancipation and improvement blended into one. The bar's program and slogan of *freie Advokatur* lay available for Gneist to adopt in 1867, and it became the mobilizing theme for the liberal legislative agenda after 1871.

This chapter, then, examines first the relationship of the German bar in private practice to other legally trained professions such as the judiciary and state service, in other words, the position of the *Rechtsanwaltschaft* within the *Juristenstand*, together with the early evolution of the private legal profession in Germany, culminating in the dramatic attempt in Prussia to abolish the profession altogether, a story perceived by nineteenth-century observers to be one of decline and need for restoration. Second, it considers how the professional project of lawyers and the middle-class project of liberal judicial reform legislation converged prior to 1848 by analyzing the prescriptions for procedural reform and reform of the private bar advanced by liberal precursors to Gneist's galvanizing call to action. Third, it depicts the complex position of agitation by lawyers for professional reform within the context of both liberal hopes for legal reform and state-initiated attempts to rationalize the German legal system. Finally, the focus narrows to the issue of *freie Advokatur*, freedom of advocacy, which Gneist's book raised as the rallying cry both for lawyers and liberals.

Structure and Early History of the Bar

Before beginning a discussion of the history of private practitioners in Germany, it is necessary to understand the position of the practicing bar in relation to the legal profession as most broadly conceived. German lawyers in private practice represent roughly one-quarter to one-third of all university graduates trained in law, in contrast to the American situation, in which roughly three-quarters of all law graduates engage in private practice. The three other principal groups in Germany, each also representing roughly one-quarter of law graduates, are (1) judges and state prosecutors, (2) lawyers serving in general administrative positions in the government bureaucracy, and (3) lawyers in private employment, often in managerial rather than legal positions.[1] This third group, lawyers in private employment, has seen its largest growth during the twentieth century.[2] Throughout the first three-quarters of the nineteenth century, the number of lawyers in private practice rarely equalled the number of judges and often was much smaller.[3] Private practitioners in Germany, then, have always represented a minority of all graduates of the law faculties of universities.

Since the rise of the administrative state in Germany in the eighteenth century, law has been considered to be a profession of high prestige, and the legal faculties of universities have had higher social status than others.[4] Law students tended to come from families high

1 Rueschemeyer, *Lawyers and their Society*, 30. This study is an indispensable starting point for someone who is accustomed to the American system of private legal practice and who seeks to understand the German system. A useful recent summary description of the German private bar in the 1980s, together with a brief sketch of its history, is Erhard Blankenburg and Ulrike Schultz, "German Advocates: A Highly Regulated Profession," in Abel and Lewis, eds., *Lawyers in Society*, 2:124–59. For other general descriptions of the contemporary contours of the German legal profession, see Haimo Schack, "Private Lawyers in Contemporary Society: Germany," *Case Western Reserve Journal of International Law* 25 (1993): 187–205, and Kaupen, *Die Hüter von Recht und Ordnung* (for circumstances in the late 1960s). See also Gneist, *Freie Advocatur*, 18, who indicates that in mid-nineteenth-century Prussia three-quarters of all judicial personnel were judges and only one-quarter lawyers in private practice.

2 Remarkably little historical research has been done into this important group, despite the notorious prominence of trained lawyers among German business leaders; see the recent sociological study by Michael Hartmann, *Juristen in der Wirtschaft. Eine Elite im Wandel* (Munich, 1990), especially 27–35 in which he surveys the history of the expansion of legally trained graduates into business, first in finance, then into other branches, all the while maintaining some of the marks of elite status.

3 See the table found at Gneist, *Freie Advocatur*, 17–18, which indicates that in 1837 there were 2,008 judges, 2,196 *Referendare* (trainees) and *Auskultatoren* (candidates), and 1,146 private practitioners in Prussia. See also Weißler, *Geschichte der Rechtsanwaltschaft*, 528–30. In the United States, according to the U.S. Census, in 1930 86.8 percent of all lawyers were in private practice and 8 percent in government and the judiciary; by 1970 the figures remained 72.6 percent and 15.9 percent; Abel, *American Lawyers*, 172, and table 37b at 299.

4 During the time of the reception of Roman law in the late fifteenth and sixteenth centuries, lawyers who had obtained the doctorate were minor nobles; Gerald Strauss, *Law, Resistance, and the State: The Opposition to Roman Law in Reformation Germany* (Princeton, 1986), 4–5, 25, 166. The high social prestige of the legal faculty of the universities, and hence of legal studies, persisted into the nineteenth and early twentieth centuries. Peter Lundgreen, "Zur Konstituierung des 'Bildungsbürgertums': Berufs- und Bildungsauslese der Akademiker in Preußen," in Conze and Kocka, eds., *Bildungsbürgertum im 19. Jahrhundert*, 79–108, 80, and Tabelle 12, 105; John E. Craig, "Higher Education and Social Mobility in Germany," in Konrad H. Jarausch, ed., *The Transformation of Higher Learning 1860–1930* (Chicago, 1983), 219–44, 224; and Johannes Conrad, "Allgemeine Statistik der Deutschen Universitäten," in Wilhelm Lexis, ed., *Die Deutschen Universitäten*, 2 vols. (Berlin, 1893), 1:115–68, 142, and Tabelle VI, 140–1.

on the social scale; many were aristocrats or children of high state officials or other lawyers. The access to state service and to other positions of power granted by a legal education, together with the privileged origin of legal graduates "facilitated the fusion of the aristocratic, wealthy, and cultivated segments into one elite."[5] This elevated status, however, applied to legal education generally and was closely connected with ideals of state service. Folk wisdom and sayings were full of contempt for and distrust of lawyers in private practice, and the popular prestige of private practitioners reached low points in both the sixteenth and eighteenth centuries.[6] Part of the professional project of the practicing bar in the nineteenth century, then, was to elevate the status of their branch of the *Juristenstand* so that it would equal state service and the judiciary in public esteem.

Within the *Juristenstand* during the eighteenth and nineteenth centuries, prestige varied in relation to the proximity to power. The position of judge ranked first, for "the judiciary in our German fatherland is counted among the most prestigious of all professions."[7] Next in prestige came the state prosecutor, resplendent in the dignity of the state official and charged with the representation of the interests of the state. Finally, less prestigious than these, but by the mid-nineteenth century usually equal in its educational requirements, was the lawyer in private practice, charged with advising clients and

5   Bruford, *Germany in the Eighteenth Century*, 246, 260–1. This discussion is based in large part upon Konrad H. Jarausch, *Students, Society and Politics in Imperial Germany: The Rise of Academic Illiberalism* (Princeton, 1982), 140–4, and an examination of the sources cited therein. Ralf Dahrendorf, "Die Ausbildung einer Elite. Die deutsche Oberschicht und die juristischen Fakultäten," *Der Monat* 14 (1962): 15–26, argues that historically and in the Federal Republic, legal faculties performed the same function of socializing and forming a leadership elite that the public schools performed in England.

6   Strauss, *Law, Resistance, and the State*, esp. 3–30 and 215–30, gives numerous examples of antilawyer folk sayings that were widespread in the sixteenth century and of profound hostility to lawyers by Martin Luther. For the eighteenth century, see the long attack on lawyers that was distributed as a broadsheet published in Berlin in 1780, reproduced in Friedrich Wilhelm Basilius von Ramdohr, *Über die Organisation des Advocatenstandes in monarchischen Staaten* (Hannover, 1801), 25–32; and Salomon Phillipp Gans, *Von dem Amte der Fürsprecher vor Gericht, nebst einem Entwurfe einer Advocaten- und Tax-Ordnung* (Celle, 1820; 2d ed., 1827), 61–78, for a discussion of the decline of the private legal profession in Germany in the seventeenth and eighteenth centuries. For a compendium of antilawyer folk sayings such as "A lawyer and a wagon-wheel both need to be greased," see Günter Grundmann, Michael Strich, and Werner Richey, eds., *Rechtssprichwörter* (Hanau [DDR], 1984); more generally see Erwin Riezler, *Die Abneigung gegen die Juristen* (Munich, 1925), who also mentions Luther's jibes at lawyers, 6.

7   Violets Berufswahlführer, *Der Jurist: Eine Übersicht über sämtliche auf Grund des juristischen Studiums ergreifbaren Berufe innerhalb und außerhalb des Staatsdienstes* (Stuttgart, 1907), 35.

representing their interests in court.[8] Although the profession itself
stressed its role as an independent and integral element of the administration of justice, its public prestige had fallen throughout the eighteenth century.

University training in the law for some practicing lawyers in the
secular courts became necessary with the beginning of the reception
of the Roman law during the late fifteenth and early sixteenth centuries. From the Roman precepts of canon law came the division of
private practice into two branches: procurators, who had the exclusive right to appear before the court and plead cases, and advocates,
who rendered office advice and prepared the cumbersome and technical pleadings required by the common law written system of civil
procedure, adopted from the Roman law.[9] Earlier Germanic institutions such as that of the lay pleader lost out to the trained Roman
lawyers, newly returned from Italian and, later, German universities.[10] The nomenclature was greatly complicated by the multitude of
German states under the Holy Roman Empire, with the definitions
of procurator and advocate being reversed in some regions. Procurators practiced before only one court, and there was usually a fixed
upper limit to the number admitted to practice, a *numerus clausus*,
determined by that court or by the justice ministry of the regional
state. This fixed number of procurators followed from the notion,
with deep roots in the Germanic institution of lay pleader, that pleading before the court was a judicial office, whereas the role of advocate, analysis of the substantive law and preparation of pleadings,

8   See the discussion of the general duties of a lawyer in Adolf Friedländer and Max Fried-
    länder, *Kommentar zur Rechtsanwaltsordnung vom 1. Juli 1878*, 3rd ed. (Munich, Berlin,
    Leipzig, 1930), 12–13.
9   Arthur Engelmann, et al., *A History of Continental Civil Procedure*, trans. and ed. by Robert
    Wyness Millar (Boston, 1927), 544–6. The German terms are *Prokurator* for the individual
    and *Prokuratur* for the occupational group; likewise, *Advokat* and *Advokatur*.
10 For an account and explanation of popular hostility toward lawyers during the time of the
    reception, see Strauss, *Law, Resistance, and the State*, esp. ch. 6, 165–90. Weißler, *Geschichte
    der Rechtsanwaltschaft*, provides the most comprehensive history of the *Vorsprecher* ("lay
    pleader"), 23–83. He also gives a clear account of the origins of the division of the profession
    into *Prokuratur* and *Advokatur* in the canonical procedure and its transfer into secular courts
    with the reception, 110–21, 168–79. A "push-pull" effect characterized the growth of the
    legal faculties of universities and of the legal profession between the sixteenth and eighteenth
    centuries. See Filippo Ranieri, "Vom Stand zum Beruf. Die Professionalisierung des Ju-
    ristenstandes als Forschungsaufgabe der europäischen Rechtsgeschichte der Neuzeit," *Ius
    Commune* 13 (1985): 83–105 (published in abbreviated form and without scholarly apparatus
    in English as "From Status to Profession: The Professionalisation of Lawyers as a Research
    Field in Modern European Legal History," *Journal of Legal History* 10 [1989]: 180–90),
    William J. Bouwsma, "Lawyers and Early Modern Culture," *American Historical Review* 78
    (1973): 303–27, and the essays in Prest, ed., *Lawyers in Early Modern Europe and America*.

was not an official function but rather a private service with which
the court did not have to concern itself.[11] There was therefore no
fixed number of advocates, and anyone who met the prescribed educational requirements could practice; hence they were less insulated
from economic competition. Because of the need for expertise in the
Roman law in order to prepare the written pleadings, advocates were
usually university-trained, commonly licentiates, and often doctors
of one or both laws (civil and canon). Procurators, in contrast,
needed no university training in the law to argue cases based upon
pleadings drafted by advocates, so that their training was usually
practical, based upon the apprentice system. The result was a lower
social rank for procurators.[12] The distinction between procurator and
advocate differed from that between barrister and solicitor in England; social and educational levels differed, as well as the legal and
institutional background of the functional division, so the German
terms will be preferred.[13]

By the beginning of the eighteenth century, both branches of the
profession, but especially the procurators, had fallen into public disrepute. The responses of the territorial states were various, all tending
toward a stricter discipline in order to prevent abuses, but none went
so far as Prussia. There, the distinction between procurator and advocate had gradually faded, so that by the beginning of the eighteenth
century most advocates were also procurators.[14] The Great Elector

11 Weißler, *Geschichte der Rechtsanwaltschaft*, 296. The *Vorsprecher* was appointed by the judge
    at the request of a party, and he remained the representative of the judge, in the service of
    justice, not of the party's interest; ibid., 27, 33–4. The correct prefix is "vor-" rather than
    "für-," for the *Vorsprecher* spoke *before* the court and *before* the party, rather than *for* the
    party; ibid., 26.
12 Strauss, *Law, Resistance, and the State*, 16–18; Döhring, *Geschichte der deutschen Rechts-
    pflege*, 120.
13 The correspondence is much closer to the French system of university or law school
    trained *avocats* and guild-like *procureurs* (later *avoués*). See Bell, *Lawyers and Citizens*, 26–40;
    Fitzsimmons, *The Parisian Order of Barristers*, 1–33; Berlanstein, *The Barristers of Toulouse*,
    4–11; Woloch, "The Fall and Resurrection of the Civil Bar"; and Werner Schubert, ed.,
    Entstehung und Quellen der Rechtsanwaltsordnung (Frankfurt, 1985), 4–6, for the French
    system under the Ancien Régime, Revolution, and Restoration. For a survey of the
    structures of the bars in various European countries in the first half of the nineteenth
    century, see H., "The Continental Bar – State of the Profession in France, Germany,
    Spain, and Italy," *The Law Magazine or, Quarterly Review of Jurisprudence* 13 (1835): 287–
    309. For the structure of the French system in the early twentieth century, see Pierre
    Prud'hon and Jean Appleton, "Frankreich," in Julius Magnus, ed., *Die Anwaltschaft*
    (Leipzig, 1929), 92–100; Paul Fuller, "The French Bar," *Yale Law Journal* 16 (1907): 457–
    70; and E. M. Underdown, *The French Judiciary and Bar* (London, 1911).
14 Weißler, *Geschichte der Rechtsanwaltschaft*, 290–1, 295–6. The *Prokuratur* was formally abol-
    ished in 1738 but later reinstated; it was finally and effectually abolished in 1748 in the
    Codex Fridericianus Marchicus, ibid., 325, 333. Most complaints about abuses by the legal

had already in the seventeenth century placed strict limits upon the number of procurators, and a legal examination was required of all procurators and advocates at the court of appeal in Berlin after 1709.[15] The strictest measures, however, were taken by King Friedrich Wilhelm I, whose attitude toward lawyers is best exemplified by the reason that he supposedly gave in promulgating a sumptuary law that required a distinctive costume for lawyers "so that you may recognize the swindlers from afar and protect yourself against them."[16] Only a month after his accession to the throne in 1713, he reduced the number of lawyers permitted to practice before the court of appeal in Berlin by two-thirds and ruled that they could charge only one-fourth of their former fee.[17] He anticipated complaints that would arise from the reduction in fees by reasoning:

> The privy council shall set the number of procurators smaller than has been the case up until now; if the advocates and procurators say that they cannot live, that is not true, because there are now only 24 advocates and 24 procurators and thus the number is three times less than before, and they can live just as well as before.[18]

Later in 1713, Friedrich Wilhelm extended his efforts to reduce the number of lawyers to the entire kingdom, and the total number of advocates in Prussia shrank from 887 to 336 and that of procurators from 165 to 82.[19]

The efforts by Friedrich Wilhelm I to reduce the number of lawyers constituted an integral part of his more general administrative reforms and of his efforts to ensure that his officials were properly trained for their tasks through the imposition of a system of state

---

profession concerned the nonuniversity-trained *Prokuratur*; university-trained *Advokaten* legally assumed the duties of pleading cases in court as they had done in practice over many years. The result was the extinction in Prussia of nonuniversity-trained practitioners, except for *Rechts-* and *Winkelkonsulenten*; Gneist, *Freie Advocatur*, 3–4.

15 Gerhard Dilcher, "Die preußischen Juristen und die Staatsprüfungen. Zur Entwicklung der juristischen Professionalisierung im 18. Jahrhundert," in Karl Kroeschell, ed., *Festschrift für Hans Thieme zu seinem 80. Geburtstag* (Sigmaringen, 1986), 295–305, esp. 297–8.

16 Kaupen, *Die Hüter von Recht und Ordnung*, 20–1. "Damit man die Spitzbuben schon von weitem erkennen und sich vor ihnen hüten möge." Weißler gives the source for this oft-quoted statement as Otto Hintze, *Acta Borussica* VI. 1, 211; *Geschichte der Rechtsanwaltschaft*, 310.

17 Friedrich W. Holtze, *Geschichte des Kammergerichts in Brandenburg-Preußen*, 4 vols. (Berlin, 1901), vol. 3, "Das Kammergericht im 18. Jahrhundert," 90–2.

18 Cited in Weißler, *Geschichte der Rechtsanwaltschaft*, 297–300, 298.

19 Ibid., 302–4. Rueschemeyer emphasizes the fiscal aspect of this measure, pointing out that the newly confirmed lawyers had to pay fees for their patents of office and that the dismissed lawyers had also paid substantial fees for their offices; *Lawyers and their Society*, 149, relying upon Weißler, *Geschichte der Rechtsanwaltschaft*, 296–310.

examinations. Between 1693 and the accession of Friedrich Wilhelm in 1713, examinations in law were imposed as preconditions first for judges at the court of appeal in Berlin, later for lower judicial officials and judges at lower courts, and finally for lawyers at the court of appeal and at lower courts. By 1723 all judges and all lawyers at royal courts had to pass examinations that proved their conversance with the law; by 1749 this requirement was extended to patrimonial courts as well. While these examinations raised the standards of legal knowledge among judges and lawyers in Prussia, they also extended the tradition of close identification with the state from judges, who were state employees, to private practitioners.[20]

The efforts of Friedrich Wilhelm I were just the beginning, however, of a series of drastic and arbitrary reforms of the private practice of law in Prussia. At the urging of Georg Friedrich Cammann, an advocate before the courts of the New Mark of Brandenburg, the king attempted to establish an expedited oral civil procedure, but the efforts failed in the face of widespread nonobservance by courts and lawyers.[21] Frederick II's famous reforming minister of justice and later chancellor, Samuel von Coccecji, followed with the *Codex Fridericianus Marchicus* and the foundations for the Prussian General Law Code of 1794, and the final dissolution of the profession of procurator.[22] Then came Johann Heinrich Casimir Carmer, minister of justice first in the province of Silesia and later the entire Kingdom of Prussia, who broached the idea of the abolition of the private practice of law. If the real duty of the lawyer was to seek the truth, no matter whose case it helped or hurt, rather than to conceal or confound the truth if it was hurtful to his client's case, then the basic relation between lawyer, client, and court must be changed. After initial defeats, Carmer succeeded in the draft of the *Corpus Iuris Fridericianum* of 1781 in abolishing the practice of law as a free profes-

---

20 The standard work in English remains Dorwart, *The Administrative Reforms of Frederick William I*; see 77–8 for the effect on lawyers of the legal reform of 1713. Regarding the imposition of the requirement of legal examinations for judges and lawyers, see Dilcher, "Die preußischen Juristen und die Staatsprüfungen," 297–8. For a more general discussion of the regularization of legal examinations as a qualification for appointment as a higher state official, see Bleek, *Von der Kameralausbildung*, 38–44, 56–61, and 79–82.

21 Holtze, *Geschichte des Kammergerichts*, vol. 3, 97–113; Weißler, *Geschichte der Rechtsanwaltschaft*, 314–16.

22 A description of Coccecji's judicial and administrative reforms can be found in Rosenberg, *Bureaucracy, Aristocracy, Autocracy*, 123–36, and a more comprehensive account in Johnson, *Frederick the Great and His Officials*, ch. 4, "Rise of the Judicial Bureaucracy," 106–33. For the long Frederician reform project, see Stölzel, *Brandenburg-Preußens Rechtsverwaltung und Rechtsverfassung*, 2:141–309.

sion; henceforth, parties in litigation would be accompanied upon their motion by "assistance counsellors," paid state officials, drawn from the ranks of the judiciary, whose primary task was to aid the court in determining the truth.

> At the very least, the assistance counsellors, who are sworn to the truth and have received the right to the trust of His Royal Majesty and the public on this single condition, must not let themselves be misused as tools of chicanery, untruth, fraud, or injustice, and if ever an assistance counsellor in even a single case makes himself guilty of such crimes, he shall not only be immediately cashiered without further proceedings, but in addition be sentenced to confinement in prison or fortress as a perjurer.[23]

The new code provided for an expedited and oral system of procedure, abolishing the old common law written procedure, and the task of the assistance counsellor was to elicit the facts from the party and present them truthfully to the court. The assistance counsellor received a salary from the state, and the party paid fees into the state treasury for his services.

In Prussia, then, this radical reform abolished the free profession of lawyer and replaced it with a category of state officials; indeed, this measure reduced the representation of parties to an auxiliary function of the judiciary. Parties possessed no influence in the selection of the assistance counsellor; instead, the court assigned one.[24] But what happened to the lawyers already in practice? The new system was only for cases of ordinary jurisdiction litigated before regular courts. For matters of noncontentious jurisdiction and office advice, the law created the new office of "justice commissar." Former lawyers who had been excluded from trial practice were thus entitled to advise and represent clients in all legal matters that were not ordinary trials.[25]

The new system of assistance counsellor was unworkable; it encountered resistance from lawyers and the public, caused confusion and delay in litigation, and was then abandoned by 1783. The Prussian General Court Ordinance of 1793 entitled the justice commis-

---

23 Gneist, *Freie Advocatur*, 9. For discussions of the legal reforms of Cammann, Cocceji, and Carmer, see Weißler, *Geschichte der Rechtsanwaltschaft*, 314–59, and Holtze, *Geschichte des Kammergerichts*, 3:244–5, 328–31. The German term that I render "assistance counsellor" is *Assistenzrat*.

24 Döhring, *Geschichte der deutschen Rechtspflege*, 114. As Weißler puts it: "Thus was the private practice of law then in Prussia brought under state control. The citizen no longer could seek legal counsel and representation from a trusted person freely chosen, but rather from a state official assigned to him by the state"; *Geschichte der Rechtsanwaltschaft*, 353.

25 Weißler, *Geschichte der Rechtsanwaltschaft*, 353. The German term that I render "justice commissar" is *Justizkommissar*.

sars, who were appointed by the ministry of justice, to appear in ordinary litigation and otherwise to perform all the functions of the former advocates.[26] Strictly localized (required to live at a particular place), they were admitted only before a particular court. Although lawyers now received remuneration by fees rather than a fixed salary, and the choice of a representative was returned to the party, in the public mind the close relation to the state apparatus was apparent; if not actually state officials, the justice commissars were clearly state-official-like. While the ministry of justice fixed no set *numerus clausus* for each court, it controlled admissions strictly to prevent oversupply of these representatives before any particular court.

The reforms of Frederick the Great, while bringing an upheaval to the world of the private legal profession, actually resulted in some benefits for the justice commissars. The principle that the educational requirements for lawyers in private practice should be the same as those for judges gained acceptance after the legislative reduction of the profession to one university-trained branch, and aspirants to both careers sat for the same three bar examinations.[27] The strict limitation imposed by the ministry of justice upon the number of private practitioners ensured a high income to those who were appointed; the result was that judges, often senior ones held in high esteem for their experience and skill, resigned from the bench and applied for appointment to the more lucrative bar.[28] A final result of the system of state appointment of lawyers was that the strict limit on their numbers led to an oversupply of candidates for legal and judicial positions, causing the beginnings of a clamor for reform. Despite subsequent legislative revisions, however, the most lasting result of the Frederician reforms remained the basic conception that private legal counsel must be bound to the state in some capacity in order to prevent abuses and to regulate the profession.[29]

Yet the abortive experiment of 1781–93, especially the chaos that reigned between 1781 and 1783, convinced many worried lawyers

---

26 For a text of the pertinent provisions of the Prussian General Court Ordinance (*Allgemeine Gerichtsordnung*) of 1793, see Alexander Brix, *Organisation der Advokatur in Preußen, Österreich, Sachsen, Oldenburg, Braunschweig, Baden, Württemberg, Mecklenburg-Schwerin und Strelitz, Schweiz, Frankreich und England, nebst einer Einleitung, quellenmäßig dargestellt* (Vienna, 1868), 6–22. The discussion here relies heavily upon Gneist, *Freie Advocatur*, 12–18.

27 Brix, *Organisation der Advokatur*, 31–45, for the test requirements as embodied in the Prussian statute of 1849.

28 Weißler, *Geschichte der Rechtsanwaltschaft*, 530.

29 Döhring, *Geschichte der deutschen Rechtspflege seit 1500*, 115; see also Weißler, *Geschichte der Rechtsanwaltschaft*, 343–85, esp. 360–71.

that a truly independent counsel, representing the interests of the party rather than abstract interests of justice, was indispensable to the orderly prosecution of civil cases. While the reforms of 1781–93 secured comfortable incomes for those admitted to the bar and established the principle of educational equality between bench and bar, they also erected a lasting infringement upon the independence of private practitioners. Lawyers in Prussia occupied their positions by virtue of governmental appointment and discretion, subject to governmental discipline, and their numbers were strictly limited, yet they were retained and employed by private parties. Practitioners experienced these restrictions as degrading and humiliating. Moreover, candidates for the bar were at the mercy of the discretion of the ministry of justice for appointment to practice, again experienced as an unworthy limitation upon a proud profession. Despite the survival of the bar after 1793, tutelage to the state remained strong. This abject position of the private bar soon attracted the attention of professional and political reformers.[30]

Convergence of the Professional and Middle-Class Projects

In the first half of the nineteenth century, the practicing bar in Germany presented a motley spectacle. There was a unified legal profession in Prussia, Austria, Saxony, and several of the smaller Thuringian states, and in these states procurators had disappeared; in the Prussian Rhineland, a bifurcated profession consisted of an unlimited number of university-trained, office-practicing advocates, complemented by *Advokatanwälte* appointed in fixed number with a monopoly on courtroom pleading; elsewhere the old system of a fixed number of procurators and an unlimited number of advocates prevailed; and in Ostfriesland in Hannover, the old Prussian justice commissar still persisted.[31]

Although it is difficult to generalize without resorting to a long list

---

30 Gneist, *Freie Advocatur*, 3. Gneist believed that the reform of the legal profession from above was necessary because the bar was too geographically dispersed and personally individualized to create a professional consciousness on its own, as judges had done in collegial courts since the sixteenth century; ibid., 2.

31 Weißler, *Geschichte der Rechtsanwaltschaft*, 424. See also the overview in the introduction to Brix, *Organisation der Advokatur*, v–xii; for Hannover, see also Chr. W. E. Freudentheil, *Zur Geschichte des Advocatenstandes des Königreichs Hannover bis zum Jahre 1837* (Stade, 1903).

of exceptions, the German bar shared numerous other characteristics during the *Vormärz*. Mandatory representation by a lawyer was the rule before higher and middle-level courts, requiring that parties be represented by counsel when appearing before them. This practice had two origins: first in the traditional privileges of the fixed body of the procurators, attached to a court, and second in the idea that, with the gradual acceptance of oral civil procedure, representation by counsel was more necessary in order to expedite the trial and guard the interests of the orderly administration of justice. Mandatory representation by a lawyer thus was seen as a necessary concomitant of oral civil procedure based upon the French model. Written procedure still prevailed in most of Germany, but increasingly, reform measures adopted an oral civil procedure.[32] Procurators and (where there was no division) the unified profession were localized, that is, each lawyer was admitted to a particular court and could appear only before it; all other lawyers, admitted before other courts, were excluded. Where the division of the profession persisted, the pleading-drafting advocates were not localized, and neither courts nor administrative bureaucracies exercised control over their number. Statutes demanded of lawyers the same educational requirements that were required of judges, usually university training and two bar examinations separated by a period of practical legal education.[33] The ministries of justice of the various governments appointed lawyers to practice, no longer the courts themselves, and many states, particularly Prussia and Austria, kept the numbers quite low. Oversight and discipline of lawyers rested with the courts, usually the superior courts, and lower-ranked clerks investigated alleged infractions, an affront to the dignity of the university-trained lawyers. Finally, fee statutes existed in almost all of the German states, and the courts possessed the power to reduce or even to deny a lawyer's fee on a case-by-case basis. The income of lawyers was adequate but not extremely high and always subject to arbitrary reduction by the courts.[34]

Against the background of this almost incomprehensible fragmen-

32 Notably in Prussia in 1833, extended to the whole kingdom in 1846; see Weißler, *Geschichte der Rechtsanwaltschaft*, 364–71. The German term that I render as "oral civil procedure" is *Mündlichkeit*; Millar translates it as the principle of "orality," but that term seems needlessly awkward; Engelmann, *A History of Continental Civil Procedure*, 49–62, 53, 595. The German term that I render as "mandatory representation by a lawyer" is *Anwaltszwang*.
33 Döhring, *Geschichte der Rechtspflege*, 127, makes the point that occasionally the requirements for passing examinations were *more stringent* for private practitioners than for judges, in an attempt to keep "unsuited" elements out of the profession.
34 Weißler, *Geschichte der Rechtsanwaltschaft*, 424–39.

tation of the legal profession, two strands of literature emerged in the first half of the nineteenth century, both of which placed the improvement of the status of the legal profession at the center of a campaign for legislative reform. First, a number of works, some of them written by practitioners, attempted to analyze the reasons for the decline of the German bar and to prescribe reforms that would restore its former glories. In the aftermath of the Prussian effort to abolish the private bar, these authors had to defend the very legitimacy of the profession before they could advance proposals to improve its status. A central tactic in the arguments of these writers was that improvement of the status of lawyers in private practice and advances in their independence, prestige, and income served the interests of the common good, of the civic community.

By adopting this tactic, these tracts merged almost seamlessly with the second body of literature that called for reform: that authored by liberal political theorists. As part of their rationalist critique of the particularism of the old regime in Germany, these liberals viewed the vast complexity of court systems (including patrimonial jurisdiction), procedural systems, and legal professions in the manifold German states as impediments to economic improvement, protection of individual liberty, the growth of civic life, and of national unity. This kaleidoscope of legal systems hindered the predictability, certainty, and uniformity of legal outcome that was central to the *Rechtsstaat*, and thus it needed reform. As these bodies of literature evolved, there emerged a generally agreed upon comprehensive reform scheme in which reform of the private bar stood as the keystone to rationalization of court organization and procedure in general and as the gateway to national legal reform. These two literatures then stood as background to Gneist's summons to reform the legal profession and framed the discourse of *freie Advokatur* in which he spoke.

Friedrich Wilhelm Basilius von Ramdohr, a Hannoverian judge, argued in 1801 that lawyers were a necessary part of the administration of justice, indispensable mediators between parties and judges, who guarded against arbitrary error by the judge and blind commitment to interest by the client.[35] He sought to refute those who contended that the profession was so corrupt that it should either be abolished or supervised with extreme scrutiny by the state, explicitly rejecting the idea that it should be made a state service. Instead:

---

35 von Ramdohr, *Ueber die Organisation des Advocatenstandes*, 3–8.

The other way [to reform the legal profession] is this: the lawyer remains independent from the state, as far as every citizen of the state can be, but the advantages that the state guarantees to the lawyer in the pursuit of his art must bind him to it.[36]

He drew an invidious comparison between the degraded condition of the profession in Germany and its elevated status in France, England, Denmark, and Holland, where lawyers, by virtue of public and oral court proceedings, enjoyed great prestige and honor.[37] Ramdohr embraced a limitation upon the total number of practitioners and public employment, but not appointment, of private lawyers.[38] Despite these concessions to the tutelage of the state, he defended two basic principles: the propriety of the existence of lawyers as representatives of parties and their independence from the state so far as possible.

In 1820 Salomon Phillipp Gans, a lawyer in private practice in the Hannoverian city of Celle, also published a book that defended the existence of the private bar, lamented its degradation in Germany, and prescribed steps, even draft legislation, for its restoration. He argued the necessity of the private bar from the very nature of judicial proceedings and traced its origins to the first appearance of courts: "The office of lawyer is thus as old and as necessary as that of the judge."[39] He also drew a negative comparison with England and France, arguing that in those lands the prestige and honor of the bar had not declined as it had in Germany, because "in the constitutions of those lands a shadow of the Roman constitution, which was the cause of the greatness of the Roman legal profession, still existed, namely a popular assembly and public court proceedings."[40] Compared to these countries, the German bar had suffered a great decline, and Gans advanced a diagnosis:

The lack of all causes for its greatness, the absence of a public popular assembly and the public administration of justice is the sole cause of the decline of the private legal profession in Germany.[41]

The prescription for the restoration of its greatness was clear: opening court proceedings to the public and ending the "complete subjection of lawyers to the courts and to despotism"; the key to restoring

36 Ibid., 38.   37 Ibid., 40–1.   38 Ibid., 61, 62–9.
39 Gans, *Von dem Amte der Fürsprecher vor Gericht*, 9.
40 Ibid., 53–4. For a discussion of Gans's perceptions of the status of the bar in England and France, see ibid., 54–8.
41 Ibid., 64.

the greatness of the bar was to grant it the "noble flower of regulated freedom and independence."[42]

Gans suggested a fourfold means of accomplishing this restoration: (1) the greatest possible independence of lawyers from the power of the court with regard to the conduct of their profession; (2) protection from arbitrary discipline at the hands of the courts; (3) an end to judicial determination of legal fees by means of a legislative fee schedule; and (4) equality of education with the judges at the level of court before which the lawyer practiced.[43] In thus formulating the professional project of lawyers, Gans set the stage for its intersection with the middle-class project of liberalism, and he prescribed the very remedy that liberal theorists began to propose in the 1830s.

At the same time that authors like Ramdohr and Gans defended the legal profession and called for reforms to increase its prestige, liberal theorists, many of whom were trained as lawyers, discovered the private bar. Private practitioners embodied many of the characteristics that liberal theory valued highly: advanced, cultivated, neo-humanistic education; eloquence and quick thinking, developed through rational argument; relative independence from the state conferred by their position in the market and by a training easily transferable to other occupations; and independence of thought and judgment. Conscious and envious of the English model, liberals from the 1830s began to hope for great accomplishments from lawyers, looking to them for leadership.

The upheavals of the Napoleonic Wars had provided great impetus for liberal theorizing about the reform and national unification of the multifarious particularist legal systems of the various German states. In the Rhineland, French occupation between 1794 and 1814 had left behind new codes of substantive and procedural law. The influence of French procedural law reached even east of the Rhine, and it conformed in many particulars to the desires of liberals for protection of the citizen from the repressive policies of the restoration governments.[44] Most specifically, French procedure was oral rather than written.

---

42 Ibid., 211–14.
43 Ibid., 211–44; Gans prescribed a divided legal profession in which some better-trained lawyers could practice before all courts while others, with less training, could practice only before intermediate or lower courts; 242–3.
44 The importance of the influence of the *Code Napoléon* on the right bank of the Rhine, including its procedural aspects, even in states in which the code was not fully introduced, is a central theme of Elisabeth Fehrenbach, *Traditionale Gesellschaft und revolutionäres Recht. Die Einführung des Code Napoléon in den Rheinbundstaaten*, 3rd ed. (Göttingen, 1983).

Vormärz liberals envisioned three interrelated procedural reforms as necessary foundations of the *Rechtsstaat*: codes of trial procedure for civil and criminal cases, a law governing court organization, and a new law governing the organization of the private legal profession. They viewed public and oral trial procedure as paramount in order to force the workings of justice out into the open and to protect the citizen from the arbitrariness of the traditional written and secret procedure of German practice.[45] The demand for publicity of proceedings was an integral part of the project of constructing a political "public sphere" for the expression of "public opinion" on matters of political import.[46] The best means to promote the ends of efficiency, clarity, and certainty in procedure was to adopt the principles of public and oral pleading from French procedure.

For the new trial procedure to work, the system of court organization required profound reform. The independence of the judiciary from the regime had to be established beyond all doubt to ensure a fearless corps of judges who would not hesitate to find in favor of the citizen against the government. Reform should eradicate all vestiges of patrimonial jurisdiction, bringing all cases into the purview of state-run courts. Trial by jury served as a further bulwark of the rights of the citizen, especially for serious crimes and for cases involving freedom of the press.[47] Carl Joseph Anton Mittermaier, professor of law at Heidelberg and later in 1848 president of the *Vorparlament,* argued in 1831 that the precondition for the protection of any rights of the citizen was the proper organization, or constitution, of the court system:[48]

45 The most accessible survey of the history of civil procedure in Germany is found in Engelmann, *History of Continental Civil Procedure*; for introductions to continental civil law systems more generally, see Merryman, *The Civil Law Tradition,* and Alan Watson, *The Making of the Civil Law* (Cambridge, Mass., 1981).
46 Jürgen Habermas, *Strukturwandel der Öffentlichkeit. Untersuchungen zu einer Kategorie der bürgerlichen Gesellschaft* (Darmstadt and Neuwied, 1962), 101–11, esp. 105–6.
47 The ideological centrality of trial by jury in creating a sense of solidarity among the Rhenish *Bürgertum* is the central theme of a very important essay by Dirk Blasius, "Der Kampf um die Geschworenengerichte im Vormärz," in Hans-Ulrich Wehler, ed., *Sozialgeschichte Heute. Festschrift für Hans Rosenberg zum 70. Geburtstag* (Göttingen, 1974), 148–61, esp. 156. See also Peter Landau, "Schwurgerichte und Schöffengerichte in Deutschland im 19. Jahrhundert bis 1870," in Antonio Padoa Schioppa, ed., *The Trial Jury in England, France, Germany 1700–1900* (Berlin, 1987), 241–304.
48 *Gerichtsverfassung* means literally "constitution of the courts." It encompasses the concept of the statutory framework setting forth courts of initial and appellate jurisdiction and defining their subject matter and territorial jurisdictions in matters both of civil and criminal law. It also was often construed to include the statutory framework for the private practice of law. Landau, "Die Reichsjustizgesetze von 1879," 196–7; Kern, *Geschichte des Gerichtsverfassungsrecht,* 92; and idem, *Gerichtsverfassungsrecht. Ein Studienbuch,* 2d ed. (Munich, 1954),

It depends upon the organization of the courts whether the citizen will receive justice in a dispute against a mighty opponent, whether he can hope to see his property truly protected by the courts, whether the courts to which he must turn afford adequate surety of their independence of power of will and intelligence.[49]

For the desired reforms of trial procedure and court organization to have meaning, the organization of the private practice of law had to be changed. Mittermaier continued:

All attempts to effect a fundamental improvement of our procedural arrangements and to introduce a meaningful form of public and oral procedure as the foundation of a new reorganization must fail if they are not based above all upon a better position for the legal profession. . . . It is the profession [*Stand*] of lawyers in private practice who appear everywhere as advisor to those in need of aid, as representative of the afflicted, as control of judges, as eternally watchful protector of all oppressed, as translator of judgments once handed down, as explicators of the law. The degree of trust that the people have in the administration of justice and in their judges depends upon the legal profession. The legal profession promotes and refines the sense of justice of the people, and it can prevent that pernicious evil, the addiction to lawsuits.[50]

Other liberal observers agreed that the role of lawyers in private practice was crucial. Friedrich List argued in the *Staats-Lexikon* in 1834 that publicity of procedure would fit lawyers in private practice for their ascribed role in the procedural *Rechtsstaat*:

Publicity of the administration of justice again proves itself to be the life's breath of all state institutions, without which nothing can thrive. The lawyer is trained by means of the publicity of proceedings and thereby receives his position in public opinion, and respect and dignity in the eyes of judges and the public – and independence in his calling with regard to public authority; by means of publicity of proceedings, the legal profession forms the natural control of the judges as well as the nursery wherein future judges are trained; finally, by means of publicity, lawyers attain the high calling of instructing the people in their rights and duties, of perfecting the state of the

164–74. The closest analog in American practice to the *Gerichtsverfassungsgesetz* of 1877 is Title 28, U.S.C. The Constitution of the Courts of 1877 was a piece of legislation rather than an integral part of the constitution of the German Empire.

49 Carl Josef Anton Mittermaier, "Ueber die Bestimmungen einer zweckmäßigen Gerichtsverfassung und Proceßordnung," *Archiv für die civilistische Praxis* 14 (1831): 398–420, 399–400 (hereafter abbreviated *AcP*).

50 Carl Joseph Anton Mittermaier, "Die künftige Stellung des Advocatenstandes," *AcP* 15 (1832): 138–50, 138–9. See also the speech by Heinrich von Gagern in the Hessian *Landtag*, 3 October 1833, in Paul Wentzcke and Wolfgang Klötzer, eds., *Deutscher Liberalismus im Vormärz. Heinrich von Gagern, Briefe und Reden 1815–1848* (Göttingen, 1959), 121–8.

law, of ever improving legal science and keeping it always in stride with the general cultivation of the people.[51]

The more civilized and politically educated a people, the higher the esteem that the legal profession enjoyed.[52] Karl Brater described them as the only realistic group in German society with the necessary legal knowledge, life experience, and personal independence to occupy leading positions in public life.[53]

Lenore O'Boyle has summarized succinctly the normative argument about lawyers as follows:

For both liberals and democrats [in 1848], the case of the lawyers became the focus of wider political considerations. An improvement in the lawyers' status was seen as inseparable from the extension of political liberty. Only in a free society, one subject to law rather than to official caprice, could the legal profession play its proper role. Oral proceedings, trial by jury, free press coverage, would give the lawyer significance in the eyes of the public. Conversely, only an honored and independent legal profession could teach the public the meaning of government under law. The lawyers came to be regarded by many not only as possible but as necessary allies in the struggle for free government.[54]

From *Vormärz*, through 1848, and into the 1860s, liberals attributed to lawyers the role of educating and leading the *Bürgertum* toward the establishment of a legal order and to political power. Procedural reform of court organization and trial procedure would culminate in a new framework for the private practice of law, and the reformed lawyers would bring life and substance to the new framework. Expressed otherwise, Gneist and other liberal reformers viewed lawyers in private practice as the shock troops, the leading edge, of the middle class project.

Legal Reform, Professional Reform, and National Unity

The close imbrication of the private bar's professional project and the middle-class project of legal reform championed by German liberals

51 Friedrich List, "Advocat," in Carl von Rotteck and Carl Welcker, eds., *Staats-Lexikon oder Encyklopädie der Staatswissenschaften* (Altona, 1834), 15 vols., I:363–77, 366.
52 List, "Advocat," 363. The future president of the Frankfurt Parliament, Heinrich von Gagern, wrote that respect for lawyers rose and fell in the same measure as the political freedom of a people and that when that freedom was high, lawyers were the first among all estates, the leaders of the people; Wentzcke and Klötzer, eds., *Deutscher Liberalismus im Vormärz*, Nr. 176, letter from Heinrich von Gagern to Heinrich Karl Hofmann, fall 1845, 294–304, 296.
53 Karl Brater, "Advokatur," in Johann Caspar Bluntschli, ed., *Deutsches Staats-Wörterbuch* (Stuttgart and Leipzig, 1851), 11 vols., I:71–82, 81.
54 Lenore O'Boyle, "The Democratic Left in Germany, 1848," *Journal of Modern History* 33 (1961): 374–83, 379.

also linked the reform of private practice to the great question of nineteenth-century German history – national unification. Any step toward legal reform, any progress toward professional reform, raised the issue of whether it should proceed on a national stage, and if so, what German nation. German liberals insisted from the very beginning that their goals included both reform and national unification of the various particularist systems of law in the various German states and hence reform and national unification of laws governing the private legal profession.[55]

Anton C. F. Thibaut sounded the tocsin for legal reform in 1814 when he advocated the drafting of a German national civil law code in his pamphlet, *On the Necessity of a General Civil Law for Germany.* He argued:

The value of mere [legal] unity would be inestimable. Even if political division must and ought to prevail, the Germans would nevertheless be highly interested in a fraternal common sentiment binding them together. Moreover, civic commerce makes [legal] unity almost a screaming necessity.[56]

Friedrich Carl von Savigny famously attacked Thibaut's call for rationalistic codification of substantive civil law, arguing instead in favor of the historical, "organic," and therefore particularistic development of law. The thought of the "historical school" founded by Savigny prevailed in legal academic circles and postponed codification of substantive law until 1896.[57] However, procedural law proved less vulnerable to organicist anticodification arguments, and hopes for national legal

55 The most comprehensive work on the history of the movement toward legal unification in Germany is Getz, *Die deutsche Rechtseinheit im 19. Jahrhundert*; for the history of court organization, see Kern, *Geschichte des Gerichtsverfassungsrechts*.
      Fundamentally important research and analysis with regard to all of the imperial justice laws has been undertaken by Werner Schubert of the University of Kiel. Among other source collections, he has edited two particularly useful volumes: *Die deutsche Gerichtsverfassung* and *Entstehung und Quellen der Rechtsanwaltsordnung*.
56 Anton C. F. Thibaut, *Über die Nothwendigkeit eines allgemeinen bürgerliche Rechts für Deutschland* (Heidelberg, 1814), cited in Karl Kroeschell, *Deutsche Rechtsgeschichte 3 (seit 1650)* (Opladen, 1989), 174.
57 Savigny's reply to Thibaut was the famous Friedrich Karl von Savigny, *Vom Beruf unsrer Zeit für Gesetzgebung und Rechtswissenschaft* (Heidelberg, 1814). Michael John provides a useful summary of the Savigny–Thibaut debate over legal codification and the victory and evolution of the historical legal school in *Politics and the Law*, ch. 2, 15–41, an expansion upon John, "The final unification of Germany," ch. 2, 10–24; see also Whitman, *The Legacy of Roman Law*, 102–10 and Theodore Ziolkowski, *German Romanticism and Its Institutions* (Princeton, 1990), 78–86. For the texts that contributed to the debate, see Jacques Stern, ed., *Thibaut und Savigny. Ihre programmatischen Schriften*, intr. by Hans Hattenhauer (Munich, 1973). For Savigny and the historical school more generally, see Susan Gaylord Gale, "A Very German Legal Science: Savigny and the Historical School," *Stanford Journal of International Law* 18 (1982): 123–46, and Hermann Kantorowicz, "Savigny and the Historical School of Law," *The Law Quarterly Review* 53 (1937): 326–43.

unity of procedural law persisted among the liberal *Bürgertum* despite
the triumph of the historical school.[58] Lawyers in private practice
consistently played an important role in keeping the goal of codification alive.[59]

The Revolution of 1848 saw, among other things, a failed effort to
confer the general power to enact national legal legislation upon the
proposed German *Reich*.[60] But momentum toward legal unity had
received new impetus from the economic changes unleashed by the
formation of the Customs Union in 1834. The necessity to coordinate
tariffs and promote trade provided numerous opportunities to harmo-
nize legal systems as well.[61] The political failure at Frankfurt in 1848–9
could not end the advance of steps toward legal unity. During the
1850s and 1860s, the middle states of the German Confederation,
recalling the strength of the Holy Roman Empire as an "incubator"
and protector of their particularisms against dominance by the two
German Great Powers, began to sponsor legal reforms within the
legislative structure of the Confederation.[62] Beginning in 1856,

58 Getz, *Die deutsche Rechtseinheit im 19. Jahrhundert*, 13–16, 16, describes the effect of
    Savigny's triumph on efforts to bring about legal unity as follows: "For the following
    thirty years, the conflict of legal schools absorbed the interest of academics, and the
    political struggles of the liberal Bürgertum for German legal unity lacked continuing
    scholarly [*wissenschaftlich*] support."
        For another brief description, in English, of the Thibaut–Savigny dispute and its out-
    come, see Various European Authors, *A General Survey of Events, Sources, Persons, and
    Movements in Continental Legal History* (Boston, 1912), 439–51; see also Wieacker, *Pri-
    vatrechtsgeschichte der Neuzeit*, 390–6. The most authoritative exposition of the careers of the
    two men remains Roderich von Stintzing and Ernst Landsberg, *Geschichte der Deutschen
    Rechtswissenschaft*, 3 vols. in 4, part 3, half-volume 2 (Munich and Leipzig, 1910), 69–88,
    186–253.

59 Getz, *Die deutsche Rechtseinheit im 19. Jahrhundert*, 79–101, stresses the importance of law-
    yers in the strivings of the liberals for legal unity in the *Vormärz*. See also Schnabel,
    Deutsche Geschichte im Neunzehnten Jahrhundert, 2:202–5.

60 Art. 64 of the 1849 Constitution of the German Reich provided: "The Reich Authority is
    charged with establishing a uniform legal system among the German people by promulgat-
    ing general codes relating to civil law, commercial and banking law, criminal law and legal
    procedure"; Elmar M. Hucko, ed., *The Democratic Tradition: Four German Constitutions*
    (Oxford, 1987), 77–117, 90–1. For a more general description of the role of legal codifica-
    tion in the debates of the Frankfurt National Assembly, see Gerhard Wesenberg, "Die
    Paulskirche und die Kodifikationsfrage (Zu §64 der Paulskirchenverfassung)," *Zeitschrift
    der Savigny-Stiftung für Rechtsgeschichte*, Germanistische Abteilung 72 (1955): 359–65. See also
    Getz, *Die deutsche Rechtseinheit im 19. Jahrhundert*, 102–26.

61 For the importance of the *Zollverein* as a step toward legal unity, see Kroeschell, *Deutsche
    Rechtsgeschichte*, 174–5, and Elmar Wadle, "Der Zollverein und die deutsche Rechtsein-
    heit," *Zeitschrift der Savigny-Stiftung für Rechtsgeschichte, Germanistische Abteilung* 102 (1985):
    99–129, which focuses especially on commercial law and the law of commercial paper
    (*Wechselrecht*).

62 The concept of the Holy Roman Empire as "incubator" of the particular rights of smaller
    German states, as the means used by the smaller states to protect themselves from the
    ambitions of Prussia and Austria is drawn from Walker, *German Home Towns*.

adopted by the Confederation and recommended to the member states for enactment in 1861, and enacted by all but two states by 1869, the General German Commercial Code represented the first great step toward legal unity.[63] Throughout the course of the movement toward German legal unity, the issues of the organization of courts, codes of procedure, and the framework for the private legal profession remained alive in the debate. Lawyers themselves, through efforts at professional organization and through political activity, helped to shape the discourse of reform to their own advantage.

The private bar faced the suspicion if not the hostility of the state as they sought both to organize themselves and to participate in political life after 1815. Both Burke and Tocqueville were convinced that lawyers had led the overthrow of the French old regime in 1789.[64] Thus, the governments of restoration Germany viewed the practicing bar as an inherently politically subversive group. German lawyers took part prominently in the constitutional struggles in Germany during the 1830s and 1840s, playing leading roles in the parliaments in many German states. They also emerged during the Revolution of 1848 as leaders of the new liberal political parties. For example, ninety members of the Frankfurt Parliament were lawyers in private practice, one-sixth of the total number; they outnumbered the professors at the so-called Professors' Parliament.[65] Lawyers provided many of the

63 For the general history of the enactment of the Commercial Code (*Allgemeines Deutsches Handelsgesetzbuch*), see Getz, *Die deutsche Rechtseinheit*, 136–40, Laufke, "Der deutsche Bund und die Zivilgesetzgebung," 1–57, and Enno E. Kraehe, "Practical Politics in the German Confederation: Bismarck and the Commercial Code," *Journal of Modern History* 25 (1953): 13–24. See also Ledford, "Lawyers, Liberalism, and Procedure," 177–8. The two German states that had not adopted the code in 1869 were Luxemburg and Limburg; Getz, *Die deutsche Rechtseinheit*, 140, and Laufke, "Der deutsche Bund," 8–11.

64 Edmund Burke, *Reflections on the Revolution in France* (Garden City, N.Y., 1973), 54, and Alexis de Tocqueville, *Democracy in America*, 2 vols. (New York, 1945), 1:284–5. David A. Bell, *Lawyers and Citizens*, 15, points out the flaws in this monolithic view of the profession. For more nuanced if varying arguments, see also Berlanstein, *The Barristers of Toulouse*, 148–82, and Fitzsimmons, *The Parisian Order of Barristers*, 196–8, in which he concludes that only the *elite* of the Parisian bar, those elected to the Estates General/National Assembly, supported the radical changes of the abolition of corporations, while the rank and file of the bar eschewed politics and preferred to live and practice within the old corporate idiom.

The conviction that French lawyers played an important role in fomenting the French Revolution has a long and persistent history; see Schnabel, *Deutsche Geschichte im Neunzehnten Jahrhundert*, 2:202–3, and Alfred Cobban, *The Social Interpretation of the French Revolution* (Cambridge, 1964), 54–5, 58–62, 172.

65 Weißler, *Geschichte der Rechtsanwaltschaft*, 474. Four hundred forty-five of the 812 delegates and substitutes to Frankfurt were *Volljuristen*, who had completed legal studies and pursued some kind of legal career; Siemann, *Die Frankfurter Nationalversammlung 1848/49*, 33–4. The figure for private practitioners is drawn from the charts at Rosenbaum, *Beruf und Herkunft der Abgeordneten*, 53, 62. Karl Demeter reckons the total number of lawyers in private

great leaders of the national assembly at the *Paulskirche*, and they also led many local revolutionary movements in 1848–9. In general, the political involvement of the private bar in the ferment of 1848–9 seemed to confirm the subversive tendencies of the profession and hence to increase state scrutiny of the bar.

The private bar had not neglected its professional project during this period of increased involvement in liberal politics. Lawyers' increased educational standards and involvement in public life, especially in the constitutional states of the south and west, contributed to a gradual increase in their prestige. "The people began to notice what an independent profession, learned in the law, could mean in the *Rechtsstaat*."[66] Evidence of the rising prestige of lawyers may be found in the substitution of the new, unified term *Rechtsanwalt* for the older term, because:

[T]he name "advocate" stood in an unpleasant connection with the concepts of trickery and cunning; one spoke of "shady-," "shifty-," and "devils-advocates;" in contrast, the word "*Anwalt*" still enjoyed a maidenly blamelessness.[67]

Encouraged by their increasing prestige and the recognition of their important role in the orderly administration of justice, lawyers in private practice began, quietly at first but with increasing vigor, to agitate for further reforms of their profession.[68]

Lawyers first sought to take advantage of the revolutionary ferment of 1848–9 to reform and unify their professional structure. They built upon the basis of two national lawyers' conventions that had been held after much struggle and in the face of government opposition in 1846 and 1847, and they summoned a third lawyers' convention to meet in Dresden on 27 August 1848. The terms of the debate on professional issues can be summed up in the

practice at no more than ninety-five, sixty-four of whom were clearly private lawyers, an additional eleven terming themselves "Justizrat," and twenty "Dr. iur."; "Die soziale Schichtung des deutschen Parlaments seit 1848," *Vierteljahrschrift für Sozial- und Wirtschaftsgeschichte* 39:1–29 (1952), fourteen; Siemann criticizes Demeter's overall figures without addressing his calculation of private practitioners. Finally, see also O'Boyle, "The Democratic Left in Germany, 1848," 375, who counts fifty-one lawyers, noting the adherence of lawyers to parties of the right as well as to those of the left, and Frank Eyck, *The Frankfurt Parliament 1848–1849* (London and New York, 1968), 57–102, especially table 1 at 95.

66 Weißler, *Geschichte der Rechtsanwaltschaft*, 436.
67 Ibid., 423.
68 Concerning agitation by lawyers for reform of the legal profession, see Edith Fließ, *Der Kampf um den numerus clausus in der Rechtsanwaltschaft* (Dr. jur. diss., Freiburg i. B., 1933), 17–18, and Müller, *Die Freiheit der Advokatur*, 17–28, as well as Huffmann, *Kampf um freie Advokatur*, and Weißler, *Geschichte der Rechtsanwaltschaft*, 458–522.

speech given at that convention by Julius Hermann Beschorner of Dresden:

[He argued] that he found the justification for lawyers in private practice in the necessity, determined by the imperfection of humankind, to allot to the judge a guardian. By virtue of this task, the lawyer is obligated to take part in political movements with the aim of upholding the law. His position demands independence, and therefore freedom from state-official status, an unlimited number, and lawyers' chambers as disciplinary authorities.[69]

Although each of these items that Beschorner mentioned found opposition, particularly among Prussian lawyers who did not want to give up the security of their limited numbers, and the convention therefore took no position on them, these demands represented the key elements of the profession's agenda of reform.[70] From the experience of failure in 1848–9, lawyers emerged with the conviction that their profession had a special mission, "the realization that the power of the state is founded upon the educated *Bürgertum* and that the able core of this *Bürgertum* is the lawyer in private practice."[71]

The institution that lawyers proposed to create to govern professional functions even before 1848 was the lawyers' chamber, whose membership would be all lawyers in private practice in the bailiwick of a superior court. Members of the lawyers' chamber would elect from their ranks an executive committee that would have jurisdiction in the first instance to hear complaints about professional misconduct and to assess punishments. Most importantly, the chamber would represent the professional interests of lawyers, provide advisory opinions to lawyers and to the ministry of justice, designate lawyers to represent indigent clients, and cooperate in oversight of the education and admission of new lawyers. By assuming responsibility for discipline over lawyers and governance of the profession, the chamber would free lawyers from direct oversight by either the court or the ministry of justice. In the absence of any traditional corporate structure for the legal profession, the lawyers' chambers would both interpose themselves between the state and

---

69 Weißler, *Geschichte der Rechtsanwaltschaft*, 521. For details regarding the issue of legal unity at the *Vormärz* lawyers' conventions, see Getz, *Die deutsche Rechtseinheit im 19. Jahrhundert*, 83–101.
70 See Huffmann, *Kampf um freie Advokatur*, 26–108. For opposition by Prussian lawyers at Dresden to the introduction of *freie Advokatur*, see Julius Hermann Beschorner, "Soll die Zahl der Anwälte und deren Wirkungskreis in einem Staate beschränkt sein oder nicht?," *AcP* 31 (1848): 474–93, 474.
71 Weißler, *Geschichte der Rechtsanwaltschaft*, 502.

individual lawyers as an intermediate body and form the basis for a collegial, corporate professional life. The restoration governments in Germany feared any such loosening of their grip on lawyers and refused to create lawyers' chambers. Lawyers responded in good *bürgerlich* fashion by creating private alternatives to public lawyers' chambers, voluntary bar associations, voluntarily submitting themselves to disciplinary authority.[72] Often the governments treated these organizations as criminal conspiracies and repressed them, so that there was little progress toward satisfying the reform goals of the practicing bar before 1848. Association aspired to corporation, and the instinctive response of the reactionary governments was to crush such intermediary bodies.

The campaign for professional self-discipline in the form of lawyers' chambers began to bear some fruit after 1848. The first *Anwaltskammerordnung* was adopted in the Kingdom of Hannover in 1850 (effective in 1852), and it was soon followed in Oldenburg, Braunschweig, and the Kingdom of Saxony.[73] Private practitioners in Prussia had achieved a very limited measure of self-discipline in the "councils of honor" (*Ehrenräte*), enacted into law in 1847. The duties of the councils were *limited* to the exercise of primary jurisdiction for the investigation and punishment of disciplinary offenses of lawyers, but its work could be superseded at any time by the judges of the court, who could impose a punishment as they saw fit. Moreover, Prussian lawyers remained under the disciplinary authority of the government, state-official-like, allowing for further political mischief. Because of the limited nature of this reform, lawyers never considered the councils to be their own institutions, regarding them rather as an additional means of oversight by the state.[74] The councils were unable to evolve into institutions capable of representing professional interests more broadly. Despite the halting and partial nature of the reform in Prussia, however, the lawyers' chamber emerged as a truly autonomous system of professional self-discipline and self-

---

72 Huffmann, *Kampf um freie Advokatur*, 35–61; Weißler, *Geschichte der Rechtsanwaltschaft*, 503–6, 541–7. See Chapter 4 for a discussion of the parallel development of voluntary bar associations and lawyers' chambers. The German term that I render as "lawyers' chamber" is *Anwaltskammer*.

73 Huffmann, *Kampf um freie Advokatur*, 46, 61; by Huffmann's count, complete or partial freedom from judicial disciplinary oversight had been achieved in Prussia, Braunschweig, Oldenburg, Hannover, Baden, the Kingdom of Saxony, and Saxe-Coburg-Gotha by 1871.

74 Ibid., 55; for a legislative history of the *Verordnung* of 30 April 1847, which created the councils of honor (*Ehrenräte*), see Weißler, *Geschichte der Rechtsanwaltschaft*, 371–9.

government in several German states, and the prestige of the profession continued to rise.[75]

Freie Advokatur

The ultimate goal of the reform agitation between 1848 and 1878 was uniform national legislation regulating the private legal profession in all of Germany. Convinced that the right regulation of the practicing bar contained the key to the growth of liberty in state and society, both lawyers and liberal reformers sought to create a *freie Advokatur*, a private bar based upon free entry for all who had undertaken a university legal education, passed the necessary bar exams, and successfully completed the period of practical legal education. In the first half of the nineteenth century, the concept of *freie Advokatur* possessed primarily a political meaning, the struggle for freedom from the disciplinary authority of the judges and for emancipation from administrative appointment and civil service status.[76] The adoption of the system of lawyers' chambers in many states solved the problem of professional self-discipline. Moreover, in some states in western and southern Germany, lawyers succeeded in having their non-state-official character recognized. Prussia had lagged behind in this process, for the councils of honor provided only partial self-discipline. Indeed, many Prussian lawyers saw their state-official status as a positive attribute, believing that it contributed to a collegiality with judges and that state oversight protected the interests of the profession.[77]

Around the middle of the century, the attention of the practicing bar turned to a second political meaning of *freie Advokatur*, freedom from state interference in the selection of the bar, freedom of lawyers

75 Although the prestige of the practicing bar was rising during the first half of the nineteenth century, that did not automatically place all lawyers in the higher reaches of German society. According to a detailed social index, of the seven lawyers in Göttingen in 1861, two belonged to the lower middle, four to the upper middle, and only one to the upper stratum. Of the twelve state prosecutors, in contrast, two belonged to the "poor" category, two to the lower middle, one to the upper middle, and seven to the upper level. Wieland Sachße, "Lebensverhältnisse und Lebensgestaltung der Unterschicht in Göttingen bis 1860. Ein Projektsbericht," in Werner Conze and Ulrich Engelhardt, eds, *Arbeiterexistenz im 19. Jahrhundert. Lebensstandard und Lebensgestaltung deutscher Arbeiter und Handwerker* (Stuttgart, 1981), 19–45, Statistischer Anhang, 40–5, 43.

76 Huffmann, *Kampf um freie Advokatur*, 80; Fließ, *Der Kampf um den numerus clausus*, 9, 19; Müller, *Die Freiheit der Advokatur*, 23–8.

77 Huffmann, *Kampf um freie Advokatur*, 72, 75. Huffmann concludes: "To summarize, one can thus see that Prussian lawyers felt overwhelmingly like state officials because of their inclusion for more than a century in the civil service, and did not possess the inner independence to shake off the familiar bonds of the civil servant."

from appointment by the state. Two elements made up this freedom: the end of the concessionary system of state appointment of lawyers to practice before particular courts and the elimination of numerical limits on the size of the bar, either at a particular court or on a state or national level.[78] The system of *numerus clausus* and state appointment had resulted in a high standard of income and guaranteed circle of clients for those lawyers who practiced under it. Indeed, during the first half of the century, petitions from lawyers to courts and ministries of justice more often called for *adoption* of the *numerus clausus* as a means of improving the profession and the lot of its practitioners than they called for its abolition and the introduction of a system of *freie Advokatur*.[79] After 1848, professional periodicals, lawyers' conventions, and bar associations began to serve as forums for debate on the merits of free entry into the bar. Prussia and Bavaria, however, closely controlled the number of lawyers and maintained it at a very low level by means of a *numerus clausus*.[80] But political intrusions into the independence of lawyers, as well as widely diffused doctrines of economic liberalism, gave new impetus to the idea of free entry. As some states began to eliminate the *numerus clausus* and introduce *freie Advokatur* (Sachsen-Coburg-Gotha in 1862, Baden in 1864, and Württemberg in 1868), lawyers and liberals in Prussia began to debate the matter more vigorously.[81] The absence of *freie Advokatur* in the two largest of the German states, but especially in Prussia, seemed to many lawyers in private practice the chief evil afflicting the profession, and there was much agitation in favor of its reform.

78 Ibid., 13, 80.
79 For the reluctance of many Prussian lawyers to forsake the security of their closed number, see the arguments at the first three Prussian Lawyers' Conventions, quoted in Georg Reidnitz, *Freie Advokatur und numerus clausus* (Mainz, 1911), 15–34. See also Beschorner, "Soll die Zahl," *AcP* 31 (1848): 474–93, and Huffmann, *Kampf um freie Advokatur*, 81–5. John, "Between Estate and Profession: Lawyers and the Development of the Legal Profession in Nineteenth-Century Germany," in Blackbourn and Evans, eds., *The German Bourgeoisie*, 162–97, gives a nuanced discussion of the ambivalent attitude of many German private practitioners to the end of the *numerus clausus*.
80 Brix, *Organisation der Advokatur*, vi–viii. For a description of the private bars in the various German states in 1868, see Heinrich Jacques, *Die freie Advocatur und ihre legislative Organisation. Eine Abhandlung zur Reform der deutschen und österreichischen Gesetzgebung* (Vienna, 1868), 101–206.
81 Ibid., 103. See also Weißler, *Geschichte der Rechtsanwaltschaft*, 527–30. Hannover, Braunschweig, Mecklenburg, the Hanseatic cities, Oldenburg, Sachsen-Coburg-Gotha, Baden, and Austria introduced *de jure* free entry before 1878. In Rhenish Prussia, Anhalt, Lippe, and Württemberg, *de facto* free entry prevailed. In Saxony there was a legislated *numerus clausus*, but it was set so high and admissions were so freely granted that the bar was *de facto* open. Notable exceptions, then, in which the bar was not open were Prussia east of the Rhine and Bavaria, in which the number admitted before each court was kept extremely low.

The decade of the 1860s saw a crescendo of agitation for the introduction of *freie Advokatur* in the German states. The Prussian Bar
Association engaged in lively debate on the issue of *freie Advokatur*
from its very beginning in 1860. Following upon a collective petition
from the ranks of the candidates for judicial positions in Prussia to
the Prussian House of Delegates in 1860, calling for *freie Advokatur* in
order to provide them employment, the Prussian Bar Association
convened its first convention in 1861.[82] Despite opposition, especially from local bar associations in Westphalia, the association endorsed the elimination of the *numerus clausus* and the opening of the
profession to economic competition at its second convention in June
of 1862.[83] A system of free entry into the profession for all who met
the educational requirements fit well with the dominant liberal economic and political doctrine of the era. Likewise the fourth German
Jurists' Convention in Mainz in 1863 approved *freie Advokatur*, adopting principles of economic liberalism and marketplace competition
which it had previously resisted.[84] Finally, the Prussian regime under
Bismarck gave new urgency to the issue by applying political tests to
private practitioners during the constitutional crisis of the 1860s,
going so far as to include lawyers in private practice in decrees concerning disciplinary measures for state officials who voted for opposition parties in elections to parliament.[85] When the Fifth Congress of
German Economists in Weimar in 1862 resolved that there was no
valid reason why the practice of law should be governed by principles different from those governing any other trade, it appeared that
the principle of *freie Advokatur*, including both freedom from political
interference and marketplace competition, had become the prevailing
dogma.[86]

An anonymous article in the liberal journal *Preußische Jahrbücher* in

82 Reidnitz, *Freie Advokatur*, 10. See also Gneist, *Freie Advocatur*, 25–6. Overcrowding of the
    judiciary and administration in Prussia had slowed promotion of bureaucrats before 1848
    and again by the early 1860s; Gillis, *The Prussian Bureaucracy in Crisis*, 41–3, 190. The
    periodic overcrowding was a chronic, cyclical, and recurrent phenomenon in Prussia;
    Thomas Kolbeck, *Juristenschwemmen. Untersuchungen über den juristischen Arbeitsmarkt im 19.
    und 20. Jahrhundert* (Frankfurt, 1978), 109–14; more generally, see Hartmut Titze, "Die
    zyklische Überproduktion von Akademikern im 19. und 20. Jahrhundert," *Geschichte und
    Gesellschaft* 10 (1984): 92–121.
83 Reidnitz, *Freie Advokatur*, 15–34; see also Weißler, *Geschichte der Rechtsanwaltschaft*, 547–55.
84 Reidnitz, *Freie Advokatur*, 35–43; Weißler, *Geschichte der Rechtsanwaltschaft*, 573–5.
85 Huffmann, *Kampf um freie Advokatur*, 72; Weißler, *Geschichte der Rechtsanwaltschaft*, 532.
86 Fließ, *Der Kampf um den numerus clausus*, 21. Rudolf Gneist declared that by 1867 a majority
    of the members of the Prussian Bar Association, but not yet a majority of all private
    practitioners in Prussia, favored free entry; Gneist, *Freie Advocatur*, 25; Weißler, *Geschichte
    der Rechtsanwaltschaft*, 573–5.

1864 presented a coherent example of the liberal critique of the position and legal structure of the private practice of law in Prussia.[87] The
author began by lamenting the fact that lawyers in private practice
had never enjoyed the importance for public life in Prussia that they
had in England and France. This had led to harm, not only in the
position of the profession but also in the development of all of public
life, for lawyers in private practice had an important role to play in
the parliamentary state. Government officials and judges had dominated the Prussian parliament instead of lawyers, and political life in
Prussia could only develop and progress when the parliament came
to be dominated by lawyers.[88]

Two main reasons stood behind the limited importance of private
practitioners in public life: a limited conception of the mission of
lawyers and the limitation of the number of lawyers through appointment and monopoly. The author argued that the profession and the
public should not view the pleading of cases as the sole business of
lawyers. Rather,

All lawyers in private practice should be the artists who should shape the
raw material of the political, social, legal life of the nation into its ever more
complete forms. In every great social undertaking, in the founding of workers' cooperatives, credit associations, railroads, building associations, in every political reform, in every agitation excited from the commercial and
trading classes, lawyers, who are completely trusted with the formal demands of the law and the real demands of commerce, should stand at the
head and mediate between the two.[89]

One consequence of the limited conception of the mission of lawyers
in private practice was the limitation of the number of lawyers.
Lawyers produced lawsuits, and lawsuits were necessary only in
limited numbers, so the number of lawyers had to be limited in order
to prevent them from bringing mischievous lawsuits just to live from
the fees generated thereby. "Thus runs the wretched argument,"
wrote the author, lamenting this interference with the "natural law of
supply and demand."[90]

The anonymous writer argued that the result of the limitation
upon the number of private practitioners was the insufficient provision of legal service to the public. Lawyers, especially in Berlin,
refused to take cases that they considered to be unimportant; they

87   Anon., "Die Advocatur in Preußen," *Preußische Jahrbücher* 14 (1864): 424–39.
88   Ibid., 425.   89   Ibid., 431–2.   90   Ibid., 432.

refused to take politically dangerous cases, protecting people and principles from intrusions of the government; and many refused to sully themselves with criminal defense work, even of those charged with political offenses, leaving the accused to rely upon a criminal defense bar of low repute. The article proposed the remedy of freeing the private practice of law, opening it to all who met the education requirements. This act would result in the provision by the market of exactly the needed number of lawyers; moreover, as the examples of England and France showed, freeing the practice of law would not result in an overfilling of the profession, and contrary examples in other German states could all be explained by peculiar circumstances.[91]

In the year of this article (1864) and the years immediately following, political events of a greater scale postponed the consideration of reforming the organization of the legal profession. Bismarck's wars and diplomacy added new provinces to Prussia and assured that any national unification would be a *kleindeutsch* one under the firm leadership of Prussia. In 1867 the convention of the Prussian Bar Association endorsed the idea of *freie Advokatur*, although there was substantial dissent at the meeting and many stressed that only a fraction of the lawyers in Prussia had attended. An anonymous Prussian lawyer stressed that the daring step of eliminating the privilege granted by the *numerus clausus* would result in the liberation of the individual and of the profession from the existing lack of independence caused by the state-official status of lawyers.[92] The author concluded that the advantages of free entry outweighed its potential disadvantages.

Thus, the concept of *freie Advokatur* was widely accepted when Gneist published his book in 1867. But Gneist advanced arguments for *freie Advokatur* that went beyond the agenda of political liberalism for creating a truly independent political grouping to lead the *Bürgertum*, for summoning into being a new general estate. He also argued that economic changes had rendered the state-official-like status of lawyers obsolete:

One should look about oneself and not close one's eyes to the fact that property, education, and self-reliance no longer today have their center of gravity in the life of a civil servant. Indeed perhaps the prediction is not too bold that a more mature view of professional dignity would consider private

---

91   Ibid.
92   Anon., "Die freie Konkurrenz in der Advokatur," *Zeitschrift für Gesetzgebung und Rechtspflege in Preußen* 1 (1867): 682–97, 685.

legal practice as the first of the free trades than the last of the judicial offices.[93]

But was the private legal profession a trade, to be pursued solely for profit, governed only by the economic law of supply and demand? To be sure, the market played an important part in Gneist's conception of the proper organization of the profession and of society. He agreed with the proposition that competition was the "life's breath for the practicing bar." He did not shy from an obvious but perhaps demeaning comparison to other legal changes in the recent past in recognizing the value of free entry into the profession:

But once more one may not completely scorn a parallel to the modest experience of our *Gewerbefreiheit* [entry into an occupation free from guild restrictions]. The century that brings *Gewerbefreiheit* to rule in Germany has also mightily prepared the ground for free competition in this realm [the private practice of law]. Lifting of mandatory membership in guilds and of the licensing system have become popular slogans and goals in most parts of Germany. The stricter the requirements of intellectual qualification are made, the more superfluous become external and mechanical limits.[94]

Gneist viewed the private practice of law, however, as more than a mere trade, more than a mere link in the chain of profitable work. It stood in a necessary connection with the realization of the law, of justice, the highest task of the state. Therefore, it could not be governed *solely* by supply and demand. The lawyer could not, should not, and did not want to accept every case.[95] He was and remained the servant of the law, and that duty took precedence over the mere earning of money.

Gneist argued that, while a lawyer's activity cannot rest solely upon supply and demand, this in no way excludes free competition. Indeed, intellectual work thrives upon competition, and the need of the justice-seeking public demands it. In a nation with a modern economy, the need for legal counsel was so great that a closed bar protected by a monopoly could never meet it. The bar as it was constituted in Prussia in 1867 would never be able to meet the demands of a growing commercial and industrial economy. It had to be freed in order to free businessmen from the necessity of choosing

93 Gneist, *Freie Advocatur*, 50.
94 Ibid., 57.
95 Ibid., 55. Although Gneist does not expand upon the point, herein lies the germ of an argument for independence "from below," from the client.

between delay in receiving legal advice from lawyers and reliance upon the advice of untrained lay practitioners who thrived in the shadow of the closed bar.[96]

Gneist's remedy for all of these evils was *freie Advokatur*.[97] He refuted the many objections that he expected to be raised, notably objections concerning the baleful effects of an anticipated oversupply of lawyers. As far as the harm to the public caused by lawyers driven to dishonorable acts by competition, he answered that such concerns fell more properly within the realm of professional self-discipline; moreover, only mediocre lawyers would suffer from competition, and they would suffer even under a monopoly. Finally, regarding objections that an oversupply would harm the welfare of the profession itself, Gneist stated that "no one can insure a sufficient income to those who enter a field of endeavor without capability and zeal, to which they have no predisposition, no real calling, and that, in the nature of human labor, *should* not be done."[98]

Gneist pointed out that professional independence did not mean elimination of all influence by the state. State intervention, however, must be limited to (1) the prescription of a long and arduous general educational pathway, thus eliminating unsuited elements, (2) the requirement of a rigorous technical legal training, on an equal level to that required for judges, (3) the creation of a system of professional self-discipline to ensure a high standard of professional ethics, and (4) the establishment of a tariff of fees for trial representation, so as to assure a just economic reward for the lawyer's efforts.[99]

Gneist thus laid out a manifesto for the future free organization of the profession.[100] In accord with liberal belief and experience, he called for an insulation of the practicing bar from the political controls of the Prussian state. He was willing to rely upon the market to correct many of the ills afflicting the profession. The market would reward the diligent, discourage the incompetent, and provide enough lawyers to meet the expanding need of the German economy for legal services. Yet in accord with German liberal doctrine, he also accepted broad limitations by the state upon the workings of the market. He accepted and endorsed rigorous educational requirements for general and legal

---

96 Ibid., 62.   97 Ibid., 82–3.   98 Ibid., 90–1.   99 Ibid., 52–5.
100 All subsequent authors salute the centrality of Gneist's work to the success and durability of the concept of *freie Advokatur* in German legal thought. See, for example, Fließ, *Der Kampf um den numerus clausus*, 20–3, and Müller, *Die Freiheit der Advokatur*, 27–8.

education, prescribed by the government, which were preconditions to sitting for bar examinations, themselves administered by the government. The expense of classical secondary education, of university legal education, and of practical legal training between the first and second state examinations served to restrict severely the social basis of those who could enter the private practice of law. Like many German liberals, he endorsed *Gewerbefreiheit* in theory and in his argument, but he readily accepted state limitations in practice.[101] For him the political goal of shifting entry to the private practice of law from a process of "appointment" in the discretion of the ministry of justice to a system of "registration" of right with the court, thereby eliminating the exercise of discretion by the government, was the paramount reform, even though the prescription of qualifications to practice still lay in the hands of the state.

The economic aspect of *freie Advokatur*, although adhered to in the face of arguments about resultant economic suffering of lawyers after the abolition of monopoly, did not encompass a complete opening of the profession to all who sought to practice.[102] Gneist valued competition as useful to regulate the profession, but only so long as earning money did not become a "goal in itself." Even the greatest champion of *freie Advokatur*, then, retained a wariness and a distance toward unlimited economic competition. While he endorsed unlimited freedom of entry into the profession, he limited the freedom of economic conduct of those already admitted to the bar. Because he never expected there to be an oversupply of lawyers, he never expected questions of economic subsistence and conduct to pose a widespread problem.[103] A National Liberal *Honoratioren* and lawyer-notable, Gneist assumed that all lawyers at all times would subscribe to his elite attitude toward economic matters, which he subsumed among the ideals of the legal profession, and that all lawyers would imitate deferentially the distance from daily economic concerns that he and other comfortably situated lawyer-notables could afford.

There was no lack of dissenting voices contesting Gneist's assertion of the centrality of *freie Advokatur*. In 1868, A. F. Haack, a

---

101 See Sheehan, *German Liberalism*, 29–34.
102 Examples of completely open bars, regulated solely by the market forces of client selection, did exist in the German-speaking world, in some of the rural cantons of Switzerland. See Siegrist, "Gebremste Professionalisierung," in Conze and Kocka, eds., *Bildungsbürgertum im 19. Jahrhundert*, 301–31.
103 Fließ, *Der Kampf um den numerus clausus*, 19.

private practitioner from Glogau in Silesia, published a reply in which he contested Gneist's arguments one by one.[104] He denied that the condition of the Prussian justice system was as dark as Gneist painted it. He countered Gneist's claim that the organization of the private legal profession was the key to the reformation of the entire Prussian justice system with the argument that targeted legislation could cure each specific ill. Most centrally, Haack argued that an end to the *numerus clausus* for lawyers in private practice would lead to overcrowding of the profession, an imbalance between large cities with many lawyers and small towns with none, misbehavior on the part of struggling practitioners, ethical violations, and less effective legal representation of the public.[105]

Other private practitioners, although endorsing *freie Advokatur* in the sense of independence of private practitioners from their state-official-like status and appointment by the state, also expressed fears about the results of abolition of limits upon the number of lawyers. Siegfried Haenle, later the long-time editor of the *Juristische Wochenschrift*, delivered an address at the ninth Lawyers' Convention at the end of 1868 in which he expressed concern about the degenerative effects of an oversupply of lawyers in private practice. He endorsed fully the importance of the independence of lawyers from political interference by the state:

If the task of the legal profession, as Mittermaier argued, consists of bringing the interest of freedom and of the rights of the individual into harmony with the interest of the civic order [*der bürgerlichen Ordnung*], it follows that the freedom of the legal profession rests upon the principle that it is the duty of the state to provide to the guardians of the rights of the individual in his or her collisions with the laws and with the civic order a position within the state in which they can best realize this task independent from any hindering influences. This independence is the life's breath of the freedom of the legal profession; it is its fundamental precondition. The lawyer must be free from the influences of state authority; free before the judge's bench, before which the lawyer must plead his case; free from the manifold considerations of the totality of his clientele; finally free with regard to each individual client, for he must be the client's guide and not his servant.[106]

104 A. F. Haack, *Ueber Dr. Rudolf Gneist's Freie Advocatur* (Berlin, 1868).
105 Ibid., 17, 22, 38–43: "But *freie Advokatur* would create a great number of needy lawyers, an evil that could be avoided by a closed number without endangering the interests of the public"; ibid., 42–3.
106 Siegfried Haenle, *Referat über die Freigabe der Advocatur erstattet auf dem IX. Anwaltstag, Sonntag, den 6. December 1868 zu Nürnberg* (Nürnberg, 1869), 13.

Accepting this as the legitimate role of lawyers in private practice and as the goal to be striven for, Haenle devoted most of his address to examining the question of whether a system of unlimited admission to the bar of all who possessed the necessary qualifications would accomplish this ideal freedom of the practicing bar. His conclusion was that it would not, and he recommended a system of admission based upon whether there was demand for more lawyers, as determined by lawyers themselves, however, rather than by the state:

Accordingly, the system of *freie Advokatur* in the sense of independence of the lawyer from the government is indispensably necessary; the system of *freie Advokatur* extended to the admission of a limitless number of competitors damages the independence of the lawyer and his position with regard to the mass of justice-seekers and with regard to his own client.[107]

Although the views expressed by the dissenters, especially by Haenle, remained important countercurrents in the discourse about the shape of the private legal profession, they did not play an important role in the debate that was to come. It was Gneist's book that set the stage for a great legislative campaign to realize the combined professional and middle-class project of national reform of the judicial system and legal profession, and that campaign began in 1871.

107   Ibid., 19.

3

Foundation of the Modern Profession: The Private Bar under the Lawyers' Statute

The process of legal unification of the German Empire was a long one, culminating with the adoption of the Civil Law Code in 1896, effective in 1900, but the first peak, of crucial importance for the organization of the legal profession, came in the years 1877–9. The Imperial Justice Laws, which the Reichstag adopted between January 1877 and July 1879, and which entered into effect together on 1 October 1879, unified the legal system of the new German Empire and changed the lives of all lawyers practicing in the country.[1] Contemporaries viewed these statutes as an interrelated whole, and they must be read together in order to understand fully the framework governing the organization of the private practice of law.[2]

This chapter traces first the legislative history of the Imperial Justice Laws, particulary of the Lawyers' Statute ("RAO"), to show how the enactment of the reform legislation intersected with the professional and middle-class projects for reform. Then it explains the legislative framework that the laws created, under which the private legal profession structured itself and operated essentially un-

---

1 A brief description of the court system created by the constitution of the courts is found in Robert C. K. Ensor, *Courts and Judges in France, Germany, and England* (Oxford, 1933), 52–75 (in which he uses the awkward term "Office Court" to translate *Amtsgericht*; this book will use the freer but more readily recognizable translation "district court"). See also J. J. Cook, "The Judicial System of Germany," *The Juridical Review. A Journal of Legal and Political Science* 1 (1889): 70–80, 184–92, 298–306. The best brief summary of civil procedure under the Code of Civil Procedure is Engelmann, *A History of Continental Civil Procedure*, 605–15. For a step-by-step guide through trials under the code, see Simeon E. Baldwin, "A German Law-Suit," *Yale Law Journal* 19 (1909–10): 69–79 (a trial before a superior court) and idem, "The German Law-Suit Without Lawyers," *Michigan Law Review* 8 (1909–10): 30–8 (a trial before a district court).

2 Civil litigation is and was the single largest source of income for German lawyers. Trial work has always represented a larger proportion of total income for German lawyers than for American; Rueschemeyer, *Lawyers and their Society*, 37–8.

changed until 1933. Both discussions will pay particular attention to inchoate tensions within the bar that the reform legislation created, setting the stage for an exploration in later chapters of how these tensions ripened and manifested themselves, creating internal and external difficulties for the private bar and interfering with its ability to succeed in either the professional or middle-class project.

The Enactment of the Imperial Justice Laws: The RAO in Context

Gneist wrote *Freie Advocatur* at a time when legal reform had moved to the center of the agenda of German state building for many competing interests besides just liberals and lawyers. Various German states had been engaged in reform of the judicial and procedural systems, as well as their legal professions, since the Kingdom of Hannover began the process in 1850.[3] During the late 1850s, the German Confederation had taken steps toward legal reform that culminated in the General German Commercial Code of 1861, and in February 1862 it appointed a commission to draw up a uniform code of civil procedure.[4] The outcome of the Austro-Prussian War of 1866, however, strengthened the role that Prussia would play in any eventual legal unification, and the Constitution of the North German Confederation granted the federal government jurisdiction to adopt "common legislation concerning the law of obligations, criminal law, commercial law and the law of exchange, and trial procedure."[5] Leaders of the National Liberal Party, including Johannes Miquel and Eduard Lasker (the former a Hannoverian trained in law and the latter a lawyer in private practice in Berlin) began immediately to seek to expand this provision by constitutional amendment granting the federal government the power to legislate with regard to all substantive civil law "including the organization of the courts." Opposition to this expansion of the power of the central government came from the governments of the German "middle states," which

3 Ledford, "Lawyers, Liberalism, and Procedure," 176–7.
4 Ibid., 177; John, *Politics and the Law*, 33–7.
5 Art. 4, ¶13, reproduced in Ernst Rudolf Huber, ed., *Dokumente zur deutschen Verfassungsgeschichte*, 3rd ed., 4 vols. (Stuttgart, 1978–   ), 2:272–85, 273. As part of the liberal reforms in the Austrian half of the Habsburg monarchy that followed upon the defeat of 1866, an *Advokatenordnung* was adopted on 6 July 1868, effective on 1 January 1869, on the basis of *freie Advocatur*, permitting unlimited admissions. For the Austrian view of the question of *freie Advocatur*, see Jacques, *Die freie Advocatur und ihre legislative Organisation*, and Kübl, *Geschichte der österreichischen Advokatur*.

feared further erosion of their sovereignty and a shift of the balance of power toward a federal government dominated by Prussia, and from the Catholic Center Party, which saw decentralization of power as the key to its liberty and protection against persecution.[6]

The Prussian government under Bismarck after 1867 perceived legal reform as a way to overcome legal division within Prussia itself, as a means of reconciling some of the middle states to their inclusion in a Prussia-dominated Reich, and at the same time as a method of building national institutions.[7] Already in 1869, the Bundesrat of the North German Confederation had approved a Prussian motion to create commissions to draft codes of civil and criminal procedure. In December 1869 Bismarck requested the Prussian Minister of Justice, Adolf Leonhardt, to draft a court organization law for the North German Confederation, and the Bundesrat assented to this step in January 1870 over the objections of Hamburg, Hessen, Mecklenburg, and Saxony that the constitution did not grant this competence to the federal government.[8]

With the Prussian victory in the war against France in 1870 came the long-dreamed-for national unification of Germany. The constitutional provision providing for central government competence to legislate in the realm of legal reform was carried over unchanged into the Constitution of the German Empire in 1871.[9] When the new Reichstag convened, Miquel and Lasker renewed their efforts to amend this provision to include substantive civil law and the organization of the courts. Although the euphoria of national unification had reinforced enthusiasm for legal unification, the opposition of the middle states and the Catholic Center Party remained strong.[10] While the middle states and the Center had become reconciled to the eventual emergence of an historically based code of substantive law, they

6   For a nuanced and thoughtful account of the politics that lay behind this protracted struggle over a constitutional amendment, see John, *Politics and the Law*, 42–72.

7   See the discussion in Ledford, "Lawyers, Liberalism, and Procedure," 178–81, 190–1; see also Pflanze, *Bismarck*, 2:347–50.

8   Letter from Bismarck to Leonhardt, 21 December 1869, reprinted in Schubert, *Die deutsche Gerichtsverfassung*, 322; see also the protocol of the Bundesrat session of 21 February 1870, ibid., 331–2, and report of Kirchenpauer, delegate from Hamburg, of the same date, ibid., 332–3.

9   Art. 4, ¶13; Huber, ed., *Dokumente*, 384–402, 387; see also Hucko, *The Democratic Tradition*, 121–45, 123.

10   Typical of the attitude of lawyers toward the importance of legal unity for national unity were the comments of Siegfried Haenle in his New Year's observations in 1877: "The statement will scarcely find any contradiction, the political unity of the Empire essentially depends upon unity in the realm of legal life"; "Zum Neujahr 1877," *JW* 6 (1877): 1.

still saw uniformity of court organization as a threat to the justice sovereignty of the individual German states. In order to allay the particularist-federalist fears of the leader of the Center Party, Ludwig Windthorst, in May 1872 Miquel and Lasker dropped the phrase "including the organization of the courts" from their constitutional amendment, which then passed in December 1873.[11]

Once the phrase "including the organization of the courts" had been dropped from the proposed Miquel-Lasker constitutional amendment, it was clear that the constitution would remain silent on the matter of federal jurisdiction to legislate comprehensively in the realm of court organization. Liberals dismissed claims by Bavaria, Saxony, Württemberg, and Braunschweig that federal legislation on court organization was tantamount to a loss of justice-sovereignty by the states, viewing comprehensive court organizational reform as an ancillary function of the constitutional power granted to the federal government to legislate reforms in trial procedure.[12] Leonhardt and the officials in the Prussian Ministry of Justice shared this view, and thus they predicated the so-called Prussian draft of a court organization law, produced in September 1872 and subject to negotiations among representatives of the ministries of justice of the various German states between December 1872 and April 1873, upon this prevailing assumption.[13] The stubborn opposition to the centralizing tendencies of the Prussian draft forced Leonhardt to retreat. Only in November 1873 did Bismarck submit a draft set of justice reform laws to the Bundesrat, and the liberals in the Reichstag saw the package of justice reform legislation only in October 1874.[14]

To the general disappointment of lawyers, this legislative package contained no comprehensive court organization law. Moreover, it made no provision for either a separate law reforming and governing the legal profession or such a framework within the law of court organization. As part of the attempt to accommodate the concerns of the middle states, Bismarck and Leonhardt now contended that the

11 John, *Politics and the Law*, 54–5, 69, and Schubert, *Die deutsche Gerichtsverfassung*, 55–8.
12 See, for example, "Begründung des Entwurfs eines Gerichtsverfassungsgesetzes und des Einführungs-Gesetzes," in Carl Hahn, ed., *Die gesammten Materialien zu den Reichs-Justizgesetzen*, 8 vols. in 11 (Berlin, 1881–98; repr. ed., Aalen, 1983), vol. 1, *Die gesammten Materialien zu dem Gerichtsverfassungsgesetz* (hereafter cited as Hahn, *Materialien GVG*), 24–187, 24.
13 The text of the Prussian draft is reproduced in Schubert, *Die deutsche Gerichtsverfassung*, 338–80; for an account of the draft and the discussions, see ibid., 71–5.
14 The debates among the states in the Bundesrat are discussed in ibid., 79–86.

Imperial Constitution as amended did not give the federal government jurisdiction over matters such as the organization of the practice of law. In introducing the package of legislation to the Reichstag, Leonhardt argued that the Imperial Constitution permitted the federal government to enact only those aspects of court organization absolutely necessary for effective procedural codes. He warned the Reichstag delegates that, as a matter of constitutional necessity "observed from a formal standpoint, the constitution of the courts appears as a subsidiary law, as a foundational law to the procedural codes."[15]

But the second Reichstag, in which the National Liberals held 152 out of 397 seats, had its own plans for justice reform. Eduard Lasker clearly outlined the program when he argued that Germany needed a comprehensive court organization law, including national regulation of qualification for the judiciary, national guarantees of the independence of judges, and a national regulation of the legal profession.[16] Lawyers in private practice too were profoundly disappointed that the draft contained no provisions governing the legal profession. The German Lawyers' Convention in Würzburg in 1874 reacted by resolving "that there is an imperative need for the relations of the legal profession to be regulated by a common German lawyers' statute."[17] In early 1875, the Reichstag referred the legislative package for study and revision to a Justice Commission, composed of twenty-eight members, twenty-seven of whom were trained in law and six of whom were private practitioners.[18]

---

15   Hahn, *Materialien GVG*, 188–90, 189.   16   Ibid., 197–211.

17   The DAV consistently criticized the failure to include a lawyers' statute in the draft Imperial Justice Laws; "Die Anwaltsordnung vor dem deutschen Bundesrathe," *JW* 3 (1874): 81–2, "Die Rechts-Anwaltsordnung," *JW* 3 (1874): 113. For secondary accounts, see Weissler, *Geschichte der Rechtsanwaltschaft*, 579; Schubert, *Entstehung und Quellen*, 25–6.

18   Hahn, *Materialien GVG*, 271–3. The commission consisted of twelve National Liberals: Johannes Miquel (lawyer-politician), Friedrich Ludwig Gaupp (judge), Isaac Wolffson (lawyer), Joseph Völk (lawyer), Karl Grimm (judge), Rudolf von Gneist (law professor), Otto Bähr (judge), Henning von Puttkamer (judge), Heinrich von Marquardsen (law professor), Eduard Lasker (lawyer), Hermann Heinrich Becker (judge), and Johannes Struckmann (judge); eight members of the *Zentrum*: Max Theodor Mayer (judge), Thomas von Hauck (prosecutor), Peter Franz Reichensperger (judge), Joseph Bernards (judge), Friedrich Christoph von Forcade (judge), Ernst Philipp Lieber (lawyer), Hugo Pfafferott (judge), and Adolf Kraetzer (judge); four Progressives: Arthur Eysold (lawyer), Moritz Klotz (judge), Carl Herz (judge), and August Friedrich Karl Zinn, (medical doctor and the only nonlawyer on the panel); two Conservatives, Wilhelm von Schöning (state official) and Gustav Wilhelm von Jagow (state official); and two Free Conservatives, Friedrich von Schwarze (prosecutor) and Karl Gustav Thilo (judge). Ibid., 274–6; Schubert, *Die deutsche Gerichtsverfassung*, 89, n. 17; Max Schwarz, *MdR. Biographisches Handbuch der Reichstage* (Hanover, 1965).

The Justice Commission of the Reichstag made enormous revisions to the draft justice laws, restoring a number of liberal and centralizing provisions that the Bundesrat had removed from the first drafts, and in many cases going much farther. Over the objections of the representatives from the Catholic Center Party, who supported the federalist concerns of the non-Prussian states, the Justice Commission reinserted a uniform national determination of the qualifications for appointment to the bench.[19] Of most crucial importance to lawyers, the commission inserted a detailed provision governing the legal profession, creating a national, unified bar, with uniform standards for admission, free from state appointment and state-imposed discipline and governance.[20]

The draft of Title IX of the proposed constitution of the courts, *Rechtsanwaltschaft*, rested upon the principle of *freie Advokatur*. Liberals advanced three reasons in favor of *freie Advokatur* as the basis of the organization of the private practice of law: first, that it would free the practicing bar and applicants for admission from political persecution by the state; second, that it would create a safe haven, equal in prestige to the judiciary, for judges and state officials who found themselves either in disagreement with the policies of the government or the victims of political persecution; and third, that free entry for all who had passed the bar examinations would more likely result in the sufficient provision and optimum distribution of private practitioners than had the old system of state appointment and *numerus clausus*. Opinion was more divided on the last point than on the first two.

Following Gneist, Title IX proposed the opening of the legal profession to all persons trained in the law and who had qualified to serve as judges by passing two legal examinations separated by a period of practical training. Self-discipline through a system of lawyers' chambers would replace the discipline formerly exercised by courts or justice ministries by virtue of the state-official-like status of lawyers. Once and for all, the draft settled the question of public office or free profession in favor of the latter. Lawyers flocked to comment upon and to endorse this plan: "This result brought forth a literary flood, a mass of assemblies and resolutions of lawyers' associations, groups of lawyers practicing before single courts, in prov-

19 Hahn, *Materialien GVG*, 371–81.   20 Ibid., 509–56.

inces, and in entire states."[21] The Reichstag exhaustively debated the draft, both in the Justice Commission and on the floor.

Discussion in the Justice Commission began with near unanimity of opinion that *freie Advokatur* should be the basis for the new organization. The National Liberal leader Eduard Lasker understood this term primarily as

the opposite of the concessionary system, that is, the system whereby the government decides in its free discretion, without the check of a statutory direction, as to the admission of a qualified applicant to the position of his choice.[22]

Lasker regarded freedom of private lawyers as necessary for political reasons, as well as in the interests of the administration of justice. The ensuing competition within the practicing bar open to talent would contain its own correctives, which, together with a strong disciplinary system, would prevent the abuses that opponents of *freie Advokatur* feared. Other speakers stressed the effect that a free practicing bar would have upon the independence of the bureaucracy:

The state official must also be allowed to become a lawyer as soon as he believes that he is unable to unite his convictions with effectiveness in service to the existing government. Therein lies an essential guarantee of the independence of state officials.[23]

The leaders of the Catholic Center Party joined in the support for *freie Advokatur*. Their political motives for endorsing it were obvious, conditioned as they were by the harsh persecution of the *Kulturkampf*. What was surprising was their ringing endorsement of economic freedom. Peter Reichensperger stated that he did not share the fears of some that the freeing of the legal profession would lead to an oversupply or a shortage of lawyers. "Our entire existence rests upon the fact that freedom, in combination with the interest of the individual, will result in the correct measure."[24]

Concern for the economic consequences of *freie Advokatur* appeared repeatedly in the debates, but it was either dismissed with economic liberal arguments or belittled as exaggerated. As shown by the statement of another National Liberal delegate, concern for poli-

---

21 Weißler, *Geschichte der Rechtsanwaltschaft*, 581.
22 "Erste Beratung der Justiz-Kommission über den neuvorgeschlagenen Titel des Gerichtsverfassungsgesetzes 'Rechtsanwaltschaft'," 7. Januar 1876, in Siegel, *Die gesammten Materialien*, 18–26, Delegate Eduard Lasker (National Liberal), 18.
23 Ibid., Delegate Otto Bähr (National Liberal), 23.
24 Ibid., Delegate Peter Reichensperger (Center), 25.

tical independence of the bar and, by extension, of the judiciary, remained paramount.

You have a whole group of people in the country who, on account of their political party position, are disqualified beforehand as unsuitable for any significant state office. The Imperial Chancellor expressly stated that here earlier; – practice teaches us each week that it is so in Prussia. Thus, gentlemen, *freie Advokatur* will make it possible that in the future even in this part of Germany people of independence, of academic education, can study law with the prospect of practicing, even when they belong to the political opposition and thereby have no desire to enter into government service.
A second political reason, gentlemen, is much more considerable. All guarantees of the independence of the judiciary, . . . are not as important as the institution of *freie Advokatur*. The awareness that a judge has, who can no longer stand it in government service, that he can take up another, similar activity as a lawyer, is the most secure guarantee of his independence. Gentlemen, in Prussia we have lacked this support until now. There in the Progressive Party still sit the gentlemen who can testify to it, Parisius and Schulze-Delitzsch; the one was expelled from the judiciary directly on disciplinary grounds, and the other preferred to quit, because he could no longer endure it on account of all kinds of disputes. Herr Twesten, the famous leader of the National Liberal party, – was he not also expelled from the judiciary in a manner which I do not fear to characterize as unworthy? Gentlemen, remember your great leader, and finally create the guarantees which still are unavailable to him.[25]

The changes made to the draft justice reform legislation in the Reichstag alarmed both the middle states and the Prussian government, and the Bundesrat's justice committee decided even before the Reichstag Justice Commission released its report that the changes were unacceptable.[26] Yet it had become apparent during the first and

25 "VII. Schlußberathung und Ablehnung des Titels XI des Gerichtsverfassungsgesetzes 'Rechtsanwaltschaft' im Plenum des Reichstags," 19. Dezember 1876, in Siegel, *Die gesammten Materialien*, 183–191, Delegate Bernhard Schröder (National Liberal), 186. Ludolf Parisius was a county judge from Gardelegen who suffered dismissal for his involvement in the leadership of the Progressive Party in the Prussian House of Delegates; see the judgment against him of 3 October 1864, in G.St.A., I HA Rep. 84a, 3059, 33–6. Hermann Schulze-Delitzsch, the great champion of workers' cooperatives and one of the founders of the *Nationalverein*, had been tried in a criminal case in 1849 for voting for the "tax refusal resolution" in the Landtag and persecuted out of the Prussian judiciary in 1850–1; *ADB* 33:18–29, 20. Karl Twesten was a judge of the *Kammergericht* in Berlin who was also a Progressive Party delegate to the House of Delegates during the constitutional crisis, who was dismissed in 1865, arrested, tried, and convicted of defaming the Prussian Minister of Justice in a speech on the floor of the parliament; he served two years' imprisonment. For an account of his travails and those of the other judges, see Hess, *Das Parlament das Bismarck widerstrebte*, 111–12, 118–19.
26 "Protokoll der Sitzung des Justizausschusses des Bundesrates 3.4.1876 und 4.4.1876," Schubert, *Die deutsche Gerichtsverfassung*, 831–42.

second readings of the bills in the Reichstag in the course of 1876 that a majority there embraced the Justice Commission's recommendations. The entire legislative enterprise was threatened with collapse. At Prussian urging, the Bundesrat informed the Reichstag that the draft laws were unacceptable on eighteen points, emphasizing particularly the unacceptability of the fragmentary title governing the legal profession. The leaders of the National Liberal Party feared that the reform process would come to an unhappy end, and they entered into negotiations with Bismarck and Leonhardt in December. The National Liberal leaders agreed to drop the title concerning lawyers, one of their most desired goals, once Leonhardt promised to draft and present to the Reichstag a new, national, comprehensive lawyers' statute substantially in accord with the draft produced by the Justice Commission. The National Liberal Reichstag fraction approved the agreement on 16 December by a large majority, and the first of the Imperial Justice Laws, the Constitution of the Courts and the Codes of Civil and Criminal Procedure, passed into law on 21 December 1876, by a vote of 194 to 100, with the National Liberals, Free Conservatives, and Conservatives voting in favor and the Center and Progressives voting against.[27]

Lawyers of course were profoundly disappointed that the Constitution of the Courts had come into being without the title governing the legal profession. The editor of the official journal of the DAV complained that although the last days of December had brought the German people the Christmas present of unified national codes of court organization and trial procedure, there was no jubilation in the land.[28] But true to his word, Leonhardt introduced a draft RAO to the Bundesrat in October 1877. After consideration in the Bundesrat, the new draft RAO was laid before the Reichstag on 6 February 1878. This draft also stood upon the principle of *freie Advokatur*. All parties understood the magnitude of the step being taken. The Prussian Minister of Justice reported to the Kaiser that by giving the right of admission to the bar to every lawyer who had passed the qualifying examinations for the judicial service in the state in which he had passed the examinations the commission had "thereby pronounced the almost unlimited opening of the profession."[29]

27 Ledford, "Lawyers, Liberalism, and Procedure," 189.
28 Siegfried Haenle, "Zum Neujahr 1877," *JW* 6 (1877): 1–2.
29 "Entwurf eines Berichts an den Kaiser (10.11.1876)," reprinted in Schubert, *Entstehung und Quellen*, 139–43, 141.

Lawyers made more of the limitations placed upon the freedom of the profession. The main restrictions were three. First, the absolute right to admission existed only so long as a lawyer applied within one year after passing the second bar examination and before he entered any state service. Second, a lawyer could move from one court to another only after five years' practice at the first.[30] The third limitation, the so-called blocking paragraph whereby admission before other courts could be barred by the ministry of justice if it determined that the number of lawyers at any one or several courts in the same state was insufficient for the orderly administration of justice, excited the most opposition.[31] Political fears, both for the practicing bar and for the judiciary, lay at the core of this opposition, for judges would be denied entry into the practicing bar as a safe haven from political persecution and new graduates could suffer from tendentious application of the "blocking paragraph." The liberals' memory of their treatment at the hands of Bismarck during the constitutional crisis kept such considerations foremost in their minds.[32]

Despite these actual limitations upon the freedom of the profession, the official ministerial report explaining the legislation began from the position that there was general agreement within the bar in favor of freeing the profession. Citing both the arguments advanced by Gneist and the public need for access to lawyers, especially in cases in which representation by lawyers would be mandatory, the report stated that the purpose of the draft was to assure the greatest

30 Weißler, *Geschichte der Rechtsanwaltschaft*, 588. A fourth limitation, that practice before the imperial supreme court was not open to all lawyers but rather to a closed group selected in the free discretion of the presidium of the supreme court, was initially opposed but later accepted. The key to its acceptance was the small number of lawyers (twenty-five) actually affected.

31 "Über den Entwurf der Deutschen Rechtsanwalts-Ordnung," *JW* 7 (1878): 17; the German term is *Sperrparagraph*.

32 Oppositional judges who were members of the Prussian House of Delegates paid the price for their political behavior during the Prussian constitutional crisis; six suffered disciplinary transfers, four were dismissed, and Twesten was imprisoned; see note 25. Just how real the present fears were was borne out in the experience after 1879, when progressive judges were also forced out of office by the conservative ministry of justice. See Eckart Kehr, "Das soziale System der Reaktion in Preußen unter dem Ministerium Puttkamer," in *Der Primat der Innenpolitik*, Hans-Ulrich Wehler, ed. (Frankfurt, 1970), 64–86, 75. Despite the success of their attack upon the thesis of the "Puttkamer purge," Anderson and Barkin have cast no doubt upon the question of the movement of politically liberal judges from the judiciary to the practicing bar after 1879; Margaret L. Anderson and Kenneth Barkin, "The Myth of the Puttkamer Purge and the Reality of the *Kulturkampf*: Some Reflections on the Historiography of Imperial Germany," *Journal of Modern History* 54 (1982): 647–86. See also Wunder, *Geschichte der Bürokratie*, 89–90, and more generally Hattenhauer, *Geschichte des deutschen Beamtentums*, 307–13.

selection of lawyers reasonably possible at any court.[33] The means of preventing misconduct by lawyers lay not in the limitation of the number of lawyers but in the redoubled strictness of discipline under the system of free entry into the profession. The report minimized the absence of any limitation on the entry of judges into the practicing bar by predicting that few judges would feel inclined so to move, especially since the new oral civil procedure would increase the strenuousness of the work of lawyers and because the replacement of the system of monopoly by one of free competition would make the private practice of law less lucrative than before.[34]

Liberal delegates in the Reichstag took issue with these claims when the bill came up for debate. Adolf Hoffmann of the Progressive Party, a district court judge from Berlin, argued that all limitations on the freedom of the private practice of law had to be eliminated:

Gentlemen, the crucial point of the regulation of the practice of law, inasmuch as it alone especially corresponds to the demands of our times and of the *Rechtsstaat*, both in regard to the assured determination of justice as well as in regard to a lawful government which holds itself free from arbitrariness, is and remains the free practicing bar.[35]

Hoffmann conceded that *freie Advokatur* did not mean an absolute freedom of entry, for admission must be made dependent upon certain strictly prescribed educational prerequisites; but it was indispensable that entry must be made independent of the discretion and arbitrariness of the government.[36] The best practicing bar was the one least regulated, with the most possible free competition. He concluded:

Yes gentlemen, the practice of law – naturally presupposing a certain education, and the requirements of this education you may set as high as you wish – *must* open a clear path for knowledge, talent, and constancy of character; the search for justice can only come into full bloom when it works to a certain extent with the sum total of those characteristics which are to be found in this realm.[37]

33 "Motive zum Entwurf einer Anwaltsordnung," *JW* 7 (1878): 33, 15 February 1878, 36.
34 Ibid., 37.
35 "Amtlicher stenographischer Bericht der ersten Berathung des Entwurfs einer Rechtsanwaltsordnung im Deutschen Reichstag," *JW* 7 (1878): 105, 107, Delegate Adolf Hoffmann.
36 Ibid.
37 Ibid., 108. Except for a tiny number of radicals, it was assumed that stringent educational and examination requirements would be necessary. As Müller, *Die Freiheit der Advokatur*, 33, notes: "The successful completion of one's legal education as a precondition for entry into the legal profession remained an unconditionally required limitation even in the full bloom of economic liberalism." Only in some Swiss cantons did no educational prerequisites prevail; Siegrist, "Die Rechtsanwälte und das Bürgertum," in Kocka, ed., *Bürgertum im 19. Jahrhundert*, 2:92–123.

Competition, then, was the necessary correlate to mandatory representation by a lawyer. Arguments such as these prevailed against the principal limitations upon the freedom of the private practice of law contained in the draft. All trace of the blocking paragraph disappeared from the final version of the bill.

Compromises occurred however, most notably the acceptance in the final bill of the principle of localization, limiting the freedom of lawyers to appear before any court in any case, and of permissive limitations upon simultaneous admission, the right of a lawyer to practice before more than one court at the same time. Conceptually, the problems were intimately linked, for arguments in favor of the localization of lawyers in Germany contradicted calls for simultaneous admission.[38] Both issues arose from the existing regulation of the legal profession. Although the systems of organization of the private practice of law in the many German states varied in the first half of the nineteenth century, most required that the lawyer be admitted (or appointed) to practice before only one court. The lawyer then assumed the duty of establishing and maintaining his residence in the town in which that court was located, unless he obtained special permission from the state ministry of justice to the contrary. Prussia followed an especially strict version of localization. Lawyers were appointed to practice before one particular court and had to live in the town in which it lay. Prussia appointed lawyers even to the courts of lowest jurisdiction, the county courts, thereby creating a class of lawyers who practiced before these courts.[39]

Other states followed different patterns. For example, after 1850 the Kingdom of Hannover pursued a policy of concentrating all lawyers in collegial court towns. Although there was no numerical limit upon the number of lawyers who could engage in office practice, they were forbidden to live in towns with lower courts or no court unless they first received permission from the ministry of justice. The govern-

---

38   Simultaneous admission is the literal translation of the term *Simultanzulassung* which was consistently used to refer to the admission to practice before a superior court of a lawyer admitted before and resident in the town of a district court in the geographic district of that superior court. The admissions need not *occur* simultaneously; the simultaneity referred to is the *status* of being admitted to the two courts at the same time. See, particularly, Verein Deutscher Amtsgerichtsanwälte (e.V.), ed., *Simultanzulassung. Handbuch zum Reichsgesetz vom 7. März 1927* (Berlin, 1931), 26–8.

39   Schubert, *Entstehung und Quellen*, 3–4; Brix, *Organisation der Advokatur*, 6–22. Localization provisions in the various German states may be found in "Motive zum Entwurf einer Anwaltsordnung," *JW* 7 (1878): 33, 15 February 1878, 38–40, 42. The German term for the Prussian county courts is *Kreisgerichte*.

ment viewed lawyers as a stimulus to litigation and sought to prevent resort to legal action by reducing the availability of lawyers. District court towns in Hannover, then, seldom had a lawyer living there.[40] During the 1850s and 1860s, other states, led by the southwest liberal states of Baden and Württemberg as well as some of the Thuringian states such as Sachsen-Coburg-Gotha, began to admit lawyers to all the courts within the bailiwick of a superior court and to allow them to choose their place of residence within that region more or less at their pleasure.[41] Prussia and Bavaria, however, adhered strictly to a policy of maintaining lawyers resident in the town of every court.

As legislative reforms of the legal profession began to be considered, the question of localization and whether the legal order needed lawyers who practiced before district courts had to be addressed. In the very first draft Lawyers' Statute, produced within the Prussian Ministry of Justice in 1872, admission was limited to a single court, because:

[T]he new civil procedure [oral and public as opposed to the old system of written and secret procedure] required "a certain ease of communication among the parties as well as between a party and the court," "so that the oral argument can be prepared for sufficiently and the proceeding guided to an end without delay." Moreover, the maintenance of an orderly trial procedure at the courts made it urgently desirable that "each lawyer devote his principal activity to a single court, so that the competing activity does not lead, as a result of the necessary presence of the lawyer in the oral hearings, to numerous continuances, often, if experience is a guide, permitted through the connivance of the opposing party."[42]

From the very beginning, the basic argument in favor of localization and against simultaneous admission remained the same: a lawyer should not be admitted to practice before two courts because he needed to cultivate close relations with the personnel of his single court, and his absence in another court would lead to delays in litigation.

This preliminary draft Lawyers' Statute was never introduced to the Reichstag because of objections by the middle states to the jurisdiction of the Reich under the constitution to pass legislation governing the private bar. When the Justice Commission of the Reichstag in

---

40 Brix, *Organisation der Advokatur*, ix–x; Roscher, "Gerichtsverfassung," 100; and Weißler, *Geschichte der Rechtsanwaltschaft*, 417. The system in Hannover maintained a limit on the number of lawyers who could appear before courts (*Advokatenanwälte*) but none on those who could maintain office practices (*Advokaten*).
41 Schubert, *Entstehung und Quellen*, 6–18.   42 Ibid., 47.

1876 drafted, debated, and inserted into the constitution of the courts Title IX on the *Rechtsanwaltschaft*, it also incorporated the principle of localization and rejected that of simultaneous admission in general, although it made simultaneous admission permissible in the discretion of the state ministry of justice in cities with more than one collegial court.[43] This provision represented a compromise engineered by the National Liberals, especially Lasker, between the positions of proponents of general admission to all courts and the more restrictive wishes of the Prussian government.

Lawyers in private practice generally favored a more radical freedom from localization. The fifth Lawyers Convention in Cologne in 1876 endorsed simultaneous admission before all courts within a court of appeal district.[44] Despite this pressure from lawyers outside the Reichstag, and despite pressure from the Bundesrat to strike the title governing the bar altogether, the Justice Commission held fast to its original decision, and the Reichstag initially endorsed the title as part of the constitution of the courts, in defiance of the Bundesrat. This draft, however, became irrelevant in December 1876 when the National Liberals agreed to strike Title IX in return for passage of the Constitution of the Courts and the Codes of Civil and Criminal Procedure and for Leonhardt's promise to present a separate lawyers' statute.

The draft RAO, introduced on 6 February 1878, called for strict localization of the bar at all levels of court. The Reichstag referred it to the Justice Commission for debate, and that body broadened the bill to provide that all admissions would be to individual collegial courts (that is, lawyers would be admitted to a superior court but could appear before all courts within its geographic district). The district court bar would thereby be eliminated. In this form, the bill returned to the plenum of the Reichstag for debate.[45]

In the debate in the Reichstag, the National Liberals, with Lasker at their head, strove to compromise with the obdurate Prussian regime, which insisted upon maintaining a district court bar. Lasker offered

---

43 Ibid., 26–8; see also "Erste Berathung des Justizkommissions über den neuvorgeschlagenen Titel des GVGs 'Rechtsanwaltschaft'," in Siegel, *Die gesammten Materialien*, 39–45.

44 "Der V. Deutsche Anwaltstag," *JW* 5 (1876): 105–14, and "Beschlüsse des Deutschen Anwaltstages. Köln, den 2. Juni 1876," ibid., 114–15. See also Schubert, *Entstehung und Quellen*, 30; Weißler, *Geschichte der Rechtsanwaltschaft*, 581–4.

45 Schubert, *Entstehung und Quellen*, 37. The revisions by the Justice Commission did not go as far as the bar association wished. That group had endorsed admission to all courts in a court of appeal district at its convention in 1878. See "Beschlüsse des VI. Anwaltstages zu dem Entwurfe einer Rechtsanwaltsordnung," *JW* 7 (1878): 157–62, 157.

an amendment whereby admission would be to a particular court, but district court lawyers could be admitted to the superior court above when the executive board of the lawyers' chamber and the court of appeal agreed that it would be in the interests of justice to permit such admission.[46] Windthorst and the Center Party led the opposition to this amendment, insisting that any form of localization was simply opportunity for political persecution by the Prussian or Reich government. Moreover, without simultaneous admission, lawyers practicing before district courts would be lawyers of a second or even third class.[47] Swayed by Windthorst's arguments, the Reichstag rejected Lasker's compromise amendment by a vote of 106 to 105 and retained the provision that admission should be to all courts in a superior court district.

The Prussian Ministry of State, and as a result the Bundesrat, declared any lawyers' statute that eliminated a separate district court bar unacceptable.[48] In the face of this threat, the Reichstag accepted Lasker's compromise amendment on the third reading, despite Windthorst's repeated warnings.[49] Because of this concession, Windthorst called the RAO "a caricature [*Zerrbild*] of *freie Advokatur*."[50] Lasker and the National Liberals fashioned the compromises with Bismarck in return for the enactment of a less-than-ideal RAO, which nonetheless established a unified private bar on a national basis. Lasker put the issue as follows:

It is my opinion that this house must divide itself into two parts: those who, for objective reasons, agree with Herr Delegate Windthorst that it is better not to agree on this lawyers' statute and to attempt to agree in some other way next year immediately before the entry into effect of the justice laws, must vote against this motion; the other half of this house on the contrary must see the way clear to accept this motion insofar as they consider the

---

46 "Zweite Berathung des Entwurfs der Rechtsanwaltsordnung im Plenum des Reichstages," in Siegel, *Die gesammten Materialien*, 485.

47 Ibid., 493.   48 Schubert, *Entstehung und Quellen*, 39, 203, 205.

49 "Dritte Berathung des Entwurfs des Rechtsanwaltsordnung im Plenum des Reichstags," in Siegel, *Die gesammten Materialien*, 624–5.

50 Fließ, *Der Kampf um den numerus clausus*, 24–5, argues that substantial limitations on *freie Advokatur* remained in the RAO. Müller, *Die Freiheit der Advokatur*, 33–9 catalogues the limitations upon lawyers' freedoms, arguing that freedom from the state was almost complete, whereas freedom from the profession (*Stand*) remained very limited. Lawyers accepted their remaining dependence upon the state as part of the bargain that created a nationally unified profession from a congeries of particularistic, functionally divided (into *Advokatur* and *Prokuratur*) state bars. Taken as a whole, the RAO largely realized the freedom of the practicing bar. For the quotation from Windthorst, see "Erste Berathung des Entwurfs einer Rechtsanwaltsordnung. 3. Sitzung," in Siegel, *Die gesammten Materialien*, 364–96, 382.

acceptance of the lawyers' statute at the present time to be a positive completion of the justice laws.[51]

With the compromises, the Prussian government dropped its opposition, and the RAO passed the Reichstag in May and was promulgated
into law by the Kaiser on 1 July 1878, to become effective together
with the other pieces of reform legislation on 1 October 1879.

The entry into effect of the RAO and the other Imperial Justice
Laws in 1879 both represented a long-fought-for triumph for the
liberal conception of the structure of the private practice of law and
initiated the legal structure under which the bar in private practice
would operate for the next fifty years. Despite the compromises, *freie
Advokatur* now prevailed as the fundamental principle of the organization of the bar. Lawyers had to accustom themselves to their new
circumstances, breathe life into the institutions set forth in legislation, and face the vicissitudes of the free market. The framework of
the bar under the RAO contained inchoate rifts that became the
terrain of contention within the profession in later years. Before
turning to a closer account of the history of the bar between 1879 and
1933 and of the debates loosed by the new structure, focus must first
turn to that legal framework for lawyers in private practice created
by the Imperial Justice Laws.

The Legal Framework for the Private Bar

The Constitution of the Courts completely restructured the judicial
system of the German Empire. It unified the system of courts by a
legislative act passed by the federal, imperial parliament; its adoption was an exercise in imperial sovereignty over the states.[52] It
erected a uniform, national pyramid of courts, with a uniform nomenclature, structure, and procedure for appellate review, which
replaced the piebald mixture that had existed before unification, in
which each state had its own system of judicial nomenclature, structure, and appellate review. The Constitution of the Courts did not
erect a massive imperial justice bureaucracy to oversee this new
court system, instead leaving the appointment and remuneration of

---

51 "Dritte Berathung des Entwurfs der Rechtsanwaltsordnung. 53. Sitzung," in Siegel, *Die
    gesammten Materialien*, 617–47, 620.
52 As such, the Imperial Justice Laws represent a high point of Bismarckian and of National
    Liberal state building; Pflanze, *Bismarck*, 2:347–50; Nipperdey, *Deutsche Geschichte 1866–
    1918*, 2:188–91, 363–4.

judges to the federal states, but it did prescribe uniform standards for qualifications to serve as judge. As will be seen, the educational requirements for judges had a direct impact upon lawyers in private practice.[53]

The Constitution of the Courts prescribed a four-tier hierarchy of courts, composed of local district courts, which were subordinate to superior courts which, in turn, were subordinate to twenty-eight courts of appeal, crowned by an imperial supreme court in Leipzig (GVG, §12).[54] District courts had exclusive initial jurisdiction in civil cases in which the amount in controversy did not exceed three hundred marks (§23). Superior courts had exclusive initial jurisdiction in civil cases not within the initial jurisdiction of the district courts, as well as appellate jurisdiction in cases from the district courts (§§70, 71). Finally, courts of appeal had jurisdiction over appeals from the superior courts (§123).

Single judges heard civil cases in district courts (§22).[55] In contrast, collegial panels of judges heard cases argued before superior courts and courts of appeal (§59, §120).[56] Each superior court consisted of at least two chambers, one for civil cases and one for criminal cases. The same division applied to courts of appeal, except that the divisions were called senates. For cases of serious criminal offenses before the superior courts, jury trials were provided in which the panel of three judges was supplemented by twelve lay jurors who served as finders of fact, alone deciding the question of guilt or innocence (§79, §81).[57]

In order to qualify for the position of judge, a candidate had to pass two bar examinations (§2).[58] This requirement superseded previous state laws concerning qualification for the office of judge, such as

---

53 The supreme imperial authority in matters of the administration of justice was not a ministry at all, but a mere "office." The official title was *Reichsjustizamt* until 1919, when it was changed to *Reichsjustizministerium*. See Hans Hattenhauer, "Vom Reichsjustizamt zum Bundesministerium der Justiz," in Bundesministerium der Justiz, ed., *Vom Reichsjustizamt*, 9–118, for an institutional history of this ministry.

54 *Amtsgericht, Landgericht, Oberlandesgericht,* and *Reichsgericht,* respectively.

55 Criminal cases were heard before panels of three persons, consisting of one judge and two lay people called *Schöffen* (§25).

56 Because cases at the superior court and court of appeal levels were heard by panels of judges, the collective term for all such courts was "collegial courts."

57 The jury trials for serious criminal offenses at the superior court level were called *Schwurgerichte* and the jurors known as *Geschworene.*

58 For a survey of the history of the educational requirements for judges and lawyers in private practice, as well as the legal education requirements in the German states as of 1911, see Georg Reidnitz, *Juristenbildung, insbesondere die Vorbildung der Rechtsanwälte in ihrer Entwicklung bis heute* (Mainz, 1911).

Prussia's requirement of three examinations, and made the prescribed sequence of legal examinations and practical legal training uniform throughout the empire. The first examination followed a three-year minimum period of study at a university, at least three semesters of which had to be spent at a German university. Following the first bar examination, the candidate became a trainee. The period of practical legal training between the first and second examinations had to be at least three years, and it was devoted to practical legal education in unpaid service with the courts and with lawyers in private practice.[59] It was permissible at the option of the trainee for part of it to be spent in service with a state's attorney. A federal state was permitted to lengthen the required periods of study and practical legal training and to require that part of the latter be spent in the administrative bureaucracy.[60] The individual federal states also determined the requisite course content of legal study at the university, making a certain course of study a prerequisite for sitting for the first examination in that state. This led to considerable variety in requirements among the various states. A candidate who had passed the first examination in one federal state was permitted (but not required) to be admitted to practical legal training in another federal state (§3), and a fully qualified candidate for the office of judge in one state was qualified to serve as judge in another state (§5). Finally, appointment to a judgeship was for life (§6).[61] At the end of practical legal training came the second bar examination, the "great state examination," after which a

59   The first state examination was known as the *erste Staatsprüfung* or the *Referendarprüfung*. Upon passing it, the candidate would become a trainee (*Referendar*), and the period of practical legal training was called the *Referendariat*. This system still obtains in Germany today.

60   Victor Berger set out the varying testing and practical education prerequisites for the federal states in 1913 in his opinion prepared for the DAV in 1913; Victor Berger, "Freizügigkeit und Simultanzulassung, Gutachten erstattet im Auftrage des Vorstandes des Deutschen Anwaltvereins für den XXI. Anwaltstag," *JW* 42 (1913): Supplement to No. 13, 1 July 1913.

61   In an important step toward legal unification of the empire, the Constitution of the Courts created an imperial supreme court (*Reichsgericht*) (§§125–141), whose seat was eventually placed at Leipzig. Because the *Rechtsanwaltschaft* at the supreme court was a closed one, appointed by the presidium of the supreme court, it represented a significant deviation from the principle of *freie Advokatur*; RAO §§98–102. The size of the supreme court bar was always small (twenty-five), and it was protected by its *numerus clausus* from the vagaries of the modern market economy which beset other lawyers. Thus despite the significance of the imperial supreme court for legal unification of the nation, the bar of the supreme court is both not large enough and sufficiently different in its organization from the rest of the practicing bar that it will not be treated at length in this work. For a description of the legal framework of the supreme court bar, see Friedländer and Friedländer, *Kommentar zur Rechtsanwaltsordnung*, 549–50, and for a discussion of its development, see Ostler, *Die deutschen Rechtsanwälte*, 83–6.

candidate awaited appointment to the bench or left state service to enter private practice.[62]

In a similar manner to the way in which the Constitution of the Courts unified and federalized the court system, the RAO unified and federalized the private practice of law. It overrode existing state law and abolished all distinctions between branches of the private legal profession where those still remained, establishing one group of private practitioners, the *Rechtsanwaltschaft*, whose duties included both the rendering of legal advice and representation in court.[63] Anyone qualified to assume the office of judge could apply for admission to the bar (§1); he *could* be admitted in any federal state (§2), but he *had to* be admitted in the federal state in which he had passed the qualifying examination (§4). Here is found the legislative adoption of the principle of free entry into the private practice of law, *freie Advokatur*.[64] The ministries of justice in the federal states decided whether an applicant for admission to a court in their territory was qualified to serve as a judge and hence be admitted to the bar. The ministries were obligated to seek and hear the opinion of the executive board of the appropriate lawyers' chamber before ruling (§3).

The RAO specified the only permissible grounds for denial of an application for admission. A set of mandatory grounds ("admission *must* be denied") included (1) conviction of crimes or serious disciplinary offenses; (2) loss of the power of disposition over one's property (whether through incompetence or bankruptcy); (3) culpability in the opinion of the executive board of the lawyers' chamber for an act that would lead to his expulsion from the bar in a disciplinary procedure; or (4) physical defect or physical or intellectual weakness that in the opinion of the executive board would render the applicant perma-

---

62 The second or great state examination was known as the *große Staatsprüfung* or the *Assessorprüfung*. Upon passing it, the candidate would become a candidate (*Assessor*), and the period of candidacy was called the *Assessorzeit*. This system also still obtains in Germany today.

63 Weißler, *Geschichte der Rechtsanwaltschaft*, 597; Schubert, *Entstehung und Quellen*, "Entwurf eines Berichts an den Kaiser (10.11.1876)," 141; and "Motive zum Entwurf einer Anwaltsordnung," *JW* 7 (1878): 33–100, 34. The traditional conception of the professional activity of lawyers, as counsel, advisor, and representative of parties in legal cases, is the one that shaped the activity of most of the profession. By 1930, many commentators were calling for steps by private practitioners to widen the scope of their professional activities, in order to respond to changes in the modern economy and the straitened economic circumstances of the bar as a whole. See, for example, Friedländer and Friedländer, *Kommentar zur Rechtsanwaltsordnung*, 12–15.

64 Friedländer and Friedländer, *Kommentar zur Rechtsanwaltsordnung*, 27.

nently unsuited to fulfill the duties of a lawyer (§5).[65] Another mandatory ground for refusal of admission was the applicant's carrying on a
business or occupying an office that, in the opinion of the executive
board, did not correspond to the dignity of the profession (§5(4)).[66]
This provision preserved discretionary room for application of many
corporate ideas of what secondary occupations or offices were consistent with the dignity of being a lawyer.

Discretionary grounds for denial of admission ("admission *can* be
denied") included (1) the situation in which the applicant had neither
practiced law, occupied a post in the general government bureaucracy
or the judicial service, nor taught law at a German university for a
period of three years after passing the qualifying examination; (2) cases
in which the applicant had lost his eligibility to serve in public offices
as a result of a criminal judgment; and (3) cases in which the applicant
had earlier been a lawyer and had been convicted of disciplinary offenses within the last two years (§6). In all cases, the discretion was to
be exercised by the state ministry of justice, *after* hearing the opinion of
the executive board of the lawyers' chamber, subject to the appeal by
an applicant of an unfavorable decision to the disciplinary panel, again
composed of members of the executive board. Through the con-
sultative power of the executive board of the lawyers' chambers, lawyers effectively became judges of admission to their profession.

65 Examples of cases in which admission had to be refused included: conviction in a German
    court of a crime that carried a sentence of imprisonment, or sentencing to an independent
    punishment of loss of eligibility to hold public office; the subjection of the applicant's entire
    estate to seizure by virtue of bankruptcy or execution, or by virtue of appointment of a
    guardian because of incompetency, disappearance, or alcoholism; and as to the last ground
    for refusal, blindness, deafness, mental illness, etc. Friedländer and Friedländer, *Kommentar
    zur Rechtsanwaltsordnung*, 31–49. For the first three grounds of refusal, the ministry of justice
    exercised its own discretion; for the latter grounds, it sought the opinion of the executive
    board of the lawyers' chamber, and that opinion was determinative.
66 This prohibition actually conflated two situations. The first case was when an applicant
    occupied a public office that was legally forbidden to be combined with the profession of a
    lawyer; an example here was when an applicant was a notary in a state that prohibited the
    combination of that office with the private practice of law. The second case was the pursuit
    by an applicant of another occupation that, in the opinion of the executive board, was
    inconsistent with the dignity of the legal profession. This second case again treated two
    situations. The first was the *Syndikus*, the salaried lawyer. The mere status of being a
    salaried employee was held not to disqualify the applicant. Only if the applicant could not
    exercise his independent legal and moral judgment before representing a position in court
    would his salaried position injure the dignity of the profession. Finally, however, some
    professions were considered simply to be inconsistent with the dignity of the legal profes-
    sion in every instance: running a saloon, an insurance agency, a provincial bank, or a
    brewery, or considerable activity in trade that brought the lawyer into close contact with
    the public. These were always considered to be beneath the dignity of a practicing lawyer.
    Ibid., 35–44.

The great charter of free entry into the private practice of law lay in the provisions of §13, which read: "Admission before the court designated in the application may not be refused on the ground of the absence of need for an increase in the number of lawyers admitted before that court." This was an express rejection of any consideration of the question of the supply of lawyers in deciding upon applications for admission. It represented a rejection of the previous Prussian and Bavarian practice of considering need before appointing new lawyers, as well as more formalized systems of *numerus clausus*. It was the greatest obstacle in the path of later proponents of the reimposition of the *numerus clausus* and other limitations on admission based upon an oversupply of lawyers.

Although the RAO made entry into the profession free, it limited the movement of lawyers. Localization was the basic concept of the statute, accepting the argument that a lawyer and the court to which he was admitted formed a unit; intimate personal acquaintance of judges and lawyers and consistent presence of lawyers during the court's term were necessary for the court to function properly.[67] Localization therefore became one of the basic principles of the new RAO. Each lawyer was admitted to only one court and, unless a special exception was forthcoming, he had to maintain his residence there (§8, §18). Most observers viewed it as the necessary concomitant of mandatory representation by a lawyer, one of the basic principles of the code of civil procedure. That law *required* parties appearing before collegial courts to be represented by lawyers, in the interests of the efficient administration of justice. Localization was no innovation but rather the embodiment in the RAO of the prior practice in many German states.[68] Lawyers traded freedom of movement for a legal monopoly of representation at collegial courts. Mandatory representation by a lawyer did *not* apply at district courts.

The RAO excluded district court lawyers in general from trial representation in civil cases before superior courts (§27).[69] Similarly,

67 "Motive zum Entwurf einer Anwaltsordnung," *JW* 7 (1878): 33, 38: "For the conduct of a lawsuit, the bench and bar form, as it were, a unit, a homogeneous whole."
68 Ibid., 38–40, 42. The *Anwaltszwang* provisions of the Code of Civil Procedure were based upon the presumption that lawyers would be localized, so that the *Motive* to the RAO presented the issue as a *fait accompli*.
69 District court lawyers could appear in criminal cases in any court in the empire except for the imperial supreme court and in civil cases before superior courts only as *Beistände* (who could appear in court in a cause and address the court *only* in the presence of their client; *any* person competent to sue and be sued could act as a *Beistand*) rather than full representatives (§26); they could appear in superior court civil cases as plenipotentiary representative

it excluded superior court lawyers from appearing before the courts of appeals. The statutes thus created three distinct groups of lawyers with competing economic interests, one at each level of court. A superior court lawyer could appear in any district court in the country and compete with district court lawyers for clients, but a district court lawyer could not represent even regular clients on appeal before the superior court. Conversely, district court lawyers could *not* compete with superior court lawyers for cases within the initial jurisdiction of the superior courts. They thereby lost the more valuable cases (amounts in controversy over three hundred marks) of their regular clients to superior court lawyers.

In addition to competition from superior court lawyers, district court lawyers faced competition from nonlegally trained lay practitioners, derogatorily referred to as "petty-foggers" or "shysters."[70] While the economic competition was no doubt real, the greater grievance of district court lawyers involved status. They felt professionally demeaned and degraded by being forced to compete with and argue against tradesmen of much lower social origin and educational background than themselves. District court lawyers feared that the public would fail to distinguish carefully between them and the lay practitioners and would forget that district court lawyers had the same educational background as superior court lawyers and were to be afforded the same degree of respect.

In accordance with Lasker's compromise amendment to §9 of the RAO, district court lawyers, *could*, however, upon application, be admitted simultaneously to the superior court whose bailiwick included their district court. Simultaneous admission could occur *only* when the court of appeal and the executive board of the lawyers' chamber agreed that such admissions were in the interests of the admin-

(*Prozeßbevollmächtigter*), but only if a lawyer admitted to the court was retained and deputized the first lawyer to argue the case before the superior court (§27).

70 With roots as ancient as the old Germanic institution of *Vorsprecher*, these practically trained practitioners were called *Rechtskonsulenten* or *Prozeßagenten* and regulated by §38 of the Trades Statute (*Gewerbeordnung*). For an overview of the extent of the practice of appointing *Rechtskonsulenten* as late as 1913, see Heinrich Dittenberger, "Die Praxis hinsichtlich der Zulassung von Prozeßagenten und der Zurückweisung geschäftsmäßig verhandelnder Bevollmächtigter gemäß §157 ZPO," *JW* 42 (1913): 1121, esp. the chart 1124–8. Theoretically, the appointment of *Rechtskonsulenten* was reserved for district courts where no lawyer had chosen to settle. As Dittenberger's chart shows, however, there often were *Rechtskonsulenten* at district courts which had one or even two lawyers. For the history of the *Rechtskonsulenten*, see Heinrich Wilhelm Kornmann, "Die Rechtsbeistände" (Dr. jur. diss., Freiburg i. B., 1938). The derogatory term in German is *Winkelkonsulenten*.

istration of justice (§9, §3).[71] The various federal states pursued differing policies regarding simultaneous admission after 1878; many states, such as Saxony, Baden, and Württemberg, routinely granted permission for simultaneous admission, but the ministries of justice of the two largest states, Prussia and Bavaria, routinely discouraged it.[72]

Thus the law created a fault line through the apparently unified legal profession. It permitted superior court lawyers to cultivate district court cases if they so desired, entering into direct competition with district court lawyers. It forbade district court lawyers to practice before superior courts, unless they went through the humiliating process of being seconded by a superior court lawyer. District court lawyers could not represent even their regular clients before superior courts on appeal from the district courts. They faced competition from litigants themselves, who could plead their own cases, and from nonlegally trained lay practitioners, a clear affront to the status and prestige of district court lawyers who had invested long years in university study and practical legal education. Applications for simultaneous admission under the permissive provisions of §9 lay to the executive board of the lawyers' chambers, whose members were almost exclusively the already privileged collegial court lawyers. Soon after the turn of the century, frictions and tensions began to develop between these classes of lawyers.

A different form of simultaneous admission was available to lawyers who were admitted before superior courts and courts of appeal. Any lawyer admitted before a collegial court was to be admitted to any other collegial court whose seat was at the same place as the seat of the court to which he was already admitted, so long as the court of appeal had made a plenary decision that such admissions were in the interests of the orderly administration of justice (§10). In practice, this meant that superior court lawyers admitted before superior courts in towns in which a court of appeal also sat could be admitted to both courts.[73]

---

71 Friedländer and Friedländer, *Kommentar zur Rechtsanwaltsordnung*, 59. See also the historical discussion in Verein Deutscher Amtsgerichtsanwälte, ed., *Simultanzulassung*, 33–58.

72 Friedländer and Friedländer, *Kommentar zur Rechtsanwaltsordnung*, 59. According to the Association of German District Court Lawyers, the Prussian government denied simultaneous admission because it wanted to divide the bar into three separate groups, one at each level of court, in order to prevent the emergence of a unitary profession and to better control the splintered bar. Verein Deutscher Amtsgerichtsanwälte, ed., *Simultanzulassung*, 45.

73 Another case in which this provision would apply was in Berlin, which was the seat of two and later three superior courts. This provision was of no practical effect in the province of Hannover, for the *Oberlandesgericht* was located in Celle, which had no *Landgericht*; the

The RAO also created the much-desired institution of professional self-government and self-discipline, the lawyers' chamber (§41). All lawyers admitted before any court in the bailiwick of a court of appeal formed a lawyers' chamber, and membership was mandatory; the best analogy from American practice is the integrated bar. The establishment of lawyers' chambers for purposes of self-government and self-discipline of lawyers, freeing them from more direct forms of supervision by the courts or ministries of justice, represented the achievement on the national level of a goal that lawyers had formerly pursued on the state level, with varying degrees of success.[74] The lawyers' chamber had an executive board of nine to fifteen members, elected by the membership at the annual meeting (§42, §43). The executive board elected from its ranks four officers: a chairman, a secretary, and a deputy for each (§46). The lawyers' chamber had the duties to draw up a procedural statute to govern its operations, to vote the necessary assessment of dues to fund its operations, and to review the financial reports from the executive board (§48). The executive board had the duty to oversee the fulfillment of their professional duties by the members of the lawyers' chamber. It exercised discipline in matters of professional ethics and administered the disciplinary authority of the chamber, mediated disputes between lawyers (and upon the application of clients, between lawyers and clients), and advised the ministry of justice in disputes between lawyers and clients in cases forwarded to the ministries by the courts (§49). Oversight over the business of both the executive board and the lawyers' chamber as a whole lay in the hands of the president of the court of appeals (§59). The chairman of the executive board had to file a written annual report with both the court of appeals and the state ministry of justice concerning the activities of the board and the chamber (§60). The system thus erected was one of substantial professional self-administration, subject only to the oversight of the court of appeal, and that oversight limited to formal violations of provisions of the RAO or other laws.[75] The professional autonomy granted by the RAO exceeded that of any existing scheme of organization within the private practice of law in Germany.

superior court for Celle sat at Lüneburg. This was the only *Oberlandesgerichtsbezirk* in Germany in which the seat of the court of appeals was not also the seat of a superior court. Ibid., 71–5.

74 Huffmann, *Kampf um freie Advokatur*, 61–7.
75 Friedländer and Friedländer, *Kommentar zur Rechtsanwaltsordnung*, 415–18.

The RAO described the professional duties of a lawyer in general terms.[76] A lawyer who violated his duties subjected himself to a disciplinary proceeding (§62).[77] The executive board elected a five-member disciplinary panel, consisting of the chairman, his deputy, and three other members (§67). This panel received initial complaints and determined whether further investigation was appropriate. If it so determined, it turned the matter over to an investigating judge appointed by the court of appeal (§71). If the disciplinary panel refused to open an investigation, the state prosecutor could appeal (§69). After further investigation, a full evidentiary hearing occurred before the disciplinary panel, with the state prosecutor conducting the case against the accused and the accused represented by counsel (§§80–8). Penalties included warning, reprimand, fines up to three-thousand marks, and disbarment, or a combination of penalties (§63). Appeal lay to a supreme disciplinary panel, composed of three judges of the imperial supreme court and three lawyers admitted before the supreme court (§90). Thus the RAO established a system of substantial self-discipline, although the power of the state intruded upon the disciplinary proceeding in the form of the investigating judge, the state prosecutor, and the judges on the supreme disciplinary panel. Although judges retained the power to impose summary penalties for infractions against order in their courtrooms, lawyers substantially achieved their goal of freedom from the disciplinary power of judges or bureaucrats.[78]

The fourth statute passed in 1879, which completed the framework of the private practice of law, was the Fees Statute for Lawyers. Prior to 1879, at least five different systems of calculating the remuneration for lawyers had existed in Germany. These systems ranged from that of free agreement between client and lawyer, which existed in Hamburg and in a modified form in the Rhine provinces of Prussia, to a system of fees for reading and drafting

---

76 RAO §28 provided:

> The lawyer is obligated to practice his professional activity conscientiously, and through his conduct in the practice of the profession, as well as outside the same, to show himself worthy of the esteem that his profession requires.

> The Friedländers describe the provisions of §28 as a general formula for the professional duties of lawyers, encompassing within it all more specific duties set forth elsewhere; ibid., 145.

77 The term used is *ehrengerichtliches Verfahren*, meaning literally "a proceeding in a court of honor."

78 The local disciplinary panel was called the *Ehrengericht* and the supreme disciplinary panel the *Ehrengerichtshof.*

pleadings and documents calculated according to their length in Schwarzburg-Sondershausen, to a system of lump-sum fees for representation at each stage in the procedure in the eastern provinces of Prussia, Baden, Waldeck, and Bremen.[79] Although there was debate within the practicing bar, with some lawyers arguing for a system of free contractual agreement as to fees, the majority sentiment always favored a statutory fee schedule.[80] Thus, the debate within the profession and within the Reichstag was not so much over the merits of free agreement versus fee schedule as over the sufficiency of the fee schedule proposed.

The Fees Statute for Lawyers set fees in civil cases in a schedule relating to the amount in controversy in the case (§9). The fee set forth in the schedule, however, was not the complete fee for the entire representation. A full or partial fee was accorded to the lawyer for each of several stages in the civil proceeding. For example, a plenipotentiary lawyer received one full fee for the overall direction of the case, one for the oral proceeding, and one for his work in attaining a final settlement before trial (§13[1],[2],[3]). He received a half fee for representation at each evidentiary hearing required by the case (§13[4]). A simple resort to the fee schedule, then, would not reveal the actual remuneration to a lawyer in any given case; that remuneration would depend in great measure upon the procedural complexity of the case.

Because lawyers' fees were set in relation to the value of the object or by the amount in controversy, there was an inherent conflict of interest between district court and superior court lawyers. Any increase in the jurisdictional limit of the district court would take cases

<hr/>

79 Ostler, *Die deutschen Rechtsanwälte*, 26–7.
80 Weißler, *Geschichte der Rechtsanwaltschaft*, 604. The idea of a fee schedule had been a centerpiece of reform proposals at least as far back as Gans, *Von dem Amte der Fürsprecher vor Gericht*, who presented a detailed outline for a legislatively enacted fee schedule, "Entwurf einer Taxordnung über die Gebühren der Fürsprecher," 264–84, in 1820. Lawyers persisted in their mixed feelings toward fee agreements after 1879. Guidelines for the practice of law published by the DAV in 1929 forbade agreement to accept a fee less than that prescribed by the fee schedule, a contingency fee, and an agreed-upon fee when the matter at hand was brought to an earlier-than-expected conclusion. Deutscher Anwaltverein, *Richtlinien für die Ausübung des Anwaltsberufs* (Leipzig, 1929), 11–12. The reason for reliance upon a fee schedule was the practice in German (and most continental) civil procedure whereby the prevailing party recovered attorney's fees from the losing party, in addition to the object of the case. Fees calculated according to a schedule were *ipso facto* reasonable and hence recoverable. The fee schedule also practically eliminated one means of economic competition among lawyers, although prominent lawyers could demand higher fees. ZPO §91, II. This recovery of attorney's fees by the prevailing party is fundamentally alien to the American practice.

and fees away from superior court lawyers. Moreover, if a party chose to be represented by a district court lawyer at the superior court level, he had to retain two lawyers and pay a fifty-percent greater fee (§42). The client and lawyer could conclude a written fee contract in derogation of the provisions of the law, but by and large the practice was to observe the fee schedule (§93).[81]

These four laws together defined the legal basis for the private practice of law in the Second Empire and Weimar Republic.[82] In them, the private bar had achieved the goals that Rudolf von Gneist had articulated and that liberals and lawyers had sought since the 1830s. They had achieved freedom from the disciplinary oversight of courts and ministries of justice. They had succeeded in separating their profession from its state-official-like position in Prussia, placing it on its own independent footing. They had achieved their aim of definitional equality with the judiciary, for both now were subject to the same educational and preparational requirements. They had attained their goal of *freie Advokatur*, free entry into the bar for all who had passed the second bar examination. It remained to be seen whether this attainment of lawyers' professional goals would lead to the political change and growth in Germany so hoped for by Gneist and so pessimistically anticipated by Wilhelm Heinrich Riehl.

81 For the permissible content and form of an agreement to pay a fee that exceeds the fee schedule, see Friedländer and Friedländer, *Kommentar zur Rechtsanwaltsordnung*, 232–4.

82 These laws have been celebrated since 1879 as charters of freedom, as the foundation of the *Rechtsstaat*, and as truly noble achievements of liberal legal reform and German nation building. Indeed, the value of all of the Imperial Justice Laws to present legislation in the Federal Republic has been consistently emphasized; as merely one example, see Wolfgang Sellert, "Die Reichsjustizgesetze von 1877 – Ein gedenkwürdiges Ereignis?" *Juristische Schulung* 17 (1977): 781–9.

4

Institutional Framework:
Lawyers and Honoratiorenpolitik

In 1882, the secretary of the German Bar Association ("DAV"), Hermann von Mecke, acclaimed the entry into effect of the Imperial Justice Laws of 1877–9 as the "formation of the practicing bar into a profession."[1] But in many ways, Mecke's pronouncement misunderstood the nature of the innovation introduced by the Imperial Justice Laws, particularly in the structure of the professional institutions of the private bar. He underestimated the degree of change that had already occurred, for the legislation of 1877–9 did not write upon an institutional *tabula rasa*. Since the 1830s, lawyers had participated vigorously in the *bürgerlich* project of creating a "bourgeois public sphere," constructing by 1871 an increasingly dense network first of local, then of state, and ultimately of national professional associations that continued to exist until 1933.[2] This web of associations formed an important part of the milieu of the lives of lawyers, and the practices that the private bar had invented in the process of their creation structured the ways that lawyers responded to the new opportunities created by the Imperial Justice Laws and by the subsequent demographic and career-pattern changes that they introduced.

1 Hermann von Mecke, "Die Gründung des Anwaltstandes (Eine zweite Neujahrsbetrachtung)," *JW* 11 (1882): 45. Von Mecke used the word *Stand* and argued that, despite the efforts of voluntary bar associations, lawyers did not become *de facto* a profession until their rights and duties were recognized by statute and guarded and protected by bodies elected by lawyers themselves.
2 Weißler, *Geschichte der Rechtsanwaltschaft*, 502, puts it this way: "It is self-explanatory that, in the century of association, the practicing bar would also seize this mighty lever of public effectiveness." For the tendency toward association in Germany, see Habermas, *Strukturwandel der Öffentlichkeit*, 50–1 (eighteenth century) and 92–4 (early nineteenth century); for the importance of the voluntary association to the bourgeois public sphere, see also Geoff Eley, "Nations, Politics, and Political Cultures: Placing Habermas in the Nineteenth Century," in Craig Calhoun, ed., *Habermas and the Public Sphere* (Cambridge, Mass., 1992), 289–339, 296–9. See also Anthony J. La Vopa, "Conceiving a Public: Ideas and Society in Eighteenth-Century Europe," *Journal of Modern History* 64 (1992): 79–116.

Mecke's assessment also overestimated the innovation created by the reforms in that he presented them as fully formed. But the Lawyers' Statute ("RAO") had only set forth a framework for the long-sought-after mandatory-membership lawyers' chamber for each court of appeal district, for the first time including every lawyer in Germany within a self-governing professional institution. Lawyers after 1879 faced the task of imbuing the chambers with real meaning as they drafted bylaws, elected officers, and embarked upon the self-government and self-discipline that they had so long sought. When it came to questions of organizational structure and institutional life, quite naturally they turned to the familiar idiom available to them from their experience in voluntary organizations. In many ways, lawyers shaped the governance of the new lawyers' chambers in the image of the voluntary bar associations that already existed; the old influenced the creation of the new.

Therefore, a more nuanced picture of the nature and history of the structure of professional institutions, of the voluntary bar associations and the lawyers' chambers, becomes an important foundation for understanding the behavior of lawyers in Germany between 1878 and 1933. It also reveals two problems that, while latent in 1882, by the 1920s caused the institutions of the bar to reflect the widening social and economic cleavages among groups of lawyers, reducing the credibility of the institutions' claims to represent the profession as a whole and damaging lawyers' self-image as the general estate. First, the very fragmentation of institutions into local and national voluntary associations and regional lawyers' chambers without a national capstone organization prevented the emergence of a single institution for the governance of the legal profession that possessed all of the attributes necessary to claim without challenge to speak with compete authority on behalf of all lawyers. Local voluntary bar associations were of limited geographic scope and often did not even include all lawyers in a given locality. The DAV, the national voluntary bar association, encompassed only part of the German bar, and most crucially it had no organizational link to local organizations. While all lawyers belonged to the official lawyers' chambers, those bodies were organized on a regional basis and lacked any unified national voice. Increasingly after the turn of the century, lawyers who felt unrepresented in existing institutions created new associations, further fragmenting the voice of the organized bar. This thicket of associations meant that most lawyers lived in multiple, sometimes overlapping institutional worlds. A lawyer who practiced in a city or town large enough to support a local bar association might belong to it and to the DAV, to a special-interest organization, and of necessity belonged to the lawyers' chamber located in the town of the nearest court of appeal. Institutional fragmentation by the 1920s paralyzed the various bar associations and reduced their effectiveness in defending or even expressing the interests of lawyers.

The second problem uncovered by the history of lawyers' professional institutions provides another important intersection of the trajectories of the private legal profession and German liberalism. Bar associations (and middle-class voluntary associations more generally) and liberal political parties emerged at the same time and shared a common structure, that of an organization of notables (*Honoratioren*), and they each pursued a form of *Honoratiorenpolitik*, a politics of notables. Both bar associations and liberal parties expected to accomplish their goals with a narrow basis of active members, an elite, who received deference from the rank-and-file members or voters. But the social and economic changes that accelerated in Germany after 1880 placed new stresses upon the organization of notables. Beginning in the 1890s a new mass politics emerged that shook the electoral prospects of the liberal political parties and called *Honoratiorenpolitik* into question. Likewise, in the first decade of the twentieth century, tensions emerged within the practicing bar that would bedevil its organizations into the 1920s and result in a decay of deference and a series of attempts to reform professional institutions so that they would better represent the "mass" of rank-and-file lawyers. In the end, the tumult of the 1920s vitiated the effectiveness of the organization of notables, famously ending the political viability of liberalism in Germany but also severely constraining the ability of the institutions of the private bar to support the pose of lawyers either to be the general estate or even to speak with one voice.[3]

Honoratiorenpolitik

As an important element of the emergent public sphere, lawyers created for themselves organizations that were typical of German

3 The definitive work on the fate of the liberal political parties during Weimar is Larry Eugene Jones, *German Liberalism and the Dissolution of the Weimar Party System 1918–1933* (Chapel Hill, 1988); see his conclusion on 476–82.

middle-class associational life. Beginning at the local level, voluntary bar associations tended to blend goals of sociability with those of reform.[4] In the context of restoration Germany, calls for reform of the legal profession amounted to calls for legal, hence political, reform.[5] As associations of lawyers, these voluntary bar associations were by definition associations of notables, for lawyers certainly numbered among local notables throughout Germany.

Because lawyers in private practice had been so closely associated with liberalism in general and especially with the emergence of liberal conceptions of justice reform, it should not be surprising that their ideas about how to build institutions shared much in common with the emerging structures of those liberal parties. German liberal parties in the middle of the nineteenth century served as vehicles for local *bürgerlich* notables to pursue political power and reform; in Thomas Nipperdey's famous phrase, they were "parties of notables" (*Honoratiorenparteien*).[6] The liberal parties emerged on the local level first usually as a self-selected electoral committee established to wage an election campaign. Small in membership, often consisting of the only politically active persons in a locality, no further organization was usually necessary unless electoral competition emerged. An alternative, but also episodic form of organization was the electoral assembly, which served as a means of candidate selection and political mobilization. A third and more durable form was the electoral association, a more permanent structure that often emerged from one of the first two forms of organization. With the association and its greater formality of structure came the inevitable division of labor

---

4 For a general discussion of the importance and development of voluntary associations for the German middle class, see Nipperdey, *Deutsche Geschichte 1800–1866*, 1:67–71; a more expansive consideration of the phenomenon of the association in the first half of the nineteenth century is idem, "Verein als soziale Struktur im späten 18. und frühen 19. Jahrhundert," in Hartmut Boockmann, et al., eds., *Geschichtswissenschaft und Vereinswesen im 19. Jahrhundert* (Göttingen, 1972), 1–44. See also Wolfgang Hardtwig, "Strukturmerkmale und Entwicklungstendenzen des Vereinswesens in Deutschland 1789–1848," in Otto Dann, ed., *Vereinswesen und bürgerlich Gesellschaft in Deutschland* (Munich, 1984), 11–50; Klaus Tenfelde, "Die Entfaltung des Vereinswesens während der Industriellen Revolution in Deutschland (1850–1873)," ibid., 55–114; and Michael John, "Associational Life and the Development of Liberalism in Hanover, 1848–66," in Jarausch and Jones, eds., *In Search of a Liberal Germany*, 161–85.
5 Hardtwig, "Strukturmerkmale und Entwicklungstendenzen des Vereinswesens," 30–3, points out the "crypto-politicization" of ostensibly unpolitical organizations in the *Vormärz*; see John, "Associational Life," 161.
6 The concept of the *Honoratiorenpartei* was first formulated in Nipperdey, *Die Organisation der deutsche Parteien*, 395, and developed further, extending to associations generally, in idem, "Verein als soziale Struktur," 1–44.

between the leadership and the rank and file, who, by electing officers, delegated decision-making authority to those officers, at least
between meetings.[7] There emerged from this tradition of the liberal
party of notables a tradition of loose associational organization and
deference to leadership by local notables. Built around practices of
sociability, local worthies who could afford to participate in politics
without compensation, such as state officials, industrialists, bankers,
rentiers, professors, and especially lawyers, assumed their right to
lead and to receive the deference and respect of those less favorably
situated than they.[8]

In the 1890s, the growth of mass politics in Germany called the
liberal parties' politics of notables into question. As the German
electorate settled into four great social groupings (Conservative
Party/East-Elbian rural, Center Party/Catholic, Social Democratic/
working class, and a fragmented Protestant *Bürgertum*), electoral turnout rose dramatically, calling for new methods of political mobilization to cement mass core constituencies.[9] The inability of either of
the liberal parties to adapt to the era of mass politics, to secure a
reliable mass constituency, caused in part by their stubborn adherence to the elitist politics of notables, led in part to their electoral
decline that culminated in the debacle of the elections of 1932.

This chapter, buttressed by the evidence of subsequent chapters,
contends that the politics of notables fared no better within lawyers'
professional institutions than it did in politics writ large. Frictions
emerged between the lawyer-notables, who had founded and continued to lead the voluntary bar associations and who now assumed the
leadership of the lawyers' chambers, and rank-and-file lawyers. After
the turn of the century, many of the rank and file began to question
the legitimacy of the professional organizations. Structural fissures

7 Nipperdey, *Die Organisation der deutschen Parteien*, 42–85. See also the depiction of the
   Progressive Party in Hessen as an *Honoratiorenpartei* in Dan S. White, *The Splintered Party:
   National Liberalism in Hessen and the Reich, 1867–1918* (Cambridge, Mass., 1976), 40–50.
8 White, *The Splintered Party*, 41–5, describes the social basis of the local notables; lawyers
   played a particularly central role.
9 The definitive work on this electoral shift is Stanley Suval, *Electoral Politics in Wilhelmine
   Germany* (Chapel Hill, 1985); see 21–2 for the growth in turnout, and 63–106 and 122–60
   for the social groupings; see also Eley, "Notable Politics, the Crisis of German Liberalism,
   and the Electoral Transition of the 1890s," 190–3. In the 1871 Reichstag election, turnout
   was 51 percent; in 1887 it was 77.5 percent and by 1912 it was 84.9 percent; Gerhard A.
   Ritter and Merith Niehuss, eds., *Wahlgeschichtliches Arbeitsbuch. Materialien zur Statistik des
   Kaiserreichs 1871-1918* (Munich, 1980), 38–43. For an innovative account of the meaning of
   electoral participation to German voters, see Margaret Lavinia Anderson, "Voter, Junker,
   Landrat, Priest: The Old Authorities and the New Franchise in Imperial Germany," *American Historical Review* 98 (1993): 1448–74.

among special-interest groups of lawyers bedeviled both the voluntary bar associations and the official lawyers' chambers, manifesting themselves in struggles for control of the machinery of the institutions or attempts to restructure or to circumvent them, and leading ultimately to an atomization of the profession into special-interest associations. The division between lawyer-notable leaders and the rank and file, together with the institutional deficiencies of the tripartite system of lawyers' organizations, contributed to a paralysis of the private bar, exacerbating the crisis within the bar during the 1920s and accelerating the decay of lawyers' institutions as agents for the protection of the interests of lawyers in private practice.

The division of responsibility among the various organizations and the legitimacy of their claims to speak with authority for the entire bar remained fundamentally unclear. Lawyers sought to reform their institutions, especially after 1900, but they achieved only limited degrees of success. The apparent unity of the life of the German practicing bar gradually eroded, revealing more fully the latent clefts created by the RAO and leading to a decentralism that weakened the collective voice of lawyers. Again and again, on questions such as the proper organization of professional associations, *numerus clausus*, and simultaneous admission of district court lawyers, the line of cleavage ran between the lawyer-notables who governed the institutions of the bar and favored the status quo and some segment of the rank and file, outside of institutional power, who sought change. As groups of insurgent lawyers challenged the leadership of the lawyer-notables, the professional bodies became the terrain of struggle for control of the direction of the profession. While these struggles racked the organizations, their authority and legitimacy to speak for the interests of the entire bar was severely compromised. When the institutions of the private bar proved unable to contain the conflicts, one party or the other sought an arbiter from outside of the profession.

Origins of the Voluntary Bar Associations, 1830s to 1879

Along with other elements of the German *Bürgertum*, lawyers in private practice began to form voluntary associations in the early part of the nineteenth century. Although a few bar associations arose in the 1820s, the real impetus came during the 1830s. Most of these associations formed locally, limited in their membership to lawyers who practiced in a particular city or before a particular court, although regional associations of lawyers appeared during the early 1840s.[10] The governments of the German Confederation inadvertently spurred this development by refusing to consider lawyers' petitions for the creation of official lawyers' chambers. The local associations represented attempts to attain privately what lawyers' chambers would have achieved as a matter of public law. Frustrated by the refusal of the governments to erect a statutory system for professional self-government and self-administration, lawyers set up a voluntary one of their own.

The aims that lawyers outlined for these "self-help" voluntary bar associations were the same ones that they set for official lawyers' chambers: to increase professional consciousness and honor by means of an evenhanded and just administration of discipline; to strengthen a feeling of professional unity and mutual responsibility among lawyers; and to attain a stronger influence upon public legislation. Private practitioners believed that they could influence public policy better by petitioning the governments in the name of the bar of an entire city or even an entire state rather than merely on behalf of individuals or small groups of lawyers.[11] Thus, the local voluntary bar associations had at least three functions in most cities: to exercise disciplinary authority over those lawyers who joined; to represent the interests of the private bar in matters of legal reform in general, and especially on the issue of reform of the legal profession; and, finally, to fulfill the function of sociability that was so integral a part of all of German associational life.

The local voluntary bar associations did not escape the attention of the suspicious governments of the German Confederation. All such associations had to disclaim any overtly political ambitions, especially after the decree against political associations of 5 July 1832.[12] The governments scrutinized the statutes of the bar associations closely and quickly forced them to strike objectionable goals that even faintly resembled political activity, for example, petitioning the

---

10 The list of cities with voluntary bar associations, together with the year of foundation, includes Stuttgart, 1829; Hannover, 1831; Giessen, 1832; Gotha, 1834; Celle, 1837; and "during the 1840s," Braunschweig, Stade, Breslau, Dresden, Leipzig, Munich, Zittau, Schwerin, and Frankfurt a.M.; Weißler, *Geschichte der Rechtsanwaltschaft*, 503.

11 Huffmann, *Kampf um freie Advokatur*, 30–1.

12 The development of the law of associations under the German Confederation as well as in the constituent states is set forth in Alfons Hueber, "Das Vereinsrecht im Deutschland des 19. Jahrhunderts," in Otto Dann, ed., *Vereinswesen und bürgerliche Gesellschaft*, 115–32, 117–18.

94

Institutional Framework

government on behalf of the practicing bar.[13] In other instances, governments prohibited the formation of local bar associations altogether. As a result of this scrutiny and the tenuousness of public life during the era of restoration, those local bar associations that did come into being remained loose and evanescent structures, quickly appearing and disappearing.

By the 1840s, however, lawyers began to form regional, provincial, or even statewide associations.[14] The success of such undertakings, particularly in the traditional south German liberal stronghold of Württemberg, led many lawyers to think of a German national voluntary bar association. On 11 September 1843, a committee of the Württemberg bar association issued an invitation to all German lawyers to attend a general lawyers' convention in Mainz on 1 July 1844, "for the purpose of lawful activity toward the introduction of a common German law." The call at first met with widespread approval from lawyers throughout Germany, but difficulties soon materialized. Although the government of Hessen had issued in December 1843 the necessary permit for the forthcoming convention, in February 1844 the Prussian Ministry of Justice prohibited all Prussian lawyers from attending either the convention in Mainz or the preparatory meeting scheduled for Königsberg. When other governments followed the Prussian lead and forbade attendance at the Mainz convention, the organizers recognized their defeat and cancelled the meeting.[15]

German lawyers did not abandon their attempts to hold a national convention to discuss the reform and establishment of uniformity of law. Under the leadership of the Leipzig Lawyers' Association, plans

13 Huffmann, *Kampf um freie Advokatur*, 33; Weißler, *Geschichte der Rechtsanwaltschaft*, 503, indicates that the government of Hannover raised objections against the statutes of both the Hannover and Celle bar associations, finding in the organizational goal of petitioning the government on behalf of lawyers in private practice an "impermissible representation of the legal profession."
14 In Oldenburg, 1839; Württemberg, 1842; Waldeck and Anhalt, 1843; Schleswig-Holstein-Lauenburg (founded in 1841, merged in 1845) and the Kingdom of Saxony, 1845; Weißler, *Geschichte der Rechtsanwaltschaft*, 503.
15 Getz, *Die deutsche Rechtseinheit im 19. Jahrhundert*, 83–99, emphasizes the importance of the plans of the Mainz conference for the movement toward German legal unity and gives details of the plans of the Württemberg lawyers. See also Weißler, *Geschichte der Rechtsanwaltschaft*, 507–10, who laments the uncanny ability of the government in *Vormärz* Prussia to make itself unnecessarily unpopular; the ministry of justice had already countenanced numerous discussions of legal uniformity within the states of the German Confederation, both by lawyers and judges, it tolerated many of the proposed reforms in civil procedure (oral, public procedure) both in the Rhineland and throughout Prussia, and it was already at work itself on a draft of a uniform German law on bills of exchange. Thus, Weißler complains, the prohibition of attendance at the lawyers' convention was an unnecessary affront to "public opinion"; ibid., 512.

began for a convention in 1846. The planners sought a city willing to host such a meeting, trying first in Leipzig, then Kiel, and finally in the liberal Hanseatic city-state of Hamburg. In August 1846, the first German Lawyers' Convention convened in that hospitable venue to discuss the "purpose, tasks, and limits of a German lawyers' convention, public and oral civil procedure, and the present status and future of the legal profession."[16] Eighty-five German lawyers (forty-seven from Hamburg) attended this first convention. The convention achieved little of substance except the call for a second meeting, which convened, again in Hamburg, in September 1847. Against strong opposition, the second convention adopted a motion to convert itself from a lawyers' convention, in the sense of being composed solely of private practitioners, into a jurists' convention, since issues of the unification and improvement of German law required the input of other legally trained persons, such as judges and government officials.[17]

Thus the difficulty in finding a meeting site that would accept them, the narrow geographic territory from which those who attended came (both because of distance and because of continued opposition to the conventions by the governments of some states), and the broad nature of their agendas limited the impact of the first two lawyers' conventions.[18] The participation of jurists other than lawyers would certainly have been appropriate if the goal of the conventions had been *merely* to discuss legal unity and reform in general; but the presence of judges and other state officials inhibited efforts by private practitioners to free their profession from the tutelage of state service and to develop an autonomous sense (or autonomous institutions) of professional identity and independence.

By the time that the third Lawyers' Convention convened in Dresden on 27 August 1848, conditions in Germany were completely different. The more general issues of German legal unification and legal reform were now under consideration at the German National Assembly in Frankfurt, and lawyers could focus more closely upon

16 Weißler, *Geschichte der Rechtsanwaltschaft*, 516. Also to be discussed at the first German Lawyers' Convention (*Deutscher Anwaltstag*) were "the advancement of jurisprudence, the awakening of legal awareness in the population, and the improvement of the profession from within"; ibid., 518. See also Getz, *Die deutsche Rechtseinheit im 19. Jahrhundert*, 99–101.
17 Weißler, *Geschichte der Rechtsanwaltschaft*, 519.
18 Weißler notes the dominance of lawyers from Hamburg and Schleswig-Holstein at the second convention, with most of the remainder coming from Hannover and Mecklenburg and hardly any from other regions. Thus, the first two conventions can hardly be termed "national"; ibid., 520.

the future of the private legal profession. Under the prevailing conditions of freedom of press and assembly, a free discussion of the liberal agenda specifically for the legal profession ensued. Speakers endorsed the independence of the legal profession from state supervision, elimination of the status of lawyers as state officials, abolition of the distinction between court pleaders and office lawyers, an end to the systems of *numerus clausus* and creation of lawyers' chambers as official organs of professional self-discipline. Other speakers vigorously opposed many of these proposals, especially the end of the *numerus clausus*, and, as a result, the assembly adopted no binding resolution. The convention founded a German Lawyers' Association, whose stated purpose was "to work toward the perfection of the legal order in Germany and to uphold the honor and dignity of their [lawyers'] mutual estate." Although this association disappeared with the failure of the Revolution of 1848, the idea of a national association of lawyers remained firmly planted in the minds of many German private practitioners.[19]

During the reactionary 1850s, lawyers centered their organizational effort on the state level. For example, a series of state-level lawyers' conventions occurred in the Kingdom of Hannover, meeting at Celle in 1858, in Göttingen in 1860, and in Hildesheim in 1861.[20] The gradual introduction of lawyers' chambers as organs of professional self-government and self-discipline in many of the states of the German Confederation achieved state sanction for some of the goals for which lawyers had formed voluntary associations during the 1830s. Some goals of the practicing bar, however, remained outside the purview of lawyers' chambers, especially in their Prussian incarnation as "councils of honor" with narrowly circumscribed powers. A dichotomy emerged for the first time between state organs of professional self-government, with limited and state-regulated powers, and the system of voluntary organizations of lawyers, more dedicated to the pursuit of a fundamental reform of the organization of the profession and, most importantly, to the advancement of the interests of its members.[21]

By 1860 the grip of reaction in Germany had loosened sufficiently

---

19   Ibid., 520–2. Weißler goes on to state: "Its foundation is the only sign of life that was ever given by this association [the *Deutscher Anwaltverein*]; it was never heard of again"; ibid., 561–2.

20   Ibid., 505. Regarding the reversion to the regional theater of activity, see also Ostler, *Die deutschen Rechtsanwälte*, 86–7.

21   For a recognition of this dichotomous system, see Ostler, *Der deutsche Rechtsanwalt*, 5.

that permanent statewide voluntary bar associations could emerge. In January 1861, lawyers meeting in Nürnberg formed the Bavarian Bar Association, for the purposes of exercising professional self-discipline (Bavaria still lacked a system of lawyers' chambers) and promoting reform of the legal profession. Out of 321 lawyers in Bavaria, 216 initially joined the bar association.[22] The association produced a draft of a lawyers' statute, which adopted the principle of a *closed* profession (free entry was repeatedly rejected at conventions throughout the 1860s and in 1870) and endorsed the creation of official lawyers' chambers. The bar association also commented upon pending legislative reforms of civil procedure and the organization of the bar. Although the Bavarian civil procedure reform was adopted in 1870, the reform of the organization of the bar was not enacted at that time and afterwards remained in abeyance pending consideration of the matter at the new imperial level.

Similarly, in August 1861, around one hundred Prussian lawyers assembled in Berlin and formed the Prussian Bar Association, one of the goals of which was the effort to achieve the "complete independence of lawyers in private practice." That first Prussian lawyers' convention, as well as subsequent ones throughout the 1860s, called for freedom of entry into the practicing bar (the abolition of the *numerus clausus*), despite the opposition of many members to such a measure; abolition of the civil-servant-like status of Prussian lawyers; and transfer of exclusive disciplinary powers to official lawyers' chambers composed exclusively of lawyers, transcending the Prussian system of councils of honor.[23] District associations formed in many localities as branches of the Prussian Bar Association.[24] The association suffered, however, from a relatively low membership and an even lower attendance at the lawyers' conventions.

Lastly, in August 1860 a completely different kind of association of persons trained in the law had come into being. At the instigation of members of the Juristic Society of Berlin, a call had been issued for a German Jurists' Convention for the express purpose of discussing

22 Weißler, *Geschichte der Rechtsanwaltschaft*, 558; generally, see ibid., 555–61.
23 Ibid., 548. Weißler treats the Prussian Bar Association and its leaders at length on 547–55. For an account of the discussion of the question of free competition within the practicing bar of the Prussian Bar Association, see Anon., "Die freie Konkurrenz in der Advokatur," *Zeitschrift für Gesetzgebung und Rechtspflege in Preußen* 1 (1867): 682–6.
24 For example in the court of appeal districts of Insterburg, Stettin, Breslau, Bromberg, Münster, Hamm, and Ehrenbreitstein; Weißler, *Geschichte der Rechtsanwaltschaft*, 553.

ways in which to promote the uniformity of German law.[25] The
response to the invitation was enormous. Seven hundred and ten
jurists responded initially, and almost eight hundred actually registered when the meeting convened in Berlin. In stark contrast to the
treatment of the abortive lawyers' convention of 1844, the governments of the various German states, led by Prussia and Austria,
greeted the call for the convention and endorsed its goal of achieving
legal uniformity. Symbolic of the euphoria of the Prussian "New
Era," the Prince Regent (later King and Emperor), Wilhelm I, provided a subvention of 2,500 talers to the convention.[26]

While the call to convention mentioned only the goal of striving
for legal uniformity throughout Germany (still conceived of in a
großdeutsch sense as including Austria), the bylaws adopted by the
lawyers assembled in Berlin stated broader goals. Section 1 of the
original bylaws provided that:

The goal of the German Jurists' Convention is: to form an association for the
lively exchange of opinion and personal intercourse among German jurists,
to obtain ever greater recognition of demands for uniform development in
the realms of private, procedural, and criminal law, to identify the impediments that stand in the way of this development, and to come to an understanding over proposals that are suited to promote the uniformity of law.[27]

The definition of those jurists who were qualified for membership was
quite broad; it included judges, state prosecutors, lawyers in private
practice, notaries, aspirants or candidates for all of those positions,
others qualified for those professions under the laws of the states in
which they lived, teachers at German universities, members of learned
academies, doctors of law, and "legally-trained members of the administrative authorities."[28] For fear of exciting insurmountable differences

25 Hermann Conrad, "Der deutsche Juristentag 1860–1960," in Ernst von Caemmerer, et al.,
    eds., *Hundert Jahre deutsches Rechtsleben. Festschrift zum hundertjährigen Bestehen des deutschen
    Juristentages 1860–1960*, 2 vols. (Karlsruhe, 1960), 1:1–36, 2–4. Getz, *Die deutsche Rechts-
    einheit im 19. Jahrhundert*, 140–4, gives much credit to the idea of the "unification of the
    German nation in the realm of law" as the impetus for the formation of the German Jurists'
    Convention. The Berlin body was named the *Juristische Gesellschaft Berlin*.
26 Thomsen, Oberlandesgerichtsrat zu Stettin, *Gesammtbericht über die Thätigkeit des deutschen
    Juristentags in den 25 Jahren seines Bestehens 1860–1885. Jubiläumsschrift im Auftrage des
    ständigen Deputations verfaßt* (Berlin, 1885), 3–4. Thomsen takes pains to illustrate at length
    the degree of official acceptance, even endorsement, enjoyed by the German Jurists' Con-
    vention from the very beginning, by quoting from the letters and speeches of welcome
    given by various ministries of justice, both in 1861 and after.
27 Statut des deutschen Juristentages, §1, in *Festschrift für den neunten deutschen Juristentag in
    Stuttgart* (Stuttgart, 1871), 7–12, 7.
28 Ibid., §3, 8.

within the ranks of its own membership, the German Jurists' Convention excluded from its scope of concern any involvement with political issues or questions of public law, recognizing also that such activity could place it in danger of interference from outside authorities.[29]

The main organ of the German Jurists' Convention was the convention itself, held annually until 1876 and biennially thereafter.[30] These conventions were especially fruitful in the 1860s and 1870s. They considered the question of unification of German law in different substantive and procedural fields and, especially after 1874, debated the drafts of the Imperial Justice Laws pending before the Reichstag. Again in the 1880s and 1890s, the conventions analyzed and discussed the drafts and final version of the Civil Law Code.[31] Secondarily, the conventions provided the opportunity for lawyers from all parts of Germany, with various legal traditions, to meet and become acquainted with one another and one another's ways. Further, the broad nature of the membership allowed members of all branches of the *Juristenstand* to intermingle: judges, state administrative officials, and professors, as well as lawyers in private practice. On the other hand, the broad membership of the German Jurists' Convention excluded the possibility that it could ever be the instrument for the promotion of the interests of the private legal profession.[32]

Encouraged by the success of the German Jurists' Convention, lawyers in private practice therefore sought once again to form a national association. Soon after the unification of the German Empire in 1871, the Bavarian Bar Association and the Prussian Bar Association, the former flourishing and the latter languishing, issued a joint call for a national lawyers' convention to convene in Bamberg on 25 August 1871. The order of business was to be the consideration of the foundation of a German bar association and, if such an organiza-

---

29   Thomsen, *Gesammtbericht,* 7.   30   Conrad, "Der deutsche Juristentag 1860–1960," 5.
31   John, *Politics and the Law,* 107–9, 114, 194, 249.
32   The German Jurists' Convention had to face the political upheavals within the German-speaking realm during the 1860s and 1870s. After 1866, after 1871, and again after the entry into effect of the Imperial Justice Laws in 1879, the convention faced the question of whether political events had rendered it superfluous, and each time it concluded that it still was a useful institution. Despite the *kleindeutsch* solution to the question of German unification, Austrian jurists remained within the convention. Throughout the period in question, the German Jurists' Convention remained a lively organization in which many lawyers in private practice were active, although not one directly concerned with the professional affairs and development of private practitioners. Thomsen, *Gesammtbericht,* 10–16; Conrad, "Der deutsche Juristentag," 7, 14–24. The membership remained relatively limited, especially when compared to the DAV; from 1,500 members in 1884 it rose to 3,700 in 1912, but it declined greatly during the First World War and remained at 800 in 1924; ibid., 8–9.

tion were formed, the selection of experts to draft opinions concerning the already existing draft civil procedure code.[33] One hundred and sixty-nine private practitioners met in Bamberg and unanimously voted to create the German Bar Association. Section 1 of the statute of the DAV stated:

> The goal of the German Bar Association is:
> I.   The advancement of the public spirit of the comrades in the profession [*Stand*] and the cultivation of the scholarly spirit,
> II. The advancement of the administration of justice and the legislation of the German Empire,
> III. The representation of the interests of the profession.[34]

Throughout all subsequent changes in the statute of the DAV, the stated purpose remained the same.[35]

Every German lawyer in private practice was entitled to membership in the DAV (§2). The DAV consisted of two organs, the convention itself, acting as a plenum, and a seven-member executive board that represented the association between the regularly scheduled conventions and supervised the execution of the decisions made by the convention (§4). Because many states within the new German Empire had already adopted the system of official lawyers' chambers, the organizers of the DAV did not charge it with any duties of disciplinary oversight, thereby distinguishing it fundamentally from the existing local associations and from the attempts to create a national bar association in the 1840s.[36] The immediate task of the DAV, much like that undertaken by the German Jurists' Convention after 1871, was to consider, draft, and criticize proposals for uniform substantive and procedural laws for the new empire. As described earlier, the DAV first directed its attention to the reform of the constitution of

33 Weißler, *Geschichte der Rechtsanwaltschaft*, 562. The texts of the calls to convention, initiated by the Bavarian Bar Association in April and responded to by the Prussians in July, are reproduced in Dittenberger, "Fünfzig Jahre Deutscher Anwaltverein. 1871/1921," *JW* 50 (1921): 969, 986.

34 Dittenberger, "Fünfzig Jahre," 987. Although only 169 lawyers attended the convention, an undetermined number of other lawyers responded in writing, declaring their support for the creation of a national association and their intention to join; Weißler, *Geschichte der Rechtsanwaltschaft*, 562.

35 Ostler notes with pride that representation of the interests of the profession was the third and last of the stated goals of the DAV: "The 'representation of the interests of the profession' was first mentioned in third place"; Ostler, *Die deutschen Rechtsanwälte*, 87.

36 Weißler, *Geschichte der Rechtsanwaltschaft*, 562. Ostler draws a sharp distinction between the organization of the DAV in 1871 and previous efforts to create a national bar association, indicating that the unification of Germany had led to a narrowing of the focus of lawyers, away from political goals and more to strictly jurisprudential and professional ones; *Die deutschen Rechtsanwälte*, 86.

the courts and of civil procedure, especially to the issue that it considered most integral to the question of the form of procedure, the organization of the private legal profession itself.

With the creation of the DAV, the Prussian Bar Association considered itself superfluous and dissolved on 29 December 1872, transferring its treasury of 1,000 talers to the new association.[37] The new DAV differed profoundly, however, from the organizational framework of the Prussian Bar Association in that it lacked any organizational connection to the various local bar associations. Many members of the DAV were also members of local associations, and after 1879 all lawyers were members of the lawyers' chambers, but no organic institutional ties existed among these different levels of associations. This essential disunity of associational expression of the legal profession on the national and local levels at first presented no problems, but after the turn of the century it gave rise to frictions and reform movements within the DAV.[38]

Nevertheless, the DAV experienced immediate acceptance among lawyers and began to grow. By 1873 the DAV had 1,476 members, and although the total had declined to 1,308 in 1878, a quarter of all German lawyers in private practice had joined (see Table 4.1).[39] At the fourth Lawyers' Convention in Würzburg in 1874, the DAV endorsed the concept of an imperial law regulating the private practice of law. The specific draft then before the Reichstag was the subject of deliberations at the fifth Lawyers' Convention in Cologne in 1876, and the final version of the RAO was the focus at the sixth Lawyers' Convention at Frankfurt a. M. in 1878. Although the RAO as finally adopted did not conform in all of its particulars to the desires of German lawyers as expressed through the DAV, especially in the strict localization of the RAO, the DAV had skillfully assembled and presented, even guided, the position of the legal profession on the many issues of professional organization and had seen its positions prevail in most instances.[40]

With the adoption of the RAO and its system of official lawyers' chambers for self-government and self-discipline, Mecke and other

---

37 Weißler, *Geschichte der Rechtsanwaltschaft*, 566. The Bavarian Bar Association continued to exist until 1883 when it finally dissolved, and its newspaper ceased to appear; ibid., 561.
38 Ostler, *Die deutschen Rechtsanwälte*, 88.
39 Ibid., 88; Weißler, *Geschichte der Rechtsanwaltschaft*, 568. By 1881 over one-third of all German lawyers were members of the DAV.
40 See generally Weißler, *Geschichte der Rechtsanwaltschaft*, 566–8, 572–603.

Table 4.1.   *Total number of lawyers and total members of the Deutscher Anwaltverein (DAV)*

Year	Total lawyers	Total DAV	Percent DAV	Year	Total lawyers	Total DAV	Percent DAV
1880	4,112	1,492	36.3	1915	13,051	10,576	81.0
1881	4,091	1,546	37.8	1916	10,310		
1882		1,635		1917	12,393	10,105	81.5
1883		1,650		1918		9,988	
1885	4,556			1919	12,030	9,758	81.1
1887	4,810			1920		9,953	
1889	5,123			1921	12,276	9,707	79.1
1891	5,349	3,043	56.9	1922		9,747	
1893	5,565			1923			
1895	5,819			1924	12,531	10,190	81.3
1897	6,176			1925	13,537	10,746	79.4
1899	6,629			1926	14,308	11,472	80.2
1901	6,831			1927	14,894	12,052	80.9
1903	7,262	4,676	64.4	1928	15,329	12,533	81.8
1905	7,863	5,125	65.2	1929	15,846	13,070	82.5
1907	8,638	5,810	67.3	1930	16,416	13,508	82.3
1909	9,607	6,830	71.1	1931	17,184	14,122	82.2
1911	10,844	8,248	76.1	1932	18,036	14,651	81.2
1913	12,324	9,574	77.7	1933	19,208	15,178	79.0
1914		10,194					

Note: The total number of lawyers in Germany *includes* those practicing before the Imperial Supreme Court (*Reichsgericht*) in years up to and including 1915; thereafter the total reported does not include these approximately twenty-five lawyers.
Source: Compiled from Reichs Justiz-Amt, *Deutsche Justiz-Statistik* (Berlin), vols. 1–17 (1883–1915); *Anwaltsblatt* (1919–33); and Jarausch, *The Unfree Professions*, table A.5a, 238.

observers believed that they had witnessed a culmination, the "completion of the formation of the German legal profession," a process that had been begun by the formation of the local bar associations and continued by the creation of the DAV. Some observers even questioned the continuing need for a voluntary national bar association. The conclusion reached in 1879, and subsequently whenever the question arose again, was that the official and voluntary institutions served different and complementary functions, so that both were needed in order to represent fully the interests of lawyers.[41] Despite the continued existence of the local associations and the creation of

41   Ostler, *Der deutsche Rechtsanwalt*, 3, 6.

official lawyers' chambers in 1879, the DAV remained recognized and accepted, both in public opinion and within the profession itself, as the principal representation of the professional *Stand* of German lawyers.[42]

Part of the appeal of the DAV was its publication of an important professional periodical, the *Juristische Wochenschrift*, begun in 1871. Part newspaper, part legal journal, the *JW* appeared first semi-monthly and later weekly. It carried news and commentary of interest to the legal profession, notices to members of the DAV, and most importantly summaries of judicial decisions from appellate courts. It also included scholarly articles expounding questions of law generally, but with particular emphasis on legal issues that affected the organization and interests of the private bar, such as procedure, jurisdiction, discipline, and the RAO. In 1914, the DAV created a new journal to carry notices to members and articles about issues of the law of the legal profession, the *Anwaltsblatt*.[43]

The DAV in Crisis, 1907–9

After 1879, the organizational life of lawyers in private practice consisted of three complex, interrelated elements: local voluntary bar associations, the official, mandatory lawyers' chambers, and the voluntary DAV. First, the local voluntary bar associations continued to exist, shorn now of their voluntary disciplinary power but still fulfilling the functions of sociability so important to all such groups.[44] They lacked, however, any connections to each other or to a unifying national voluntary bar association (after 1871, the DAV). Second, the lawyers' chambers by statute encompassed all German lawyers, but they were both supralocal and subnational. Since they included all

---

42 Ostler, *Die deutschen Rechtsanwälte,* 88.
43 From 1914 through 1925, this paper, usually published monthly, was called *Nachrichten für Mitglieder des Deutschen Anwaltvereins;* from 1926 to 1933, it appeared under the title *Anwaltsblatt;* and after coordination the title changed to *Mitteilungsblatt der Reichsfachgruppe Rechtsanwälte des Bundes nationalsozialistischer deutscher Juristen.* The German term translated as "law of the legal profession" is *Standesrecht.*
44 Dittenberger in 1921, perhaps with the benefit of hindsight after living through the "crisis" of 1907–9, indicated that the founders of the DAV had never intended to replace the local and regional bar associations, for their continued existence was important in view of the differences in substantive law among the various German states. Although this reason for the continued existence of the local associations had diminished in importance as more and more areas of the law received uniformity through codification, nonetheless he argued that the local organizations remained important for the success of the national bar association; Dittenberger, "Fünfzig Jahre," 972–3.

lawyers within the bailiwick of a court of appeal, they lacked both the sociability of the local associations of lawyers in the same town and also any focus on the national interests of the bar. Since there was no unifying lawyers' chamber at the national level, each chamber tended to speak for the parochial interests of the lawyers in its district, and each was in turn usually dominated by the lawyers from the court of appeal. Thus, the lawyers' chambers often lacked legitimacy to represent the interests of all lawyers in the eyes of many of their members. Third, the only national organization for lawyers in private practice was the DAV, a voluntary bar association that lacked any institutional tie to the local associations or to the official lawyers' chambers and that at the outset could claim only one-quarter of all private practitioners as members.

Soon after its foundation, the DAV became the subject of complaints by some of its members that associational life was confined to the biennial (and for a period of time after 1879, triennial) conventions. Moreover, some complained that the executive board of the DAV, seated at first in Berlin but after 1879 in Leipzig and dominated by elite lawyers from the Court of Appeal in Berlin and the Imperial Supreme Court in Leipzig, was out of touch with the members of the association.[45] Between conventions, the DAV remained remote from the lives of most lawyers, as the members of the executive board carried out the business of the association in Leipzig and reported little to the membership through the *Juristische Wochenschrift*.[46] Although membership grew steadily (some believed as a result of lawyers joining the DAV in order to obtain subscriptions to the *Juristische Wochenschrift* at a reduced rate), attendance at the lawyers' conventions remained generally low until 1896, and lawyers who lived at the convention site always predominated (see Table 4.2).

45   There was substantial justice to this latter claim. Of the members of the executive board of the DAV between its foundation and 1920, their court of admission was as follows, compiled from ibid., 990–1:

Imperial supreme court	10
Superior court Leipzig	4
Collegial court in Berlin	8
Other court of appeal	17
Other superior court	10
District court	3
Total	52

46   Ibid., 971–2.

Table 4.2. *Attendance at German lawyers' conventions,*
1871–1920

Number	Site	Year	Attendance
I	Bamberg	1871	169
II	Berlin	1871	138
III	Eisenach	1873	117
IV	Würzburg	1874	116
V	Cologne	1876	251
VI	Frankfurt	1878	227
VII	Berlin	1879	323
VIII	Heidelberg	1881	155
IX	Dresden	1884	128
X	Munich	1887	165
XI	Hamburg	1890	355
XII	Stuttgart	1894	172
XIII	Berlin	1896	996
XIV	Mainz	1899	375
XV	Danzig	1901	311
XVI	Strassburg	1903	275
XVII	Hannover	1905	384
XVIII	Mannheim	1907	640
1st Extraord.	Leipzig	1907	1,192
XIX	Rostock	1909	281
2nd Extraord.	Leipzig	1909	442
XX	Würzburg	1911	1,049
XXI	Breslau	1913	919
3rd Extraord.	Leipzig	1919	475
XXII	Leipzig	1920	408

Source: Heinrich Dittenberger, "Fünfzig Jahre Deutscher Anwaltverein. 1871/
1921," *JW* 50 (1921): 969, 993–1016.

Increasingly after 1879, problems of the profession began to occupy the attention of the lawyers' conventions. At first, the questions were technical ones such as the administration of self-discipline
by the disciplinary panels. As the 1890s passed, however, the concern more and more became the economic condition of the private
legal profession. Confusion reigned as to which body, the lawyers'
chambers or the DAV, was better suited to represent the economic
interests of lawyers. In 1887, a member of the executive board of the
DAV argued that the lawyers' chambers should assume the lead role
in the "representation of the interests of the profession," because

they were not open, as the DAV was, to the objection that decisions
were dependent upon accidental majorities determined by the location of the meetings.[47] In general, however, the lawyers' chambers
proved unwilling, with one notable exception in 1886, to take the
lead role in protecting the economic interests of lawyers and the
field of legal practice against legislative incursions. Many lawyers
felt that the unclear division of responsibility among the three levels
of professional organization had led to a neglect of the representation of lawyers' economic concerns, and restiveness grew among
the membership of the DAV after 1900.[48]

The tensions created by this disjuncture came to a head in the
"crisis" of the DAV between 1907 and 1909.[49] In late 1906, rumors
began both to circulate among lawyers and to appear in the popular
press that the imperial government was considering a far-reaching
reform of the Constitution of the Courts and the Civil Procedure
Code. Among the rumored reforms was an increase in the amount-
in-controversy jurisdiction of district courts from 300 marks, where
it had stood since 1877, to some higher sum such as 800, 1,000, or
even 1,200 marks. Lawyers who practiced exclusively before district
courts greeted this possibility with approval; lawyers who practiced
before collegial courts viewed it with alarm.[50] Lawyers practicing

47 Ibid., 974.
48 Perhaps the clearest exponent of this belief that neither the lawyers' chambers nor the DAV
    represented the economic interests with sufficient vigor was Hans Soldan of Mainz. For a
    representative expression, see Hans Soldan, *Neue Ziele, Neue Wege. Ein Vorschlag zur Hebung
    des deutschen Anwaltstandes* (Mainz, 1909), 2–4. His concern led him to form a separate
    lawyers' association, the Economic Association of German Lawyers (*Wirtschaftlicher Verband
    Deutscher Rechtsanwälte*) for the express purpose of promoting their economic security.
49 Accounts of this "crisis" stressing the urgency of the situation may be found both in
    Dittenberger, "Fünfzig Jahre," 977–8, and Ostler, *Die deutschen Rechtsanwälte*, 90–2.
50 Schulze (Delitzsch), "Die Reform des Amtsgerichtsprozesses und ihre Bedeutung für die
    Anwaltschaft," *JW* 36 (1907): 65, recounts the rumors concerning the origin of this reform
    bill in the Imperial Justice Office and its distribution to the states for comment. He
    indicates his understanding that the jurisdictional amount would be raised to 1,000 marks,
    whereas the first draft bill issued in October 1907 raised the limit only to 800 marks. For
    another statement of the position of district court lawyers, see Böhm (Sagan), "Zur
    Eingabe des Kammervorstandes zu Nürnberg," *JW* 36 (1907): 121, in which he argues that
    the executive boards of lawyers' chambers could not act in a disinterested manner in the
    question because, he claimed, they were dominated by superior court lawyers. For articles
    stating the positions of superior court and court of appeal lawyers, see Alfred Lots
    (Altenburg), "Erweiterung der amtsgerichtlichen Zuständigkeit und die Gebühren der
    Rechtsanwälte bei den Landgerichten. Entgegnung auf den Artikel des Herrn Justizrat
    Koffka, Berlin in Nr. 10," *JW* 36 (1907): 471; Emil Koffka (Berlin), "Erweiterung der
    amtsgerichtlichen Zuständigkeit und die Gebühren der Rechtsanwälte bei den Oberlandes-
    gerichten," *JW* 36 (1907): 297, and Friedeberg (Stettin), "Erhöhung der amtsgerichtlichen
    Zuständigkeit in ihrer Wirkung auf die Rechtsanwälte bei den Oberlandesgerichten," *JW*
    36 (1907): 163 (representing the point of view of lawyers at courts of appeal). Court of

before superior courts were particularly worried, fearing that they would lose up to seventy-five percent of their cases of initial jurisdiction under a reform that raised the jurisdictional amount for district courts to 1,000 marks.[51]

In March 1907, the Imperial Justice Office announced that it was engaged in preparation for a reform of district court procedure, and that when a draft bill had been prepared it would be submitted in confidence to the state governments and to the executive boards of the lawyers' chambers for comment. Thereafter, the practicing bar (meaning here the DAV) would be given a chance to comment upon the draft.[52] Led by Rhenish lawyers, and in particular by the local Association of Lawyers in Bonn, 2,304 members of the DAV, almost half of the total membership, signed a petition asking the executive board to convene an extraordinary convention to discuss the proposed reforms.[53] After the executive board of the DAV received this petition in April, it declined to call an extraordinary convention, for in the meantime the preliminary draft of the proposed changes had been referred to the lawyers' chambers and state governments for review. Since no action would be taken in the Reichstag with regard to the reform proposals before the regularly scheduled convention, the executive board thought it proper to await the opinions of the lawyers' chambers, declined to call an extraordinary convention, and placed the matter on the agenda for the regular convention in Mannheim in September.[54]

The decision of the executive board not to convene an extraordinary convention evoked a firestorm of criticism. Many of the critics were enraged at the high-handed act of the executive board, imposing its own judgment on the merits of an extraordinary convention when according to the statute it had only the ministerial function

appeal lawyers were concerned because the increase in district court jurisdiction would remove from their jurisdiction appeals in cases involving amounts between 300 marks and the new limit, directing those cases instead to the superior courts.

51 "Zur Frage der Erweiterung der amtsgerichtlichen Zuständigkeit. Eingabe des Vorstandes der Anwaltskammer Nürnberg an das Königliche Bayerische Justizministerium," *JW* 36 (1907): 93, 94. It is important to remember that actions such as that of the lawyers' chamber in Nürnberg, meeting to consider the possible increase in jurisdictional amount and petitioning the ministry of justice, took place *before* any intention to do so was announced and *before* any draft reform bill was introduced or announced. This attempt at preemptive action demonstrated the depth of concern that such a proposal evoked among private practitioners.

52 "Vereinsnachrichten," *JW* 36 (1907): 161.

53 Under §5 of the statute of the DAV, a minimum of ten percent of the members of the association had to sign a petition to call an extraordinary convention.

54 "Vereinsnachrichten," *JW* 36 (1907): 321; "Vereinsnachrichten," *JW* 36 (1907): 378.

of selecting a site and date. Other critics took a broader view of the
crisis, however, focusing upon the lack of any intermediate body
between the plenary conventions, held roughly biennially, and the
executive board, concentrated in Leipzig and dominated by lawyers
who practiced before the supreme court or in Berlin. Reliance upon
the convention as the decision- and policy-making body of the DAV,
it was feared, led to a devaluation of the opinion of the DAV on the
part of the government, public opinion, and sectional interests
within the bar itself. Because lawyers from the site of the conventions usually preponderated, majorities at those conventions could be
dismissed as "accidental majorities."[55] The fact that majorities depended upon the chance of the location of conventions tempted the
losers at one convention to raise the same issue again at the next one,
in hopes that changed geography might lead to a changed majority.
This gave rise to an image of inconstancy and led the Imperial Justice
Office and the ministries of justice, as well as public opinion, to look
to some source other than the DAV in their efforts to find the representative voice of the legal profession. Since the current structure of
the DAV seemed incapable of representing the status and professional
interests of lawyers in private practice, immediate reform was necessary to strengthen the claim of the DAV to be the unified national
voice of the bar. One commentator summarized the shortcomings:

The rich activity and serious strivings at the German bar conventions must
lead one to wonder at the fact that the decisions reached there, in contrast to
those of other professional associations, are not accorded, either by government authorities or by the German bar as a whole, the singular importance
that should be wished for in the interest of the bar in private practice and the
orderly administration of justice.

   The reason for this regrettable but indisputable fact lies above all in the
fact that the DAV counts among its members only a *part* of the German
bar, albeit a very large part, and that the decisions of the bar conventions
rest more or less upon "accidental majorities," as a result of the organization of the association, because those who attend the bar conventions come
in large part for numerous apparent reasons from the town or region
where the bar convention meets, and decisions on each matter for discussion on the agenda regularly turn upon the attitude of lawyers in the
region of the meeting site.

   The outcome of decisions is not determined by the totality of the DAV
nor by an assembly that represents in relatively equal numbers all German
lawyers, but rather the lawyers of the region where the meeting is held; in

55   The German term is *Zufallsmehrheiten.*

this way, successive bar conventions have often reached conflicting decisions on the same issues.[56]

The solution for this problem was to create a representative assembly between the plenary convention and the executive board, a "parliament," composed of representatives elected in some fashion. One proposal suggested that the existing local bar associations or lawyers' chambers elect representatives. This idea raised the problem that not all members of local associations or lawyers' chambers had joined the DAV, so that either nonmembers would have to be allowed to vote for the members of the DAV representative assembly or some mechanism would have to be created to exclude them from voting. Despite the difficulties, there arose a consensus that some step in this direction would be necessary.[57]

The eighteenth German Lawyers' Convention met in Mannheim in September 1907 and heatedly debated the proposed reforms to the Constitution of the Courts and the Code of Civil Procedure.[58] Although the convention refused to adopt a vote of no confidence in the executive board of the DAV for its refusal to call an extraordinary convention, the need seemed clear to all to revise the statute of the DAV. Near the end of the convention, it endorsed a motion to create a special commission to draft suggested changes in the statute, which would provide for an intermediate representative body. In the press of time, the convention postponed discussion of the questions of the exact structure of the commission and its membership until an extraordinary convention to be held in Leipzig in November.[59]

At the first Extraordinary Lawyers' Convention in Leipzig in November 1907, the assembled members of the DAV elected a special commission consisting of fifteen lawyers and one representative of the executive board to study the reform of the statute and to

56 Wilhelm Rosenthal (Munich), "Der Deutsche Anwaltverein. Eine Anregung zum Mannheimer Anwaltstage," *JW* 36 (1907): 498, 499. Dittenberger describes these feelings as widespread throughout the bar; Dittenberger, "Fünfzig Jahre," 977.
57 Rosenthal, "Der Deutsche Anwaltverein," 500. See also Dittenberger, "Fünfzig Jahre," 977.
58 The deep division between the district and superior court lawyers emerged most sharply during this debate, for the change in jurisdictional amounts was perceived as a zero-sum action by the two groups; "Verhandlungen des XVIII. Deutschen Anwaltstages zu Mannheim am 11. und 12. September 1907. Stenographischer Bericht," *JW* 36 (1907): 592–652. For a more extensive discussion of the district-superior court split, see Chapter 7.
59 Ibid., 645–6. For a summary of the actions taken at the Mannheim lawyers' convention, see Fischer I (Köln), "Der XVIII. Deutschen Anwaltstag, abgehalten zu Mannheim, 10. bis 14. September 1907," *JW* 36 (1907): 568.

report at the next convention.[60] It published its initial recommendations for proposed changes in the DAV statute in the *Juristische
Wochenschrift* in 1909. The first draft called for creation of "branch
associations" (*Zweigvereine*) of the DAV both by inviting the existing local bar associations to affiliate with the DAV and by founding
new branch associations. The branch associations would then elect
delegates to the representatives' assembly (*Vertreterversammlung*) pro-
portionate to their memberships. The representatives' assembly
would take over almost all of the discretionary functions heretofore
carried out by the executive board.[61] The executive board opposed
the proposed revision altogether, contending that there was no need
for branch associations and that incorporation of existing local bar
associations was problematic because of the number of non-DAV
members within them.[62] Instead of a representatives' assembly, the
executive board proposed the creation of a "committee," elected by
the members of the DAV voting in districts, to carry out many of
the same duties proposed in the commission's draft but also to serve
as spokesmen of the executive board with the members in their
districts, convening district assemblies at least once a year.[63] The
commission thereafter revised its draft, abandoning the idea of
branch associations but retaining the representatives' assembly, now
elected by the members of the DAV within each superior court

60 "Verhandlungen des XIX. (außerordentlichen) Deutschen Anwaltstages zu Leipzig. Sonn-
    abend, den 23. November 1907. Stenographischer Bericht," *JW* 36 (1907): 768–821, 819–
    21. Two of the members of this commission were district court lawyers. Ostler interprets
    the selection of a supreme court lawyer as its representative by the executive board as
    evidence of the distance between that body and the sentiments of the membership; Ostler,
    Die deutschen Rechtsanwälte, 92.
61 "Entwurf der neuen Satzung des Deutschen Anwaltvereins," *JW* 38 (1909): 210. The
    commission identified in its deliberations the deficiencies in the existing structure of the
    DAV:

    1 There lacks any connection between the Association's leadership and the members,
       especially between the Association's leadership and the local bar associations, present
       everywhere in the Reich;
    2 There lacks any readiness of action for the rendering of opinions publicly and quickly
       on draft legislation which is of considerable importance for the administration of justice
       or the legal profession, because only the sluggish means of an extraordinary lawyers'
       convention is available for this purpose. . . .

    Neumann, "Zur Änderung unserer Satzungen," *JW* 38 (1909): 209.
62 Neumann, "Zur Änderung der Satzungen des Deutschen Anwaltvereins," *JW* 38 (1909):
    442.
63 "Anträge des Vorstandes des Deutschen Anwaltvereins zu dem in Nr. 8 der Juristischen
    Wochenschrift veröffentlichten, von der Kommission ausgearbeiteten Entwurf der neuen
    Satzungen des Deutschen Anwaltvereins," *JW* 38 (1909): 345. The German term translated
    as "spokesmen" is *Vertrauensmänner*.

district in which at least fifty members practiced.[64] This proposal created an entirely new local level of connection, based neither upon the single-town-based local bar associations nor upon the court of appeal district-based lawyers' chambers. Instead, electoral districts of DAV members within each superior court district would be represented at the national level.

The proposed revision came before the nineteenth German Lawyers' Convention in Rostock for consideration in September 1909. Although a minority of lawyers opposed the revisions, the Convention adopted a version that created a representatives' assembly, with one representative for each superior court district with fifty or more DAV members and one for the remaining superior courts within a court of appeal district, so long as they contained fifty DAV members together.[65]

The DAV thus possessed a new decision-making body, and the representatives' assembly quickly assumed a position of real importance in the life of the DAV. Lawyers' conventions became less frequent in the 1920s, as most of the business of representing the interests of lawyers was taken care of by the representatives' assembly.[66] While the representatives' assembly improved the functioning of the DAV and allowed it to respond more quickly to proposed legislative reforms that posed threats to the interests of lawyers, it did not resolve the underlying conflicts within the DAV and the bar. At first the new body attracted little interest from members of the DAV. Participation in elections to the representatives' assembly remained quite low: 15.1 percent in January 1910 (1,050 out of 6,251), 11.4 percent in December 1910 (854 out of 7,781), 16.9 percent in December 1911 (1,442 out of 8,530), and 13.6 percent in December 1919 (1,279 out of 9,422).[67] The rate of participation rose only after the rules for conducting the elections were changed in 1923. The increase in turnout was dramatic; in 1927 it was 81.4

---

64 "Entwurf der neuen Satzung des Deutschen Anwaltvereins," *JW* 38 (1909): 444.

65 "Verhandlungen des XIX. Deutschen Anwaltstages zu Rostock am 9. und 10. September 1909. Stenographischer Bericht," *JW* 38 (1909): 545, 619.

66 Between 1909 and 1914 the representatives' assembly met seven times, whereas there were only two lawyers' conventions. No lawyers' convention was held between 1913 and 1919, whereas the representatives' assembly met six times. After 1913 and before 1933 (in reality before 1949), only four conventions met, while most of the work of the DAV was done by the assembly; Dittenberger, "Fünfzig Jahre," 1010–16; Ostler, *Die deutschen Rechtsanwälte*, 401–2.

67 Dittenberger, "Die Wahlen zur Vertreterversammlung des Deutschen Anwaltvereins," *JW* 41 (1912): 215–16; "Mitteilungen über die Vertreterwahlen 1919/20," *Abl* 7 (1920): 53.

Table 4.3.   *Court of admission, members of DAV representatives'*
assembly

	1910	1912	1920	1923	1928	1932
Court of Appeal	25	24	25	40	51	65
Superior Court	34	42	45	17	28	35
District Court	4	2	1	15	21	23
Supreme Court	1	1	1	1	1	1
Total	64	69	72	73	101	124

Source: "Die Ergebnisse der Wahlen zur Vertreterversammlung," *JW* 39 (1910): 169–73;
"Vertreterversammlung," *JW* 41 (1912): 161–5; "Vertreter-Versammlung," *Abl* 7 (1920): 54–9;
"Vertreterversammlung," *Abl* 10 (1923): 149–50; "Ergebnis der Wahlen zur Vertreter-Versammlung," *Abl* 15 (1928): 42–5; and "Ergebnis der Wahlen zur Abgeordneten-Versammlung," *Abl*
19 (1932): 46–9.

percent (9,922 out of 12,179) and in 1931 88.5 percent (12,433 out
of 14,041).[68] The composition of the representatives' assembly also
changed with the increase in turnout. Table 4.3 shows that a dominance by superior court lawyers was replaced with a dominance by
court of appeal lawyers, as the number of district court representatives also grew. As the representation of the warring district and
superior court lawyers became more equal, power shifted to the
court of appeal lawyers. Creation of the representatives' assembly
created a link between the national DAV and lawyers at a local
level, but the same lawyer-notables assumed control of the new
body. Electoral districts to the assembly assumed a parallel place
beside the local voluntary associations and lawyers' chambers.

Fundamental confusion remained over which of these institutions
really represented the interests of the entire bar. Local bar associations continued as before without any organic tie to the DAV. The
lawyers' chambers, although working closely with the DAV in many
regards, still lacked any direct organizational tie to the voluntary
association. Moreover, as will be seen in Chapters 7 and 8, special-
interest associations of segments of the bar began to emerge and to
express the interests of their members both within the DAV and
directly to government authorities. The reforms flowing from the
great crisis of the DAV in 1907–9 did not resolve these conflicts.[69]

68 Dittenberger, "Die Wahlbeteiligung bei den Wahlen zur Abgeordnetenversammlung vom
    31. Dezember 1931," *Abl* 19 (1932): 76.
69 Despite the dissatisfaction of many lawyers with the performance of the DAV, the percentage of all lawyers who were members of the DAV grew steadily. See Table 4.1. This

The Mandatory-Membership Lawyers' Chambers

At the same time that the DAV sought to modernize its structure in response to initiatives "from below" within the bar, the executive boards of the lawyers' chambers searched for a solution to their fragmentary existence. In 1886 the executive boards had sent delegates to Berlin to debate proposed changes in the fees statute for lawyers and to communicate the sentiments of the bar as a whole to the Imperial Justice Office.[70] At this assembly, however, there was no discussion regarding creation of a permanent body uniting the lawyers' chambers. No subsequent meeting of delegates from the executive boards occurred until 1907. In that year, delegates met, again in Berlin, to debate the proposed reform in civil procedure before district courts and increase in the jurisdictional amount.[71] The assembled representatives resolved to meet every two years for the purpose of mutual discussions of the interests of the professions, especially disciplinary matters, and founded the Association of Executive Boards of German Lawyers' Chambers (hereafter referred to as "Association of Executive Boards").[72] A new national organization thus entered the lists in 1907 to protect the interests of German lawyers.

The Association of Executive Boards occupied a peculiar place in public law. Although there was no specific statutory authority for its existence, the leading commentators on the RAO were of the opinion that §50 of that law, which permitted the executive boards of lawyers' chambers to direct proposals and petitions concerning the interests of the administration of justice or of the private bar to

"degree of organization" is comparable with that of physicians during the same time period; Huerkamp, *Der Aufstieg der Ärzte*, Tabelle 15, 251.

70 A letter from the "delegates assembly" to the Bundesrat, as well as a protocol of the meeting and a list of the participants is reproduced at "Hoher Bundesrath!" *JW* 15 (1886): 427. See also "Exkurs zu §61. Vereinigung der Kammervorstände und Reichsanwaltskammer," in Friedländer and Friedländer, *Kommentar zur Rechtsanwaltsordnung*, 421–3.

71 Buhmann (Munich), "Die Vereinigung der deutschen Anwaltskammervorstände und die Rechtsanwaltsordnung. (Ein Rückblick und ein Ausblick.)," *JW* 46 (1917): 881, 882. Buhmann notes that this assembly convened in response to the request by the Imperial Justice Office for the opinions of the various executive boards on the district court reforms.

72 Friedländer and Friedländer, *Kommentar zur Rechtsanwaltsordnung*, 422. The purposes of the Association of Executive Boards (*Vereinigung der Vorstände der deutschen Anwaltskammern*) were:

1 Discussions concerning the obligatory duties and authority of the executive boards under the RAO;
2 Preparation of common petitions to the justice administration;
3 Promotion of the interests of the German bar in private practice.

the ministries of justice, supported the authority of those boards to create the Association of Executive Boards as a means of advancing those purposes. It quickly became recognized by lawyers and by the government as an important voice in the expression of the interests of the bar. It rendered opinions on matters such as the introduction of the *numerus clausus* (unanimously rejecting it in 1909) and insisted that the Imperial Justice Office consult with the "elected representatives" of the bar before it submitted certain new legislative proposals to the Reichstag.[73]

The Association of Executive Boards believed that it had two important functions: to comment upon pending legislation that would improve the administration of justice or further the interests of lawyers and to propose such legislation. Nevertheless, it recognized a vague division of labor between its duties and those of the DAV. Particularly in matters of the economic well-being of the legal profession, it conceded that the DAV had more freedom to act than it did, because of the legally prescribed and circumscribed sphere of activity of the executive boards. The Association of Executive Boards, however, claimed to speak with more authority to public agencies, both because of the position of the lawyers' chambers as corporations of public law that included all lawyers and because the DAV, a creature purely of private law, spoke for only a part (albeit a considerable and influential part) of the private bar.[74] In general, relations between the two bodies were cordial. The DAV often co-opted representatives from the executive boards onto its commissions, and in many cases the delegates to the Association of Executive Boards were influential members of the DAV and of local bar associations as well.

The Association of Executive Boards sought to establish its authority as the chief voice of the entire bar, but it failed to assume many of the functions that would have strengthened its claim.[75] It failed to establish a newspaper, instead relying upon the *Juristische Wochenschrift* for publication of its pronouncements. It agreed upon a uni-

---

73 Ostler, *Die deutschen Rechtsanwälte*, 57.   74 Buhmann, "Die Vereinigung," 882–3.
75 For example, in "Vereinigung der Vorstände der deutschen Anwaltskammern," *JW* 39 (1910): 48, the association is reported to have resolved that the Imperial Justice Office should feel obligated to consult with the "berufene Vertreter der Anwaltschaft" before introducing legislation limiting appeals to the imperial supreme court. Similarly, in considering the need for a general reform of the RAO, the association called for creation of a legislatively recognized "lawyers' chamber committee" to be created to represent the entire practicing bar; "Örtliche Anwaltsvereinigungen," *JW* 42 (1913): 288.

form format for the annual reports of the lawyers' chambers but left it to the *Juristische Wochenschrift*, organ of the DAV, to publish an annual overview of the reports. The DAV continued to compile and publish the decisions of the supreme disciplinary court, although disciplinary matters fell within the exclusive jurisdiction of the lawyers' chambers. In short, the Association of Executive Boards remained a "loose collective organ," and it assumed jurisdiction only when there was a true necessity.[76]

Local and Special-Interest Bar Associations

Despite the attempts of both the DAV and the Association of Executive Boards to make themselves more representative and more effective in their representation of the interests of lawyers, special-interest and local bar associations arose at an accelerating rate after 1909. A national organization of district court lawyers had already emerged, and it provoked counterparts among superior court and court of appeal lawyers immediately after the war. Hans Soldan's Economic Association of German Lawyers, and other special-interest groups such as the Association of Rhenish-Westphalian Lawyers, advocated some form of limitation upon admission to the bar as a means of ameliorating the economic distress of lawyers. Local bar associations persisted and new ones were formed. Ostler reports that in 1913 eighty-five local bar associations existed, and the editor of the *Juristische Wochenschrift* expressed the need for an organic connection between the DAV and the local groups, calling for the creation of permanent local chapters of the DAV in each superior court district.[77]

By 1928 there were twenty-eight special-interest or regional bar associations, ranging from the Association of German District Court Lawyers with 1,930 members and the Association of German Superior Court Lawyers with 2,394, to the Association of South Holstein Lawyers with 25 members and the Association of District Court Lawyers for the Superior Court District of Lüneburg with 15. Fully 176 local associations existed, most including all the lawyers in a particular locality. The largest local association was the giant Berlin Bar Association with 2,170 members; the smallest was in Schwäbisch-Gmünd

76 Ostler, *Die deutschen Rechtsanwälte*, 57.
77 Ostler, *Die deutschen Rechtsanwälte*, 93; Dittenberger, "Der Deutsche Anwaltverein im neuen Jahre," *JW* 42 (1913): 3, 5–6.

Table 4.4.   *Local bar associations, Province Hannover, 1928*

Name of association	Headquarters city	Year founded	Members 1 May 1927
Advokatenverein Celle	Celle	1837	27
Göttinger Anwaltsverein	Göttingen	1910	29
Rechtsanwaltsverein zu Hannover, e. V.	Hannover	1831	155
Verein Harburger Rechtsanwälte	Harburg	1919	17
Hildesheimer Anwaltverein	Hildesheim	1908	27
Rechtsanwaltsverein	Lüneburg	1920	16
Anwaltsverein zu Osnabrück	Osnabrück	1898	34
Anwaltverein Verden	Verden	1911	11
Total membership			316
Special interest bar associations, Province Hannover, 1928			
Verein der Amtsgerichtsanwälte des Landgerichtsbezirks Göttingen	Göttingen	1921	15
Verein der Amtsgerichtsanwälte für den Oberlandesgerichtsbezirk Celle	Hannover	1921	207
Verein der Amtsgerichtsanwälte des Landgerichtsbezirks Lüneburg	Uelzen	1921	15
Total membership			237
Total membership, all associations			553

Source: Deutscher Anwaltverein, ed., *Verzeichnis der Rechtsanwälte, Notare, und Gerichtsvollzieher* (Leipzig, 1928), 60–70.

with 5. The province of Hannover, for example, had 8 local associations with 316 members (see Table 4.4).[78] Some of these local bar associations were venerable, such as the Advocates' Association of Celle, which dated from 1837, but most dated from the twentieth century, and 87 of the 176, almost half, had been organized since 1910. While the concept of local bar associations, then, predated the foundation of the DAV and the lawyers' chambers, the organizational and economic circumstances of lawyers in the twentieth century had led to a new efflorescence.

78 Deutscher Anwaltverein, ed., *Verzeichnis der Rechtsanwälte, Notare und Gerichtsvollzieher, geordnet nach Gerichtsbehörden, nebst Mitteilungen über die Organisation der Rechtsanwaltschaft und einem Verzeichnis der Gerichtsorte* (Leipzig, 1928), 60–70. Almost all of the special-interest regional associations were various chapters of the Association of German District Court Lawyers, organized in superior court districts. For further details about this group, see Chapter 8.

With the new growth of local bar associations, many lawyers and leaders of the DAV came to believe that the organizational changes made in 1909 needed to be reexamined. The sense was strong that the only way to build a close relationship with a broader spectrum of lawyers in the localities was to create "branch" or "district" chapters of the DAV for each superior court. Forty local associations applied for corporate membership in the DAV. The Lawyers' Convention in Stuttgart in 1927 debated the issue, but the real discussion occurred at the National Conference of German Lawyers in Leipzig in November 1927. That gathering recommended the further revision of the statute of the DAV to allow local bar associations to be recognized as district groups of the DAV. The DAV adopted this reform in 1928, finally creating a direct link between the local bar associations and a national umbrella group.[79]

Conclusion

The institutional framework of German lawyers in private practice after 1879, then, contained chronic flaws that were caused by its structure as an organization of notables and exacerbated by the economic crises of the private bar. As a result, the influence of the institutions of the bar decayed during the 1920s. The DAV had arisen as a national association rather than as an umbrella organization, and as such it lacked organic connections to the local bar associations. Domination of leadership positions by lawyer-notables who practiced before collegial courts in larger cities, especially in Berlin and Leipzig, aggravated the gap between the activities and policies of the DAV and the lives of average lawyers.[80] The decision by the founders of the DAV to establish membership on an individual basis meant that the national bar association depended upon notable individuals rather than group expression

79 Ostler, *Die deutschen Rechtsanwälte*, 224. For the debates at the National Conference, see Deutscher Anwaltverein, ed., *Stenographischer Bericht über die Reichskonferenz der deutschen Anwaltschaft vom 12. und 13. November 1927 zu Leipzig* (Leipzig, 1928).
80 Other professions developed their professional institutions differently. Medical doctors, for example, formed the Federation of German Physicians' Associations in 1873, specifically "to unify the scattered medical associations of Germany to give mutual stimulus to and promote common participation in the scientific, practical, and social relations of the medical profession." This group functioned as an umbrella organization (*Dachverband*) in that delegates to the medical conventions represented local associations rather than only themselves as individuals. Huerkamp, *Der Aufstieg der Ärzte*, 241–54, 249. For outlines of the more fragmented organizational structure of engineers, see Jarausch, *The Unfree Professions*, McClelland, *The German Experience of Professionalization*, and Gispen, *New Profession, Old Order*, especially the conclusion at 333–6.

for leadership. Opinions of individuals can be dismissed more readily as unrepresentative than resolutions of substantial groups.[81]

Lawyers also triumphed relatively early in their campaign for official self-government. Medical doctors in Prussia achieved self-government through doctors' chambers only in 1899.[82] Yet the regional framework of lawyers' chambers hindered their emergence as accepted representative bodies of lawyers, as an authoritative voice for the profession. Moreover, lawyers' chambers were reluctant to become the strong advocates of the economic interests of lawyers, partly because of the statutory definition of their scope of activity, partly because of the existence of the DAV as an alternative advocate, and partly because of the internal divisions within the bar (lawyer-notables versus rank and file, district versus superior court lawyers).[83]

The result of these overlapping layers of professional institutions was the decentralization of the functions of associations. Local bar associations provided both sociability and an easily accessible forum for discussion of professional issues. The lawyers' chambers provided a locus of self-discipline and a source of direct comment to the government on matters of legislation, but they served only a regional constituency. The DAV provided an instrument for the expression of the will of the bar as a whole, but it lacked organic ties to the localities, not all lawyers were members, and, increasingly after the turn of the century, many lawyers believed it to be dominated by groups within the profession whose economic interests were opposed to their own. The multiple layers of professional institutions, then, hampered the efforts of German lawyers to speak with one voice and encouraged those centrifugal tendencies that already existed.

81 Lawyers recognized this weakness, expressly comparing the organization of the DAV unfavorably with that of the medical doctors' organization; Ernst Plum, "Die Abstimmung auf den Anwaltstagen," *Abl* 1 (1914): 41–4, 42–3.
82 Huerkamp, *Der Aufstieg der Ärzte*, 270.
83 An opposite course of development of professional association obtained among schoolteachers. No dominant organization ever emerged which combined both secondary and primary schoolteachers. Representation of economic interests was so much the principal goal of the primary schoolteachers' professional association that it declared itself a "professional trade union" in 1921. Teachers' organizations also suffered a party-political fragmentation that never afflicted the DAV. See especially Rainer Bölling, *Sozialgeschichte der deutschen Lehrer. Ein Überblick von 1800 bis zur Gegenwart* (Göttingen, 1983), 44–52, 80–91, 125–35; Christoph Führ, "Gelehrter Schulmann – Oberlehrer – Studienrat. Zum sozialen Aufstieg der Philologen," in Conze and Kocka, eds. *Bildungsbürgertum im 19. Jahrhundert*, 417–57; William Setchel Learned, *The Oberlehrer. A Study of the Social and Professional Evolution of the German Schoolmaster* (Cambridge, Mass., 1914), 101–19; and Jarausch, *The Unfree Professions*.

5

Growth and Diversification: Lawyers in the Province of Hannover, 1878–1933

In the same way that the Imperial Justice Laws in 1879 grafted new institutions onto a preexisting framework, the reforms faced a practicing bar in Germany that already consisted of 4,091 lawyers. But the new rules of *freie Advokatur*, combined with demographic growth, economic change, and political upheaval between 1879 and 1933 to change dramatically the shape and texture of the bar and the nature of private practice. Free entry and economic opportunity offered new vistas of opportunity for ambitious young men and drew new social elements into the private practice of law. Economic dynamism in large cities made them magnets that attracted many new practitioners, while other cities, formerly important, fell into stagnation because economic growth passed them by. Some previously sleepy towns grew into economic powerhouses, thus inevitably attracting lawyers to serve new clients. As the bar grew, lawyers devised new career strategies and penetrated markets for legal services that they formerly had neglected. Overall, the era of *freie Advokatur* saw growth and diversification in the practicing bar.

But the changes unleashed in 1879 became apparent only gradually. Persons who had been lawyers under the old system continued to practice under the new, although they faced immediate choices with regard to the place and shape of their legal practices. New members of the bar had to decide where to open their practices and how to seek their livings in entirely changed circumstances and based upon expectations rather than a record of experience. The sons of certain social groups still had distinct advantages in entering legal practice, while sons of previously less-represented groups had new opportunities. Over time, the process of growth and diversification of the bar in its social origins, geographic distribution, confessional makeup, and position within the hierarchical system of courts created complications and concerns regarding the governance of the bar at first and ultimately the frictions and conflicts that divided and paralyzed the institutions of lawyers in private practice. Growth and diversification ultimately exploded the myth that the bar was the unified and monolithic general estate and exposed it as not merely one of many competing special interests in German society but as *several* mutually antagonistic special-interest groups. The lawyer-notables who led the bar, who had played the greatest role in estab-lishing the myth of the bar as the general estate, and who had the greatest stake in preserving it, fought with remarkable success a forty-year battle to maintain the image and with it their power.

Later chapters will pursue the story of the decline of the power of lawyers' claim to be the general estate. In order to understand the forces that worked beneath the surface in that process, however, one must have a detailed knowledge of the changes within the bar and within professional self-conception and self-administration. Only a close examination of the growth and diversification of the bar in private practice between 1879 and 1933 and how these changes worked themselves out within the profession in a manageable local study can illuminate the deeper meanings of the institutional and professional conflicts on the national level after 1879. This chapter explores the demographic changes of the private legal profession in the Prussian province of Hannover during the period of *freie Advo-katur*, while Chapter 6 examines how lawyers administered and disci-plined themselves.

The province of Hannover provides a particularly suitable locus for a detailed exploration of the development of the practicing bar after 1879.[1] Hannover proudly claimed a long history as a leader among German states in the development of the law of civil proce-dure, organization of the courts, and structure of the private legal profession. For the century and a half before its incorporation into the Kingdom of Prussia in 1866, Hannover had always featured

---

1 The actual focus of this chapter is upon the bailiwick of the court of appeal at Celle (*Oberlandesgerichtsbezirk Celle*). That district included the entire province of Hannover, as well as the principalities of Lippe-Detmold, Waldeck, Pyrmont, and several counties from Hessen, and after 1909 the principality of Schaumburg-Lippe. For purposes of this chapter, the non-Hannoverian territories have been excluded because the number of lawyers in-volved was minuscule (rarely more than fifteen) and because lawyers from Lippe were by treaty between the principality and the Kingdom of Prussia accorded certain rights (such as simultaneous admission to district courts, the superior court at Detmold, as well as the court of appeal at Celle or the right to practice before the court of appeal in Celle while maintaining one's residence in Detmold) that were not granted to lawyers in Hannover.

prominently in the discussions of legal reform in Germany. The strong Hannoverian tradition of private practitioners serving in prominent positions in administration and government carried over after annexation. Hannoverian lawyers such as Rudolf von Bennigsen, Johannes Miquel, and Ludwig Windthorst provided leadership for political parties both in the Prussian House of Deputies and the Reichstag. A former Hannoverian lawyer and ministry of justice official, Adolf Leonhardt served as Prussian Minister of Justice from 1867 to 1879 and was responsible for the drafting and passage of the Imperial Justice Laws. Those laws, moreover, while encompassing much of the liberal agenda with regard to procedural and professional reform, were based in large part upon Hannoverian reforms that had been in place since 1852. Hannoverian legal traditions, then, exercised a strong influence upon the legislation of 1877–9.[2] These new laws, however, introduced sufficient innovation that Hannoverian lawyers shared in the challenges and disruptions faced by all German lawyers between 1878 and 1933.

Hannover also provides a geographic, confessional, and economic microcosm of the new, Prussian-dominated German Empire. In 1879, Hannover was still a largely agrarian economy, with a stable population and little evidence of an economic take-off. Blessed with ample waterway transport and significant commerce centered upon North Sea ports and the city of Hannover, the province experienced remarkable growth in industry after 1879. This rapid development led to tensions and frictions between still agrarian regions, such as East Frisia and the Lüneburg Heath, and industrial and commercial centers, such as the city of Hannover, Harburg, and Geestemünde-Lehe (later consolidated into the city of Wesermünde and now

---

2 The most comprehensive commentary upon the Hannoverian justice reform statues was written by the minister of justice who oversaw their enactment, Leonhardt, *Die bürgerliche Processordnung*. After the annexation of Hannover by Prussia in 1866, Leonhardt advocated the use of the Hannoverian laws to reform those of Prussia, and of course he later presided over that reform as Prussian Minister of Justice; idem, *Betrachtungen über die hannoversche Justizverwaltung mit Rücksicht auf die Vereinigung des Königreichs Hannover mit der Preußischen Monarchie* (Hannover, 1866). See also Ledford, "Lawyers, Liberalism, and Procedure," 176, 190. Lawyers in Hannover continue to claim this connection with pride. See for example, Karl Kroeschell, "Geschichte der Advokatur in welfischen Landen," in Ernst Benda, et al., :ds., *Hundert Jahre Rechtsanwaltskammern. Festsprachen bei den Hundertjahrfeiern einiger Rechtsanwaltskammern* (Munich, 1981), 1–24, 23–4: "The importance of the year 1879 does not lie in the mere fact that lawyers' chambers were first founded. Much more it lies in the fact that in that year the Hannoverian model of lawyers' chambers was extended, not only to Prussia, but to the entire empire. When one remembers this path-breaking role of Hannoverian legal legislation, one ought to say with full right, that the lawyers' chamber in Celle not only is entitled, but obligated, to commemorate this day with a celebration."

known as Bremerhaven). These tensions between rural and small-town life and the modern industrial city found resonance in tensions within the bar itself.

The province of Hannover also affords typicality in its confessional makeup. Like the rest of Prussia, it was predominantly Protestant, although its traditions were Augsburg Confession-Lutheran rather than those of the Prussian Evangelical United Church. Since the beginning of the nineteenth century, however, Hannover had gained territories that had Catholic majorities, such as the Archbishoprics of Osnabrück and Hildesheim. Confessional divisions, as well as local particularisms, must be considered in Hannover as in the rest of Germany in seeking explanations for patterns of behavior among social actors such as lawyers.[3]

The province possessed one of the most renowned legal faculties in the empire at its University in Göttingen.[4] Despite the attraction of law faculties at other German universities, notably the University of Berlin, the academic wanderings of many German law students included a stop at Göttingen for at least a semester. In particular, there was a high degree of identification with that university by citizens of Hannover, and most Hannoverian private practitioners spent a considerable portion of their academic careers there.

In sum, Hannover provides an important and revealing focus for an examination of the life of lawyers in Protestant Prussia. Despite lingering particularism after the forced annexation in 1866, Hannoverian legal life was quickly integrated into that of the whole of Prussia, especially after 1879, and without any of the lingering peculiarities evidenced in Rhenish Prussia. This chapter proceeds first with a short account of the history of the development of the judicial system, civil procedure, and the organization of the legal profession in Hannover, down to the reconstitution of the private bar in 1879. Next, it traces the growth and distribution of the practicing bar throughout the province during the period 1878–1933. Then the focus shifts to the diversification of the social origins of lawyers in Hannover and to changes in the pattern over time. It also considers the diversification of the confessional identity of lawyers. Next, it

3 For the confessional composition of the province, see Hans A. Schmitt, "From Sovereign States to Prussian Provinces: Hanover and Hesse-Nassau, 1866–1871," *Journal of Modern History* 57 (1985): 24–56, 35.
4 For the national significance and social selectivity of the legal faculty at Göttingen in the late nineteenth century, see Titze, "Die zyklische Überproduktion," 103, and Lundgreen, "Zur Konstituierung," Tabelle 12, 105.

examines the geographic origins and mobility of lawyers. This discussion will include an examination of the career patterns of Hannoverian lawyers. Finally, the emphasis turns to the executive board of the lawyers' chamber in Celle as a means of investigating lawyer-notables, the elite of the bar.

Organization of Courts and Bar in Hannover

The story of modern judicial development in Hannover and of the development of the bar in private practice must begin in the early eighteenth century. When Duke Ernst August secured the unification of the territories of the two lines of the Guelph family and thereby attained the ninth electoral dignity in the Holy Roman Empire in 1692, the new electoral state obtained the *privilegium de non appellando*. Since litigants could no longer appeal cases of ordinary jurisdiction to the highest courts of the Empire, the elector had to make provision for a territorial supreme court of appeal.[5] Thus he created the High Court of Appeal in Celle in 1711.[6]

The organization of the High Court of Appeal in Celle displayed in

5   The best discussions in English of the Imperial Cameral Tribunal (*Reichskammergericht*) and Imperial Aulic Council (*Reichshofrat*) are found in Michael Hughes, *Law and Politics in Eighteenth Century Germany: The Imperial Aulic Council in the Reign of Charles VI* (Woodbridge, Suffolk, 1988), and John G. Gagliardo, *Reich and Nation: The Holy Roman Empire as Idea and Reality 1763–1806* (Bloomington, Ind., 1980), 26–32. For the uses of the imperial courts in maintaining small state sovereignty within the Empire in the eighteenth century, see also Walker, *Johann Jakob Moser and the Holy Roman Empire of the German Nation*.

6   The definitive history of the Kingdom of Hannover remains Erich Rosendahl, *Geschichte Niedersachsens im Spiegel der Reichsgeschichte* (Hannover, 1927). Particularly useful for the history of the organization of and procedure before the courts in Hannover are Ernst Spangenberg, *Das Oberappellationsgericht in Celle für das Königreich Hannover, nach seiner Verfassung, Zuständigkeit und nach dem bei demselben Statt findenden Geschäftsgange und Proceßverfahren dargestellt* (Celle, 1833); Theodor Roscher, "Gerichtsverfassung und Anwaltschaft im einstmaligen Kurstaat und Königreich Hannover," in *Festschrift zum siebzehnten Deutschen Anwaltstage. Hannover 1905* (Hannover, 1905), 5–116; Karl Gunkel, *200 Jahre Rechtsleben in Hannover. Festschrift zur Erinnerung an die Gründung des Kurhannoverschen Oberappellationsgerichts in Celle am 14.10.1711* (Hannover, 1911); and Helmut Coing, *Zur Geschichte des Oberlandesgerichts in Celle* (Celle, 1951). Another short sketch of the history of the court can be found in Karl Lühr, "Die ersten zweihundert Jahre," in *250 Jahre Oberlandesgericht Celle 1711–1961* (Celle, 1961), 1–61. For a brief overview of the earliest period of development of the private bar (before 1711) see Kroeschell, "Geschichte der Advokatur in welfischen Landen," 1–19. See also the various essays in *Festschrift zum 275jährigen Bestehen des Oberlandesgerichts Celle* (Celle, 1986). Finally, a short description of the legal history of Hannover can be found in G. Ludewig, et al., *Wirtschaftliche und kulturelle Zustände in Alt-Hannover*, 2nd ed., (Hannover, 1929), 167–94, esp. 167–74. An invaluable bibliographical and biographical reference for the study of the Kingdom and Province of Hannover is the massive volume edited by Walther Hubatsch, *Grundriß zur deutschen Verwaltungsgeschichte 1815–1945*, 22 vols. (Marburg, 1975–83), Series A: Prussia, vol. 10: Hannover (1981).

microcosm the structure and division of power within Hannover. The elector (after 1815, the king) held the right to appoint a certain number of judges and bore the costs of maintaining the court building and other physical appurtenances. The estates of the several Hannoverian duchies, dominated by the landed nobility, possessed real political power well into the nineteenth century, and they retained the right to appoint a certain number of judges. Moreover, they bore the costs of the salaries of the judges and other personnel of the court at Celle. At no time during the history of the High Court of Appeal did the elector nominate a majority of the judges; the estates always had the right to appoint a majority, and at times their share amounted to two-thirds of the bench.[7]

The High Court of Appeal itself was a third independent actor in this separation-of-powers drama. It possessed from the beginning of its existence, and guarded until the annexation by Prussia in 1866, the right to examine both the character and legal qualification of nominees to its ranks and to reject nominees whom it considered in its sole discretion, to be unqualified.[8] Thus, the High Court of Appeal enjoyed a degree of political independence from both sovereign and estates in which Hannoverians took great pride.

In accord with common practice in the Holy Roman Empire since the time of the creation of the Imperial Cameral Tribunal in 1495, the Celle court consisted of a noble and a learned bench. The judges of ancient noble families who sat on the noble bench were required after 1711 to have a legal education. From early in the eighteenth century, in fact, candidates for both benches had to pass court examinations of their character and their legal knowledge.[9]

Below the level of the High Court of Appeal lay a varied array of lower and intermediate courts. The lower courts consisted of "courts" (*Ämter*) administered by the elector, patrimonial courts, and municipal courts, all of which combined judicial and administrative functions.

---

7 Roscher, "Gerichtsverfassung," 21, and Coing, *Zur Geschichte*, 6–7. The elector always retained the power to name the president and vice-president of the court. Although the estates as a whole had the right to appoint the majority of the judges, no *single* estates of one of the territories ever had the right to appoint more judges than the elector. One author adds: "The independence of the court from the ruler was in the final analysis the price that Georg Ludwig [the elector] had to pay to his estates; a supreme court dominated by the monarch was exactly as unacceptable for the estates as an imperial court dependent upon the [Holy Roman] Emperor was for the princes"; Peter Jessen, "Die Gründung des Oberappellationsgerichts und sein Wirken in der ersten Zeit," in *Festschrift zum 275jährigen Bestehen des Oberlandesgerichts Celle*, 21–59, 41.
8 Coing, *Zur Geschichte*, 7; Roscher, "Gerichtsverfassung," 22–3.
9 Roscher, "Gerichtsverfassung," 22–3.

At the intermediate level were both electoral courts (*Justizkanzleien*, which had exclusive jurisdiction over criminal cases) and parliamentary courts (*Hofgerichte*), competing with each other for jurisdiction over civil cases.[10] Each of the component duchies and principalities of the province had its own scheme and jurisdictional rules. The only unifying principle of court organization was that final appeal lay to the High Court of Appeal.[11]

Courts at all levels in Hannover followed the civil procedure set out by the common law of the Empire since the time of the reception of Roman law. That procedure provided for trial based upon written pleadings and conducted in secret. At the High Court of Appeal, this meant that it would accept the written record for appeals from the intermediate courts and for cases of plain error based upon bald violations of procedural rules from the courts of first instance. Two members of the court were assigned the task of abstracting the case and preparing draft opinions for discussion and decision by the entire court sitting *en banc*.[12] Such a system of procedure carried obvious consequences for the structure and nature of the private practice of law.

The practicing bar in Hannover during the eighteenth century shared the division, common in Germany since the reception of Roman law, into procurators (*Prokuratur*) and advocates (*Advokatur*). Procurators (also called *Anwälte*) received the power of attorney from the client to represent him at trial and were closely related and bound to the court before which they practiced. Advocates were the learned legal counsel who prepared the written pleadings upon which the case was tried, carried out the minimal oral arguments permitted by the written civil procedure, and provided nontrial related legal advice. Advocates could appear before a court, in writing or in person, only with the signature or presence of the procurator. The practice was common in Hannover for a procurator to be an advocate also.[13]

10 Although the German name of these latter courts would imply that they were under the control of the electoral court (in the nonjudicial sense), they were actually creatures of the various estates; ibid., 15–16.
11 Ibid., 13–19. The district courts (*Ämter*) and *Justizkanzleien* mixed judicial and administrative functions in a manner that was common in many German territorial states during the eighteenth century.
12 Coing, *Zur Geschichte*, 10–11. For a detailed discussion of the common law procedure, see Engelmann, *A History of Continental Civil Procedure*, 544–74; for a description of procedure in Celle, see Jessen, "Die Gründung," 46–8.
13 Roscher, "Gerichtsverfassung," 68–9. After the foundation of the University at Göttingen in 1737 and for most of the remainder of the eighteenth century, the High Court of Appeal in Celle regularly required that candidates for the *Prokuratur* who wished to practice before

Because the procurator was conceived of as an integral part of the mechanism of the court, the principle of mandatory representation by a lawyer applied at the High Court of Appeal, meaning that a party had to retain one of the procurators admitted before that court in order to prosecute an appeal there. Because of the mandatory representation requirement, the procurators were localized, admitted only before the High Court of Appeal and required to live in Celle. Their number was fixed, first at six, rising to eight by 1800.[14] The court itself exercised disciplinary jurisdiction over procurators. Each intermediate court regulated its own procurators differently, but the systems were essentially the same as the one at the High Court of Appeal. At courts of initial jurisdiction, there were usually no procurators, and litigants could be represented by anyone they chose.

While the number of procurators was fixed by the courts and closed, the principle governing advocates was freedom of admission. Although at first the only requirement for practice as an advocate was proof of study at a university, the High Court of Appeal soon set up a system of examinations to probe the legal knowledge of a candidate before he enrolled in the registry of lawyers.[15] The number of advocates was much greater than that of procurators. Advocates shared the same educational background as candidates for state service; because connections were needed to obtain positions in the state service, the profession of advocate became a place of refuge for disappointed office seekers. Over the period 1711 to 1800, the number of registered advocates totalled 1,333, and the profession was considered to be quite overcrowded. Around 1800 there were eighty advocates in the city of Hannover, which had a population of 20,000, and forty in the much smaller city of Celle.[16]

The events of the Napoleonic era upset the autonomous develop-

it obtain a doctoral degree in law. Successful candidates usually already had the degree; otherwise appointments were made conditional upon the attainment of the degree within a given period of time; ibid., 69–70. Possessors of a doctoral degree in law from Göttingen were exempt from examination from 1737 until the reform of 1832; Spangenberg, *Das Oberappellationsgericht in Celle*, 127, 131, 138–43.

14 Roscher, "Gerichtsverfassung," 69–70. Spangenberg, *Das Oberappellationsgericht in Celle*, 112, 127, differentiated between the two by classifying the *Prokuratoren* as *Nebenpersonen* ("auxiliary personnel") like counsel for the estates, while *Advokaten* were *gerichtsverwandten Personen* ("court-related personnel"), like notaries and the "bonded bookbinder."

15 Roscher, "Gerichtsverfassung," 73–5.

16 Ibid., 80. Although the foundation of the High Court of Appeal led to a "flood of lawyers" (*Advokaten*) in Celle, the written nature of civil procedure meant that *Prokuratoren* actually had little to do other than forward pleadings drafted by *Advokaten*, so "the boundaries between the *Advokaten* and *Prokuratoren* faded"; Jessen, "Die Gründung," 42–3.

ment of procedure and profession in Hannover. While the French occupation and incorporation of Hannover into the Kingdom of Westphalia had little permanent effect upon the formal organization of the practicing bar, it introduced new and modern forms of civil procedure that had a lasting impact upon the self-conception of Hannoverian lawyers and upon Hannoverian legislative thought. In place of the common law written and secret procedure, the Kingdom of Westphalia adopted the French system of oral and public civil procedure.[17] Although *Prokuratoren* were still viewed as adjunct personnel of the courts and *Advokaten* were still examined by the courts before admission and subject to judicial discipline after admission, the oral procedure placed new emphasis upon the rhetorical and forensic skills of lawyers and elevated them to a higher status in the legal system. Although the old common law procedure returned under the Restoration after 1815, the practicing bar in Hannover had experienced an invigorating stimulus that had raised its self-consciousness and self-confidence.

The experience of the Restoration, however, disappointed practicing lawyers, particularly the advocates. They suffered from overcrowding, from the old low degree of social status, from the superior attitudes of fellow legal graduates who had entered into preparation for state service, and from the heavy hand and degrading implications of court-imposed discipline. During the Revolution of 1830, which found great resonance in Hannover, lawyers proposed that candidates for the practicing bar and for state service be subjected to the same educational and examination requirements. Further, they demanded that the practicing bar be closed to non-Hannoverians, for the openness of admission had led to extreme overcrowding, evidenced by the presence of more than 800 *Advokaten* in the Kingdom.[18] A royal proclamation of 9 April 1832, realized these goals. Thereafter in Hannover, both candidates for the bar and for state

17 Ibid., 28; see also Bernhard Heile, "Die Zeit von 1733 bis 1866," in *Festschrift zum 275jährigen Bestehen des Oberlandesgerichts Celle*, 63–111, 80–4, and Spangenberg, *Das Oberappellationsgericht in Celle*, 128–31.
18 Roscher, "Gerichtsverfassung," 89; Spangenberg, *Das Oberappellationsgericht in Celle*, 132, gives the figure 800–900. Another author indicates that in 1830, when the city of Hannover had a population of 24,000, there were ninety-six *Advokaten*; out of the eighty *Advokaten* in the city of Hannover in 1852, six were appointed *Prokuratoren* before the new superior court of the city of Hannover; Rudolf Göhmann, "150 Jahre Advokaten- und Rechtsanwaltsverein Hannover (1831–1981) – Ein Bericht zum 150. Gründungstag am 1.7.1981," in Rechtsanwaltsverein Hannover, ed., *Festschrift zur 150-Jahr-Feier des Rechtsanwaltsvereins Hannover e.V. (1831–1981)* (Hannover, 1981), 1–41, 2–3, 6.

service had to study law at a German university for three years and pass two state examinations. The government set quotas for the number of candidates who would be accepted each semester into preparatory service for both career paths.[19] Despite the efforts of practicing lawyers and others, however, further reforms remained thwarted until the Revolution of 1848.

The most lasting consequence of the Revolution of 1848 in Hannover was the justice reform legislation of 8 November 1850, effective on 1 October 1852. Helmut Coing has described the effect of the new constitution of the courts, civil procedure statute, and lawyers' chamber statute as nothing less than the establishment of the modern principles of procedure in the jurisprudence of Hannoverian courts.[20] The reform statutes finally established a system of intermediate and lower courts on the basis of royal authority, replacing the former system of patrimonial, municipal, parliamentary, and royal courts. The court of general initial jurisdiction was the district court with exclusive jurisdiction in cases concerning 100 talers or less.[21] Intermediate courts called superior courts were created to replace the *Hofgerichte* and *Justizkanzleien*, and they were classified as "large" or "small" superior courts. By 1859 there were ten large superior courts, seated at Aurich, Celle, Göttingen, Hannover, Hildesheim, Lüneburg, Meppen, Osnabrück, Stade, and Verden, and two small ones, at Hameln and Nienburg.[22]

The civil procedure reform of 1852 reintroduced the oral and public procedure on the French model.[23] Whereas formerly the written pleadings had bound the parties exclusively to the issues set forth therein (*Eventualmaxime*), now the pleadings assumed a merely preparatory nature, and counsel could exceed the scope of the pleadings or even amend them orally at trial.[24] The oral presentation of the case became

19 Roscher, "Gerichtsverfassung," 91; Spangenberg, *Das Oberappellationsgericht in Celle*, 132–43.
20 Coing, *Zur Geschichte*, 12.
21 Roscher, "Gerichtsverfassung," 47. The term translated as "district court" is *Amtsgericht*. In 1859 the jurisdictional amount was increased to 150 talers. The laws of 1852 established the preposterously large number of 168 district courts, a number reduced to 144 in 1859 and further to 107 in 1879; Ludewig, *Wirtschaftliche und kulturelle Zustände*, 170–1.
22 The term translated as "superior court" is *Obergericht*. The Prussians abolished the superior court in Meppen in 1875; Roscher, "Gerichtsverfassung," 49.
23 Ibid., 42; see also Weißler, *Geschichte der Rechtsanwaltschaft*, 416.
24 For an explanation of the principle of the *Eventualmaxime*, also translated as "the principle of contingent cumulation," see Engelmann, *A History of Continental Civil Procedure*, 27–9, 538–40, 545. Some remnants of this principle survived the reforms in Hannover in 1852 and in the Empire in 1877; ibid., 608.

the determinative event rather than the written presentation in the pleadings, and an increased premium was placed upon the courtroom skill and eloquence of the lawyer. The Hannoverian procedure of 1852 closely resembled the civil procedure established by the Code of Civil Procedure of 1877.[25] It was in many ways the model for the latter enactment, and indeed, the Prussian Minister of Justice who oversaw the adoption of the Code of Civil Procedure in 1877, Adolf Leonhardt, was the same man who had been responsible, as state secretary in the Hannoverian Ministry of Justice, for drafting the former law.[26]

The revised civil procedure required a revised organization of the legal profession. The Hannoverian reforms divided practicing lawyers into two groups: *Anwälte*, who were the courtroom pleaders, and *Advokaten*, who were office lawyers and who helped prepare cases for trial. This structure was no mere perpetuation of the common law procurators and advocates, for the *Anwälte* had to appear and plead the cases of their clients orally and publicly in the stimulating presence of an articulate adversary rather than merely subscribe to and file pleadings prepared by an advocate, receive and transmit counterpleadings, and receive the final judgment, reached in private by the judges. The law imposed upon both advocates and *Anwälte* the same educational and examination qualifications as judges, namely three years' study at a German university and two state examinations, surrounding a four-year period of practical legal study.[27] The consideration of need by the ministry of justice, in effect a general *numerus clausus*, was eliminated as a precondition for admission to the first examination.

A specific *numerus clausus* persisted, inasmuch as the Ministry of Justice appointed *Anwälte* to practice before the High Court of Appeal at Celle and before the twelve superior courts in numbers that it fixed for each court, after consultation with the lawyers' chamber on

---

25 Hannoverian pride in the reforms of 1850–2 is a constant theme in appreciations of these laws; see, among many examples, Heile, "Die Zeit von 1733 bis 1866," 99–106.

26 Leonhardt had also taken the lead in drafting a proposed civil procedure reform for the German Confederation in the early 1860s; Ledford, "Lawyers, Liberalism, and Procedure," 177–8.

27 For a description of the new organization of the bar in Hannover, see Weißler, *Geschichte der Rechtsanwaltschaft*, 413–17. The text of the provisions of the *Gerichtsverfassungsgesetz* for Hannover that governed the practicing bar, as amended in 1859, may be found in "Motive zum Entwurf einer Anwaltsordnung," *JW* 7 (1878): 33, Anlage D, "Zusammenstellung der landesgesetzlichen Vorschriften über Zulassung, Ernennung, Anstellung der Rechtsanwälte, sowie Lokalisierung der Rechtsanwaltschaft," 77–8. Finally, an overview of the Hannoverian system is presented by Stegemann (Obergerichtsrath zu Göttingen), "Kurze Darstellung der Justizverfassung des ehemaligen Königreichs Hannover," *Zeitschrift für Gesetzgebung und Rechtspflege in Preußen* 1 (1867): 255–63, with the provisions governing lawyers found at 260–2.

the question of need. *Anwälte* could practice only before one court and had to reside there. Mandatory representation by a lawyer applied before superior courts and the High Court of Appeal, meaning that the *Anwälte* had a monopoly of representation there.[28]

In contrast, no *numerus clausus* limited entrance into the ranks of advocates: all lawyers who fulfilled the educational and testing requirements could practice. Unlimited admission, however, existed *only* at the seats of collegial courts (superior courts or the High Court of Appeal); advocates could practice in towns having district courts or towns without courts *only* if the ministry of justice determined that the need for a lawyer existed.[29] Advocates could appear before any district court in the state as well as before collegial courts if accompanied by an *Anwalt*. *Anwälte* were appointed by the ministry of justice from among the ranks of advocates, based upon seniority.[30]

The final attainment of which Hannoverian lawyers were justifiably proud was the creation of a system of lawyers' chambers. The lawyers admitted before each collegial court formed a lawyers' chamber, to which was entrusted the disciplinary oversight of the profession as well as numerous advisory functions in the ministry of justice's administration of professional affairs.[31] Despite the name of the institution, all practicing lawyers, *Anwälte* and *Advokaten* alike, were members. The erection of the lawyers' chambers did not evoke the invigorating response from lawyers for which proponents of the institution had hoped, a phenomenon most often attributed to the tiny size of the membership of most of the chambers (for the province was divided into twelve lawyers' chambers).[32] Reactionary amendments to the justice laws carried out by Börries in 1859 reduced the autonomy of the chambers, but nonetheless, the lawyers' chambers in Hannover

28 Roscher, "Gerichtsverfassung," 101.
29 Brix, *Organisation der Advokatur*, ix–x, comments upon the singularity of this arrangement. See also Roscher, "Gerichtsverfassung," 100, and Weißler, *Geschichte der Rechtsanwaltschaft*, 417.
30 Roscher, "Gerichtsverfassung," 100, and Gebhard von Lenthe, "Die Rechtsanwaltschaft am Oberlandesgericht Celle," in *250 Jahre Oberlandesgericht Celle*, 179–208, 188.
31 The text of the statute governing the lawyers' chambers in Hannover, as amended in 1859, is found in "Motive zum Entwurf einer Anwaltsordnung," *JW* 7 (1878): 33, Anlage E, "Zusammenstellung der landesgesetzlichen Vorschriften über Anwaltskammern (Anwalts-verein, Anwaltsausschuß, Disziplinarrath, Ehrenrath, etc.)," 88–9. For details of the efforts of lawyers in Hannover to attain the creation of lawyers' chambers, see Weißler, *Geschichte der Rechtsanwaltschaft*, 541–4, and Huffmann, *Kampf um freie Advokatur*, 40–8.
32 By 1867 there were only nine, one for the *Obergerichte* at Hannover, Hameln, and Nienburg, one for the *Obergerichte* at Osnabrück and Meppen, and one each for the *Obergerichte* at Aurich, Celle, Göttingen, Hildesheim, Lüneburg, Stade, and Verden; Stegemann, "Kurze Darstellung," 261–2.

went far toward establishing the legal profession on a more prestigious and independent footing, to the pride of Hannoverian and the envy of many other German lawyers.[33] The constitution of the courts and of the legal profession established by the reforms of 1852 survived even the upheaval surrounding the loss of sovereignty by the Kingdom of Hannover and its annexation by Prussia as a province (as a result of the 1866 Austro-Prussian War). The High Court of Appeal in Celle lost its character as a court of last resort, for the Prussians erected a special court of final review in Berlin for cases arising in Hannover. Part of Bismarck's strategy for thwarting the forces of Guelph loyalism, however, involved a respect for native Hannoverian institutions other than the monarchy. The administrative reforms that he imposed were moderate and based upon traditional Hannoverian forms. As part of this policy, Bismarck left the judicial structure, civil procedure code, and organization of the practicing bar unchanged.[34] Despite the momentous changes in political organization during the years 1866 to 1878, the private practice of law continued relatively undisturbed.

The adoption of the Imperial Justice Laws in 1877–9 brought far-reaching change to the lives of lawyers in Hannover.[35] It abolished the distinction between *Anwaltschaft* and *Advokatur*. The *numerus clausus* on practice before collegial courts disappeared and lawyers could move at will to settle anywhere they wished so long as they settled at the seat of the court before which they sought admission. The strict control of the number of lawyers practicing in small district court towns also disappeared. A single lawyers' chamber for the entire bailiwick of the court of appeal at Celle replaced the tiny chambers at each superior court, so that for the first time all Hannoverian lawyers united into one institution charged with the

---

33 Roscher, "Gerichtsverfassung," 105–7. For the constitutional conflict under the ministry of Börries, see Ernst Rudolf Huber, *Deutsche Verfassungsgeschichte seit 1789*, 8 vols. (Stuttgart, 1957–90), vol. 3, *Bismarck und das Reich*, 215–17.
34 For an account of Bismarck's moderate strategy favoring "the preservation of all local institutions that did not threaten Prussian interest," see Stewart A. Stehlin, *Bismarck and the Guelph Problem 1866–1890: A Study in Particularist Opposition to National Unity* (The Hague, 1973), esp. ch. VII, "Bismarck and the New Province," 158–93, and Schmitt, "From Sovereign States to Prussian Provinces," 41. The relatively minor amendments to the Hannoverian justice laws between 1866 and 1879 are recounted in Roscher, "Gerichtsverfassung," 115–16. See also Lühr, "Die ersten zweihundert Jahre," 48–52, and Peter Schmid, "Oberappellationsgericht, Appellationsgericht und Oberlandesgericht in der Zeit von 1866 bis 1933," in *Festschrift zum 275jährigen Bestehen des Oberlandesgerichts Celle*, 113–142, 114–25.
35 Gunkel, *200 Jahre Rechtsleben in Hannover*, 438.

representation of professional interests and the exercise of professional self-discipline and self-government. The transitional provisions of the RAO granted every lawyer the right to admission to the superior court in whose district he lived, without requiring him to move his residence to the town of the superior court so long as he applied within three months after the entry into effect of the justice laws. These provisions also required that the new lawyers' chambers convene their organizational meetings within three months after the entry into effect of the new laws on 1 October 1879.[36]

The Imperial Justice Laws replaced the previous twelve superior courts with eight new superior courts. The small superior courts in Hameln and Nienburg, as well as the large one in Celle, were eliminated, and the lawyers who had practiced there as *Anwälte* faced the choice of changing the court of their admission or practicing henceforth as district court lawyers. About half of the affected lawyers in Celle moved to the court of appeal, while the other half began to practice exclusively before the district court there. The same ratio applied in Hameln and Nienburg, with half moving to Hannover and Verden respectively and half remaining to practice before the district court.[37] In the remaining eight cities, Aurich, Göttingen, Hannover, Hildesheim, Lüneburg, Osnabrück, Stade, and Verden, the reforms established new superior courts, and these cities served as judicial centers for their districts until after 1933.[38]

The Eight Superior Court Districts

The eight superior court districts in the province of Hannover varied greatly in population and economy, and therefore the practice of law varied as well. Each superior court was the successor to an older court and found its roots in a long history of judicial organization with its own particularities. Each functioned as the judicial "capital" of a geographic region, and the characteristics of each region must be understood in order to understand the nature of the bar and the character of legal practice there.

36 RAO §107, §106.
37 *Handbuch über den königlichen preußischen Hof und Staat für das Jahr* ——— (Berlin), 1878/79, 649–61, 1879/80, 645–57, 1880/81, 638–46. The list of Hannoverian lawyers who registered with the new lawyers' chamber in Celle in early 1880 is found at G.St.A. I HA Rep. 84a, 21912, 23–7.
38 For a brief description of economic, social, and political conditions in the province of Hannover around 1880, see Manfred Hamann, "Politische Kräfte und Spannungen in der Provinz Hannover um 1880," *Niedersächsisches Jahrbuch für Landesgeschichte* 53 (1981): 1–40, esp. 3–12.

The court of appeal in Aurich represented a continuation of a long tradition of East Frisian judicial particularity. The inhabitants had hoped for reunification with Prussia after the Napoleonic Wars, but the region instead had been attached to the newly elevated Kingdom of Hannover.[39] Although East Frisia was the site of the construction of the new military port at Wilhelmshaven, as well as other seaborne commerce from ports such as Emden, between 1878 and 1933 it remained primarily a thinly populated agrarian region, the least populous of the superior court districts. The city of Aurich remained one of the smallest of the seats of superior courts.[40]

Likewise, the promontory between the mouths of the Weser and the Elbe was and remained a largely agrarian area, with certain exceptions. The small city of Stade was the seat of the superior court and the administrative center for the region. The most economically vital centers, however, were the growing port and industrial cities of Harburg on the Elbe opposite Hamburg and Geestemünde-Lehe on the Weser. Part of this region, moreover, fell within the district of the superior court at Verden, a governmental town even smaller than Stade. In both of these districts, growing industrial cities which possessed only district courts overshadowed stagnant superior court seats.[41] Together, the three districts of Aurich, Stade, and Verden comprised a thinly settled agrarian segment of the province with very small superior court cities.[42]

The territory of the superior court at Lüneburg occupied an inter-

39 A. Tecklenburg and K. Dagefÿrde, *Geschichte der Provinz Hannover* (Hannover, 1921), 135; Georg Schnath, et al., *Geschichte des Landes Niedersachsens* (Würzburg, 1973), 104. For the history of the courts in East Frisia, see Roscher, "Gerichtsverfassung," 33–4.

40 Business circles in East Frisia had suggested after 1866 that the region be incorporated into the Prussian province of Westphalia rather than Hannover, because of economic ties, but that solution was not adopted; Schnath, *Geschichte des Landes Niedersachsens*, 105. The city of Aurich was one of the smallest seats of superior courts in the province, having a population of 4,264 in 1871, 6,141 in 1905, and 6,558 in 1933; Gustav Uelschen, *Die Bevölkerung in Niedersachsen 1821–1961* (Hannover, 1966). The role of lawyers in the social and administrative life of the city in the period before 1878 is explored in Friedrich-Wilhelm Schaer, *Die Stadt Aurich und ihre Beamtenschaft im 19. Jahrhundert, unter besonderer Berücksichtigung der Hannoverschen Zeit (1815–1866)* (Göttingen, 1963).

41 The population of Stade was 8,424 in 1869, 10,837 in 1913, and 19,470 in 1944, while that of Harburg was 13,179 in 1869 and 67,202 in 1913. Verden numbered 6,037 in 1869 and 9,728 in 1913; Geestemünde-Lehe (these two towns, with their separate two district courts, were combined into the city of Wesermünde in 1924) totalled 7,698 in 1869, 44,417 in 1913, and 112,831 in 1944; Hubatsch, *Grundriß*, 769, 776, 781, 737, 674.

42 Despite their thin populations, all three of these regions were rich agrarian areas with a positive agricultural ability to support a larger population. Their population density increased relative to the rest of the province until after 1871, when their populations began to decrease relative to the province as a whole; Hans Linde, "Das Königreich Hannover an der Schwelle des Industriezeitalters," *Neues Archiv für Niedersachsen* 24 (1951): 413–43, 425–6.

mediate position between the three agrarian districts and more industrialized ones. It possessed two urban centers of note, Lüneburg and Celle. Outside of those administrative and industrial cities, the economy remained primarily agrarian, although the industrial aspects of the economy received a boost from the discovery of petroleum under the Lüneburger Heath.[43]

The three superior court districts of Göttingen, Hildesheim, and Osnabrück each contained a medium-sized city that dominated the remainder of the territory. Each city was an administrative and cultural center, and each experienced the growth of industry over this period. Hildesheim and Osnabrück were the main centers of Catholicism in the Protestant province. These two areas, moreover, had been added to Hannoverian territory since the beginning of the nineteenth century, so that particularist traditions persisted and received reinforcement from the confessional difference.[44]

Finally, in its own category stood the superior court in the city of Hannover. Far and away the largest urban concentration in the province, Hannover experienced the most rapid population growth and economic expansion between 1878 and 1933. The bar of the superior court there utterly dominated the district and to some extent the bar of the entire province, despite the substantial district court bar in nearby Hameln. This industrial and commercial center presented an entirely different environment for the practice of law than did the rest of the province.[45]

Size, Distribution, and Composition of the Bar

By the end of January 1880, 222 lawyers in the province of Hannover had signed the registry at the new lawyers' chamber in Celle and had been sworn in at their respective courts.[46] Because the distribution

43 Wilhelm Treue, *Niedersachsens Wirtschaft seit 1760. Von der Agrar- zur Industriegesellschaft* (Hannover, 1964), 55–6.
44 Half of the Catholics in the province of Hannover lived in Osnabrück, and it was the only region with a Catholic majority; Schmitt, "From Sovereign States to Prussian Provinces," 35.
45 The most comprehensive account of the industrial development of the city of Hannover is Ewald Brix, *Vom Markt zur Metropole. Werden und Wandlung im 7 Jahrhunderten stadthannoverscher Wirtschaftsentwicklung* (Hannover, 1951), esp. 110–58. The population of the city of Hannover exploded, growing from 117,000 in 1871 to 188,000 in 1885, to 345,000 in 1905, to 426,000 in 1925. Hannover was consistently the tenth-largest city in Germany; Uelschen, *Die Bevölkerung in Niedersachsen.*
46 Mundt gives the initial registration as 236 lawyers, *100 Jahre Rechtsanwaltskammer*, 18. The archival documents do not support such a figure, and the total on 20 October 1880, was no

and composition of the bar changed over the fifty-year period under consideration, with consequent ramifications for intraprofessional relations, it is appropriate to examine the initial distribution and composition more closely.

Table 5.1 shows the distribution of lawyers in 1880, by superior court district, including the court of appeal in Celle as well.[47] The superior court district of the city of Hannover already dominated the bar of the province with over one-quarter of all lawyers, while far fewer lawyers practiced in the thinly populated areas of East Frisia (Aurich) and the area between the mouths of the Weser and the Elbe (Stade and Verden). As industry expanded in the city of Hannover after 1881 and these rural superior court districts remained backwaters, the natures of the practice of law in the urban and rural areas began to diverge.

The numerical balance between district court and collegial court lawyers in Hannover, however, was considerably more equal than in the rest of Prussia. There was no immediate exodus from the seats of district courts to those of superior courts as there was elsewhere. The previous practice in Hannover of refusing to permit lawyers to settle in very tiny district court towns probably explains this phenomenon. Of the 222 lawyers in the province, 110 practiced before a superior court (49.5 percent), 103 before a district court (46.4 percent), and 9 before the court of appeal (4.1 percent). The city of Hannover dominated among the eight superior courts, representing 46 of the 110 lawyers (20.7 percent of *all* lawyers in the province), leaving 64 practicing before the other seven superior courts (28.8 percent of all lawyers). District court lawyers settled unevenly, for the 103 lawyers practiced before only forty-nine of the ninety-eight purely district courts, leaving forty-nine district court towns with no lawyer at all.[48] Few district

more than 224. The number 222, moreover, is based upon the exclusion of lawyers in Detmold, whom Mundt may have included in his total.
47 These figures are derived from G.St.A. I HA Rep. 84a, 21912, and *Handbuch über den königlichen preußischen Hof und Staat für das Jahr 1879/80* (Berlin, 1880), 645–57.
48 At a district court before which no lawyer was admitted, the legal needs of the public could be met in three ways. First, lawyers from nearby district courts or from a superior court could appear before the district court and represent clients in civil cases. Second, parties could appear and represent themselves, based upon advice from a lawyer in a neighboring town if they wished, for *Anwaltszwang* did not obtain. Finally, these small district courts were the classic locus of the nonlegally trained *Rechtskonsulenten*, who represented clients for a fee if permitted by the court. Each superior court, as well as the court of appeal in Celle, sat in a town which also possessed a district court. The collegial court bar, in most cases, served the district court as well. The "purely" district courts, then, were those in towns *without* any collegial court (107 − 9 = 98).

Table 5.1. *Number of lawyers in Province Hannover,
1881, by superior court district*

Court district	Total	Superior court	District court
OLG Celle	9		
Aurich	19	4	15
Göttingen	23	8	15
Hannover	56	46	10
Hildesheim	27	17	10
Lüneburg	21	9	12
Osnabrück	32	14	18
Stade	15	9	6
Verden	20	3	17
Total	222	110	103

courts attracted more than one or two lawyers, the only exceptions being such commercial centers as the seaport of Harburg, which had five. The initial distribution of the bar in Hannover, then, was more even than in the older provinces of Prussia, in which lawyers streamed in from the countryside to big cities such as Berlin. In the prosperous but still agrarian economy of the province of Hannover in 1880, the city of Hannover did not immediately exert the attraction upon lawyers that commercial, administrative, and industrial centers exerted elsewhere.[49]

In the first years after the introduction of the new regime, the composition of the practicing bar in Hannover changed little. Indeed, the first few years saw a slight decline in the total number of lawyers. When the Prussian Ministry of Justice in 1885 first sought the opinions of the executive boards of the lawyers' chambers on the introduction of limitations upon admission to the bar, the executive board in Celle readily denied the need for such a measure.[50] Table 5.2 and Figure 5.1 show that steady, moderate growth in the size of the bar began in 1885 and continued until 1904.[51]

49 For a description of the economy of the province of Hannover around 1880, see Treue, *Niedersachsens Wirtschaft seit 1760*, 28–9.
50 Mundt, *100 Jahre Rechtsanwaltskammer*, 19–23; G.St.A. I HA Rep. 84a, 21912, 117R.
51 *Handbuch über den königlich Preußischen Hof und Staat für das Jahr* ——— (Berlin), 1878/79–1918; *Handbuch über den Preußischen Staat für das Jahr* ——— (Berlin), 1922, 1925, 1926, 1931, 1935; "Jahresberichte" of the *Anwaltskammer* in Celle, 1880–1934, G.St.A. I HA Rep. 84a, 21912–13 (1880–1928) and N.H.St.A., Hann. 173, Acc. 30/87, 30.

Table 5.2. *Growth in the private bar, Province Hannover, 1879–1934*

Year	Total bar	Superior court	District court	Year	Total bar	Superior court	District court
1879	229	114	107	1907	287	164	109
1880	221	110	103	1908	299	166	118
1881	213	112	92	1909	321	176	129
1882	211	110	91	1910	333	187	129
1883	211	110	92	1911	357	196	141
1884	210	114	87	1912	390	213	157
1885	215	114	92	1913	416	224	172
1886	226	122	95	1914	441	229	188
1887	223	124	89	1915	438	220	193
1888	232	134	88	1916	434	222	186
1889	235	134	90	1917	418	214	179
1890	243	130	101	1918	417	218	175
1891	244	132	100	1919	463	236	201
1892	248	133	105	1920	499	256	214
1893	247	137	97	1921	529	278	219
1894	250	138	100	1922	517	276	213
1895	250	141	98	1923			
1896	245	135	99	1924			
1897	246	140	95	1925	566	308	230
1898	251	145	94	1926	588	333	227
1899	257	151	93	1927	607	338	241
1900	261	149	98	1928	628	348	251
1901	252	143	96	1929	638	352	252
1902	258	146	99	1930	657	357	264
1903	257	147	97	1931	692	371	279
1904	272	157	101	1932	738	391	303
1905	274	158	102	1933	721	368	310
1906	283	162	108	1934	781	395	333

Beginning in 1904 and accelerating to the beginning of the First World War, the rate of growth of the bar increased rapidly, so that between 1904 and 1914 the number of lawyers grew from 272 to 441. The war brought about a slight reduction in the number of lawyers. This was not the consequence of lawyers resigning from the bar in order to serve in the army, for the lawyers at home sought to maintain the practices of their colleagues at the front, but rather it was a consequence of the emptying of the universities and the absence of new candidates. New admissions fell from forty-one in 1913 and thirty-six

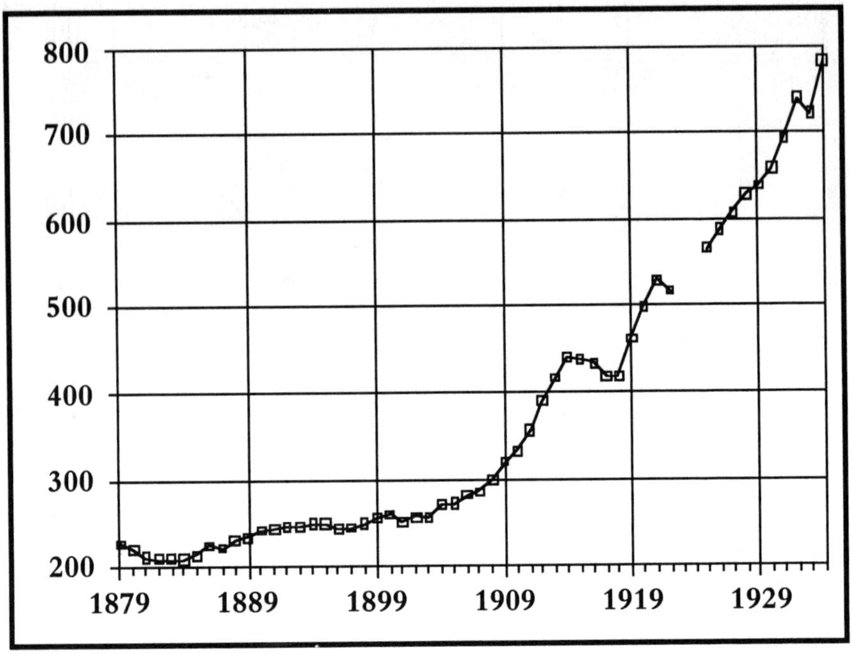

Figure 5.1. Growth in the private bar, Province Hannover, 1879–1934

in 1914 to twelve in 1915, ten in 1916, seven in 1917, and eighteen in 1918.[52] Rapid growth resumed after the war. Expansion slowed somewhat during the period of inflation, but it increased thereafter at an accelerating rate.

The growth of the private bar during the 1920s *must* have been the result of a higher proportion of law graduates entering private practice than before. The number of candidates who passed the second bar examination in both Prussia and Germany returned to prewar levels by 1920 and then declined until 1928.[53] The number of judicial and bureaucratic positions for law graduates, however, *declined* for budgetary reasons, especially after the Personnel Reduc-

52 Between 1880 and 1914, the reporting year for the lawyers' chamber in Celle ran from 1 October to 30 September of the following year. In 1915, this was changed to a calendar year, so that the figure for 1915 represents the period 1 October 1914, to 31 December 1915. G.St.A. I HA Rep. 84a, 21912, 179. See the statistics on the number of candidates for the second state examination (*Assessorprüfung*) in Prussia between 1914 and 1920 in Kolbeck, *Juristenschwemmen*, Anhang, 116–19, 118. The number of candidates for examination peaked at 1,763 in 1914, a number swelled by the *Notprüfung* administered to candidates on an accelerated basis before they departed for the front, and then declined to 708 in 1915, 326 in 1916, 239 in 1917, and 233 in 1918. It returned to its prewar levels only in 1929.
53 Kolbeck, *Juristenschwemmen*, Anhang, 116–19, 118–19.

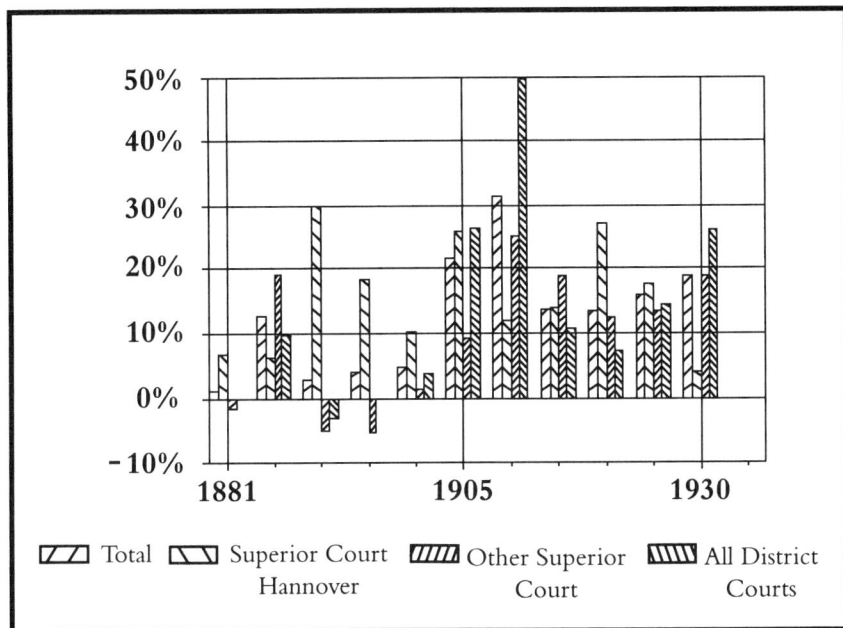

Figure 5.2. Rate of growth

tion Decree of 27 October 1923, which dismissed tenured state officials at an early age, producing a new source of candidates for the bar.[54] Two new categories of candidates flooded into the bar: young men, embarking upon their careers, who would have chosen to enter state service but found their paths blocked by the fiscally

54 Ibid., 103–9, Tabelle III, 124; Wunder, *Geschichte der Bürokratie*, 127–35, esp. 130. See also Hattenhauer, *Geschichte des Beamtentums*, 373–6. The relationship of the number of judges in Germany to the number of lawyers varied as follows:

Year	Judges	Lawyers
1919	10,569	12,030
1923	9,912	12,729
1927	9,383	14,963
1929	9,719	15,881

Rudolf Friedländer, *Der Arbeitspreis bei den freien Berufen, unter besonderer Berücksichtigung der deutschen Rechtsanwaltschaft* (Munich and Leipzig, 1933), Tabelle vi, 192.

For a general account of the reduction in government bureaucracy in the 1920s, see Andreas Kunz, *Civil Servants and the Politics of Inflation in Germany, 1914–1924* (Berlin and New York, 1986), and Jane Caplan, *Government without Administration: State and Civil Service in Weimar and Nazi Germany* (Oxford, 1988).

austere personnel policies of the national and state governments, and middle-aged judges and state officials, prematurely retired because of personnel reductions, whose pensions were insufficient to support them.[55] Reduced opportunities in the judiciary and bureaucracy, at a time when opportunity in industry was also depressed, especially before 1924 and after 1929, pushed law graduates into private practice.

The sector of the bar that experienced the fastest rate of growth varied over time. Figure 5.2 shows that the superior court in the city of Hannover led the growth of the bar as a whole until roughly 1910 and again during the 1920s. The district court bar, however, began to expand more rapidly than the bar as a whole after 1896, and it experienced a spectacular 50 percent increase during the years 1911–15. It lagged during the 1920s, but it had established itself as a vital sector of the bar prior to the war. The only segment of the bar that consistently grew less than the bar as a whole was that of lawyers practicing before the seven superior courts *other than* the one in the city of Hannover. This segment expanded during the first ten years of the new regime, but it never thereafter equalled or exceeded the overall rate of growth.

Figures 5.3 and 5.4 show the effect over time of the differential rates of growth upon the composition of the bar. In 1888 and again in 1899, the share of the superior court bar reached its peak at more than 58 percent of all lawyers, while the share of district court lawyers shrank to its nadir in both years at less than 38 percent. Thereafter, the proportion of district court lawyers began a steady rise, levelling off during the war and retreating only slightly during the Weimar Republic. The share of superior court lawyers gradually fell toward 50 percent, increasing again after 1922. The segment of the bar practicing before the court of appeal in Celle remained remarkably constant.

Superior court lawyers outside of the city of Hannover, however, experienced a squeeze between the rapidly growing bars of that city and the district courts. Constituting 29 percent of the bar in the province in 1879, lawyers at these seven superior courts expanded to

---

55 Lawyers complained most bitterly about competition from this latter group of former officials; Ostler, *Die deutschen Rechtsanwälte*, 207–8, and esp., Louis Levin, *Schutz der freien Rechtsanwaltschaft! Untersuchungen, Folgerungen und Forderungen auf der Grundlage ihrer gerichtsverfassungsmäßigen Stellung* (Leipzig, 1930), 101–4.

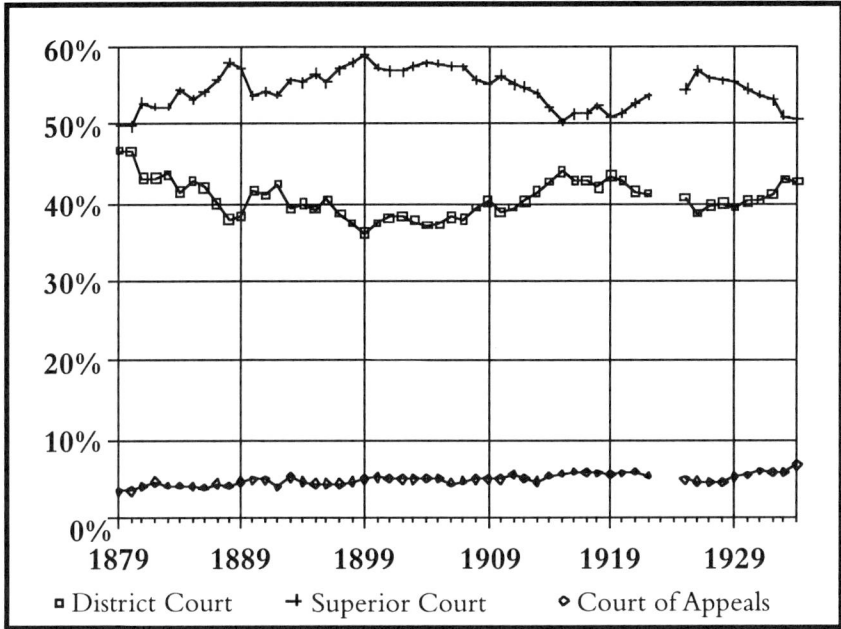

Figure 5.3. Composition of the bar by level of court

more than 35 percent of the total in 1888, during a period in which the bar in the city of Hannover rose only from 21 to 23 percent. Thereafter, however, the share of the former declined inexorably, while that of the latter rose fairly steadily. Although the gap closed a little during the war, by 1932 the relative positions had been reversed, with the superior court in the city of Hannover accounting for more than 30 percent of all lawyers in the province and all other superior court lawyers accounting for only 23 percent. The share of district court lawyers, from its low of 36 percent in 1899 (compared to more than 34 percent for the seven superior courts), rose to above 40 percent in 1931, nearly double the percentage of lawyers at the seven superior courts. A fundamental geographical restructuring of the practicing bar had taken place during the half century between 1878 and 1933, with the seven superior courts shrinking in importance when compared with both the district courts and the superior court in the city of Hannover.

Among the seven superior court bars that felt this squeeze, the bars in the small cities located in agrarian regions saw their numbers drop

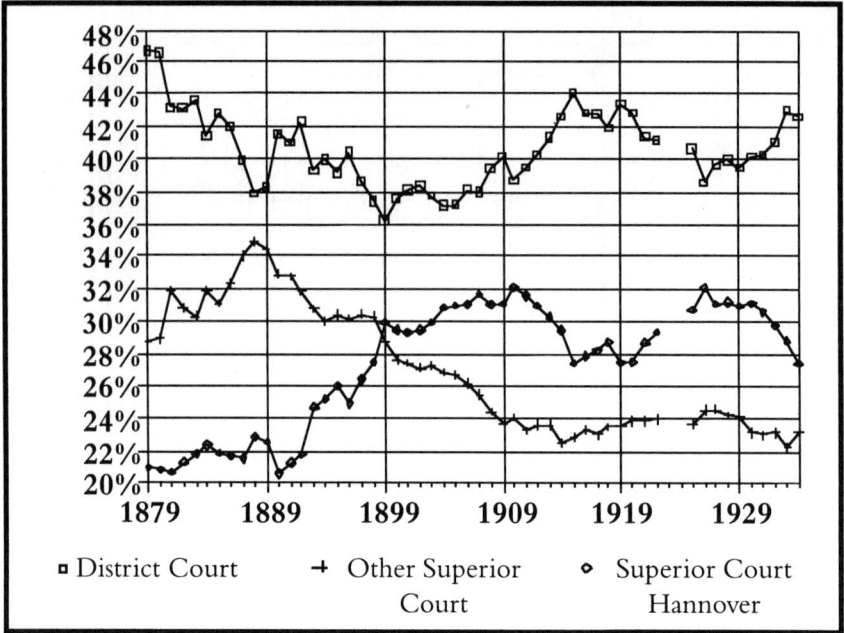

Figure 5.4. Composition of the bar, city of Hannover, other superior courts, district courts

the most sharply. The four rural superior courts, Aurich, Lüneburg, Stade, and Verden, bore the brunt of the shrinkage of the superior court bar. From their peak proportion of 16 percent of the total bar in 1888, they dwindled below 8 percent by 1914. The three "urban" superior courts, in Göttingen, Hildesheim, and Osnabrück, larger cities which were either administrative or industrial centers, maintained their share of the total more successfully. Initially more than 17 percent of the total, they increased to more than 19 percent but then declined, comprising approximately 15 percent of the provincial total with remarkable stability from 1900 to 1931. Lawyers at the four rural courts had represented almost half of all lawyers at these seven superior courts in 1881. By 1930 they were only one-third (8 percent out of 23 percent). See Figure 5.5. Lawyers at these four courts experienced most keenly the beleaguerment of their middle position, between the expanding bars at district courts and the superior court of the city of Hannover. Increasingly outnumbered both by district court lawyers and the giant bar in the city of Hannover, superior

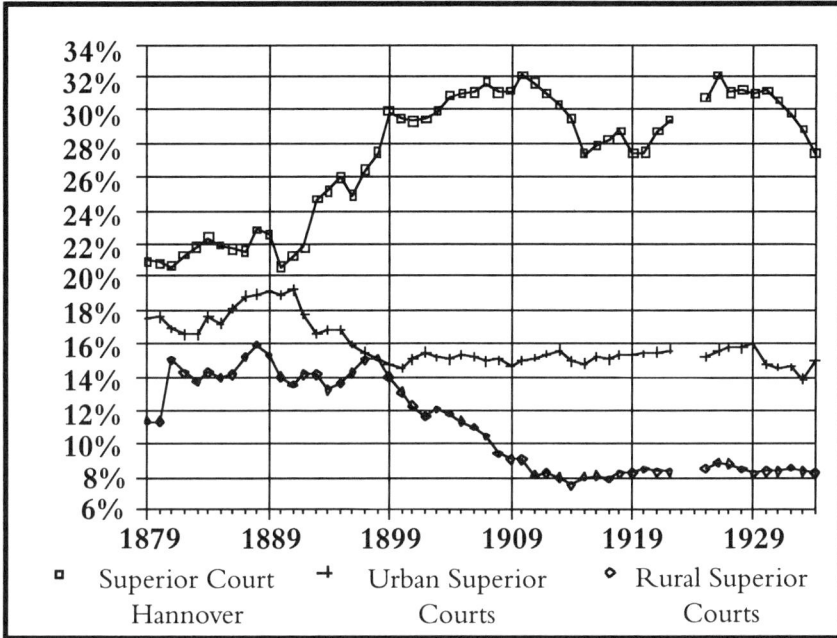

Figure 5.5. Proportion of total bar, rural superior courts, urban superior courts, superior court city of Hannover

court lawyers from these four rural courts faced challenges in the 1920s to their privileged representation on the executive board of the lawyers' chamber *and* to their monopoly on practice before their own courts.

Social Origins

The general assumption of historians has been that the onset of industrialization and the modern market economy led to a greater degree of social mobility in Europe and presumably to a change in the social origins of free professionals. The quickening pace of commerce and industry, urbanization, and the elimination of barriers to free entry into trades, occupations, and professions allowed sons from lower social levels to climb into higher social reaches by dint of their own hard work and dedication. If such mobility was not evident in the lifetime of a single person, a two-generation rise could perhaps be discerned, with the father gaining wealth through trade or industry and the son status through education and position, made possible by the father's wealth.[56]

Hartmut Kaelble has forced a modification of this assumption. Although growth in the number of members of the "higher strata" of society exceeded that of the population as a whole between 1850 and 1914, the general claim that opportunities for upward social mobility increased does not hold. Indeed, he concludes that German society was *not* forced to rely primarily upon recruitment from the middle and lower strata in order to fill the expanding demand for new members of the higher strata.[57]

While Kaelble indicates that the most fruitful directions for new studies of social mobility seem to lie with the petty bourgeoisie, there nonetheless remain groups among the upper strata of society whose social origins remain unexplored. Lawyers in private practice are one such group. The social origin of lawyers and changes during the period 1878–1933 help to illuminate both the internal tensions within the bar and the manner in which the bar related to society as a whole.[58]

Table 5.3 shows fathers' occupations for private practitioners newly admitted before all courts in the province of Hannover between 1881 and 1933, broken down into ten-year cohorts.[59] This table clearly reveals that, as one might have expected, in 1881 the overwhelming majority of private practitioners came from social groups with a historical propensity to study at universities. Fully a third were self-recruited from lawyers' families. The next third came from families of state officials, other university-educated professionals, and agricultural landowners. Lower state officials, another traditional source of university attenders and a source of social

---

56 The leading work on social mobility in Germany is Kaelble, *Soziale Mobilität und Chancengleichheit*, translated into English with new material included in idem, *Social Mobility in the 19th and 20th Centuries: Europe and America in Comparative Perspective* (New York, 1986). For a discussion of the expansion of enrollment at German universities, see Hartmut Titze, "Enrollment Expansion and Academic Overcrowding in Germany," in Konrad H. Jarausch, ed., *The Transformation of Higher Learning*, 57–88, and idem, "Die zyklische Überproduktion." Generally, see Jarausch, *Students, Society, and Politics*, 23–151.

57 Kaelble, *Soziale Mobilität*, 47, 57–8.

58 Claudia Huerkamp explored closely the social origins of medical doctors in *Der Aufstieg der Ärzte*, 61–78. As indicated below, university students have attracted much interest, as in the work of Hartmut Titze cited in note 56, John E. Craig, "Higher Education and Social Mobility in Germany," Jarausch, ed., *The Transformation of Higher Learning*, 219–44, and, most notably, Jarausch, *Students, Society, and Politics*.

59 For a discussion of the issues involved in identifying the father's occupation of lawyers and for the derivation of the occupational categories used here, see the methodological appendix.

Table 5.3. *Father's occupational group: All courts, 1881–1933*

	1881	1882–90	1891–1900	1901–10	1911–20	1921–30	1931–3	Total
Not given	78	53	60	78	102	238	106	715
Lawyer	48	20	12	6	12	30	3	131
Official	18	6	5	8	7	23	14	81
Academics	23	15	15	32	25	44	20	174
Agriculture	7	9	7	13	10	12	8	66
Businessmen	17	27	33	38	34	84	19	252
White collar	3	1	1	3	5	7	9	29
Mittelstand	6	6	7	12	9	20	10	70
Misc.	2	3	6	5	3	10	1	30
Low official	20	7	14	10	7	26	13	97
Total known	144	94	100	127	112	256	97	930
Total	222	147	160	205	214	494	203	1645
Percentage (of known)								
Lawyer	33.3	21.3	12.0	4.7	10.7	11.7	3.1	14.1
Official	12.5	6.4	5.0	6.3	6.3	9.0	14.4	8.7
Academics	16.0	16.0	15.0	25.2	22.3	17.2	20.6	18.7
Agriculture	4.9	9.6	7.0	10.2	8.9	4.7	8.2	7.1
Businessmen	11.8	28.7	33.0	29.9	30.4	32.8	19.6	27.1
White collar	2.1	1.1	1.0	2.4	4.5	2.7	9.3	3.1
Mittelstand	4.2	6.4	7.0	9.4	8.0	7.8	10.3	7.5
Misc.	1.4	3.2	6.0	3.9	2.7	3.9	1.0	3.2
Low official	13.9	7.4	14.0	7.9	6.3	10.2	13.4	10.4

climbers, accounted for 14 percent, with businessmen comprising only one-eighth.[60]

The social source of private practitioners quickly changed after 1881. The proportion of self-recruitment began a decline that lasted

60 Compare these results to Henning's data on social origins of all independent university trained professionals in Hannover:

	Officials					
Period	High	Low	Professionals	Landed	Industry	Other
1860–90	35.3%	0.0%	11.7%	23.6%	29.4%	0.0%
1890–1914	18.2%	9.1%	27.2%	0.0%	45.5%	0.0%

Henning, *Das westdeutsche Bürgertum*, 419. Among lawyers in Hannover, then, self-recruitment was more important in 1880 and the contribution of high officials was less important than among professionals as a whole.

until 1910, when a modest resurgence set in. Nonetheless, by 1930 self-recruitment was only a third of its initial proportion and it fell to 3.1 percent for the period 1931–3. The proportion of sons of higher state officials fell by half and then remained stable at the lower level until after 1920, when it rose. The immediate impact of *freie Advokatur* in Hannover, then, was an opening up of access to the practicing bar.[61] New lawyers came from a more diverse social background than that from which lawyers had previously come. Dramatic growth in the share of sons from commercial and industrial families ensued after 1881. Their proportion more than doubled immediately and then remained stable. The most dramatic change in the social origins of lawyers, then, was a shift from the traditional groups (lawyers and high state officials) to industrialists, merchants, and investors. The shift became apparent immediately after the enactment of the RAO and persisted throughout the next fifty years. Both in periods of stability and periods of growth in the size of the bar, *freie Advokatur* meant that the social basis of the practicing bar shifted away from traditional groups and toward the new *Bürgertum* of property.

This transformation in the social basis of the practicing bar did not occur equally at all levels of courts. Initially, the proportion of sons of lawyers was higher at district courts than at superior courts. Immediately after 1881, however, the proportion of new admittees before district courts who were second-generation lawyers fell from almost 40 percent to less than 10 percent, where it remained until 1933. Sons of lawyers, therefore, tended to seek admission at the seats of superior courts more than in district court towns. District court lawyers tended more after 1881 to come from families of university-educated persons other than lawyers, agricultural landowners, nonuniversity-educated officials, and, especially after 1910, the traditional *Mittelstand*, than did superior court lawyers. The proportion of sons of businessmen was initially much higher at the superior courts than at district courts and, after some convergence in the first decade after 1881, the divergence increased, despite a dramatic increase in their proportion even at district courts. Superior court lawyers after 1900 were far more likely than district court lawyers to be sons of lawyers or businessmen. University-trained professionals other than lawyers

61   This opening up, the decline in self-recruitment, was not solely a function of an expanding bar. In fact, the proportion of lawyers' sons among new admittees decreased from 33.3 percent in 1881 to 21.3 percent during the period 1882–90, during which the size of the bar remained stable or even declined.

Table 5.4.   *Father's occupational group: District courts, 1881–1933*

	1881	1882–90	1891–1900	1901–10	1911–20	1921–30	1931–3	Total
Not given	47	29	35	46	53	109	0	319
Lawyer	21	4	3	1	4	9	2	44
Official	8	4	2	3	3	5	5	30
Academics	5	9	10	17	12	22	8	83
Agriculture	2	6	3	8	9	9	6	43
Businessmen	3	11	11	16	11	28	6	86
White collar	3	0	0	0	2	2	7	14
Mittelstand	2	3	2	4	7	14	5	37
Misc.	1	0	5	3	2	3	0	14
Low official	9	4	7	6	5	15	7	53
Total known	54	41	43	58	55	107	46	404
Total	101	70	78	104	108	216	46	723
Percentage (of known)								
Lawyer	38.9	9.8	7.0	1.7	7.3	8.4	4.3	10.9
Official	14.8	9.8	4.7	5.2	5.5	4.7	10.9	7.4
Academics	9.3	22.0	23.3	29.3	21.8	20.6	17.4	20.5
Agriculture	3.7	14.6	7.0	13.8	16.4	8.4	13.0	10.6
Businessmen	5.6	26.8	25.6	27.6	20.0	26.2	13.0	21.3
White collar	5.6	0.0	0.0	0.0	3.6	1.9	15.2	3.5
Mittelstand	3.7	7.3	4.7	6.9	12.7	13.1	10.9	9.2
Misc.	1.9	0.0	11.6	5.2	3.6	2.8	0.0	3.5
Low official	16.7	9.8	16.3	10.3	9.1	14.0	15.2	13.1

contributed significant but virtually equal shares to both groups of lawyers after 1900. Tables 5.4 and 5.5 show the number and proportions of fathers' occupations for district and superior court lawyers, respectively.

These data lead to some conclusions that highlight the differences between the social origins of district court and superior court lawyers. First, district court bars appear to have been somewhat more open to social mobility than superior court bars. Self-recruitment of lawyers remained higher at superior courts, and the rise in the proportion of the entrepreneurial group, while indicating a social openness, also indicates a dominance by an economically prosperous and dynamic group. The district court bars, however, relied more heavily upon the traditional *Mittelstand*, lower state officials, and agricultural landowners for recruitment. The divergence only increased over time.

Table 5.5. *Father's occupational group: Superior courts, 1881–1933*

	1881	1882–90	1891–1900	1901–10	1911–20	1921–30	1931–3	Total
Not given	29	22	23	30	46	118	0	268
Lawyer	23	14	6	5	7	21	1	77
Official	8	2	2	4	2	16	8	42
Academics	17	6	5	13	11	19	9	80
Agriculture	5	3	4	5	1	2	2	22
Businessmen	14	13	21	22	22	51	12	155
White collar	0	1	1	3	3	5	1	14
Mittelstand	3	3	4	8	2	5	5	30
Misc.	1	3	1	2	1	7	1	16
Low official	9	3	6	2	2	11	5	38
Total known	80	48	50	64	51	137	44	474
Total	109	70	73	94	97	255	44	742
Percentage (of known)								
Lawyer	28.8	29.2	12.0	7.8	13.7	15.3	2.3	16.2
Official	10.0	4.2	4.0	6.3	3.9	11.7	18.2	8.9
Academics	21.3	12.5	10.0	20.3	21.6	13.9	20.5	16.9
Agriculture	6.3	6.3	8.0	7.8	2.0	1.5	4.5	4.6
Businessmen	17.5	27.1	42.0	34.4	43.1	37.2	27.3	32.7
White collar	0.0	2.1	2.0	4.7	5.9	3.6	2.3	3.0
Mittelstand	3.8	6.3	8.0	12.5	3.9	3.6	11.4	6.3
Misc.	1.3	6.3	2.0	3.1	2.0	5.1	2.3	3.4
Low official	11.3	6.3	12.0	3.1	3.9	8.0	11.4	8.0

Practice before superior courts carried more prestige for several reasons. First, historically in Hannover the closed body of procurators had practiced only before the collegial superior courts. Continuity of tradition meant that practice before superior courts maintained the prestige of the old system. Second, because of the rule of mandatory representation by lawyers, lawyers before superior courts did not have to argue cases against parties representing themselves or against lay practitioners. Third, the jurisdictional limits on initial jurisdiction meant that superior court lawyers handled cases involving larger objects in controversy, represented clients who, if not of a higher social status than those whose cases involved less than 300 marks, at least were wealthier and earned larger fees per case (and larger incomes in general, as will be seen). Fourth, since superior court lawyers handled appellate cases referred to them by district court lawyers who were barred from handling them on appeal, they

could claim a closer connection with the more theoretical, jurisprudential kind of law associated with appellate practice (as opposed to
the more practical orientation of practice in the initial instance), and
with a more intellectually sophisticated appellate court. Finally, since
many superior court lawyers were sons of lawyers, they no doubt
felt a sense of social and professional superiority to district court
lawyers. This basic distinction between the social origin of district
court and collegial court lawyers must be considered, along with
structural rivalries created by the RAO, in seeking the explanation
for professional tensions within the bar.

Finally, the superior court in the city of Hannover must be considered separately, for it occupied a dominant place in the scheme of the
Hannoverian provincial bar because of its size. After 1890 it accounted for more than half of all superior court lawyers. More than
the remaining seven superior courts, Hannover's expansion was
caused by an increase in the proportion of sons of businessmen (Table
5.6). While sons of lawyers accounted for around one-tenth of new
admittees after 1890, sons of businessmen composed around four-
tenths. Even more than the other superior courts, that in Hannover
possessed a bar increasingly composed of the sons of lawyers, other
university trained professionals, and businessmen. This placed it at
the polar extreme from the district court bar.

Confessional Identity

If the advent of the RAO in 1879 caused profound change in the size,
distribution, and social origin of the Hannoverian bar over the next
fifty-five years, it also brought confessional diversification to the
legal profession. Catholics and Jews had traditionally been disproportionately excluded from the legal profession, Catholics through their
underrepresentation among university students and Jews through
statutory, legal exclusion.[62] Although Prussian Minister of Justice

62 For the Catholic underrepresentation in university study, see Jarausch, *Students, Society, and
Politics*, 96–9, and table 3–3, 97; see also Peter Pulzer, "Religion and Judicial Appointments
in Germany, 1869–1918," *Yearbook of the Leo Baeck Institute* 28 (1983): 185–204, 189. Jews
had been excluded from the practice of law in Hannover by legislation until the French
occupation in the early nineteenth century, and thereafter they were admitted "in individual
cases and through special dispensation of the King"; Spangenberg, *Das Oberappellationsgericht in Celle*, 127–9. Although the terms of the Prussian constitution of 1850 guaranteed
equal rights regardless of religious confession and thus, presumably, the rights of Jews to
enter the practice of law, the Prussian system of appointment by the ministry of justice and
numerus clausus permitted widespread discrimination against Jews; Tillmann Krach, *Jüdische
Rechtsanwälte in Preußen. Bedeutung und Zerstörung der freien Advokatur* (Munich, 1991), 8–14.
Jews thus were among the leaders in the nineteenth century campaign for *freie Advokatur*.

Table 5.6.   Father's occupational group: Superior court Hannover, 1881–
1933

	1881	1882–90	1891–1900	1901–10	1911–20	1921–30	1931–3	Total
Not given	13	9	10	19	25	57	0	133
Lawyer	8	5	5	3	2	12	0	35
Official	5	0	2	4	2	7	4	24
Academics	7	2	3	8	5	12	2	39
Agriculture	0	1	1	3	1	1	0	7
Businessmen	4	4	15	14	12	40	9	98
White collar	0	0	1	3	1	2	1	8
Mittelstand	1	1	4	3	1	3	2	15
Misc.	1	1	0	2	1	4	1	10
Low official	5	1	4	1	1	6	3	21
Total known	31	15	35	41	26	87	22	257
Total	44	24	45	60	51	144	22	390
Percentage (of known)								
Lawyer	25.8	33.3	14.3	7.3	7.7	13.8	0.0	13.6
Official	16.1	0.0	5.7	9.8	7.7	8.0	18.2	9.3
Academics	22.6	13.3	8.6	19.5	19.2	13.8	9.1	15.2
Agriculture	0.0	6.7	2.9	7.3	3.8	1.1	0.0	2.7
Businessmen	12.9	26.7	42.9	34.1	46.2	46.0	40.9	38.1
White collar	0.0	0.0	2.9	7.3	3.8	2.3	4.5	3.1
Mittelstand	3.2	6.7	11.4	7.3	3.8	3.4	9.1	5.8
Misc.	3.2	6.7	0.0	4.9	3.8	4.6	4.5	3.9
Low official	16.1	6.7	11.4	2.4	3.8	6.9	13.6	8.2

Adolf Leonhardt appointed the first three Jewish judges in 1870 after
the adoption of the Emancipation Law of 1869 by the German Confederation, Jews continued routinely to be discriminated against in
appointment to judicial positions.[63] As a result, Jewish university
graduates with law degrees after 1879 flocked overwhelmingly to the
newly freed private bar. Always less than one percent of the German
population in the period 1879 to 1933, Jewish lawyers, who had
constituted only 3 percent of the Prussian bar in 1872, rose to 28.3
percent in April 1933.[64]

63 Pulzer, "Religion and Judicial Appointments," 188, 194–202; Krach, *Jüdische Rechtsan-
    wälte*, 14–23. For the story of one Jewish lawyer who enjoyed a judicial career, see Werner
    E. Mosse, "Albert Mosse: A Jewish Judge in Imperial Germany," *Yearbook of the Leo Baeck
    Institute* 28 (1983): 169–84.
64 According to tables 1–3 in Krach, *Jüdische Rechtsanwälte*, 414–16, the growth of the Jewish
    percentage of the total Prussian bar was as follows:

This disproportionate overrepresentation of Germans of Jewish religion in the practicing bar soon led to public comment, most notably from those outside of the profession. Catholics particularly were concerned in their campaign for "parity" of opportunity for the confessions in public employment and also in the free professions. Overrepresentation of Jews hampered the efforts of politicians of the Catholic Center party to maintain proportionality of representation between the Catholic (roughly one-third) and Protestant (the other two-thirds) populations.[65] Moreover, in certain cities, the proportion of the bar that was Jewish was truly astounding: in 1933, 48.3 percent of lawyers in Berlin were Jewish and 45.3 percent of those in Frankfurt am Main.[66] Despite widespread prejudice, Jewish private practitioners enjoyed prestige and acceptance within the profession. Many rose to positions of leadership within the DAV, such as Martin Drucker (longtime chair), Adolf Heilberg, Max Hachenburg, Max Friedländer, and Julius Magnus.[67]

The changes in the confessional composition of the bar of the province of Hannover represented an opening to talent and an end to civil disabilities against Jews, but the changes were not so dramatic as elsewhere in Germany. Table 5.7 shows that *freie Advokatur* indeed led to an increase in the proportion of Jewish lawyers at the expense of the proportion of Catholics. Jewish lawyers were more likely to practice at superior courts, especially the superior court of the city of Hannover, than at district courts (Tables 5.8,

Year	Percentage
1872	3.0%
1880	7.3%
1893	25.4%
1904	27.4%
1925	26.2%
1933	28.5%

65 Pulzer, "Religion and Judicial Appointments," 190–202, provides an insightful discussion of the Center Party's policy of parity. The emphasis in confessional parity caused courts, lawyers' chambers, and justice ministries to maintain detailed records on the confessional composition of the various court districts. See, for example, N.H.St.A., Hann. 173, Acc. 30/87, 195, "Generalakten betreffend Wahrung der Konfessionellen Parität bei der Besetzung von Stellen," 23a–23f, compiled in 1929 from the 1925 census data. Each district court and superior court district is recorded separately.

66 Konrad H. Jarausch, "Jewish Lawyers in Germany, 1848–1938 – The Disintegration of a Profession," *Yearbook of the Leo Baeck Institute* 36 (1991): 171–90, 177.

67 Ibid., 177; Udo Reifner, "The Bar in the Third Reich: Anti-Semitism and the Decline of Liberal Advocacy," *McGill Law Journal* 32 (1986): 96–124, 104–7, emphasizes in particular the important role of Jewish lawyers in leading the DAV before 1933.

Table 5.7.   *Confession of lawyers, all courts*

	1881	1882–90	1891–1900	1901–10	1911–20	1921–30	1931–3	Total
Lutheran	38	51	77	132	173	189	34	694
Catholic	9	11	6	23	30	29	4	112
Jewish	2	15	7	22	23	18	0	87
Reformed	1	4	2	5	10	9	3	34
Total	50	81	92	182	236	245	41	927
Percentage								
Lutheran	76.0	63.0	83.7	72.5	73.3	77.1	82.9	74.9
Catholic	18.0	13.6	6.5	12.6	12.7	11.8	9.8	12.1
Jewish	4.0	18.5	7.6	12.1	9.7	7.3	0.0	9.4
Reformed	2.0	4.9	2.2	2.7	4.2	3.7	7.3	3.7

Table 5.8.   *Confession of lawyers, all superior courts*

	1881	1882–90	1891–1900	1901–10	1911–20	1921–30	1931–3	Total
Lutheran	30	25	31	56	93	70	7	312
Catholic	6	5	4	15	17	16	0	63
Jewish	2	13	6	20	18	10	0	69
Reformed	0	0	0	1	3	1	2	7
Total	38	43	41	92	131	97	9	451
Percentage								
Lutheran	78.9	58.1	75.6	60.9	71.0	72.2	77.8	69.2
Catholic	15.8	11.6	9.8	16.3	13.0	16.5	0.0	14.0
Jewish	5.3	30.2	14.6	21.7	13.7	10.3	0.0	15.3
Reformed	0.0	0.0	0.0	1.1	2.3	1.0	22.2	1.6

5.9, and 5.10).[68] In addition, the lawyers who practiced at the four rural superior courts (Aurich, Lüneburg, Stade, and Verden) tended to be more Protestant than those at other courts (Table 5.11). Finally, Catholic lawyers tended to practice in those locales with significant Catholic populations, such as Hildesheim and Osnabrück (Table 5.12).

In sum, although the RAO did not bring to the bar confessional

68   These tables are derived from N.H.St.A., Hann. 173, Acc. 30/87, 211/4, "Zulassung zur Rechtsanwaltschaft, Allgemeines," Bd. 5.

Table 5.9.   *Confession of lawyers, all district courts*

	1881	1882–90	1891–1900	1901–10	1911–20	1921–30	1931–3	Total
Lutheran	7	24	37	68	73	97	26	332
Catholic	3	6	2	7	13	10	4	45
Jewish	0	2	1	1	4	7	0	15
Reformed	1	4	1	4	7	8	1	26
Total	11	36	41	80	97	122	31	418
Percentage								
Lutheran	63.6	66.7	90.2	85.0	75.3	79.5	83.9	79.4
Catholic	27.3	16.7	4.9	8.8	13.4	8.2	12.9	10.8
Jewish	0.0	5.6	2.4	1.3	4.1	5.7	0.0	3.6
Reformed	9.1	11.1	2.4	5.0	7.2	6.6	3.2	6.2

Table 5.10.   *Confession of lawyers, superior court of Hannover*

	1881	1882–90	1891–1900	1901–10	1911–20	1921–30	Total
Lutheran	11	9	20	32	57	34	163
Catholic	2	0	1	4	6	5	18
Jewish	1	7	6	15	14	9	52
Reformed	0	0	0	0	1	0	1
Total	14	16	27	51	78	48	234
Percentage							
Lutheran	78.6	56.3	74.1	62.7	73.1	70.8	69.7
Catholic	14.3	0.0	3.7	7.8	7.7	10.4	7.7
Jewish	7.1	43.8	22.2	29.4	17.9	18.8	22.2
Reformed	0.0	0.0	0.0	0.0	1.3	0.0	0.4

change of similar magnitude to that in some other large German cities, it nevertheless perpetuated some old and introduced some new differentiations within the profession. The bars that practiced before district courts and rural superior courts remained more Protestant than the bar as a whole. Practice in the city of Hannover approved most attractive to Jewish lawyers. Finally, the Court of Appeal in Celle remained a citadel of Protestant lawyers (Table 5.13). These confessional differentiations, perhaps not important in themselves, had the potential to combine with other interest and

Table 5.11. *Confession of lawyers, rural superior courts*

	1881–1900	1901–33	Total	Percentage 1881–1900	1901–1903	Total
Lutheran	26	48	74	92.9	88.9	90.2
Catholic	1	3	4	3.6	5.6	4.9
Jewish	1	2	3	3.6	3.7	3.7
Reformed	0	1	1	0.0	1.9	1.2
Total	28	54	82			

Table 5.12. *Confession of lawyers, superior courts in Catholic areas*

	1881–1900	1901–33	Total	Percentage 1881–1900	1901–33	Total
Lutheran	11	32	43	45.8	50.0	48.9
Catholic	10	23	33	41.7	35.9	37.5
Jewish	3	7	10	12.5	10.9	11.4
Reformed	0	2	2	0.0	3.1	2.3
Total	24	64	88			

status concerns and lead to tensions and frictions among various subgroups of the bar.

Geographic Origins

Another sort of shift in the composition of the bar that might be expected as a result of the introduction of *freie Advokatur* would be a change in the geographic origins of lawyers. Officials in Prussia, for example, feared that new admittees would shun the small district court towns and flock to the metropolis. Urbanization models would lead one to believe that the bars in large cities would be more fluid and open, less dependent upon connections in order to establish a viable professional practice. Conversely, one would expect the bars in small district court towns to be largely self-replicating, as local students returned to practice in their hometowns in response to a family oppor-

Table 5.13.   *Confession of lawyers, court of appeal in Celle*

	1881–1900	1901–33	Total	Percentage 1881–1900	Percentage 1901–33	Percentage Total
Lutheran	12	38	50	92.3	84.4	86.2
Catholic	0	4	4	0.0	8.9	6.9
Jewish	0	3	3	0.0	6.7	5.2
Reformed	1	0	1	7.7	0.0	1.7
Total	13	45	58			

tunity or to a need known to them. The changes that occurred in the bar in Hannover after 1881, however, contradict these hypotheses. In 1881 about one-third of the Hannoverian bar practiced in their hometowns. A greater proportion of superior court lawyers were in hometown practices than district court lawyers. Throughout the era in question, this one-third ratio remained stable, and it showed evidence of increasing during the 1920s (Tables 5.14, 5.15, and 5.16). A further twenty percent of lawyers practiced before a court that lay in the same superior court district as their hometowns, and this proportion also persisted over fifty years. Another third moved to their practices from a hometown outside of the bailiwick of the superior court of their practice but within the province of Hannover. The remaining practitioners came to Hannover from elsewhere in Prussia or in relatively rare cases elsewhere in Germany.[69] The Hannoverian bar, then, was primarily Hannoverian in origin and inclined to settle close to the ancestral home.

A closer examination of the data regarding geographic origins, however, reveals some surprises. Superior court lawyers were much likelier to practice in their hometowns than were district court lawyers (38.3 percent to 29.1 percent in 1881; 62 percent to 25.5 percent for new admittees in the period 1921–30; compare Tables 5.15 and 5.16). Even if the geographic realm of a superior court district is accepted as the definition of a lawyer's "home" territory, superior court lawyers had a greater propensity to stay home, 66 percent to 47

---

69 Not surprisingly, the lawyers who were born outside of Hannover were born nearby. Of the sixty-three non-Prussians, thirteen came from the Hanseatic cities of Bremen, Hamburg, and Lübeck, eight from the Duchy of Braunschweig, and seven from the Grand Duchy of Oldenburg.

Table 5.14. *Geographic origin, all courts*

	1881	1882–90	1891–1900	1901–10	1911–20	1921–30	1931–3	Total
Not given	74	52	61	80	103	239	0	609
Same town	49	27	38	47	38	112	32	343
Same dist.ct.	4	2	2	0	3	7	3	21
Same sup.ct.	29	15	13	17	21	35	28	158
Province	52	32	33	42	36	68	18	281
Prussia	4	7	7	10	9	17	8	62
Germany	7	12	6	9	4	16	9	63
Total	145	95	99	125	111	255	98	928
Percentage (of known)								
Same town	33.8	28.4	38.4	37.6	34.2	43.9	32.7	37.0
Same dist.ct.	2.8	2.1	2.0	0.0	2.7	2.7	3.1	2.3
Same sup.ct.	20.0	15.8	13.1	13.6	18.9	13.7	28.6	17.0
Province	35.9	33.7	33.3	33.6	32.4	26.7	18.4	30.3
Prussia	2.8	7.4	7.1	8.0	8.1	6.7	8.2	6.7
Germany	4.8	12.6	6.1	7.2	3.6	6.3	9.2	6.8

Table 5.15. *Geographic origin, all superior courts*

	1881	1882–90	1891–1900	1901–10	1911–20	1921–30	1931–3	Total
Not given	28	23	22	30	46	118	0	267
Same town	31	20	30	38	31	85	22	257
Same dist.ct.	2	0	1	0	0	0	1	4
Same sup.ct.	14	4	2	8	2	16	9	55
Province	28	16	14	10	13	22	4	107
Prussia	1	2	1	4	3	9	4	24
Germany	5	5	3	4	2	5	4	28
Total	81	47	51	64	51	137	44	475
Percentage (of known)								
Same town	38.3	42.6	58.8	59.4	60.8	62.0	50.0	54.1
Same dist.ct.	2.5	0.0	2.0	0.0	0.0	0.0	2.3	0.8
Same sup.ct.	17.3	8.5	3.9	12.5	3.9	11.7	20.5	11.6
Province	34.6	34.0	27.5	15.6	25.5	16.1	9.1	22.5
Prussia	1.2	4.3	2.0	6.3	5.9	6.6	9.1	5.1
Germany	6.2	10.6	5.9	6.3	3.9	3.6	9.1	5.9

Table 5.16.   *Geographic origin, all district courts*

	1881	1882–90	1891–1900	1901–10	1911–20	1921–30	1931–3	Total
Not given	46	27	37	44	58	110	0	322
Same town	16	5	5	8	7	27	9	77
Same dist.ct.	2	2	1	0	3	7	2	17
Same sup.ct.	15	11	11	8	20	18	19	102
Province	17	14	16	27	21	36	9	140
Prussia	3	4	6	2	8	7	4	34
Germany	2	7	2	4	2	11	3	31
Total	55	43	41	49	61	106	46	401
Percentage (of known)								
Same town	29.1	11.6	12.2	16.3	11.5	25.5	19.6	19.2
Same dist.ct.	3.6	4.7	2.4	0.0	4.9	6.6	4.3	4.2
Same sup.ct.	27.3	25.6	26.8	16.3	32.8	17.0	41.3	25.4
Province	30.9	32.6	39.0	55.1	34.4	34.0	19.6	34.9
Prussia	5.5	9.3	14.6	4.1	13.1	6.6	8.7	8.5
Germany	3.6	16.3	4.9	8.2	3.3	10.4	6.5	7.7

percent over the entire period. The divergence was small in the beginning and increased over the period in question. District court lawyers, therefore, contained a larger proportion of new admittees who came from outside the superior court district, but elsewhere in Hannover, to practice there. To a greater extent than superior court lawyers, they came into their practices as strangers.

The propensity of superior court lawyers to settle in the town of their birth was most pronounced in the city of Hannover (Table 5.17). In 1881, over half of the lawyers there had been born in the province but outside the jurisdiction of the superior court in the metropolis. The proportion of new admittees who came from the city of Hannover itself began to rise immediately, surpassing two-thirds by 1900 and reaching three-quarters by 1930. The bar in the city of Hannover did not grow because of the attractive power of the thriving economy, drawing new graduates in from the hinterlands. Instead, city residents studied law and returned to Hannover to practice there. The growth of the bar in the city of Hannover, then, *must* be explained by the entry of new social elements who were native to the city rather than an immigration of sons of lawyers from outlying courts.

Table 5.17. *Geographic origin, superior court, city of Hannover*

	1881	1882–90	1891–1900	1901–10	1911–20	1921–30	1931–3	Total
Not given	13	9	9	19	25	57	0	132
Same town	10	6	24	29	17	65	6	157
Same dist. ct.	0	0	0	0	0	0	1	1
Same sup. ct.	2	0	1	2	0	4	2	11
Province	16	4	8	9	8	11	0	56
Prussia	1	2	1	0	0	5	0	9
Germany	2	3	2	2	0	2	2	13
Total	31	15	36	42	25	87	11	247
Percentage (of known)								
Same town	32.3	40.0	66.7	69.0	68.0	74.7	54.5	63.6
Same dist. ct.	0.0	0.0	0.0	0.0	0.0	0.0	9.1	0.4
Same sup. ct.	6.5	0.0	2.8	4.8	0.0	4.6	18.2	4.5
Province	51.6	26.7	22.2	21.4	32.0	12.6	0.0	22.7
Prussia	3.2	13.3	2.8	0.0	0.0	5.7	0.0	3.6
Germany	6.5	20.0	5.6	4.8	0.0	2.3	18.2	5.3

The fact that law graduates from superior court towns tended to set up practice in their hometowns should not be surprising. Those who were sons of lawyers or sons of businessmen either had a practice to go to at the beginning of their careers or a ready-made clientele of family members and enterprises. Especially in the city of Hannover, the booming economy presented opportunity to lawyers who, as sons of businessmen, were not afraid of competition for clients and cases.[70] Moreover, the rule of mandatory representation by lawyers protected superior court practice from some degrading forms of competition. Superior court lawyers returned to their hometowns to practice because they had contacts and potential clients there and were unafraid of competition from other lawyers in familiar territory.

Of the admissions for whom geographic origin is known, 71.8 percent listed as their hometown one of the 108 cities and towns that were the seats of some level of court. The share of the nine collegial court towns was 48.8 percent, and that of district court

70 For one example of how a young war-veteran lawyer entered practice in the city of Hannover in 1922, as an associate of an established two-member law firm, see Ulrich Beer, *Versehrt, verfolgt, versöhnt: Horst Berkowitz, ein jüdisches Anwaltsleben* (Essen, 1979), 48–50.

towns was 23 percent. A further 13 percent moved into Hannover from outside the province. This means that only 15.2 percent of all lawyers between 1880 and 1930 came from a town without any court or from the countryside. Collegial court towns, then, were the principal source of new lawyers, with the city of Hannover the likeliest of all (24.5 percent, more than all the other collegial court towns combined). Lawyers, therefore, came largely from the urban centers of the province and they returned to those urban centers to practice.

Significantly, forty-one of the ninety-eight "purely" district courts produced no lawyer during this entire period and a further nineteen produced only one. Four district court towns made significant contributions to the recruitment for the bar, Hannoversch-Münden with ten, Geestemünde-Lehe and Leer with thirteen each, and Hameln with eighteen. This is in marked contrast with the three small superior court seats of Aurich and Verden with ten each and Stade with only nine. As a result, except for such places as the four district court towns just named, almost all district courts were net importers of lawyers, as were the small superior court towns. District court towns thus presented opportunities to outsiders to build practices. Despite competition from lay practitioners, small objects-in-controversy, and the lack of prestige of district court practice, small district court towns provided fields of limited competition from other lawyers. The steady decline of the number of district court towns with no lawyers shows the expansion of the bar into this new arena of practice.

Another way of focusing upon the propensity of lawyers to move around is to look at where they settled after growing up in the thirteen towns which produced the most lawyers during this period (the nine collegial court towns and the four district court towns mentioned). These towns together produced more than half of the lawyers for whom biographies can be constructed. Most of these courts did not absorb into the bar more than half of the lawyers who grew up there. The superior court of the city of Hannover, as usual, absorbed the greatest proportion of locally produced lawyers. Of the fourteen lawyers in 1881 who had been born in Hannover, ten (71 percent) practiced in their home city; of the fifty-one admitted between 1882 and 1905 who had been born there, thirty-eight (74.5 percent) practiced there; of the 136 between 1906 and 1930, 104 (76.5 percent) chose to return home to practice. This stands in stark contrast to the other cities. Over the entire time span, Celle absorbed only 44 percent (eleven of twenty-five) of the lawyers who grew up there, Göttingen only 39 percent (sixteen of forty-one), Lüneburg only 36.8 percent (seven of nineteen). Hildesheim and Osnabrück managed to surpass 50 percent with 52.8 percent (twenty-eight of fifty-three) and 51.4 percent (eighteen of thirty-five) respectively, but their rate of absorption remained far lower than that of the city of Hannover.[71] The degree of localization increases somewhat when lawyers who settled at district court towns within the territory of their home superior court are taken into account (for example in Aurich, where only half of the ten lawyers produced returned to the superior court, but all of the remainder settled elsewhere within the district), but the fact clearly emerges that most of these towns were exporters of lawyers elsewhere. The gigantic bar in Hannover absorbed some of these excess lawyers (seventy-four over the whole period), but the others had to look elsewhere for their practices.

Career Patterns and Strategies

A final means of approaching the data is to examine the settlement patterns of lawyers. It might be presumed, for example, that sons of lawyers tended to settle in their home-towns, entering into practice with their fathers upon admission to the bar. Family dynasties indeed were not unknown. Five members of the Beitzen family entered into practice in Hildesheim between 1881 and 1925. Four members of the Dyckhoff family were in practice in Osnabrück in 1881. In at least four other instances, three succeeding generations of the same family practiced before the same court. In at least sixty-four cases, father and son (and in one case, father and daughter) practiced before the same court. Clearly, the advantages of entering into an existing practice or opening a new practice in a town in which one's father had an already established reputation were great. Yet not all sons of lawyers returned to their hometowns to practice. At least twenty-seven cases existed in which a son of a lawyer opened a practice in a different town. The tendency to leave home was more pronounced for lawyers who had been born in district

71 The fact than Hildesheim and Osnabrück provided employment for more than 50 percent of the lawyers who grew up there can probably be accounted for by the fact that both were centers of Catholicism within the province of Hannover and therefore relatively self-contained communities.

court towns. Between 1881 and 1900, six of twenty-seven sons of district court lawyers returned home to practice; between 1901 and 1930, eight of eleven did so. In contrast, in the earlier period, thirty-two of fifty-one sons of superior court lawyers opened practice in their hometowns, and twenty-nine of thirty-four did so after the turn of the century. Thus, the greater propensity of lawyers from superior court hometowns to return home to practice is borne out as well when only sons of lawyers are considered.

Not surprisingly, sons of high officials did *not* tend to return to their hometowns to practice. The policy of the Prussian government was to ensure that high officials did not administer their home regions, so the ties of their children to their places of birth were looser. Both at the district and superior court levels, fewer than half of all lawyers from this social group returned to their given hometown to practice.

Finally, lawyers from entrepreneurial families tended to return home to practice if they came from superior court towns; they tended to leave the superior court *district* of their birth if they came from district court towns. Here the influence of the city of Hannover is clear. Between 1881 and 1900, only five of twenty-four lawyers who were sons of businessmen remained in their district court hometowns to practice while thirteen left the superior court district. The figures for 1901–30 are twelve of fifty-seven sons of businessmen remaining, thirty-two leaving. In contrast, eighteen of fifty-two businessmen's sons left superior court hometowns to set up practice elsewhere in the earlier period while twenty-five remained. The outflow *decreased* greatly after the turn of the century, when sixty-two of one hundred sons of businessmen remained in superior court hometowns and thirty left. Superior court towns, then, provided a greater opportunity than district court towns for a beginning lawyer who had no ties to the legal profession (such as the son of a businessman) to establish a practice, and the stark contrast sharpened after 1900. Superior court towns retained lawyers who grew up there as sons of businessmen and attracted lawyers from the same social background who grew up in smaller towns.

The declining number of district courts without a lawyer reveals another career strategy that lawyers adopted. In 1889, fifty-four of the ninety-eight purely district courts had no lawyer admitted before them. As late as 1905, forty-two had no lawyer. New admittees, weighing the options open to them, clearly preferred to accept the

Table 5.18.   District courts with no lawyer,
Province of Hannover

Year	Courts	Year	Courts
1880	49	1913	11
1887	54	1914	10
1889	54	1915	8
1891	53	1916	10
1893	53	1917	11
1899	52	1918	10
1901	53	1919	7
1903	43	1920	8
1905	42	1921	6
1907	32	1922	7
1909	28	1925	11
1911	18	1926	12
1912	18	1931	10

Source: Reichs-Justizamt, *Deutsche Justiz-Statistik* (Berlin), vols. 3–6, 9–15, 17 (1887–93, 1899–1911, 1915); *Handbuch über den königlichen Preußischen Hof und Staat für das Jahr* ——— (Berlin), 1912, 1913, 1914, 1922, 1925, 1926, 1931; and "Jahresbericht über die Tätigkeit der Anwaltskammer Celle und des Vorstandes dasselben," 1915–21, G.St.A., I HA Rep. 84a, 21913.

risks of greater competition in the larger bars of the superior court towns. As the pace of growth of the bar in the province as a whole grew, especially that of the bar in the city of Hannover, aspiring practitioners came to view the district courts as promising fields of practice, for the number of lawyerless courts fell to eighteen in 1911 and 1912 and below ten in 1915 and 1919–22. The district courts that remained without a lawyer were in tiny localities close to superior courts or other sources of legal advice. Lawyers reacted to the rapidly expanding bar and increased competition in the larger cities by settling in small towns that had formerly lacked legal practitioners. Rather than face the competition of those rapidly growing bars in the large cities, again especially in Hannover, some lawyers sought out lawyerless district court towns to set up practice. (See Table 5.18.)

A final career strategy that was open to lawyers was to move the site of their practice. Although lawyers could practice only before one court, they could seek admission to a new court upon condition of relinquishing admission before their former court and moving their residence to the new town. Since such a move could not be prohibited because of overcrowding at the new court, lawyers could make such a move virtually at will. One hundred and thirty-four lawyers in the sample moved at least once in their careers. Sixteen moved twice, five three times, and one lawyer moved six times in the span of twenty years. The new regime of the RAO granted lawyers a substantial measure of geographic mobility in the pursuit of economic advantage, and ten percent of Hannoverian lawyers took advantage of that opportunity at some point in their careers.

Proof that the movement among courts was not based simply upon a career progression up the ladder of courts lies in the fact that only seven lawyers moved to the court of appeal in Celle (one from a district court and six from superior courts), while three moved *from* that court to either a district or superior court. The bulk of the moves (62 out of a total of 158) involved transfers from one district court to another, usually nearby. Indeed, the lawyer who moved six times moved from one small district court to another, across the boundaries of superior court district lines, but all within the boundaries of the economic unit of the Harz Mountains. A further thirty-three moves were from a district to a superior court, usually the one in whose territory the district court lay. Conversely, thirty-four moves were from a superior to a district court. Often these moves, however, came late in the lawyer's career and involved a move from the scene of a life's practice back to that lawyer's ancestral home, seemingly a form of retirement.

Executive Board

The RAO provided that the plenary assembly of each lawyers' chamber should elect an executive board to oversee the self-administrative functions conferred upon the chambers by that statute. The executive board conducted the everyday business of the organized bar, preparing opinions upon request for the ministry of justice and the courts, as well as reviewing complaints about members of the chamber and conducting disciplinary hearings when the need arose. Membership in the executive board, therefore, was evidence of the esteem in which a lawyer was held by other members of the bar. Lawyer-notables who were members of the executive board may be considered to have been an elite among Hannoverian lawyers, and as such, their social and geographic origins deserve special attention.

By the end of 1880, the executive board consisted of fifteen members, and it remained at that size until it expanded to twenty in 1924. From the very beginning, lawyers in Hannover sought geographic balance in the composition of the executive board, and by unspoken tradition at least one member of the board came from each superior court. The bylaws of the chamber required that the chairman and secretary of the executive board always be elected from among the lawyers living in Celle, thus, in effect, from among the court of appeal lawyers.[72] District court lawyers, however, were consistently unrepresented on the executive board, gaining membership in 1904 for one of their number only by threat of collective action. Even after the expansion of the size of the executive board, district court lawyers remained underrepresented.[73] (See Table 5.19).

Eighty lawyers served on the executive board between its organization in 1881 and 1933. Before 1900, more than half practiced either before the court of appeal in Celle or the superior court in the city of Hannover (nine and eight respectively, out of a total of thirty-two). The remaining superior courts averaged two representatives each during this period. After the turn of the century and until 1930, slightly more balanced representation prevailed, as Hannover produced six and Celle six of thirty-one members, and as five district court lawyers joined the board at one time or another. Each member who was elected, however, tended to be re-elected until death or retirement. Terms were long, mitigated only by the fact that lawyers were usually older when they were first elected, again contributing to the image of the executive board as an honorific office for senior and well-esteemed members of the profession.

The social origins of members of the executive board reflected to some extent the social composition of the bar as a whole. The proportion of sons of lawyers declined after the turn of the century and that of sons of businessmen rose. Lawyers from traditional backgrounds such as high government officials, university-educated professionals,

---

72 Mundt, *100 Jahre Rechtsanwaltskammer*, 18–19. See the *Geschäftsordnung* of the lawyers' chamber in Celle, §8, ¶ 2, G.St.A., I HA Rep. 84a, 21912, 20.

73 Mundt, *100 Jahre Rechtsanwaltskammer*, 29.

Table 5.19.   *Members of executive board, Anwaltskammer Celle, by court of admission*

Court		1881–1900	Court		1901–30	Court		1931–3
LG	Aurich	3	LG	Aurich	0	LG	Aurich	0
LG	Göttingen	2	LG	Göttingen	1	LG	Göttingen	1
LG	Hannover	9	LG	Hannover	6	LG	Hannover	5
LG	Hildesheim	1	LG	Hildesheim	2	LG	Hildesheim	1
LG	Lüneburg	2	LG	Lüneburg	3	LG	Lüneburg	1
LG	Osnabrück	2	LG	Osnabrück	3	LG	Osnabrück	0
LG	Stade	2	LG	Stade	2	LG	Stade	1
LG	Verden	2	LG	Verden	3	LG	Verden	1
OLG	Celle	8	OLG	Celle	6	OLG	Celle	3
AG	Norden	1	AG	Harburg	2	AG	Geestemünde	2
			AG	Neustadt	1	AG	Hameln	1
			AG	Goslar	1	AG	Norden	1
						AG	Lüchow	1
Total		32			31			17

and agricultural landowners were disproportionately highly represented on the executive board, however, and those from business backgrounds relatively underrepresented. The executive board was certainly no vehicle for upward social mobility.[74]

Over ninety percent of all members of the executive board during this fifty-year span were natives of the province of Hannover, including all who served before 1900. One-quarter of the members who served before 1900 had been born in the city of Hannover; that proportion decreased to one-eighth between 1901 and 1930 before rebound-

74   The occupations of the fathers of the members of the executive board were as follows:

	1881–1900	1901–30	1931–3
Not given	3	5	8
Lawyer	8	3	2
Officials	4	2	1
Academics	5	7	1
Agriculture	2	3	1
Businessmen	5	6	2
White collar	0	0	1
Mittelstand	0	1	1
Miscellaneous	1	3	0
Off.Low	4	1	0
Total	32	31	17

ing to one-third between 1931 and 1933. A new element entered into
the executive board, lawyers who were not native to the province, but
they remained a tiny minority. The geographic mobility of executive
board members exceeded that of the bar as a whole, in that over forty
percent of members practiced outside the superior court district of
their birth, both before and after 1900, while the proportion practicing
in their hometowns shrank from 41 to 20 percent.[75]

While the composition of the executive board did not differ radi-
cally from that of the bar as a whole, there were some contrasts. The
executive board remained slightly more elite, less business-based in
social origin than other lawyers in the province. It preserved a geographically representative character with respect to all eight superior
courts during a time when the superior court in Hannover came
more and more to dominate that sector of the bar. The result was that
the bar in Hannover was underrepresented, while that in the small
cities of Aurich, Lüneburg, Stade, and Verden was overrepresented.
District court lawyers attained some representation after 1904, but
they remained at all times severely underrepresented in proportion to
their numbers within the provincial bar.

Women in the Bar

One final change occurred within the social composition of the bar
during the Weimar Republic. The "Law Concerning the Admission
of Women to the Offices and Vocations of the Administration of
Justice" of 11 July 1922, forbade discrimination in access to the legal

---

75 The geographic origins of members of the executive committee, by the superior court
    district in which their given hometown is listed, is as follows:

	1881–1900	1901–30	1931–3
Not given	3	5	9
Aurich	2	1	1
Göttingen	3	3	1
Hannover	8	4	5
Hildesheim	6	4	0
Lüneburg	3	3	1
Osnabrück	4	4	0
Stade	2	1	0
Verden	1	2	0
Other	0	4	0
Total	32	31	17

profession on the basis of gender, so that women could for the first time be admitted to the *Referendariat* preparatory to careers in government service or the private practice of law.[76] Theoretically, the legal faculties of German universities had been open to women since 1908, but the absence of career opportunities caused by the refusal of the government and lawyers in private practice to countenance the admission of women, as well as other social barriers, had kept female attendance at the legal faculties of universities quite low.[77] No women, then, were immediately able to take advantage of the new opportunity to enter private law practice.[78]

The official position of the lawyers' chamber in Celle was one of hostility to the admission of women to the bar. When requested in 1919 to render an opinion as to the proposed admission of women to practice, the executive board "expressed itself resolutely against the admission of women to the bar."[79] The private bar could not prevent the ultimate entry of women into private practice, however, and the first woman achieved admission to the bar in the province in September 1927 when Berta Schmidt of Duderstadt swore her professional oath before the district court there. Her father was a longtime district

76 See the discussion "Die Frau Rechtsanwalt," in Ostler, *Die deutschen Rechtsanwälte*, 169–74. For a discussion of the legal reforms necessary before women attained equal right of admission to the bar, see Margarethe Freiin von Erffa and Ingeborg Richarz-Simons, "Der weibliche Rechtsanwalt," in Magnus, ed., *Die Rechtsanwaltschaft*, 471–85, 471–7. More generally, see Deutscher Juristinnenbund, ed., *Juristinnen in Deutschland. Eine Dokumentation (1900–1989)*, 2d ed. (Frankfurt, 1989), 1–16.

77 At the University of Göttingen, the first record of a woman matriculating in the legal faculty is found during the winter semester 1908/09, when one woman enrolled out of a total of 411. That woman came from the province of Hannover, along with 169 men. Although the number of women studying law rose somewhat during the war, increasing to 9 out of 661 in the winter semester 1918/19, the real increase came after the war, and the enrollment peaked at 33 out of 829 in the summer semester 1922. Women law students, then, never constituted a large proportion of the total; *Amtliches Verzeichnis des Personals und der Studirenden der königlichen Georg-August-Universität zu Göttingen* (Göttingen), summer semester 1899–summer semester 1930, Universitätsarchiv der Georg-August-Universität zu Göttingen, and Niedersächsische Staats-und Universitätsbibliothek, Göttingen.

78 The period before 1922 has been summarized: "The history of women in the legal profession in Imperial Germany is thus almost no history at all"; James C. Albisetti, "Women and the Professions in Imperial Germany," in Ruth-Ellen B. Joeres and Mary Jo Maynes, eds., *German Women in the Eighteenth and Nineteenth Centuries* (Bloomington, Ind., 1986), 94–109, 95–6 (the quotation is from 96).

79 "Further, the executive board issued an opinion regarding the intended inclusion of women in the administration of justice. The executive board expressed itself decidedly against the admission of women to the private bar and declared other assistance of women in the administration of justice undesirable and not unobjectionable, with the exceptions of assistance as law judges in juvenile courts, with the decisions of the guardians' courts in cases under §§1666, 1673, and 1838 of the Civil Law Code, and in the jurisprudence in marital cases." G.St.A. I HA Rep. 84a, 21913, 207.

court lawyer in Duderstadt. Three other women effected their admission to the bar in 1931, two in the city of Hannover and one in Lüneburg, but the period of National Socialist rule ended the opportunity for women to enter the legal profession.[80] Although the admission of women to the bar furthered the realization of the liberal notion of "free path to the diligent," it had little social impact upon the bar in Hannover in the period in question.

Income

The question of the income of lawyers in private practice is one about which much was written and little can be precisely said. Lawyers filled the legal press, especially after 1900, with complaints about insufficient incomes. As subsequent chapters show, war, inflation, depression, and legislative reforms convinced lawyers that the state of their incomes had worsened.

Clearly, the income of lawyers was likely to vary greatly between individuals. Reputation for skill and success, good relations with other lawyers who might refer clients, and actual superiority in skill, knowledge, and discipline all increased a lawyer's chance for higher earnings, as a lack of any of these decreased his chance. Nevertheless, social observers tended to treat the private bar as a homogeneous group when classifying the German population by income level, as Gustav Schmoller did in 1897.[81] Lawyers themselves were very aware of the stratifications within the bar, especially as they manifested themselves in differences in the level of income among lawyers admitted to differing levels of courts.

---

80 See Mundt, *100 Jahre Rechtsanwaltskammer Celle*, 26–7. The proportion of women among German lawyers is still discouragingly low, amounting to 103, 5.7 percent, in the territory of the lawyers' chamber at Celle in 1979; ibid.

81 Schmoller included in his *oberer Mittelstand* of families with incomes between 2,700 and 8,000 marks (the highest group was that of families with incomes of more than 8–9,000 marks) "many members of the liberal professions." Although he did not refer specifically to lawyers, he expressly included medical doctors, and observers agreed that *average* lawyers' incomes exceeded average doctors' incomes. Gustav Schmoller, "Was verstehen wir unter dem Mittelstande? Hat er im 19. Jahrhundert zu- oder abgenommen?," *Verhandlungen des 8. Evangelisch-sozialen Kongresses 1897* (Göttingen, 1897), 132–61, 157–9. Huerkamp observed that in Saxony in the 1890s, lawyers' incomes were both higher than doctors' and also spread over a larger range, that some lawyers had extremely high incomes while others had extremely low ones; *Der Aufstieg der Ärzte*, 212–13.

In the summer of 1913, the DAV sent a questionnaire to all members inquiring as to their gross and net incomes from civil practice during the year 1911. Although 994 lawyers expressly refused to reveal their incomes, 432 returned the forms with complete responses. Those completed responses showed the average net income for the number of lawyers at the given level of court as shown in Table 5.20. According to this survey, then, income varied directly with the level of court before which a lawyer practiced.[82] Moreover, the largest proportion of respondents had relatively low incomes (Table 5.21). Of the respondents, then, more than three-quarters earned less than 6,000 marks while an elite of only five percent enjoyed *gross* incomes of more than ten-thousand marks.[83]

Incomes of lawyers actually appear to have improved after the First World War. Table 5.22 shows the gross receipts income (*Umsatz*) for lawyers in Germany the province of Hannover, and the cities of Hannover and Harburg for the year 1927. In Germany, fully 13.3 percent of all lawyers, and in the province of Hannover 10.7 percent, earned less than 3,000 RM net annually from law practice. In 1927, with the cost of living index standing at 148 percent of that of 1913, these lawyers earned in reality the same as lawyers earning 2,250 marks in 1913.[84] This proportion was significantly lower than the percentage of respondents to the 1913 questionnaire. Almost half of lawyers in the province, and more than half in the city of Hannover, earned more than 8,000 marks in constant terms; this is in marked contrast to the 5 percent who earned more than 10,000 and 23 percent who earned more than 6,000 in 1911.

Data concerning the income tax declarations of lawyers in 1928 confirmed this trend. More than half (54.4 percent) of all lawyers earned more than 12,000 RM annually, and the annual per capita income of lawyers was 18,428 RM (in contrast to 12,616 RM for medical doctors). Notably, however, lawyers' income varied in accordance with the size of the town in which they lived.[85] Law-

---

82 "Ergebnis der Umfrage über die Einkommensverhältnisse der Rechtsanwälte (Einkommen aus bürgerlichen Rechtsstreitigkeiten und Bureauunkosten)," *Abl* 1 (1914): Zugabe zu Nr. 6, June 1914, Tabelle II, 8–9.
83 Ibid., Tabelle VI, 12.
84 Gerhard Bry, *Wages in Germany 1871–1945* (Princeton, 1960), table A-1, 325–9, 326–7.
85 Statistisches Reichsamt, *Wirtschaft und Statistik* 12 (1932): 242–43, "Die Einkommensverhältnisse in einigen freien Berufen."

Table 5.20.   *Average net income from civil cases,*
1911

Level of court	Responses	Average income
Court of appeal	63	7,009.68 marks
Superior court	242	4,934.62
District court	127	3,464.48
All lawyers	432	4,805.06

Table 5.21.   *Income distribution, 1911*

Income	Number of lawyers	Percentage
< 3,000 M.	158	36.6
3–6,000 M.	175	40.5
6–10,000 M.	75	17.3
> 10,000 M.	24	5.6
Total	432	100.0

yers who practiced in larger cities, usually the seats of superior courts and courts of appeal, earned more money on the average than lawyers in small towns. All lawyers earned more on the average, in constant terms, than the respondents to the questionnaire of 1913 (see Table 5.23).

Observers, however, interpreted these statistics as confirmation of the severely straitened economic circumstances of German lawyers.[86] No doubt 1927 and 1928 had been the best years of the postwar period for the German economy in general, so that the material condition of lawyers could have worsened appreciably by 1931 and 1932. Regardless, despite apparent real gains in income, lawyers and others remained convinced that their economic situation was deteriorating frighteningly in the early 1930s.

The few available archival sources on the incomes of lawyers in the province of Hannover show that, while the income of lawyers was often low during the first years of their careers in private practice, in many cases it would rise to high levels later in their

86 Karl C. Thalheim, "Die Einkommenslage der deutschen Rechtsanwälte," *JW* 60 (1931): 3497–3500, and idem, "Neues Material zur Wirtschaftslage der Anwaltschaft," *JW* 61 (1932): 3554–8.

Table 5.22.   *Gross receipts income for lawyers and notaries, 1927*

Income (1,000 RM)	Number lawyers	Percent lawyers	60% of Income	Constant value (1913=100)
Germany				
< 5	1,847	13.3	<3	<2
5–20	6,052	43.6	3–12	2–8.1
20–50	4,547	32.8	12–30	8.1–20.3
50–100	1,150	8.3	30–60	20.3–40.5
100–500	283	2.0	60–300	40.5–202.7
Total	13,879	100.0		
Province of Hannover				
< 5	62	10.7	<3	< 2
5–20	238	41.2	3–12	2–8.1
20–50	206	35.6	12–30	8.1–20.3
50–100	61	10.6	30–60	20.3–40.5
100–500	11	1.9	60–300	40.5–202.7
Total	578	100.0		
City of Hannover				
< 5	20	11.0	<3	< 2
5–20	63	34.6	3–12	2–8.1
20–50	74	40.7	12–30	8.1–20.3
50–100	18	9.9	30–60	20.3–40.5
100–500	7	3.8	60–300	40.5–202.7
Total	182	100.0		
City of Harburg-Wilhelmsburg				
< 5	3	17.6	<3	< 2
5–20	3	17.6	3–12	2–8.1
20–50	7	41.2	12–30	8.1–20.3
50–100	4	23.5	30–60	20.3–40.5
100–500	0	0.0	60–300	40.5–202.7
Total	17	100.0		

Source: Statistisches Reichsamt, *Statistik des Deutschen Reichs*, vol. 361 (Berlin, 1931), "Umsatz und Umsatzsteuer in Deutschland nach den Umsatzsteuerveranlagungen 1926 bis 1928," 113.

careers. According to his income tax declarations, Carl Böning (born in 1863), who practiced before the court of appeal in Celle, earned 2,400 marks during his first year of practice in 1893. The son of a lawyer at the district court in Emden, his income first exceeded 10,000 marks in 1897, 25,000 marks in 1909, and peaked at 30,390 in 1914 before receding to roughly 25,000 annually dur-

Table 5.23. *Lawyers' income in 1928*

Size of town		Number of lawyers	Average income
Under	2,000	322	11,873 RM
2,000 to	5,000	1,058	11,455
5,000 to	10,000	1,008	12,959
10,000 to	25,000	1,409	15,535
25,000 to	50,000	1,264	18,373
50,000 to	100,000	1,222	18,187
over	100,000	8,379	20,749
All lawyers		14,662	18,428 RM

ing the war.[87] In contrast, the practice of his colleague at the court of appeal, Hans Naumann (born in 1864), did not prosper as quickly. From 3,536 marks in his first year of practice, 1894, his income exceeded 11,000 marks both in 1897 and 1898 but fell below 10,000 marks the next year and remained below that figure until 1904. A third-generation lawyer, whose father had also practiced in Celle (but who had died in 1892) and whose uncle practiced in Lüneburg, Naumann's income soared after 1910 to 24,634 marks in 1911, 37,396 in 1913, and 42,156 in 1915 before falling sharply during the remaining years of the war (5,167 marks during 1918).[88] Similarly, in August Borchers' first five years of practice before the court of appeal (1900–4), his income never exceeded 6,600 marks. Thereafter, it was approximately 10,000 marks annually until 1910, when it jumped to almost 20,000. His peak income was 25,100 marks in 1914 before it declined during the war.[89] In both Naumann's and Borchers' cases, their income from investments rose to the point at which it exceeded their income from law practice, at which point their income from professional activity began to decline.

A lawyer from the superior court in the city of Hannover, Hermann Poppelbaum, had the most spectacular increase in professional earnings. In his first year of practice, 1897, he earned 5,000

87 N.H.St.A., Hann. 141, 67. Böning served as chair of the executive board of the lawyers' chamber from 1925 to 1928.
88 N.H.St.A., Hann. 141, 117.
89 N.H.St.A., Hann. 141, 72. Borchers served on the executive board of the lawyers' chamber from 1925 to 1933, from 1928 to 1933 as secretary.

marks. By 1901 his income exceeded 11,000 marks, reaching 21,195 in 1908, 39,635 in 1913, 58,363 in 1914, and remaining in excess of 40,000 marks through 1919.[90] Poppelbaum, a member of the executive board of the lawyers' chamber in Celle from 1914 to 1933, depended more than Naumann and Borchers upon his income from fees rather than investments for his total income. Finally, Felix Rosenberg was first admitted to practice before the superior court in Berlin in 1887. His income there between 1893 and 1897 averaged around 7,000 marks. In 1898 he moved to Hameln and set up a practice before the district court. His first year's income (1898) was 4,552 marks and his second even lower, 2,332. By 1903, however, his income exceeded 10,000 marks and averaged around 15,000 marks annually until 1919.[91] The move to Hameln, where he had no apparent local ties, allowed him to support his father, a retired lawyer, as he built a successful practice. Modest in comparison to the other examples given here, his income nonetheless placed him in the upper economic reaches of the bar, according to the survey of income in 1911.

While it cannot be shown that these few data are representative of the bar as a whole, they do support several conclusions. Many lawyers earned a handsome living. While incomes were low as lawyers first built their practices, they often increased dramatically as their careers matured. Often lawyers saved and invested or inherited wealth, and as their investments grew they came to rely less upon their professional income. Lawyers who practiced before collegial courts earned more than those who practiced before district courts, although the greatest opportunities for very high earnings appear to have been concentrated in the city of Hannover. This difference from the national pattern can be explained by the fact that Celle was one of the smallest seats of courts of appeal in Germany and there was no superior court there to augment lawyers' incomes. Thus, Hannover varied in this particular from the national pattern. Finally, an outsider could come into a district court town, albeit a large one, even in midcareer, and earn a very comfortable living. Although the First World War in many cases disrupted practices and reduced lawyers' incomes, legitimate complaints about sinking or threatened incomes must have come from lawyers other than these lawyer-notables.

---

90 N.H.St.A., Hann. 141, 315.   91 N.H.St.A., Hann. 141, 234.

Conclusions

On the surface and in the broadest terms, the bar in the province of Hannover shared the experience of the German bar as a whole between 1879 and 1933 as it grew dramatically in size (especially after 1900), diversified in social origin and confessional identity, and accelerated in geographic mobility. The social base of the Hannoverian bar as a whole shifted away from the traditional classes of university attenders in Germany and toward entrepreneurial business groups, as *freie Advokatur* convinced businessmen-fathers that open career paths could reward investment in legal education for their sons. Jews too could now study law secure in the knowledge that they could not be denied entry into the profession for invidious reasons. This expansion of the bar permitted hitherto excluded groups to enter the private practice of law. In geographic terms, expansion meant that lawyers penetrated new markets for legal services, especially moving into smaller district-court towns but also serving the seemingly insatiable needs of the industrial-commercial cities of Hannover, Harburg, and Geestemünde-Lehe. Lawyers increasingly launched themselves into practice in these new markets, far afield from their town of birth.

But a closer analysis of the patterns of change in the private bar in Hannover reveals differentiations that help to explain many of the tensions and frictions among lawyers that played themselves out on the national level. Growth was not evenly distributed among the various levels of courts or even among the courts at the same level. The superior court of the city of Hannover expanded fastest until 1910 and again in the 1920s, while the district court bar expanded sharply between 1905 and 1914. As a result, lawyers who practiced in the seven superior courts *other than* Hannover, especially the rural superior courts in Aurich, Lüneburg, Stade, and Verden, saw their numerical importance diminish; in other words they experienced a *relative* decline as they were squeezed between these two more dynamic sectors. Small-city superior court lawyers thus developed inchoate interest conflicts both with large-city superior court lawyers and all district court lawyers. Similarly, district court lawyers and lawyers in the city of Hannover each had separate and sometimes conflicting interests.

Moreover, diversification of social and geographic origin and confessional identity added another layer of differentiation to the bar. More sons of businessmen sought admission to practice before superior courts than district courts, introducing a new form of social mobility from *Besitzbürgertum* to *Bildungsbürgertum*. The vastly more pronounced tendency of sons of businessmen to practice in the city of Hannover, however, makes even this generalization deceptive. At the seven other superior-court cities, self-recruitment of lawyers' sons and recruitment from other traditional social groups (especially other university-trained academics) remained far more important sources of new lawyers. The greatest diversity of social origin characterized the district court bar, although these courts remained the stronghold of a more traditional form of social mobility, as they welcomed the largest proportion of sons of lower government officials and of the *Mittelstand*. Confessionally, too, a segmented bar emerged, as rural superior courts remained mostly Lutheran, the bar in Hannover opened the most to Jews, and Catholics remained clustered in cities with high Catholic populations.

Under the hard-won terms of the RAO and the Imperial Justice Laws, this increasingly large, diverse, and segmented Hannoverian bar faced the necessity of governing itself through the lawyers' chamber. As the analysis of the geographic, social, and confessional characteristics of the executive board reveals, its composition did not change over time to reflect the diversification of the bar, although some reform measures occurred. Through the tradition of geographic representation of each superior court on the executive board in Celle, superior court lawyers enjoyed institutional influence and power disproportionate to their share of the bar as a whole. As a result, while these lawyers, and those at the court of appeal in Celle, were overrepresented, those in the city of Hannover and in district courts were underrepresented. Such an arrangement could work as long as lawyers conceived of themselves as a unitary profession with common interests; the underrepresented groups would thus elect the lawyer-notables at the annual assemblies of the lawyers' chambers and defer to their judgment in making decisions throughout the year. But as the inchoate conflicts of interest among the various segments of the bar became sharper, conflict would emerge that would express itself in efforts to control the shaping of professional ideology, the application of professional self-discipline, and ultimately in a struggle for control of professional institutions. The growth and diversification of the Hannoverian bar thus tended to reinforce certain structural conflicts of interest already inherent in the framework created for lawyers by the RAO.

6

Elites and Professional Ideology: Self-Discipline and Self-Administration by the Anwaltskammer *Celle*

In the same way that the Imperial Justice Laws changed the circumstances in which individuals had to make decisions about entering the private legal profession, structuring their careers, and leading their lives, lawyers in the newly created lawyers' chambers faced corporate decisions about how to structure professional life. The lawyers' chamber, a juridical person under public law, with its seat in the city in which the court of appeal lay, was the principal organ for the new self-government.[1] The provisions of the Lawyers' Statute (RAO) provided lawyers laconic guidance and a bare framework for self-government, leaving it to their own initiative how to flesh out the direction and governance of their professional and even their private lives.

The ways that lawyers in the province of Hannover invented and administered rules for self-government and self-discipline between 1879 and 1933 reinforce the picture of a hierarchical profession, whose elite governed and expected deference to their governance and used the institutional structures of *Honoratioren-politik* to perpetuate their power and corporate conceptions of honor. By the twentieth century, and especially by the 1920s and early 1930s, inchoate conflicts among groups of lawyers began to be reflected in contests for influence within and control of professional institutions. As dissent and dissatisfaction emerged into the open, the legitimacy of those professional institutions and of their control by lawyer-notables at the higher courts fell into question. In order to understand how those struggles played out on the national level, one must first analyze how they manifested themselves on the local level.

1   Friedländer and Friedländer, *Kommentar zur Rechtsanwaltsordnung*, 336–7.

Between 1879 and 1933, a group of lawyer-notables who practiced before the various higher, collegial courts of the province dominated the Hannoverian lawyers' chamber in Celle, jealously guarding the new independence of the bar from state interference, promoting the economic interests of the bar as a whole, and protecting its public reputation. They also exerted their efforts wherever possible to limit admission to the bar, closely regulated the acceptable forms of economic competition among lawyers, enforced corporate principles of the importance of private personal behavior to professional status and reputation, and expected deference to their actions from all other members of the provincial bar. Because of the conflict of interests between groups of lawyers who practiced before different levels of courts (especially between lawyers at small rural superior courts and district court lawyers), exacerbated by their difference in social origin, a gap opened between the lawyer-notables who formed the establishment of the bar and much of the rank and file. The resulting tensions and conflicts proved detrimental to the claim of the lawyer-notables and the organizations that they dominated to speak on behalf of the entire bar. While the following three chapters explore the principle conflicts and cleavages within the bar, which exploded lawyers' claim to represent the common interest, this chapter examines the emergence of the rules of professional behavior and governance in the record of the lawyers' chamber in Celle and the frictions and tensions that arose as lawyers created their new professional existence and administered their corporate life during the professional, political, and economic changes between 1878 and 1933.

The Hannoverian lawyers' chamber in Celle throughout this period pursued at least three clearly discernible policies: to protect the traditional field of employment of lawyers from challenge from competitors or from new legislative intrusions; to limit or eliminate economic competition among lawyers, even if that meant the acceptance of some limitations upon free entry to the bar; and to punish behavior in the professional or private lives of lawyers that might bring the profession into disrepute in the eyes of the public or that violated generally held norms of collegial and moral behavior. In the course of institutionalizing these policies, it both confirmed and created inchoate cleavages that eroded the unified voice of the bar and contributed to the marginalization of the influence of professional institutions.

The Statutory Framework

The RAO charged each lawyers' chamber with the drafting of bylaws to govern its actions, the levying of dues on its members to pay for its necessary activities (§48), and the election of an executive board (§43, §42). The executive board wielded the principle administrative responsibility and power of the lawyers' chamber. It exercised oversight over lawyers' fulfillment of their professional duties and administered disciplinary authority; it mediated in disputes among chamber members and between chamber members and clients; it rendered advisory opinions upon request by the ministry of justice or a court in disputes between lawyers and clients; and it administered the property of the chamber (§49). Most importantly, it elected from within its ranks a disciplinary panel to hear disciplinary cases against members of the chamber (§67). Although ultimate authority lay with the plenary membership of the chamber through the election of the executive board by absolute majority (§54), in reality the board exercised almost total power. The actions of the plenary assemblies of the membership of the chamber in Celle, held only annually, or, in extraordinary cases, more frequently (but only to elect replacements for deceased board members) were limited almost entirely to the election (usually reelection) of the members of the board, the approval of the annual report, and the approval of the amount of dues for the next year. The few initiatives that arose at annual meetings at the instance of lawyers *other than* those on the executive board met with defeat. The plenary assembly thus delegated almost complete authority to the executive board as a self-perpetuating panel of lawyer-notables, whose actions became the official policy of the bar of the province of Hannover.

The important functions that the executive board exercised gave it great power and influence over the newly freed private bar. First, by rendering advisory opinions to the ministry of justice on applications for admission (§3), giving it the first opportunity to invoke the mandatory (§5) or permissive (§6) grounds for denial of admission, the executive board effectively served as the new gatekeeper for admission into the profession. Appeals from a denial of admission lay to the disciplinary board, elected by and composed of members of the executive board (§16, ¶2). Second, the general public, clients, courts, or other governmental authorities who had complaints about the conduct of a lawyer lodged them with the executive board, which either dismissed them or found them to be well grounded. If the board ruled a complaint well grounded, it either rebuked the accused lawyer or referred the case to the state prosecutor to consider whether to open a disciplinary case. Thus, the executive board was both the public face of the legal profession for private citizens who sought redress from malfeasance by lawyers and also the wielder of disciplinary authority over lawyers. Third, in its function of providing advisory opinions to authorities, ostensibly the opinion of the entire bar in its bailiwick, the executive board served as the official voice of the bar in matters of attorney's fees, legislation, economic interest, and other professional concerns. This chapter focusses particularly upon the positions taken by the executive board of the lawyers' chamber in Celle regarding the internal organization of the bar, its gatekeeping functions in admission cases, disciplinary complaints and cases, and in its advisory opinions on matters of importance to lawyers to reveal more closely the attitudes of Hannoverian lawyers toward their new free-market professional organization, and the generally accepted standards of personal and professional conduct held by lawyers in Hannover.

The lawyers' chamber for the court of appeal at Celle met first on 29 November 1879, and again on 31 January 1880. At the second meeting, the chamber elected an executive board of fifteen members (all of whom practiced before higher courts) and adopted a set of bylaws governing the functioning of the chamber.[2] The bylaws set forth no institutional purpose for the activity of the chamber, adopting *sub silentio* those enumerated in the RAO. With these initial organizational efforts, however, the story of the existence and development of the Hannoverian practicing bar entered its modern phase.

Reflecting both the pre-1879 (indeed pre-1866) centrality of the court of appeal in Celle to the bar and to the entire legal system in the

---

2 *Geschäftsordnung* (1880; hereafter cited as "GO [year]"), G.St.A. I HA Rep. 84a, 21912, 9–27. Hermann Mundt gives an account of this meeting in which he emphasizes the fact that already at this early date, district court lawyers made up a majority of the practicing bar in Hannover; Mundt, *100 Jahre Rechtsanwaltskammer*, 18–19. Mundt, the former office manager (*Geschäftsführer*) of the lawyers' chamber between 1945 and 1975, based his work in sources including "documents of the court of appeal and lawyers' chamber in Celle" and "protocols of the plenary meetings and executive board meetings of the lawyers' chamber in Celle"; ibid., 107. No such records were available upon inquiry at the court of appeal, and the lawyers' chamber indicated that it had no records for the period in question. Letters from Schröder, Geschäftsführer der Rechtsanwaltskammer für den Oberlandesgerichtsbezirk Celle, to author, 11 November 1985, and 27 May 1986.

province of Hannover, the bylaws provided that the chairman and secretary of the executive board "shall regularly be elected from among the members of the chamber living at the seat of the chamber" (By-Laws [1880] §8). In effect, the bylaws required that the two presiding officers be elected from among lawyers who practiced before the court of appeal in Celle. The peculiarly Hannoverian situation, in which the town of the court of appeal did not also host a superior court, thus limited eligibility for these high offices to a small group of lawyer-notables.[3] The executive board elected its officers (chairman, vice-chairman, secretary, and vice-secretary) from within its ranks. The custom arose whereby the chairman and secretary were always members of the bar in Celle, as required, while their deputies were always members of the bar in the city of Hannover, the site of the largest concentration of lawyers in the province and the commercial and transport hub of the province.[4]

Meetings of the board could occur at the seat of the chamber or in a town that was the seat of a superior court (By-Laws [1880] §9). For purposes of mediating disputes between lawyers or between lawyer and client (RAO §49, ¶¶ 2 and 3), the board appointed individual members from among lawyers practicing before the appropriate superior court as delegates for each superior court district (By-Laws [1880] §11). Thus, from the very beginning and throughout the period in question, lawyers conceived of and operated the executive board of the lawyers' chamber in Celle as a geographically representative institution; at all times, at least one member of the board came from among the lawyers practicing before each of the superior courts. As will be considered further on, this idea of representativeness did not include district court lawyers, and this proved to be an increasing source of contention after 1900.

The executive board also elected from its midst the disciplinary panel (literally "court of honor," *Ehrengericht*) to hear and decide disciplinary cases. The RAO determined its membership in part, for the chairman and vice-chairman (hence, one lawyer from Celle and one from Hannover) were automatically members (§67); the board elected three additional members. Each year the board designated the

---

3 Mundt indicates that every chairman of the executive board until 1977 came from among the court of appeal lawyers in Celle; ibid., 19.
4 This pattern is discerned from the annual activity reports of the lawyers' chamber from 1880 to 1933, found at G. St. A. I HA Rep. 84a, 21912–13, and N.H. St. A., Hann. 173, Acc. 30/87, 30, *passim.*

order in which its remaining members would serve as substitutes. Nevertheless, the dominance of collegial court lawyers on the executive board ensured that they would also dominate the disciplinary panel.

The RAO provided that the executive board should have a minimum of nine members and a maximum of fifteen (§42), with the exact number to be determined by the bylaws. At the organizational meeting of the chamber in Celle on 29 November 1879, it elected an executive board of nine members, but the bylaws of 31 January 1880, increased the size to the maximum of fifteen (By-Laws [1880] §2).[5] Incumbents held the powerful position of chairman until retirement or death, and the incumbent secretary usually succeeded them.[6] Incumbent members of the executive board as a whole tended to serve until they stepped down. Elections were not contested and changes occurred only when members chose not to stand for reelection, retired or otherwise left the bar of the district, or died. Long terms of service were thus the rule, as the same members conducted the business of the board, and hence the chamber, year after year.[7] Members of the executive board, then, constituted a self-perpetuating corps of lawyer-notables, increasingly unrepresentative of the bar as a whole.

Admission Policy

Perhaps the most important and revealing of the activities of the executive board was its function of rendering advisory opinions on the merits of applications for admission to the bar. Under the terms of the RAO, the ministry of justice of a federal state decided whether

5   G.St.A. I HA Rep. 84a, 21912, 1a, 9. An amendment to the RAO in 1923 raised the maximum permissible number to twenty, and another in 1927 to thirty-six; Friedländer and Friedländer, *Kommentar zur Rechtsanwaltsordnung*, 344. The lawyers' chamber in Celle took this opportunity in early 1924 to expand to twenty members; G.St.A. I HA Rep. 84a, 21913, 229; a copy of the 1924 bylaws is found in N.H.St.A., Hann. 173, Acc. 30/87, 30, 50–5. The board adopted proportional representation in 1928, requiring that three members come from the court of appeal in Celle, six from the superior court in Hannover, eight from the remaining superior courts, and six from district courts outside of superior court towns. Mundt, *100 Jahre Rechtsanwaltskammer*, 29–30, indicates that the board expanded to twenty-three in 1928, but the archival record nowhere reflects such an action.

6   In one case in which the secretary did not succeed (and instead the vice-secretary did), he remained secretary and became chairman the next time the position fell vacant.

7   For example, Dr. Gustav Meyer of Celle served on the executive board from 1893 to 1924, as secretary from 1893 to 1907 and as chairman from 1907 to 1924.

to grant applications, but only after receipt of advice from the executive board *before* making its decision (§3).[8] The RAO thereby gave the executive board an opportunity to attempt to shape policy regarding the interpretation of the mandatory and permissive grounds for refusal of admission (§5, §6). Moreover, other provisions of the RAO presented opportunities to the executive board to restrict admission by means of strict interpretation and application of the rules if it so desired. An analysis of how the executive board of the lawyers' chamber in Celle exercised its gatekeeping function over entry into the profession reveals both the kinds of behavior that lawyers believed disqualified applicants from admission and the types of persons whom those lawyers considered undesirable colleagues.

Application for admission to the bar necessarily specified a particular court under the system of localization set up by the RAO. Thus, applications could occur (1) when a candidate who had passed the second bar examination decided to enter private practice, (2) when a lawyer from another court of appeal district first sought admission to the bar in Hannover, or (3) when a lawyer already admitted before a court in Hannover sought admission before another court, that is, sought to move from one court to another. Similar but separate provisions of the RAO governed these situations (§5, §6 for first-time applicants, §15 for applicants for admission at "another" court). Each event, either initial application for admission or subsequent move, evoked a review by the executive board of the applicant's suitability. Such reviews occupied much of the time of the board in Celle, and, although negative decisions were relatively rare, the grounds for denial displayed the means by which the board sought both to protect the integrity and professional standards of the bar and, especially in later years, to invoke the letter of the law as stringently as possible in order to limit as best they could the growing flood of admissions.

In the first thirty years of the chamber's existence, the executive board denied only nineteen applications for initial or subsequent admission (compared to 518 total admissions). These denials fell into three categories: cases in which disciplinary cases were pending against the applicants (1882, 1894), cases in which the applicant also occupied a state or communal office that created or could create a conflict of interest with his private legal practice (1883, 1884, 1891,

---

8 Friedländer and Friedländer, *Kommentar zur Rechtsanwaltsordnung*, 26–7, were of the opinion that such consultation was in fact mandatory.

1895, 1901, 1902), and cases in which the applicant was not a Prussian citizen and had not passed the second bar examination in Prussia (1888, 1901). The executive board thereby established three policy rules for applications for admission. First, the board would not permit a lawyer against whom a disciplinary case was pending to be admitted to practice at another location before its resolution. It applied this rule in one case even when the disciplinary proceeding was in its investigatory stages (1894).[9] The board in effect adopted as a mandatory rule the permissive provision of RAO §15, ¶2. A lawyer who stood accused of a disciplinary offense thus could not move to a new court until his case had been concluded.

The second rule can be discerned from the denial of admission to applicants who occupied state or communal offices, the exercise of which might conflict with the free practice of law or somehow bring obloquy upon the legal profession. In both 1883 and 1884, the board refused admission to an applicant who sought to practice before the same district court at which he served as *Amtsanwalt* or lower-court prosecutor, declaring that the two professions were not compatible (RAO §5, ¶4).[10] Moreover, in eight additional cases the board refused admission to applicants who either were or were about to become *Bürgermeister* of small towns.[11] The board first confronted the issue in three cases in 1891 and stated:

The executive board ruled that the private practice of law *for* and *against* residents of the city in which the lawyer wished to serve as *Bürgermeister* was contrary to the interests of the bar in private practice, adding however that admission could not be denied as long as the applicant did not serve as *Bürgermeister*.

Despite this opinion against admission by the executive board, the ministry of justice granted unlimited admission to the applicants. By 1895 the board and the ministry had reached an agreement on the issue. This time, three applicants who were already *Bürgermeister* sought admission. The board repeated its position that for a communal official to appear as a lawyer in cases involving citizens of the town in which he served would be damaging to the public image of the legal profession. The board placed the onus on the applicants, ruling

9   G.St.A. I HA Rep. 84a, 21912, 216, expressly invoking RAO §15, ¶2.
10 Ibid., 52R, 83R. An *Amtsanwalt* was an official who could perform the functions of state prosecutor (*Staatsanwalt*) only before a district court (*Amtsgericht*), and generally only in cases heard by a single judge (thus excluding jury trials, etc.); GVG, §142, §145.
11 1891 (three cases), 1895 (three cases), 1901, and 1902. G.St.A. I HA Rep. 84a, 21912, 195R, 231, 305, 314R.

that the office of *Bürgermeister* can only be combined with the private practice of law when the lawyer renounces the acceptance of briefs for and against members of the city commune in which he serves as *Bürgermeister*.[12]

Two applicants made the required renunciation and were admitted. The third applicant declined to renounce such briefs, and the ministry of justice refused to admit him. This result settled the issue, for similar outcomes were reached in 1901 and 1902. The executive board thereby established the second rule that the private practice of law was not compatible with the holding of official positions when the duties of those offices could cause actual or apparent conflict of interest with the duties of a lawyer to represent his client impartially and aggressively.

Finally, between 1881 and 1910 the executive board established the third rule that the permissive provisions of RAO §2 would *not* be exercised in the district of the court of appeal in Celle to grant admission to persons who had not passed the second bar examination *in Prussia*. The "freedom of entry" into the bar established by the reforms of 1877–9 entitled a person who had passed the second bar examination to admission as a matter of right *only* in the federal state in which he had passed it (RAO §4). Admission in a different federal state was a matter left to the discretion of the ministry of justice of that state, after hearing the opinion of the executive board of the appropriate lawyers' chamber (RAO §2). The executive board in Celle in 1888 advised against the admission of an applicant who had passed the second examination in the Duchy of Braunschweig (which had close historical and geographic ties to the province of Hannover) rather than the Kingdom of Prussia.[13] Again in 1901, a *Bürgermeister* of a town in another federal state applied for admission before a nearby district court in Hannover, and his application was refused altogether.[14] Thus, as the executive board interpreted the RAO, entry into the bar was open, but only to those who had undergone their training and testing in Prussia.[15]

12 G.St.A. I HA Rep. 84a, 21912, 231.
13 G.St.A. I HA Rep. 84a, 21912, 160R. The applicant in question apparently had other unspecified objectionable material in his official record from the *Referendariat* and *Assessorenzeit*; ibid.
14 G.St.A. I HA Rep. 84a, 21912, 305.
15 Particularly in southern Hannover and in the Harz Mountains, but also in western Hannover and East Frisia, the boundaries between the province and the Duchy of Braunschweig and the Grand Duchy of Oldenburg were extremely convoluted, with numerous enclaves and exclaves. Where political and administrative borders did not coincide with natural economic regions, occasions for frictions and competition among law-

After 1910, and especially after 1918, the pace at which the executive board refused admission increased. The board rejected 101 applicants (as compared to 878 total admissions), but the principles for refusing admission remained much the same as before. The board in Celle refused admission to applicants from other lawyers' chambers who had been convicted of disciplinary offenses within the past two years (RAO §6, ¶1).[16] Between 1915 and 1932, twenty-four applicants met refusal under the provisions of RAO §5 and §6 because of moral failures or physical or mental debility.[17] The board denied the applications of six lawyers who sought to move to new courts.[18] Likewise, it refused to admit six applicants who had passed the second bar examination in states other than Prussia.[19] The board also had to face a new and growing phenomenon: the so-called *Syndikusanwälte*, who were salaried lawyers in the employ of commercial enterprises, voluntary associations, or other institutions. Beginning in 1921, the board considered and rejected the applications of twelve such lawyers, five in 1925 alone.[20] While commentators, the German Bar Association, and the supreme disciplinary court in Leipzig all agreed that salaried employment did not automatically disqualify an applicant from admission to the bar, the executive board in Celle did not inquire into the particulars of the employment contract to see whether the position were so subordinate as to be beneath the dignity of a lawyer or whether the compensation were so low as to represent unfair competition. The board rejected the applications of *Syndiken* out of hand, thereby attempting to limit to a small degree the flood of lawyers into the profession in the 1920s.

Thus, the pattern of decision making by the executive board on questions of admission reveals two goals. The first goal was to protect the bar from the admission of unsavory or disreputable

yers of different federal states multiplied. For criticism of the confused borders, see Kurt Brüning, *Niedersachsen im Rahmen der Neugliederung des Reiches*, vol. 2, *Beispiele über Auswirkungen der Ländergrenzen auf Verwaltung und Wirtschaft*, 2d ed. (Bad Pyrmont, 1931), esp. 21–30 regarding court administration.

16   In 1912, 1913, 1917, and 1919.
17   One each in 1915, 1916, 1918, 1921, and 1924; two in 1919 and 1927; three in 1926; six in 1928; one in 1929; one in 1931; and three in 1932.
18   1915, 1916, 1919, 1925, 1928, and 1931.   19   1912, 1913, 1920, 1925, 1926, and 1930.
20   One each in 1921 and 1927; three in 1924, five in 1925, and two in 1926. Friedländer and Friedländer, *Kommentar zur Rechtsanwaltsordnung*, 36–44, indicate that the "so-called *Syndikus* problem" had attained an extraordinarily practical importance in the postwar period, for during those unsettled times many lawyers sought the security of salaried positions.

persons. The objections, however, always spoke to the conduct or condition of the applicant or to real or potential conflicts of interest, and never openly to the person of the applicant, in terms of social or geographic origin. The board denied admission to judges or other state officials who had been dismissed for misconduct, to candidates who had received bad evaluations during their period of practical legal training, and to lawyers from other court of appeal districts who were the subject of pending disciplinary proceedings or who had been convicted of such offenses within the previous two years. It thereby protected the reputation and prestige of the bar in the eye of the public and avoided future problems that could arise if successful applicants proved to be repeat offenders. The board rejected some applicants for health reasons also in order to prevent possible conflict with the public in the case of disappointed expectations. It refused to permit lawyers to move to another court while disciplinary proceedings pended, again to localize the potential or actual damage to the reputation of the profession. Finally, the board sought to avoid problems of actual or potential conflict of interest by refusing to admit state and communal officials whose official responsibilities might interfere with their loyalty as representatives in private legal matters. All of these refusals had at their heart the avoidance of any diminution in the public's esteem for the private bar.

The second aim of the executive board in Celle was to do as much as was in its power to reduce economic competition among lawyers within the chamber by restricting admission in those cases in which it had some influence. The board could do nothing about applicants who had been trained and tested in Prussia and therefore possessed a right to admission. But from early on it refused admission to those who had passed the second examination in another federal state. Moreover, during the 1920s and early 1930s, when the economic crisis of the bar deepened and grew chronic, the executive board consistently denied admission to salaried lawyers. While the number of refusals of admission paled compared to the number of effected admissions, the actions of the executive board showed that it was sensitive to the problem of overcrowding. The board thus pursued the double purpose of the jealous protection of the public reputation of the bar *and* the limitation of economic competition among members of the bar, to the extent permitted by the free-entry principles of the RAO.

Complaints and Disciplinary Cases

Perhaps the most important function of the executive board was its duty to receive and decide upon complaints about the conduct of lawyers and to constitute a disciplinary panel to try the facts of more serious violations. In this capacity, the board served as the protector of the public interest *and* of the professional interests of the bar. It resolved disputes between lawyers and clients, thus preserving the reputation of the bar as a self-policing body. It mediated between the bar as a whole and state officials who retained supervisory functions over lawyers, thus guarding the bar from state interference.

The RAO (§28) described the professional duties of a lawyer only in vague terms:

The lawyer is obligated to practice his professional activity conscientiously, and through his conduct in the practice of the profession, as well as outside the same, to show himself worthy of the esteem that his profession requires.[21]

The precise meaning of the general obligation for a lawyer to act in a manner "worthy of the esteem that his profession requires" remained for lawyers themselves to fill in. The leading commentary on the profession emphasized that the sources of its ethics were rarely found in positive law but instead in "norms" and "customary law"; collective opinion (*communis opinio*) elevated the morals of the profession (and the term tellingly used is *Stand*) to the status of law.[22] Thus, the decisions of the individual lawyers' chambers and of the appellate disciplinary court in Leipzig created a kind of common law of discipline. No codification of disciplinary rules appeared until 1929, when the DAV, the *voluntary* national bar association, published its *Guidelines for the Practice of the Legal Profession*.[23] The practice of disciplinary panels like that of the lawyers' chamber in Celle thus constituted the *communis opinio*, the common law of professional discipline, and is the most important source of evidence on lawyers' view of the proper relationship among state, profession, and client. It both expressed and established generally accepted norms of personal and professional behavior,

---

21 Friedländer and Friedländer, *Kommentar zum Rechtsanwaltsordnung*, 132, described the whole section that describes the rights and duties of lawyers as the "most fragmentary of the law," in no way encompassing the entire scope of the regulation of rights and duties. They inserted for reference a "Short Code of Honor" (*Exkurs II zu §28, Kleiner Ehrenkodex*), in which they presented a code of professional ethics; ibid., 166–201.

22 Friedländer and Friedländer, *Kommentar zur Rechtsanwaltsordnung*, "Exkurs II zu §28. Kleiner Ehrenkodex," 166–201, 167–8.

23 Deutscher Anwaltverein, *Richtlinien für die Ausübung des Anwaltsberufs* (Leipzig, 1929).

determining which shortcomings were deemed most serious and which were forgivable. In its administration of the self-discipline of the bar, the executive board of the lawyers' chamber in Celle sought to protect lawyers from criticism from without and indiscipline and corruption within and to establish and enforce hegemonic patterns of behavior.

COMPLAINTS

The executive board as a whole bore the responsibility to receive and rule on complaints about the conduct of lawyers from clients, members of the general public, courts and other governmental authorities, and the state prosecutor (RAO §49, ¶¶ 1, 2, 3). In Celle the chairman conducted the initial review, with authority to reject complaints from private persons that were "openly unsuitable," subject to later confirmation by the board as a whole (By-Laws §14, ¶2). The plenary board ruled upon complaints from courts or other authorities and the more serious complaints from private persons. It requested the accused lawyer to respond to the charges and to justify his actions.[24] If the explanation was satisfactory, the matter ended. If not, the board sought always to resolve the dispute through mediation. If the complaint proved true and substantial, the board had four options. It could simply find the complaint meritorious and warn the lawyer against any repetition. It could disapprove or condemn the conduct (*Mißbilligung*) or censure or reprimand the lawyer (*Rüge*). Finally, for the most serious offenses, it referred the matter to the superior state prosecutor in Celle to determine whether formal disciplinary proceedings should be instituted.[25]

Complaints against the conduct of lawyers are an inevitable part of the practice of law. Some clients will always be disappointed with the efforts of their counsel to prosecute their cases. Others will also dispute the calculation of the fees that they owe for professional services. Disappointment is almost always compounded by defeat in the underlying case. Moreover, lawyers commit malpractice; they

---

24 RAO §58 empowered the executive board to order such responses and issue summonses and to impose fines for failure to respond to its orders or summonses.

25 Objections to a decision of the executive board with regard to a complaint were directed to the president of the court of appeal; RAO §59. Moreover, the state prosecutor could institute a proceeding before the disciplinary panel without first going through the process of filing a complaint with the executive board.

Table 6.1.   *Annual number of complaints received by executive board*

Year	Total lawyers	Total complaints	Year	Total lawyers	Total complaints
1881	223	57	1908	317	125
1882	219	70	1909	333	115
1883	219	70	1910	357	135
1884	220	65	1911	388	156
1885	233	64	1912	416	171
1886	229	68	1913	444	187
1887	236	52	1914	464	198
1888	240	71	1915	447	210
1889	250	68	1916	443	117
1890	253	66	1917	435	78
1891	252	63	1918	436	62
1892	251	76	1919	479	112
1893	257	85	1920	511	140
1894	262	98	1921	542	170
1895	256	106	1922	546	219
1896	259	103	1923	543	183
1897	263	101	1924	585	216
1898	267	98	1925	608	261
1899	268	94	1926	624	318
1900	259	108	1927	655	306
1901	262	95	1928	682	304
1902	263	90	1929	699	315
1903	276	77	1930	734	345
1904	287	86	1931	771	388
1905	291	102	1932	820	446
1906	298	98	1933	805	512
1907	301	95			

Source: G.St.A., I HA Rep. 84a, 21912–13; N.H.St.A., Hann. 173, Acc. 30/87, 30.

neglect cases, neglect clients, overreach regarding fees, and some are corrupt. The record of disciplinary complaints in the province of Hannover shows that the matters considered by the executive board in Celle went far beyond client disappointment and lawyer malfeasance and included the construction of corporate notions of proper conduct, unrelated to professional practice, that occasioned intrusion by the board into lawyers' private lives.

Table 6.1 shows the total number of complaints received by the executive board each year. Although the number increased over the period in question, the proportion to the total size of the bar remained remarkably constant, at roughly one complaint for every three lawyers. During only two periods did the rate of complaints consistently exceed this ratio: during the last years before the First World War and up until 1915, and later during both the period of economic recovery under the Weimar Republic (1924–8) and the years of increasing economic and political crisis (1929–33).[26] These were periods of explosive growth in the overall size of the bar in Hannover as well as times of increased competition among lawyers, resulting in a loosening of the limits of ethical professional conduct.

The proportion of complaints dismissed by the chairman of the executive board regularly exceeded half, rising at times to three-quarters and more. Invariably, the executive board endorsed these dismissals. The fact that half of all complaints met summary dismissal indicates either that the public was ill-informed about what was to be expected of lawyers and regularly lodged trivial complaints or that the chairman viewed his role more as protector of individual lawyers than of the interests of the "justice-seeking public." Particularly after the war, the adjudication of complaints by the plenary executive board became very burdensome. When an amendment to the RAO in 1923 permitted the establishment of functionally specific panels within it for carrying out its duties, the lawyers' chamber in Celle in 1924 created such a panel to review complaints.[27] By 1931 the executive board felt moved to remark about the increased number of complaints:

The high number of unsuccessful complaints show how much the public tends to display its mistrust of lawyers and to express this mistrust through unfounded complaints. A disproportionately high number of the cases involve submissions of quarrelsome and uninstructable (*unbelehrbar*) persons, who regularly file improper and unfounded complaints with the executive committee of the lawyers' chamber and with other authorities, thus causing a great expenditure of effort. The large number of complaints does not, however, give any reason for an unfavorable view of the bar, such as regrettably is often expressed by the enemies of the profession. These expressions must be countered at every opportunity by stressing that the bar continues

26 The large number of complaints in 1915 is a reporting anomaly, caused by a shift in the fiscal year of the lawyers' chamber from 1 October–30 September to a calendar year. Accordingly, the report for 1915 covered fifteen months, 1 October 1914–31 December 1915; G.St.A. I HA Rep. 84a, 21913, 178.

27 RAO §58a; see Friedländer and Friedländer, *Kommentar zur Rechtsanwaltsordnung*, 405–12; the action of the lawyers' chamber in Celle is recorded at G.St.A. I HA Rep. 84a 21913, 229, and Mundt, *100 Jahre Rechtsanwaltskammer*, 32.

192 *Elites and Professional Ideology*

to be morally unshaken, although the economic crisis has landed an especially destructive blow squarely upon our profession.[28]

From the shifting composition of the kinds of complaints received, it appears most likely that the board and its chairman were burdened with many complaints that were in fact trivial.

The subject matter of the complaints varied greatly. The bulk of complaints, however, fell into three categories: fee disputes with clients, usually overreaching on the part of lawyers; various forms of neglect of clients' cases; and defamation of opposing parties, witnesses, and opposing counsel. The remainder of cases involved other breaches of standards of professional conduct and behavior in private life that the executive board considered to be likely to bring disrepute upon the profession.

To choose a representative early year, ten of the sixty-eight complaints received in 1886 involved differences between clients and lawyers over the calculation of fees, five delays in settling accounts with the client, thirteen delays in returning documents to clients, twenty-three delays in the execution of mandates or cases or in communication of requested information to clients, one suspected irregularity in an employment certificate for a clerk, two refusals to carry out mandates, one instance of improper conduct "within or without" professional duties, and thirteen miscellaneous complaints.[29] This general pattern of complaints repeated itself in subsequent years. Thus in 1926 the three hundred and eighteen complaints included sixty-five differences over fees, one hundred and thirty-one instances of defamation of the opponent in pleadings or oral argument and prosecution of frivolous, irrelevant, or impertinent lawsuits (*unsachgemäßes Prozessieren*), sixty-one accusations of inadequate execution of mandates, neglect in answering inquiries, delay in rendering bills or returning documents and violation of collegial duties, two cases of conflict of interest (representing both parties in the same matter, *Prävarikation*), fifteen impermissible advertisements or associations with prepaid legal insurance schemes, two improper associations with clients, and forty-two miscellaneous matters.[30] From this mass of complaints, some well grounded and some frivolous, we can discern something of the policies that the executive board pursued with regard to the governance and protection of members.

---

28 Annual activity report for 1931, N.H.St.A., Hann. 173, Acc. 30/87, 30, 59.
29 G.St.A. I HA Rep. 84a, 21912, 132.   30 G.St.A. I HA Rep. 84a, 21913, 241R.

The executive board rigorously sought to avoid in disciplinary complaints, as in admission cases, real or apparent conflicts of interest that would tend to bring the bar into public disrepute. Accordingly, the board endorsed the admissions opinion that required elected officials such as *Bürgermeister* and city council members to decline to represent parties against the city whose officials they were.[31] Yet the board exercised remarkable lenience when members faced criminal charges. In cases in which the accused was acquitted, and frequently in cases in which convictions were for lesser offenses (*malum prohibitum* rather than *malum in se*), the board declined altogether to act. Thus, in 1883 the board took no steps against members who had been acquitted of criminal defamation and of aiding and abetting usury, and also declined to censure a lawyer who stood convicted of defamation of a district court and had been fined sixty marks and costs because "the act appear[ed] to have been atoned for by means of the adjudged punishment."[32] Similarly, the board refused to censure lawyers convicted of violations of the stamp tax law in 1885, 1887, and 1889, slander of the state (*Staatsverleumdung*) in 1891, playing in a foreign lottery and defamation in 1892, and other "trivial transgressions" in 1909.[33] Very occasionally, the executive board censured a member for behavior that had resulted in a criminal charge and acquittal, but the standard response after an acquittal was to decline further action.[34] By establishing this pattern, the board showed that its concern for the reputation of the bar lay only with serious criminal offenses. Conviction of serious crimes brought swift and decisive punishment from the governing body of the profession. Acquittals and convictions for minor offenses rarely elicited any action. In this regard, the concern of the board for the reputation of the bar seemed rather lax.

In the realm of personal behavior that did not result in any criminal charges, the board was not so tolerant. Appearing in court while drunk and challenging another lawyer to a duel met with censure.[35] Aspects of private life unrelated to the practice of law also fell within

---

31 G.St.A. I HA Rep. 84a, 21912, 251R (1897), and 263 (1898).
32 G.St.A. I HA Rep. 84a, 21912, 51.
33 G.St.A. I HA Rep. 84a, 21912, 115, 147R, 176; 195; 200; 21913, 70R.
34 Aiding and abetting the escape of a prisoner, G.St.A. I HA Rep. 84a, 21912, 185 (1890), and defamation of a state official, ibid., 185R. In both instances, the board warned the member against the consequent loss of trust between the legal profession and the state officials involved.
35 G.St.A. I HA Rep. 84a, 21913, 37 (1907); 21912, 183 (1890), 230R (1895).

the realm of oversight by the executive board. Lewd or improper behavior toward women drew rebukes when substantiated.[36] The opening of bankruptcy proceedings against a lawyer drew its attention and comment.[37] By emphasizing forms of behavior normally considered to be part of the private, nonprofessional life of citizens, the executive board applied corporate conceptions of honor to the governance of the legal profession. It conceived of honor and status in terms of private modes of behavior. The executive board often considered these matters serious enough to warrant formal disciplinary cases and serious punishments. Breach of the code of honor brought action on the part of the self-disciplinary organ of the profession; breach of the law, or sufficient evidence to institute criminal proceedings, did not necessarily do so.

The executive board in Celle showed remarkable tolerance with regard to the political behavior of lawyers. The ever-vigilant state prosecutor reported in 1895 that a member of the bar was active "in the interests of Social Democracy." The board ruled that such information was not ground for disciplinary action.[38] Similarly, when the police reported in 1899 that a lawyer had a subscription to the "anarchist newspaper," *Der Socialist*, the board refused any action.[39] When the superior state prosecutor's office in Celle alerted the board in 1903 that a member of the lawyers' chamber was a member of the Social Democratic Party and active in agitation on its behalf, the board "found this no cause to take measures against the member."[40] The executive board in Celle thus refused to cooperate in any form of political testing for lawyers, thereby guarding to the extent that it could the bar's freedom from political interference by the government, which had been one of the goals of the drafters of the legal reforms of 1877–9.[41]

Finally, the board made clear in its responses to complaints its policy regarding innovative forms of economic behavior such as the affilia-

36 G.St.A. I HA Rep. 84a, 21912, 275R (1899); 21913, 52 (1908).
37 G.St.A. I HA Rep. 84a, 21913, 38 (1907).   38 G.St.A. I HA Rep. 84a, 21912, 229.
39 G.St.A. I HA Rep. 84a, 21912, 276; the lawyer concerned responded to the board's inquiry by declaring that he was an opponent of anarchism and read the newspaper only for his own instruction.
40 G.St.A. I HA Rep. 84a, 21912, 342; the board did condemn the conduct of the same lawyer in making statements in a public meeting that led to a charge of defamation of the throne, although that criminal charge was later dropped.
41 This policy was fully in accord with the generally accepted interpretation by the profession; see Friedländer and Friedländer, *Kommentar zur Rechtsanwaltsordnung*, 182, and DAV, *Richtlinien zur Ausübung des Anwaltsberufs*, 4.

tion of lawyers with private associations. As early as 1890 the board received reports that two lawyers had entered into contracts with private associations to provide legal advice and trial representation for association members free of charge, in return for payment of a set fee or salary.[42] Although this first charge proved to have been untrue, the executive board declared such arrangements to be impermissible. The matter arose again in 1897, and the board expressly condemned such contracts and ordered any lawyer who had entered into one to cancel it.[43] Here the economic concerns of lawyers clearly superseded any desire to make legal services available and affordable to the public. The board condemned salaried or similar arrangements with private associations as unethical underbidding, contrary to the traditions of the bar and to the interests of the administration of justice. The policy of the executive board acted as a brake upon competition among lawyers for clients, using ethical claims to place limits upon the competitive devices that could be employed.[44]

In its disposition of complaints about the personal and professional conduct of lawyers, therefore, the executive board established a pattern that, while insisting upon protection of the liberal achievement of independence from state tutelage, nevertheless created and confirmed corporate (and increasingly old-fashioned and elitist) notions of professional ideology. The board guarded the bar against undue interference at the hands of state officials by refusing to apply political tests as measures of proper professional conduct. Yet it also restricted entry into the bar wherever possible. Non-Prussians and lawyers with any hint of moral shortcoming and even lawyers in public office encountered resistance from the executive board. Private conduct often seemed more important than professional competence in the board's judgment of a lawyer or a candidate. This pattern emerged even more clearly in the formal disciplinary proceedings before the disciplinary panel.

42 G.St.A. I HA Rep. 84a, 21912, 182.
43 G.St.A. I HA Rep. 84a, 21912, 252R. The issue arose again in 1909 and became rampant in the 1920s.
44 The executive board similarly censured lawyers for advertising to sell their practices, G.St.A. I HA Rep. 84a, 21912, 228R (1895), for placing their names in a newsletter sent to members of a private association, ibid., 194 (1891), and even for permitting their names to be included in 1897 in a "Roster of Lawyers Who Appear Regularly in Neighboring District Courts," published by the DAV, ibid., 253R. Friedländer and Friedländer, *Kommentar zur Rechtsanwaltsordnung*, 192–3, distinguish between a *Hausanwalt*, employed by a business company, and a *Vereinsanwalt*, employed to represent members of a voluntary association, arguing that the latter status was more susceptible to abuses such as these.

196 *Elites and Professional Ideology*

DISCIPLINARY CASES

Every profession has its pathology of unsanctioned and punishable behavior, and the bar in Hannover was no exception. One of the main reform goals had been to create self-disciplinary bodies, whereby lawyers could judge the conduct of their own, separate from the disciplinary authority of government agencies, which had proved in Prussia to be susceptible to political abuse. The RAO charged the lawyers' chambers with that responsibility. The executive board of each chamber selected from its ranks the disciplinary panel of five members, composed of the chairman, the vice-chairman, and three other members of the board (RAO §67).[45] The procedure for initiating a disciplinary proceeding was as follows. When the facts alleged in a complaint by a private individual against a lawyer appeared to be true and to be serious, the executive board referred the record to the superior state prosecutor in Celle for further consideration. If upon this review, or upon its own motion, the state prosecutor found probable cause to initiate formal proceedings, he opened a preliminary investigation (RAO §69).[46] A single investigating judge, chosen by the president of the court of appeal, conducted the preliminary inquiry. At the close of that investigation, the disciplinary panel held a hearing to determine whether a formal trial should occur. At the trial the superior state prosecutor acted as prosecutor, and the accused could be represented by counsel (RAO §§80–8). Appeal lay to the supreme disciplinary panel in Leipzig, composed of judges of the imperial supreme court and lawyers from the closed corps admitted to practice before that court (RAO §§90–1). The range of possible disciplinary penalties included warning, reprimand, fines up to 3,000 marks, reprimand and fine, and disbarment (RAO §63).

Between 1878 and 1933, the disciplinary panel of the executive board of the lawyers' chamber in Celle tried 270 disciplinary cases to judgment.[47] Only in 1880 and 1907 were no verdicts rendered, and

---

45 In Celle these elections took place every two years; GO (1880) §8, ¶5.
46 Although the RAO was not completely clear, Friedländer and Friedländer, *Kommentar zur Rechtsanwaltsordnung*, 426, 470–1, indicate that the governing interpretation left the initiation of disciplinary cases solely with the state prosecutor.
47 This total includes only the cases in which lawyers who were already admitted were accused of wrongdoing. Applicants for admission to the bar could appeal a denial by the executive board to the disciplinary panel, present evidence, and receive a full hearing (RAO §16, ¶2). Disappointed applicants in Hannover availed themselves of that remedy in numerous cases, but those outcomes have already been considered above in the discussion concerning admission.

Table 6.2.   *Disciplinary cases*

Year	Total cases	Year	Total cases	Category of offenses		
1881	1	1908	4	None given	7	2.6%
1882	2	1909	2	Neglect of client	51	18.9%
1883	6	1910	4	Dispute w/other lawyer	15	5.6%
1884	5	1911	7	Breach prof. etiquette	42	15.6%
1885	7	1912	7	Private behavior	26	9.6%
1886	3	1913	9	Defiance of exec. bd.	39	14.4%
1887	2	1914	8	Conviction of crime	15	5.6%
1888	4	1915	6	Defamation	35	13.0%
1889	5	1916	4	Off. ag. gov. auth.	21	7.8%
1890	1	1917	1	Competitive offense	19	7.0%
1891	1	1918	1			
1892	3	1919	3	Total	270	
1893	1	1920	5			
1894	4	1921	9	*Outcome and Punishments*		
1895	3	1922	6			
1896	4	1923	10	Acquittal	37	13.7%
1897	2	1924	10	Warning	42	15.6%
1898	1	1925	12	Reprimand	65	24.1%
1899	1	1926	6	Rep. & fine to 500 M.	64	23.7%
1900	3	1927	9	Rep. & fine over 500 M.	33	12.2%
1901	4	1928	10	Disbarment	16	5.9%
1902	5	1929	8	Fine only	13	4.8%
1903	6	1930	5			
1904	7	1931	14	Total	270	
1905	8	1932	13			
1906	9	1933	21			
1907	0					

Source: G.St.A., I HA Rep. 84a, 21912–13; N.H.St.A., Hann. 173, Acc. 30/87, 30.

most years saw more than one. The patterns found in the decisions to commence main disciplinary proceedings, in the judgments reached, and in the punishments meted out reveal again the mixture of traditional and modern, corporate and liberal in the behavior and thought of the lawyer-notables who led the bar in Hannover.

In comparison with the total number of lawyers, the number of disciplinary cases in any given year was quite small (see Table 6.2). As might be expected, the largest single category of offenses consisted of offenses against clients – such matters as neglect of cases, delay in answering inquiries from clients or rendering bills for fees after a request, and fee disputes, usually with the lawyer standing accused of charging an improperly high fee. The number of cases of offenses against clients was actually larger, because the third largest category of offenses, defiance of the executive board, usually concerned failure to respond in a timely fashion to the board's inquiry about a complaint lodged against the lawyer by a client. The board generally imposed more severe penalties when a lawyer thus compounded his offense by adding defiance of an order of the executive board.[48] One-third of all disciplinary cases thus dealt with lawyers' breaches of their duties toward their clients.

A second large group of offenses encompassed professional relations within the bar and between the bar and bench. In fifteen cases the board examined conduct that breached the profession's code of honor for intraprofessional conduct, such as lying or misrepresenting intended actions in court to another lawyer, attempting to have direct contact with the opposing party while knowing that the party was represented by counsel, or even engaging in fistfights and other disorderly conduct with other members of the bar.[49] In a further thirty-five cases, lawyers stood accused of defaming the opposing party, a witness, or the opposing attorney, either in pleadings or in oral address and argument to the court. Forty-two cases consisted of breach of professional duty toward the courts, such as abuse of process, improperly accelerated resort to enforcement mechanisms such as execution of a money judgment without permitting the opposing lawyer reasonable time to secure satisfaction by his client, and breach of confidentiality by informing one's client of information entrusted

---

48 The consensus within the profession strongly sanctioned obedience to the executive board. DAV, *Richtlinien für die Ausübung des Anwaltsberufs*, 8, provided:

E. Relations to professional colleagues.
  I. Executive Board of the Lawyers' Chamber.
  a) The lawyer owes esteem, respect, and candor to the executive board of the lawyers' chamber as the official representative of the *Stand* and as the bearer of the discipline of the *Stand*.
  b) Nonobservance of summonses of the executive board, nonobservance of its inquiries, etc., constitute transgressions of the duties of a member of the *Stand*.

Friedländer and Friedländer, *Kommentar zur Rechtsanwaltsordnung*, 197, argue that this duty does *not* require unconditional obedience.

49 DAV, *Richtlinien für die Ausübung des Anwaltsberufs*, 9, subsumes these duties under the rubric "Duty of Collegiality"; see also Friedländer and Friedländer, *Kommentar zur Rechtsanwaltsordnung*, 178–80.

to the lawyer by the court in confidence. Finally, twenty-one cases involved the relations of the bar with governmental authorities, ranging from contempt of court citations to covert delivery of letters to prisoners awaiting trial, offenses considered likely to endanger the trust of authorities for members of the practicing bar. Altogether, these offenses against professional comity and professional duties to authorities amounted to forty-two percent of the total.

The board, however, extended its reach into the private lives of lawyers, their conduct outside of the practice of their profession as strictly defined. In twenty-six cases the disciplinary panel heard evidence about this private conduct. All private behavior was considered the proper basis for disciplinary action.[50] This category consisted primarily of two sorts of offenses: immoral relationships with women, either married women or minors, and participating in public disorders, usually involving brawling and drunkenness. The executive board punished these offenses severely, indicating its great concern for the reputation of the bar in the eye of the public with regard to such private conduct. It disbarred one lawyer for the offense of publicly beating his wife and fighting in the street with his relatives.[51] It disbarred another for immoral sexual behavior with an adolescent.[52] In three further cases, the disciplinary panel imposed the penalty of reprimand and substantial monetary fines (1,000, 2,000, and 3,000 marks, the maximum allowed by the RAO) for immoral relations with women or defamation of one's own wife through one's conduct with other women.[53] Other cases involved improper behavior while drunk

---

50 RAO §28 provided clear statutory authority to examine private behavior of lawyers. It was also clear that custom was largely the determinant of what extraprofessional behavior was consonant with the dignity of the bar. The leading commentators on the RAO assumed without question that certain forms of behavior were unacceptable, providing almost a catalog of the kinds of offenses that the disciplinary panel in Celle punished: "It goes without saying that a lawyer may do nothing, within or without his profession, that would be unworthy of any upstanding and cultivated person. If he surrenders himself to drink, if he excites scandal by immoral acts, if he mistreats his wife, he thus injures his human dignity and thereby at the same time the dignity of his *Stand*." Friedländer and Friedländer, *Kommentar zur Rechtsanwaltsordnung*, 151.

51 G.St.A. I HA Rep 84a, 21913, 228, 230, Redmer in Tostedt. The full charge was "on account of conduct unworthy of the profession, brawling with his own wife and relatives, and severe breach of his professional duties."

52 N.H.St.A., Hann. 173, Acc. 30/87, 30, 116 (1933).

53 Gustav Tripmaker of Göttingen in 1885, G.St.A. I HA Rep. 84a, 21912, 122, and also N.H.St.A. Pattensen, Hann. 173, Acc. 84/59, Nr. 388, received the penalty of reprimand and a fine of 2,000 marks for immoral conduct with the wife of a restaurant owner in Göttingen.

in public (nine cases), the accumulation of gambling debts, and duel-
ing. By means of its supervision of the private moral lives of lawyers,
and by the imposition of stiff penalties for conduct deemed to be
beneath the dignity of the profession, the disciplinary panel perpetuated guild ideas of proper behavior of members of a corporate body,
grafting them onto the modern, market-oriented structure of the bar
created by the RAO.

The disciplinary panel considered yet another category of intra-
professional offenses that also revealed its concern for corporate
values, the category of economic and competitive offenses by lawyers against each other. These breaches of professional ethics encompassed arrangements with lay practitioners, whereby lawyers
accepted referrals and in return split fees with the nonlegally trained
practitioners who sent clients their way, advertising and other
impermissible means of obtaining a practice, offering to represent
clients at fees less than those of the tariff in the fees statute for
lawyers, improper business connections with nonlawyers, and fee
splitting among lawyers.[54] While the penalties assessed were not
always draconian, the disciplinary panel made clear its claim to be
the watchdog of the manner in which lawyers competed with each
other economically. The RAO made the market the determining
force in the question of how many lawyers there were, but the
disciplinary panel in Celle took steps to regulate by ethical standards
the means by which competition among those within the profession
would be carried out. Anticompetitive ethical standards are typical
of modern professions, but they were also typical of the guild spirit.
The disciplinary panel viewed unlimited free-market competition
within the practice of law as a threat to the ethical standards of the
bar and thus resisted to the extent that it could the application of
market standards of judging behavior to the judgment of professional conduct.[55]

54 Doing business with *Rechtskonsulenten* did not always constitute a breach of professional
ethics, but the instances in which it was permitted were narrowly circumscribed; DAV,
Richtlinien für die Ausübung des Anwaltsberufs, 10; Friedländer and Friedländer, *Kommentar
zur Rechtsanwaltsordnung*, 183–4. Fee splitting was always forbidden, DAV, *Richtlinien*, 13,
although Friedländer and Friedländer, 191–2, distinguish between "genuine" fee splitting
between individual lawyers, which was impermissible, and agreements among "several
lawyers' organizations," which was allowed.
55 Max Weber treats insightfully the tension inherent between corporate concepts of personal
relations and the market conception of such relations. While the market does not recognize
or value ideas such as collegial duty, focusing instead upon the money-commodity transac-
tion, a corporate conception of relations emphasizes values such as collegial fair play;
Rheinstein, *Max Weber on Law*, 191–7, esp. 191–3; *ES* 1:635–40.

Approaching the pattern of disciplinary judgments from another angle, it is reasonable to presume that the board reserved the most severe penalties for those offenses that it believed most serious. It almost invariably imposed a reprimand and monetary fine of more than 500 marks upon repeat offenders in cases of client neglect, lawyers with previous disciplinary offenses, lawyers who refused to respond to requests from the disciplinary panel or executive board for explanations, and lawyers involved in immoral relations or unacceptable behavior in public. By following this pattern, the panel rigorously protected the public against repeat offenders within the bar and aggressively protected the reputation of the bar from private behavior of lawyers that would tend to bring it into public disrepute. The fines imposed were considerable. Individual fines included ones of 1,000 marks in 1883, of 2,000 marks in 1885, and of 3,000 marks in 1896, 1911, and 1915. These fines are more onerous in view of the fact that the average net income from civil cases of ordinary jurisdiction for lawyers responding to a questionnaire from the DAV for the year 1911 was 4,187.35 marks.[56] The magnitude of the fines indicates the determination of the disciplinary panel to deter repeat offenders and immoral private behavior.

The ultimate penalty within the power of the disciplinary panel was disbarment. In sixteen cases between 1880 and 1933 the panel considered the offense so serious as to warrant this sanction.[57] The principal offense that resulted in disbarment was conviction of embezzlement with a consequent prison sentence. The panel disbarred all ten lawyers who came before it convicted of such a breach of trust. The other cases of disbarment involved one instance of neglect of a client and delay in remitting money, in which the defendant had a long record of prior offenses and disci-

---

56 "Deutscher Anwaltverein. Ergebnis der Umfrage über die Einkommensverhältnisse der Rechtsanwälte," *Abl* 1 (1914): Zugabe zu Nr. 6, June 1914, Tabelle III, 3 (see Tables 5.20 and 5.21 in Chapter 5). Four hundred and thirty-two lawyers completed this questionnaire fully, and the income varied according to the level of court before which the respondent practiced.

57 In two instances, the sentence of disbarment imposed by the disciplinary panel was overturned. In one instance the disciplinary appeals court in Leipzig (1919, G.St.A. I HA Rep. 84a, 21913, 207R) did not consider the offense serious enough to warrant disbarment (the offense was "in addition to other offenses . . . to have solicited for practice in a manner dangerous to the prestige of the *Stand*"). In another, the accused had been accused of embezzlement of funds from an estate when the amnesty order of 3 December 1918, halted the criminal trial. The disciplinary panel nonetheless convicted and disbarred him, the disciplinary appeals court ruled that punishment too harsh, and retrial was barred by the amnesty order pardoning disciplinary offenses of 16 February 1919; G.St.A. I HA Rep. 84a, 21913, 212R.

plinary convictions; another case of repeated instances of client neglect; the already mentioned case of bringing the profession into disrepute by brawling in public with his wife and relatives; one case of improper acquisition of a practice; one case of repeated serious offenses; the case of immoral behavior with an adolescent; and one case of forgery of documents. In other instances, lawyers stood convicted of crimes such as contempt of court or even contributing to the delinquency of a minor, but they never suffered the ultimate penalty of disbarment. The disciplinary panel established the rule, therefore, that it would regard only conviction of the ultimate offense striking at the heart of the attorney-client relationship – breach of the client's trust regarding his money – as sufficient ground for automatic disbarment. Other extremes of unacceptable behavior, including repeated offenses showing a contempt for the "justice-seeking public" as well as of the executive board and disciplinary panel, constituted sufficient cause for disbarment, but then only in exceptional cases.

In summary, the disciplinary activity of the executive board of the lawyers' chamber in Celle reflected a threefold concern on the part of the establishment of lawyers within the chamber. First, these lawyer-notables sought to maintain high ethical standards in the relations of lawyers to the public. They gave some hearing to even the most trivial complaint; they punished repeat and other serious offenders against the trust of clients as severely as they could. In this way the practicing bar endeavored to prevent the reentry of state authority into its internal disciplinary affairs. Second, the executive board and the disciplinary panel sought to control admission to the bar and the methods of competition among lawyers in whatever ways they were able, in order to preserve the ethics of community within the bar and to shield lawyers from the harshest forms of marketplace competition. They excluded non-Prussians whenever possible; they discouraged and punished unacceptable forms of competition such as agreements with lay practitioners and private associations; and they condemned practices such as fee splitting. In this way corporate ideas of an economy of sufficiency survived into the market-oriented professional structure of the RAO which might have been expected to tend to encourage lawyers to maximize their incomes in whatever ways were possible. Third, the lawyer-notables who governed the executive board of the lawyers' chamber in Celle perpetuated the corporate tradition of supervision of the private lives of members. Reasoning that private behavior that would meet with disapproval from the general public would tend to bring the entire profession into disrepute, the executive board and disciplinary panel both inquired into the private activities of lawyers and punished severely those actions of which they disapproved. Again, traditional conceptions of honorable conduct, administered by an elite of lawyer-notables who practiced before the court of appeal in Celle and the eight superior courts, overlay a market-based professional structure, inevitably leading to tensions.

Advisory Opinions

A final method by which the lawyers' chamber defined its conception of how the bar in private practice ought to govern itself was in its advisory opinions, generally by the executive board and very occasionally by the plenary assembly of members, with regard to major issues of interest to the profession. Advisory opinions appeared in at least two forms: precedents shaped by the board in recurrent admission and complaint cases, and in formal advisory opinions delivered to the court or to the ministry of justice in response to a request (RAO §49, ¶4). In its advisory opinions, the board announced the official position of the Hannoverian bar with respect to issues and conflicts that affected the German private bar as a whole and in so doing both created and confirmed tensions and frictions within the bar in the province.

The advisory activity of the executive board falls into two clear periods, an earlier one of relative inactivity between its foundation and roughly 1910, and a period of greatly increased activism as the scope and volume of advisory concern expanded between roughly 1910 and 1933, accelerating after the end of the First World War. Certain issues persisted, however, throughout the years in question, while in later years the board extended its interpretation of the reach of its mandate to include new subjects.

During the entire fifty-year span, the board rendered advisory opinions to the ministry of justice and the courts concerning pending legislation that would affect the practicing bar. In early years it usually responded only to requests for such advice; after the formation of the Association of Executive Boards of German Lawyers' Chambers in 1907, it more frequently volunteered its advice. As early as 1882, the Prussian Ministry of Justice requested an opinion on the need for a reform of the fees statute for lawyers, which the board provided.[58] Similarly, in 1887 the board advised the ministry concerning a draft of legislation to revise that act, responding unfavorably to the draft and sending its written opinion to the ministry as well as to "all German lawyers' chamber executive boards, . . . the president of the royal court of appeal [in Celle], the German Reichstag, individual delegates to the Reichstag and other appropriate persons."[59] The board rendered further opinions on the subject of lawyers' fees in 1898, 1909, and 1911, arguing in this latter year that:

a) the presently valid regulations for the *appellate* level [emphasis added] contain a suitable compensation for the activity of lawyers,
b) otherwise, however, the fee tariff contained in §9 of the Fees Statute must be increased at least 15 per cent.
   In criminal cases, an increase in fees of one hundred per cent is necessary.[60]

The executive board thus took great care to represent the economic interests of the bar by commenting upon draft legislation that would affect the incomes of lawyers, although it rendered advisory opinions on other draft legislation as well. This stands in sharp contrast with the reluctance of the Hannoverian bar to participate in so crucial a task as the drafting of the advisory opinion of the private bar with regard to the newly released draft of the proposed Civil Law Code. When the board polled the membership in 1888 to discover who was willing to participate, only three lawyers responded.[61] Narrow matters of economic interest appear to have excited much more enthusiasm among the lawyers in Hannover than more abstract legal matters such as codification of substantive civil law.

Indeed, the board devoted much of its effort in rendering advisory opinions before 1910 to professional matters (*Standesfragen*). Already in 1885 the executive board responded to an inquiry from the minister of justice as to the advisability of introducing a limitation upon admission to the bar. Although the opinion of the members of the

58 G.St.A. I HA Rep. 84a, 21912, 44.
59 Ibid., 150. None of the proposed revisions to the fees statute was adopted before 1909, much to the disappointment of the executive board in Celle and most German lawyers; Ostler, *Die deutschen Rechtsanwälte*, 58–9.
60 G.St.A. I HA Rep. 84a, 21913, 102.
61 G.St.A. I HA Rep. 84a, 21912, 163R. This lack of interest stands in contrast to the flood of public comment that publication of the draft Civil Law Code evoked; see John, *Politics and the Law*, 105–7. The DAV endorsed adoption of the draft; ibid., 107, and Ostler, *Die deutschen Rechtsanwälte*, 49–50.

board was divided, the majority endorsed a limitation in the sense that admission of a lawyer could be denied when the court of appeal and the lawyers' chamber unanimously agreed that the need for such an admission to the particular court in question did not exist, "because as a result of the unlimited right of admission, the integrity of the bar appears to be threatened."[62] Again in 1894, in response to an inquiry from the ministry of justice, the board supported a revision of the RAO to permit a limitation upon admissions when the court of appeal and the lawyers' chamber agreed that there was no need for new lawyers, even while admitting that there was no general overcrowding of the bar in the province of Hannover, merely in some large cities.[63] Finally, in 1896, the opinion of the board with regard to a proposed Prussian law concerning the regulation of judges' salaries and the appointment of judicial candidates reflected its continuing concern with a perceived decline in the quality of lawyers under the system of free entry and called for limitation upon admission to the bar in order to prevent serious damage to the administration of justice.[64] Thus, at this very early stage in the experience with the free bar and even before any overcrowding began to afflict the bar in Hannover, the executive board sought to abandon the absolute entitlement of every candidate who had passed the second bar examination to admission to practice and to widen its authority and discretion as gatekeeper to the profession by obtaining the authority to rule upon the question of whether need existed for yet another lawyer.

62 G.St.A. I HA Rep. 84a, 21912, 117R. The entire report is found in N.H.St.A, Hann. 173, Acc. 30/87, 312, 6–8. The president of the court of appeal in Celle concurred in a report to the Prussian Ministry of Justice on 14 July 1885, G.St.A., I HA Rep. 84a, 38, 327–44.

63 "Zur Frage der freien Advokatur. I. Celle," *JW* 23 (1894): 252; the original is found at G.St.A., I HA Rep. 84a, 39, 93–102.

64 "The executive board of the lawyers' chamber for the district of the court of appeal of Celle makes no mistake about the fact that the present overcrowding of the legal profession, which has not yet reached its zenith, is well-suited to introduced objectionable circumstances both into the judiciary as well as into the bar. For this reason, the executive board considers the provisions of §8 of the draft Law Concerning the Regulation of Judicial Salaries and Appointment of Judicial Candidates [*Assessoren*] thoroughly objectionable, because the necessary result would be the introduction of unworthy elements into the legal *Stand*.
     The executive board is of the opinion that if efforts are made either through legislation or administrative decisions to avoid the admission of unworthy elements into the judiciary, simultaneous ways and means must be found to avoid the entry of the same into the bar; that national legislation must expand the authority of executive boards of the lawyers' chambers regarding admission to the bar; and that in addition perhaps a limitation of admission to the *Referendariat* based upon the level of demand should take place; all in order to protect the entire administration of justice from severe damage." G.St.A. I HA Rep. 84a, 21912, 241R.

The board also devoted itself to the protection of the economic and status interests of lawyers by establishing guidelines for professional behavior in relation to nonlegally trained practitioners before the district courts. These practitioners presented both economic competition, especially to lawyers who practiced before district courts, and an economic temptation, to lawyers who might accept mandates from them for trial work on behalf of the client of the lay practitioner. The board regarded any association with such practitioners, who were without university training, who had to pass no state-sanctioned examinations, and who generally came from the lower social ranks, as inevitably damaging to the prestige of the bar.[65] In response to a circular from the president of the court of appeal in Frankfurt a. M. to all Prussian courts of appeal, the board considered drawing up guidelines to regulate contacts between lawyers and these competitors.[66] The issue resurfaced in 1914, when the board "resolutely" expressed its opposition to proposals to establish concessionary positions for lay practitioners in Prussia and to establish a fee schedule for their practices. The board also circulated a set of guidelines to members, governing their relations with lay practitioners.[67] In 1925 the board opposed the appointment of lay practitioners in legal aid cases, "out of protection of the interests of members of the chamber, especially those of colleagues admitted before district courts."[68] Finally, in 1927 the executive board endorsed the "Theses on Professional Intercourse between Lawyers and Lay Practitioners (including Trial Agents)" adopted by the Association of Executive Boards of German Lawyers' Chambers. This guideline severely restricted, while not prohibiting, professional contact between the two groups, taking care to guard the prestige of the lawyer, and prohibiting any professional contact in places where there were sufficient numbers of lawyers to represent the public.[69] The executive board remained steadfast, then, in pursuing its dual goals of

65 For a discussion of the institution of the *Rechtskonsulent* or *Winkelkonsulent*, see Döhring, *Geschichte der deutschen Rechtspflege*, 128–9. Ostler, *Die deutschen Rechtsanwälte*, 101, discusses the relations between the bar and the *Rechtskonsulententum*. Generally, see Franz Hoffmann, *Der Gewerbebetrieb des Rechtskonsulenten* (Berlin, 1929), and Heinrich Wilhelm Kornmann, "Die Rechtsbeistände" (Dr. jur. diss., Freiburg i.B., 1938), 16–19, 34–8.
66 *JW* 14 (1885): 257–64; G.St.A. I HA Rep. 84a, 21912, 117.
67 G.St.A. I HA Rep. 84a, 21913, 166, 177.   68 G.St.A. I HA Rep. 84a, 21913, 234R.
69 DAV, *Leitsätze über den beruflichen Verkehr zwischen Rechtsanwälten und Rechtskonsulenten (einschl. Prozeßagenten)* (Leipzig, 1927). G.St.A. I HA Rep. 84a, 21913, 250; the executive board also reminded members of the lawyers' chamber of these guidelines in May 1929; N.H.St.A., Hann. 173, Acc. 30/87, 30, 12. See also DAV, *Richtlinien für die Ausübung des Anwaltsberufs*, 10, and Friedländer and Friedländer, *Kommentar zur Rechtsanwaltsordnung*, 183–4.

protecting the prestige and social position of the entire bar and the economic interests of district court lawyers, for whom the lay practitioners represented serious competition. Repeated pronouncements on the subject, however, indicated that the board's steadfast efforts did not always meet with success.

Just as the executive board sought to protect lawyers from the economic competition of lay practitioners, it also acted to preserve traditional fields of activity that were threatened either by the government or by the entry of new competitors into the marketplace. In Prussia, by traditional practice the office of notary could be combined with the private practice of law. Income from notarial practice was a major supplement to income from legal practice for many lawyers, especially those practicing before district courts.[70] In the first decade of the twentieth century, the Prussian ministry of justice began to make appointment of a lawyer as a notary conditional upon the abandonment of the practice of law. The lawyers' chamber in 1907 objected to this innovation.[71] In 1908 the plenary assembly adopted the following resolution:

The plenary meeting of the Lawyers' Chamber of the Court of Appeal in Celle views the introduction of the "exclusively notary" [*nur-Notar*] form of the *Notariat*, recently introduced by the Prussian Ministry of Justice, as jeopardizing the interests of the justice-seeking public and as an unjustified curtailment of an historical field of activity of lawyers in private practice.[72]

The Prussian ministry followed its new policy only fitfully in the remaining years before the war, and notarial practice remained a significant source of income and professional activity for many lawyers.[73]

After the war the role of notarial income became even more important for lawyers in private practice. In 1919 the executive board

70 For the practice of combining the *Notariat* with the *Rechtsanwaltschaft*, see Döhring, *Geschichte der deutschen Rechtspflege*, 173–7. Ostler, *Der deutschen Rechtsanwälte*, discusses the relations between the two functions at 99; he stresses its importance to the district court bar at 69. In the lawyers' chamber in Celle in 1915, 180 out of 447 lawyers were also notaries. The relative importance for different classes of lawyers can be seen from the fact that of 25 court of appeal lawyers, 3 were notaries; of 238 superior court lawyers, 55 notaries; of 184 district court lawyers, 122 notaries. G.St.A., I HA Rep. 84a, 21913, 180R.
71 G.St.A. I HA Rep. 84a, 21913, 39R; Mundt, *100 Jahre Rechtsanwaltskammer*, 37.
72 G.St.A. I HA Rep. 84a, 21913, 54.
73 Some lawyers in Hannover advocated the institution of the *nur-Notar*; for arguments in favor of such an institution, see Karl Wilhelm Lütkemann, "Anwalt-Notariat oder reines Notariat," *Zeitschrift des Deutschen Notarvereins* 9 (1909): 137–62, found in G.St.A., I HA Rep. 84a, 2399, "Notare und Notariat 1908–1913 – Errichtung Selbständiger Notariat 1908," 68–80.

advised the ministry of justice to adopt a uniform regulation, conferring the office of notary upon every lawyer with fifteen years' practice and ten years' residence in the same place, with special provisions for war veterans. The ministry adopted such a rule.[74] The board refused to endorse a proposal made by the Bremen Bar Association to nationalize the notarial office, arguing that this was not in the interest of the public.[75] During the 1920s competition for notary positions also began to come from new sources, first, salaried lawyers in the employ of business enterprises or institutions and, second, state officials who had been retired from state service during the reductions in the bureaucracy that occurred under the Weimar Republic, who now entered the private practice of law and sought appointment as notaries. The executive board opposed the appointment of either group to notarial office, calling upon the ministry to refuse appointment to salaried lawyers in 1925, 1926, 1927, and 1928, and encouraging the ministry to apply the same standard of length of service in the private practice of law and residence in one place to applicants for notarial positions who had been state officials as to those who had always been lawyers in private practice.[76] The board thus tenaciously and successfully protected this field of activity and income for lawyers.[77]

In other matters of economic interest to the bar, the board was less successful. Annually after 1920, the board advised the ministry of justice, as well as the Reichstag, against the creation of special Labor Courts (*Arbeitsgerichte*) to hear cases involving employment contracts and labor disputes, and especially against the prohibition of the representation of parties before that court by lawyers.[78] Its efforts were

74 G.St.A. I HA Rep. 84a, 21913, 207. Years in military service during the war counted as two for purposes of determining eligibility to be appointed notary under this policy; Mundt, *100 Jahre Rechtsanwaltskammer*, 38.

75 G.St.A. I HA Rep. 84a, 21913, 217 (1921). What the Bremen Bar Association meant by "nationalization" is not immediately clear. It could have meant making notaries into full-time state officials, remunerated by salary rather than by fees, or it could have meant the regulation of notaries at the national rather than the state level. In either case, the executive board in Celle would have opposed it.

76 G.St.A. I HA Rep. 84a, 21913, 234R, 242, 249R, 260R, and 261R.

77 Although the board succeeded in reserving most notarial positions to lawyers, the number and proportion of lawyers who were also notaries rose dramatically, so that the victory may have been pyrrhic in economic terms. From 1915, when 180 lawyers out of 447 were notaries (40.3%), the number rose to 349 out of 542 in 1921 (64.4%). G.St.A. I HA Rep. 84a, 21913, 180R, 216.

78 Lawyers had suffered previous defeats in this arena with the erection of *Gewerbegerichte* and *Kaufmannsgerichte* before the war. The *Arbeitsgerichtsgesetz* was adopted by the Reichstag on 23 December 1926, with the provision prohibiting representation by lawyers, §11. The

unavailing. With the effectiveness of the Labor Court Law in 1927, lawyers lost a significant field of practice.

Finally, in its advisory opinions, the executive board continually sought to regulate the means by which lawyers competed among themselves. As mentioned, as early as 1890 the board expressed its disapproval of connections between lawyers and private associations in which the lawyers agreed to represent association members free in return for a salary or retainer. Before the First World War, the issue was considered on a case-by-case basis as a disciplinary matter.[79] By 1925 the complaints had become so numerous that the board issued a blanket condemnation of most such arrangements:

The executive board has had to consider repeatedly in the past year the question of the relationship between members of the chamber and economic interest groups. In the overwhelming majority of cases that have been brought to the attention of the board, the contracts into which lawyers have entered with the economic interest groups have been objected to as incompatible with §28 of the RAO because, according to their terms, they amount to an impermissible solicitation for practice. The executive board considers it incompatible with the duties of a lawyer for him to lend his cooperation to the service of such solicitation.[80]

The board repeated this warning in 1926, 1927, and 1928.

Other unseemly means of competition also met the condemnation of the executive board. It declared the sale of a law practice impermissible and subject to disciplinary action in 1919.[81] Publication of one's name in a directory or calendar that did not also include the names of all lawyers who practiced before the court in whose region the publication circulated amounted to unfair competition and was also impermissible.[82] Placement of a newspaper advertisement announcing that a lawyer was "back from vacation" or other similar messages constituted forbidden advertising.[83] Finally, the board took great pains to regulate the opening of branch offices

advisory opinions of the executive board in Celle are at G.St.A. I HA Rep. 84a, 21913, 212, 217, 235, 241, and 245. See the discussion in Chapter 9.

79 G.St.A. I HA Rep. 84a, 21912, 182 (1890), 252R (1897), I HA Rep. 84a, 21913, 10R (1905), and 70R (1909).

80 G.St.A. I HA Rep. 84a, 21913, 235R.

81 G.St.A. I HA Rep. 84a, 21913, 207. This decision was in accord with the prevailing opinion in the profession at the time. By 1930, however, the profession recognized that in exceptional circumstances sale of a practice could be permitted; DAV, *Richtlinien für die Ausübung des Anwaltsberufs*, 5; Friedländer and Friedländer, *Kommentar zur Rechtsanwaltsordnung*, 193–6.

82 G.St.A. I HA Rep. 84a, 21913, 242R.

83 N.H.St.A., Hann. 173, Acc. 30/85, 30, 20R (1929).

and holding of office hours by lawyers in towns other than the ones in which they lived, prohibiting them in almost all cases.[84] Although a ruling by the supreme disciplinary court in Leipzig in 1916 permitted such activities, the executive board in the 1920s returned to its policy of refusing to permit branch offices or office hours in outlying towns.[85] The board thus sought to protect district court lawyers from unseemly competition among themselves for clients who lived in towns other than the seats of the district courts. It thereby adhered strictly to the concept of localization reflected in its opinion of 1928:

> The Ministry of Justice will only permit the admission of lawyers in towns that are not the seats of courts when the administration of justice requires it; in principle, a lawyer shall live at the seat of the court, so that he will not lose touch with the court and with his colleagues.[86]

By means of all of these policies, the executive board tried to limit as much as it could economic competition among lawyers.

Conclusion

The record of the lawyers' chamber in Celle shows that lawyers in Hannover reacted with a certain amount of ambivalence to the new freedom that they found after 1879. They valued highly the freedom from governmental interference that had been the chief goal of the reformers. The executive board often chose not to impose disciplinary punishment when courts or other authorities complained about the conduct of lawyers or even when lawyers stood convicted of criminal offenses. It also refused to consider the political activity of lawyers appropriate ground for professional discipline. The board

84 G.St.A. I HA Rep. 84a, 21913, 149 (1913), and 176R (1914).
85 G.St.A. I HA Rep. 84a, 21913, 189 (1916), 235 (1925), 243 (1926), 249R (1927); N.H.St.A., Hann. 173, Acc. 30/87, 30, 15 (December 1929). Office hours in outlying towns were permissible if the lawyer holding them was the only lawyer admitted within the district in which the court town and outlying town lay *or* if all other lawyers admitted before the district court in question agreed to his holding such office hours. See also Friedländer and Friedländer, *Kommentar zur Rechtsanwaltsordnung*, 200–1. Disputes over branch offices and office hours in outlying towns could be very acrimonious. See the correspondence between lawyers Kühns and Appel in Herzberg a.H. and the executive board during 1934 and 1935, seeking approval for the holding of such office hours in Gieboldehausen and Bad Lauterberg, and the letters opposing such hours by lawyers Weber and Wander in Bad Lauterberg. Eventually, permission to hold such office hours was denied. Akten des Oberlandesgerichts Celle, Oberlandesgerichtsbibliothek, Celle.
86 G.St.A. I HA Rep. 84a, 21913, 261R.

directed most of its energy, however, toward the maintenance of the economic and status position of lawyers, thereby revealing its ambivalent attitude toward the free marketplace.

The executive board applied corporate conceptions of economic relations and private conduct to its regulation of the lives of lawyers. In its policing of professional misconduct, it proved most assiduous and harsh in punishing moral failings that either created tensions within the profession (defamation) or tended to lower the bar in the esteem of the public (immoral private behavior). It made clear that qualification to practice law did not consist alone of technical professional qualification, but also of proper personal conduct at all times.

The board pursued corporate ideals when it tried at all times to limit economic competition from outside of the bar and also among lawyers. It believed in a strict interpretation of the principle of localization, amounting to a geographic division of markets, strict adherence to the fee tariff (price fixing), and traditional forms of professional behavior (no advertising, no fee splitting). Among the corporate ideals of the lawyer-notables on the executive board was the expectation by superior court lawyers, who dominated the board, of a substantial degree of deference on the part of district court lawyers. This expectation of deference, as well as the economic privilege of collegial court lawyers built into the Imperial Justice Laws, ran contrary to the economic and especially the status concerns of district court lawyers. More and more after 1900, the energies of the board were occupied with the containment of the disputes that arose between these factions. Far from creating a new, unified, strong, and independent bar, the RAO and other reforms of 1877–9 created in the province of Hannover a bar that was ambivalent toward its new framework and split internally. Thus hampered, it was poorly suited to perform the functions of leadership of the *Bürgertum* that the advocates of *freie Advokatur* had expected of it in the 1860s.

7

Simultaneous Admission: The Limits of Honoratiorenpolitik

The goal of the reformers whose efforts culminated in the Imperial Justice Laws had been to create a unified, self-administered, and self-disciplined national bar that could fulfill its ascribed role as the "Archimedean point" for the reform of German society and polity, one that could serve as the general estate. The Imperial Justice Laws in many ways represented the great victory of liberal reform doctrine. In the years after 1879, the growth, maturation, and increasing institutional and professional sophistication of the private legal profession, as evidenced both by national trends and in Hannover, seemed to justify the high hopes of the nineteenth-century liberal reformers. The path was indeed opened to talent; social mobility and diversity increased at the same time that the public status and professional competency of the private bar rose.

But the liberal machine set in motion in 1877–9 reached the limits of its adaptability and its power to accomplish the goals of the reformers in the early years of the twentieth century. From three perspectives, liberal ideas of deference and proceduralism proved too limited to adapt to the changing circumstances of German society and economy. This chapter addresses the first of the three limits of liberalism, the limits of *Honoratiorenpolitik* and the deference upon which it was based as it played out in the conflict within the legal profession over simultaneous admission of district court practitioners to practice before superior courts.[1]

Beneath the facade of institutional growth of professional self-government and self-discipline, behind the image of a unified and

---

1 For an earlier version of this discussion, see Kenneth F. Ledford, "Conflict within the Legal Profession: Simultaneous Admission and the German Bar 1903–1927," in Geoffrey Cocks and Konrad H. Jarausch, eds., *German Professions, 1800–1950* (Oxford, 1990), 252–69. See also the illuminating account of the long history of the issue of simultaneous admission in Jarausch, *The Unfree Professions*, 12, 34–5, and 72–3.

vital free profession that rose above both the individual interests of its members and the interests of the profession to represent the general interest, a solvent was at work that eventually eroded the self-conception of the practicing bar as the general estate and revealed the legal profession to be a congeries of conflicting interests. After 1900 a dispute emerged between two segments of the bar, lawyers who practiced before district courts and those who practiced before superior courts. As the dispute became ever more vituperative and bitter, it polarized and paralyzed the institutions of the private bar, rendering them irrelevant to the outcome of the underlying policy dispute. Facing two firmly held notions of justice, the DAV and lawyers' chambers could attempt only procedural solutions to the conflict, none of which satisfied the determined parties. The combatants first made the institutions of the private bar the terrain of their struggle, as those institutions became the object of a battle for power within the profession. But soon the locus of the struggle shifted to the direct appeal by new, special-interest associations to government agencies and to the Reichstag to intervene by legislation to resolve the irreconcilable struggle. The conflict that raged over simultaneous admission destroyed the legitimacy of *Honoratiorenpolitik*, as district court lawyers challenged the hegemony of the lawyer-notables who led the DAV and the lawyers' chambers; it rendered those institutions irrelevant to the final outcome and left a legacy of bitterness and distrust that lasted until 1933; and it unmasked the private legal profession, demystifying its ideology of disinterest. No longer the general estate, the bar was at best simply another special interest, at worst a quarrelling amalgam of many special interests.

The Structure of the Conflict

The RAO and the other laws of 1877–9 created a structural cleavage within the legal profession, a fundamental conflict of interests between district and superior court lawyers. Each lawyer was admitted to only one court and had to reside in the town in which it was located (RAO §8, §18). Thus, upon seeking admission each lawyer had to choose whether to practice before a court of appeal, a superior court, or a district court. Mandatory representation by a lawyer admitted before that court applied in civil cases at the court of appeal and superior court; thus a party *had* to hire a lawyer from among the bar of that court. Conversely, the rule of mandatory representation did *not* apply in civil cases at the district court level. This meant that superior court lawyers could represent clients before district courts, but district court lawyers could not represent even their own regular clients in cases pending in superior court. Superior court lawyers, therefore, could compete with district court lawyers on the latter's home turf, but not vice versa, even when the district court lawyer's client sought representation in an appeal to superior court. The law thus created an asymmetrical relation of power between superior and district court lawyers.

As detailed in Chapter 3, the issue of localization and simultaneous admission of district court lawyers had provoked much contention during the Reichstag debates on the Imperial Justice Laws.[2] Lawyers themselves had advocated the widest possible standards of simultaneous admission, but concerns by the Prussian and Bavarian governments about delays in judicial proceedings caused by lawyers who appeared in far-removed courthouse towns, especially in sparsely populated rural areas, had led the proponents of reform, despite the forceful warnings of Windthorst and the Center party, to concede that RAO §9 should read:

A lawyer admitted before a district court *can* be admitted at the same time before the superior court in whose bailiwick the district court is located. . . . The admission *must* occur when opinions of the court of appeal and the executive board of the lawyers' chamber agree that it would promote the interests of the administration of justice [emphasis added].

Under this provision, then, the ministry of justice of each federal state, which officially effected admission, had discretion to grant simultaneous admission either generally or in specific cases ("*can* be admitted"); agreement by the court of appeal and the executive board of the local lawyers' chamber made it mandatory ("*must* occur"). In general then, the power to determine whether simultaneous admission would be the rule in a German state lay in either the hands of the ministry of justice or jointly in the hands of the judges of the court of appeal and the executive board of the lawyers' chamber.[3]

Soon after the enactment of the RAO, two policies emerged in Germany regarding simultaneous admission. In smaller and middle

---

2 Chapter 3, 70–4.
3 District court lawyers later accepted it as a given that the absence of simultaneous admission in 1879 stemmed from the political fear that rural areas would be flooded by "democratic" lawyers if simultaneous admission became generally available; Verein deutscher Amtsgerichtsanwälte to Rechtsausschuß des Reichstags, May 1925, G.St.A., I HA Rep. 84a, 72, 591–7, 595.

states, in which distances, travel times, and increased costs were not likely to be considerable, the ministry of justice often routinely granted petitions by district court lawyers to be admitted also at the appropriate superior court. This became the practice in Baden, Braunschweig, Bremen, Hamburg, the two Lippes, Lübeck, Mecklenburg, Oldenburg, and Saxony. The two largest German states, however, Bavaria and Prussia, routinely refused to grant simultaneous admission unless special circumstances applied.[4] In 1894 the Prussian Ministry of Justice explained its policies toward granting simultaneous admission. In the absence of the mandatory conditions (namely the concurrence of the court of appeal and executive board of the lawyers' chamber that simultaneous admission was in the interest of the administration of justice), the ministry routinely denied applications because:

The lawyer is to provide his advice and legal representation in the first instance to residents of the place at which he has been admitted. If he travels to the superior court, he fragments his professional activity and more or less deprives those who in the first instance and principally depend upon his assistance of the opportunity for representation.[5]

The ministry would exercise its discretion only when it thought it to be in the best interests of the "justice-seeking public." Such instances included: (1) when a particular substantive law applied at the district court that did not apply at the superior court (a circumstance obviated by the effectiveness of the Civil Law Code in 1900); (2) when the public in a locale made great clamor to be represented in superior court by their local district court lawyer; and (3) in other special circumstances, such as complicated legal relationships among the parties or when simultaneous admission was necessary in order for the district court lawyer to earn a satisfactory living.[6]

Although these conflicting policies among the several German states posed no difficulty at first, the latent cleavage within the bar became the cause of a great upheaval within the private bar after the turn of the century. The growth of a new district court bar laid the foundation for a conflict that would paralyze the institutions of the bar and shake its claim to represent the public interest.

---

4 *Simultanzulassung*, 28; the ministries of justice of Hesse and Thüringen also routinely refused applications for simultaneous admission in certain areas, but the key battleground was in the largest German state, Prussia.
5 Prussian Ministry of Justice to Prussian Minister of State, Foreign Minister, and Imperial Chancellor Caprivi, 23 May 1894, G.St.A., I HA Rep. 84a, 71, 223–9, 225–6.
6 Ibid.

The Emergence of a District Court Bar, 1878–1900

Little friction between district court and superior court lawyers arose in the first years after the legal reforms for three reasons. First, the transitional provisions of the RAO granted any lawyer who had entered practice before 1 October 1879, admission as a matter of right to the superior court in whose district he lived (RAO §107). Thus, district court lawyers who were already admitted as of 1 October 1879, were entitled to simultaneous admission, and those who wished to do so took advantage of the opportunity. Second, few lawyers already in practice lived in district court towns as a result both of the policies of many state governments before 1879 to concentrate lawyers at the superior courts, for fear of stimulating trivial and unnecessary litigation, and as a result of the prior strict limitation in Prussia upon the number of lawyers at *any* court.[7] The result was that a very high proportion of district courts had no trained lawyer admitted before them. As Table 7.1 shows, on 1 January 1880, only 263 of the 1,735 district courts in the empire were served by a lawyer. Out of a total of 4,091 lawyers in all of Germany, only 165 practiced solely before a district court (Table 7.2). District court lawyers, therefore, were initially a tiny group, with no distinct corporate voice.

The third reason for the initial lack of friction between district court and superior court lawyers was the practice of fee splitting. When a district court lawyer referred a regular client to a superior court lawyer with a trial case (with an amount in controversy that exceeded the district court's jurisdictional amount) or an appeal, the two lawyers often agreed to split the fee. According to the strict terms of the Fees Statute for Lawyers, the superior court lawyer as plenipotentiary should have received three fees, while the district court lawyer would have received one and one-half fees as correspondent and for attending one evidentiary hearing. Superior court lawyers, in return for a steady stream of referrals, agreed to an equal division of the total fee. Some superior court lawyers, however, disputed the practice and argued that fee splitting was a violation of professional ethics. The disciplinary panels of the lawyers' chambers, under the control of collegial court lawyers, began to enforce the view that this practice was unethical. A decision of the supreme disciplinary panel for lawyers in 1888 upset this practice by ruling

---

7   Weißler, *Geschichte der Rechtsanwaltschaft*, 525.

Table 7.1.   *District courts in Germany without lawyers*

Year	Total courts	With lawyers	No lawyers
1880	1,735	263	1,068
1885	1,738	579	972
1887	1,737	665	950
1889	1,732	748	901
1891	1,734	786	881
1893	1,738	818	868
1895	1,743	844	845
1897	1,746	901	799
1899	1,749	965	751
1901	1,751	957	771
1903	1,752	986	746
1905	1,753	1,044	703
1907	1,760	1,119	637
1909	1,762	1,194	573
1911	1,765	1,316	449
1913	1,765	1,451	313
1915	1,769	1,484	283

Note: The column "Total Courts" includes those towns that possessed *only* a district court and excludes those that possessed collegial courts as well.
Source: Reichs Justiz-Amt, Deutsche Justiz-Statistik (Berlin), vols. 1–17 (1883–1915).

that fee splitting constituted unethical competition by underbidding on the part of the superior court lawyer.[8] Although fee splitting persisted, the official ethical position of the bar remained that it was impermissible.[9]

The expanding German economy after 1879 created a rapidly growing demand for legal services, with two results. First, the total number of lawyers in Germany grew rapidly in absolute terms, as reflected in

8 "Ehrengerichtliche Bestrafung zweier Rechtsanwälte wegen Gebührenteilung," *JW* 17 (1888): 92. For an historical overview of the practice of fee splitting, see Robert Held, *Die Gebührenteilung. Referat der 3. Abteilung des 4. Ausschußes des Deutschen Anwaltvereins* (Leipzig, 1928).
9 See the discussion in Richard Finger, *Die Kunst des Rechtsanwalts. Eine systematische Darstellung ihrer Grundfragen unter besonderer Berücksichtigung der ehrengerichtlichen Rechtsprechung* (Berlin, 1912), 53–4. Observers expressed surprise at the proscription of a practice that many had viewed as acceptable and predicted dire consequences for both the prestige and income of district court lawyers; "Gebührentheilung und Lokalisierung," *JW* 17 (1888): 193–4.

Table 7.2.   *Growth of the district court bar in Germany*

Year	Total lawyers	Sup.ct. only	Same town	Diff. town	Dist.ct. only
1880	4,091	485	378	165	
1885	4,536	469	346	588	
1887	4,787	2,650	483	334	757
1889	5,097	2,773	514	311	931
1891	5,317	2,802	593	305	1,060
1893	5,542	2,915	654	299	1,129
1895	5,795	3,005	691	319	1,196
1897	6,166	3,132	767	361	1,302
1899	6,602	3,250	890	414	1,411
1901	6,800	3,281	1,003	453	1,411
1903	7,235	3,428	1,144	484	1,490
1905	7,835	3,373	1,325	537	1,643
1907	8,608	2,737	1,572	666	1,749
1909	9,578	2,928	2,004	744	2,028
1911	10,817	3,191	2,320	832	2,459
1913	12,297	3,533	2,754	888	2,947
1915	13,024	3,595	3,067	898	3,123

Note: The figures for the total number of lawyers do *not* include the approximately twenty lawyers who practiced before the Imperial Supreme Court (*Reichsgericht*).
Source: Reichs Justiz-Amt, *Deutsche Justiz-Statistik* (Berlin), vols. 1–17 (1883–1915).

Table 7.2. Much of this growth went to accommodate demand for legal services that had been left unsatisfied under the former system of *numerus clausus*, but much of it too was a response to an expanding market for legal representation. Concern soon arose about a possible overcrowding of the profession, and the long struggle over the issue of limitations upon admission began (see Chapter 8).

Second, lawyers from this expanding pool increasingly began to seek admission before district courts. The district court bar became the fastest growing segment of the legal profession. Whereas in 1880 only 15 percent of all district courts had lawyers admitted to practice before them, by 1915 84 percent had lawyers (Table 7.1). By law, these practitioners lived in the small towns in which the district courts were located, becoming integral and respected members of the local community.[10] Nationwide, the bar that practiced solely before

10   For an illuminating local study of the influence of local notables of the *Bildungsbürgertum* in small towns, albeit in the twentieth century, see Lawrence D. Stokes, "Professionals and National Socialism: The Case Histories of a Small-Town Lawyer and Physician, 1918–1925," *German Studies Review* 8 (1985): 449–80.

Table 7.3.   *Growth of the district court bar in Prussia*

	Total lawyers		Sup.ct.lawyers		Dist.ct.lawyers	
Year	Prussia	Celle	Prussia	Celle	Prussia	Celle
1880	1,863	215	1,693	148	100	59
1881	1,951	212	1,731	148	132	56
1882	2,009	207	1,720	144	199	56
1883	2,130	206	1,757	143	279	56
1884	2,258	205	1,777	141	382	56
1885	2,429	214	1,832	145	487	62
1886	2,560	217	1,877	150	570	60
1887	2,692	217	1,913	146	652	63

Note: The number of district court lawyers in the district of the court of appeal in Celle differs in this table from the number given in Table 5.2 because of those lawyers whose simultaneous admission was grandfathered under the provisions of RAO §107.
Source: G.St.A., I HA Rep. 84a, 10344–5, "Gesetzliche Ordnung der Verhältnisse des Anwalts- und Advokatenstandes, 1881–3, 1884–7."

district courts increased tenfold between 1880 and 1905, while the bar as a whole less than doubled. In Prussia the changes in the early years were even more dramatic. Table 7.3 reveals that the district court bar grew fivefold in the first eight years after the Imperial Justice Laws, accounting for two-thirds of the total growth of the Prussian bar. Superior court lawyers expanded into district court practice as well, seeking formal simultaneous admission, usually to the district court in the same town as their superior court.[11] The number of lawyers admitted to a superior court and a district court *not* in the same town, the true class of simultaneously admitted district court lawyers, grew at a much slower rate, and that growth lay almost entirely outside of Prussia and Bavaria.[12]

District court lawyers, then, emerged as a separate and numerically significant group for the first time after 1879. After the turn of the century, they began to express themselves in the organs and associations of the legal profession. They began a struggle for status,

11   The result was that, even in Prussia, by 1913 there were generally no separate district and superior court bars in the seats of superior courts.
12   In 1894, in all of Prussia there were only seventy-six district court lawyers who were simultaneously admitted to superior courts in towns other than that in which the district court was located, and only one in the province of Hannover; Prussian Minister of Justice to Prussian Minister of State, Foreign Minister, and Imperial Chancellor Caprivi, 23 May 1894, G.St.A., I HA Rep. 84a, 71, 221, 223–9, 228.

income, and power within the profession that culminated with the adoption of mandatory simultaneous admission in 1927.

The Dispute Breaks Out

Around the turn of the twentieth century, concern began to grow about the position of district court lawyers. Although Prussia promoted the settlement of lawyers in small district court towns by early conferral of the notarial office, many observers feared that a combination of gradual inflation, the prohibition upon fee splitting, and competition from lay practitioners would cause a migration of lawyers from district courts to collegial courts.[13] District court lawyers expressed their resentment at the inequity of a system of admission that barred them from representing their regular clients before superior courts while permitting superior court lawyers to compete with them for cases at their district courts. They began to agitate for reform within the DAV and succeeded in having the topic "How can the position of lawyers admitted before the district courts be strengthened?" placed on the agenda for the sixteenth Lawyers' Convention in Strassbourg in 1903.[14] Because of a full agenda and the press of time in Strassbourg, however, the DAV postponed consideration of that issue until the next convention, to be held in Hannover in 1905. Articles in the *Juristische Wochenschrift* in 1903–5 established both the specific arguments and the rhetorical tone of the debate that lasted until 1927.

A district court lawyer named Bamberger, from Aschersleben in Prussia, published in 1903 the position paper that he would have presented at Strassbourg. District court lawyers, he argued, looked like second-class lawyers. While the rule of mandatory representation by counsel protected lawyers at collegial courts from competition, district court lawyers not only had no such advantage but had to compete with all of the 7,500 lawyers in the empire, with litigants representing themselves, and with every lay practitioner that the

13 Ostler, *Die deutschen Rechtsanwälte*, treats the struggle for simultaneous admission of district court lawyers at some length, 68–78; his statement about the fear of a withdrawal of lawyers from district courts is found on 71. For the Prussian policy of early conferral of the notarial office in order to encourage lawyers to serve small district court clients, see *Simultanzulassung*, 35.
14 Ibid., 72. See also the footnote to the article by Bamberger (Aschersleben), "Durch welche Mittel ist die Stellung der Amtsgerichtsanwälte zu stärken?" *JW* 32 (1903): 377.

court saw fit to admit.[15] Moreover, the Code of Civil Procedure confined the jurisdiction of the district court to petty cases (*Bagatellsachen*). These restrictions necessarily diminished the prestige of district court lawyers. Bamberger argued that this problem was serious enough to justify reform, regardless of any consequent disadvantage to the income of the superior court lawyer. The injury to prestige was the key grievance; district court lawyers disclaimed any interest in increasing their income. Bamberger recommended two legislative reforms to answer the question posed in his title; the first and most important remedy was to adopt simultaneous admission as a matter of right, and the second was to increase the jurisdictional amount for district courts from 300 to 500 marks.[16] Bamberger closed his article with a proposed strategy for district court lawyers to pursue in seeking simultaneous admission. He called upon district court lawyers to demand proportional representation on the executive boards of the lawyers' chambers. District court lawyers distrusted these bodies, believing that they were dominated by collegial court lawyers who used their majority to advance their own interests. Until the adoption of simultaneous admission, district court lawyers would have to resort to self-help.

A superior court lawyer, Hans Stölzle of Kempten in Bavaria, quickly responded.[17] Setting a pattern that spokesmen for superior court lawyers would consistently follow, Stölzle treated the issue solely as one of economics. While it was indeed true that district lawyers enjoyed no statutory rule of mandatory representation, it was also indisputable that they usually enjoyed a *de facto* monopoly; in fact, the increasing number of district court lawyers was driving superior court lawyers out of the district court practice. Superior court lawyers were likewise limited to one court and also had to

15　Ibid., 377. Arguments in *favor* of simultaneous admission, which remained remarkably consistent from the debates in the Reichstag in 1876–8 to 1927, are recapitulated in *Simultanzulassung*, 30–3, and Georg Reidnitz, *Lokalisation und Simultanzulassung* (Mainz, 1911). See also Hermann Raabe (Barmstedt), *Die Simultanzulassung der Amtsgerichtsanwälte beim Landgericht. Eine Entgegnung auf die gleichlautende Schrift von Justizrat Goldschmidt-Breslau* (Altona, 1921).
16　He argued that this represented no real increase in jurisdictional amount, but rather it was merely an adjustment for inflation; ibid., 379.
17　Hans Stölzle, "Durch welche Mittel ist die Stellung der amtsgerichtlichen Anwälte zu stärken? Entgegnung auf den Artikel des Herrn Rechtsanwalts Bamberger von Aschersleben im Nr. 46 und 47 S. 377 der *Juristischen Wochenschrift* vom 4. November 1903," *JW* 32 (1903): 428. The counter-arguments of superior court lawyers *against* simultaneous admission are all assembled in Martin Goldschmidt, *Die Simultanzulassung der Amtsgerichtsanwälte beim Landgericht* (Berlin, 1921).

relinquish their clients to other lawyers when their cases went up on appeal. District court lawyers usually were the only lawyers in their towns, whereas the number of lawyers in each superior court town had grown quite rapidly, resulting in more competition. The cost of living in the small district court towns was much lower. If district court lawyers considered it a slight that they had to compete with or argue against parties who argued their own cases and against lay practitioners, Stölzle noted that they had known from the beginning the situation into which they were getting, so that their lot was self-chosen.[18] He agreed that the admission of lay practitioners affronted the prestige of the entire legal profession, not just district court lawyers; the remedy, however, was to eliminate the occupation of lay practitioner.

Stölzle saved his harshest words for the proposal to widen the jurisdiction of district courts. To raise the limit to 1,000 marks would mean nothing less than the annihilation of the superior court bar; such a proposal was simply indiscussible.[19] He then attacked district court lawyers for employing strategies such as jurisdiction by consent (*Prorogation*) and the division of larger disputes into multiple cases of less than 300 marks (*Objektenteilung*) to expand the jurisdiction of district courts by subterfuge.

In 1904 and 1905, the disputing factions filled the pages of the *Juristische Wochenschrift* with the debate. District court lawyers repeatedly insisted that the issue was one of professional status, not of income.[20] Since the income of district court lawyers was no consideration, any damage to the income of superior court lawyers by simultaneous admission should also be disregarded.[21] District court lawyers needed simultaneous admission immediately to rectify their status as second-class lawyers, both in the eyes of the public and of other lawyers.[22] Simultaneous admission would increase the public's selection of lawyers for superior court cases, which was in the best interest of justice

---

18 Ibid.
19 Ibid., 430. Interestingly and revealingly, Stölzle referred to district court matters as *Bagatellobjekte* ("petty amounts in controversy"), showing remarkable insensitivity to the status concerns of district court lawyers whose practices were limited to handling such matters.
20 Eduard Rose (Harburg), "Die Stärkung der Stellung der ben den Amtsgerichten zugelassenen Rechtsanwälte," *JW* 33 (1904): 49; Balzer (Lorsch), "Die Stellung der nur bei einem Amtsgerichte zugelassenen Rechtsanwälte und deren Verbesserung," *JW* 33 (1905): 380, 381, 382; Schulze (Delitzsch), "Die Stellung der nur bei einem Amtsgerichte zugelassenen Rechtsanwälte und deren Verbesserung," *JW* 33 (1905): 384–5.
21 Rose, "Die Stärkung," 51; Balzer, "Die Stellung," 381, 382.
22 Ibid., 380; Rose, "Die Stärkung," 49; Schulze-Delitzsch, "Die Stellung," 383.

and of the justice-seeking public; it would reduce the cost of trying cases; and it would fulfill the "right" of the public to have a lawyer in their hometown who could handle all of their legal matters at the trial-court level.[23] It would eliminate the danger that the present system would reintroduce the old system of procurators and advocates by the backdoor, with district court lawyers preparing cases for superior court lawyers, who then had the exclusive right to appear before the court and plead them.[24]

The initial tone of the debate was harsh and hostile on both sides. District court lawyers accused the executive boards of lawyers' chambers, dominated by superior court lawyers, of insensitivity to their needs and of failure to push hard enough with the ministry of justice for simultaneous admission.[25] They warned superior court lawyers not to reduce the argument to a matter of money, for this could lead to a split in the profession. Most ominously, these leaders of the district court lawyers already threatened an organizational split within the practicing bar if they did not soon achieve their goal of simultaneous admission.[26] The acrimonious tone of debate made the crucial nature of the question of simultaneous admission clear when the seventeenth Lawyers' Convention convened in Hannover on 13 September 1905, to debate the topic "The situation of lawyers admitted only before a district court and its improvement."[27]

At this convention the great champion of the cause of district court lawyers, Eduard Rose of Harburg, delivered the principal address.

23 Balzer, "Die Stellung," 381; Rose, "Die Stärkung," 50.
24 Rose "Die Stärkung," 50, 49; Arnold Ziese, "Die Stellung der nur bei einem Amtsgerichte zugelassenen Rechtsanwälte und deren Verbesserung," *JW* 34 (1905): 386.
25 Balzer, "Die Stellung," 381. District court lawyers were certainly correct in their belief that they were underrepresented on the executive boards of the lawyers' chambers. In the district of the court of appeal of Celle (encompassing the Prussian province of Hannover), only one *ever* served on the fifteen-member executive board before 1904. Eduard Rose of Harburg was elected in 1904, at a time when there were 101 district court lawyers out of a total of 272, over a third of the total membership. He remained the sole district court lawyer on the board until 1924, when an amendment to the bylaws increased the size of the board.
26 Ibid., 382; Rose, "Die Stärkung," 51.
27 Superior court lawyers replied in print to the arguments of the district court lawyers before this lawyers' convention. They argued: (1) superior court lawyers also competed with lay people and lay practitioners when they practiced before district courts, and they did not feel that their prestige was thereby damaged; (2) a greater proportion of district court lawyers had busy practices than superior court lawyers; (3) disciplinary offenses and unethical conduct were temptations to be avoided, and not cause for a change in ethical standards; and (4) the public prestige of most district court lawyers was raised in most cases by the fact that most of them were also notaries. Karl Wilhelm Lütkemann (Hannover), "Noch einmal die Stellung der 'nur bei den Amtsgerichten' zugelassenen Rechtsanwälte," *JW* 33 (1904): 225–6.

His argument was calm and clear, but even in the beginning he emphasized what was at stake:

I believe, gentlemen, that as a result of this consideration, the entire bar, even beyond the district court lawyers, would have to be favorably disposed toward these wishes [of district court lawyers] and have to contribute to their fulfillment, in order to nip in the bud a schism within the bar, which is only distantly possible at this time.[28]

Rose strongly denied that the issue was one of money. District court lawyers, he argued, would not dare bring before the assembly of all German lawyers the mere question of money. Rather, what was at stake was a pure question of status (*eine reine Standesfrage*). It was simply unjust and inequitable that a district court lawyer, who had exactly the same secondary education and who had to apply the same diligence and pay the same costs for a legal education as a collegial court lawyer, should be excluded from superior court cases and confined in his sphere of professional activity merely because he had been admitted to a district court: "Where the duties are the same, the rights should also be the same."[29]

One by one, Rose answered the objections to simultaneous admission.[30] He argued that superior court lawyers had often asserted but never proved that simultaneous admission would result in significant economic damage to them. The improved position of district court lawyers could *lessen* the overcrowding of the superior court bars by drawing lawyers off to district court towns.[31] Ultimately, however, the economic interests of superior court lawyers could never be decisive but would have to give way to the ideal interests of district court lawyers in status, prestige, and equality with collegial court lawyers.[32]

Simultaneous admission, Rose argued, was the only effective countermeasure to the degraded position of district court lawyers. Raising the jurisdictional competence of district courts would not address the issue of status and prestige; winning election to the executive boards

---

28   "Verhandlungen des XVII. Deutschen Anwaltstages zu Hannover am 13. und 14. September 1905," *JW* 34 (1905): 569, 601; these proceedings are also reprinted in part in *Simultanzulassung*, 158–79.

29   Ibid., 603. Although Rose denied that the question was one of economics, he argued that it was inequitable to exclude district court lawyers from the lucrative superior court practice without compelling justification.

30   Regarding one of the principle objections, namely that simultaneous admission would lead to a delay in cases because lawyers would be in one place when their cases came on for hearing in another, Rose argued that the increasing use of the telephone and automobile reduced that possibility; Rose, "Die Stärkung," 52.

31   "Verhandlungen des XVII. Deutschen Anwaltstages," 607.   32   Ibid., 615.

of lawyers' chambers was merely a small first step on the way to the goal of equality with collegial court lawyers. Finally, he rejected the suggestion that superior court lawyers be excluded from district court practice, thereby freeing district court lawyers from their competition and creating an exclusive district court bar.[33] Such a solution was the *opposite* of what district court lawyers wanted; they wanted instead to eliminate the barriers that held them in the position of second-class lawyers.[34]

Rose's address provoked a short and sharp response from a superior court lawyer. Siegfried Krimke, who practiced at the superior court of Verden, not far from Harburg, dismissed the arguments concerning prestige. Every lawyer, like every person, he argued, has the social position that he makes for himself, and any district court lawyer who does his duty to the fullest has the highest level of prestige in the eyes of the public. He agreed that being forced to compete against lay practitioners injured a lawyer's prestige and he endorsed a resolution to outlaw that trade, but its elimination was a governmental matter, not a professional one. He then sounded the theme that became the standard retort of superior court lawyers to the aspirations of district court lawyers: "Gentlemen, just as the entire social question is essentially no completely ideal question, we are also dealing here with a pure question of money."[35] If simultaneous admission were introduced, superior court lawyers in small superior courts would suffer great economic hardship. The interests of superior court lawyers were no less important than those of district court lawyers, and the former should not be injured in order to rectify the hardships of the latter.

Despite Krimke's arguments, the Lawyers' Convention endorsed simultaneous admission as a matter of right with only a few contrary votes, and charged the executive committee of the DAV with the task of lobbying the "legislative bodies" of the empire to adopt the necessary amendment to RAO §9.[36] The victory of district court lawyers was, however, not as complete as it seemed.

33 Adolf Weißler, "Die Amtsgerichtsanwaltschaft der Kern der Anwaltfrage," *DJZ* 10 (1905): 767–8.
34 "Verhandlungen des XVII. Deutschen Anwaltstages," 608.   35 Ibid., 610.
36 Ibid., 615. See also "Bericht des Referenten Justizrat Schatz, Leipzig," Anlage B, in Deutscher Anwaltverein, ed., *Um die Simultanzulassung. Bericht über die Ausschußverhandlungen im Deutschen Anwaltverein (Erster Teil)* (Leipzig, 1925), 22–43, 22 (hereafter cited as *Um die Simultanzulassung I*; the report will be cited "Schatz, 'Bericht' "). As Ostler indicates, the outcome of the Lawyers' Convention in Hannover is all the more remarkable

The eighteenth Lawyers' Convention in Mannheim in September 1907 examined proposed reforms of the Constitution of the Courts, the Code of Civil Procedure, and the Fees Statute for Lawyers, and in the course of its discussion again addressed simultaneous admission. After the airing of the usual arguments for and against the proposition, the convention adopted with an "overwhelming majority" the resolution that "all lawyers admitted to a court within the district of a superior court are to be granted admission to that superior court."[37] Despite this apparent continuation of the success of the district court lawyers, the tide was beginning to turn against them. At the nineteenth Lawyers' Convention in Leipzig in November 1907, an extraordinary convention called to discuss the draft reforms at greater length, the proposed increase in the jurisdictional competence of the district courts to 600 or even 1,000 marks led to sharp conflict between district and superior court lawyers. The proposed jurisdictional change mobilized superior court lawyers and caused them to attend the conventions in greater numbers than ever before, increasing the already overwhelming preponderance that they enjoyed.[38] The Reichstag adopted the reforms despite the opposition of the DAV and doubled the jurisdictional limit for district courts to 600 marks (effective 1 June 1909). Relations between district court and superior court lawyers deteriorated rapidly.

A parallel erosion of relations between the district and superior court bars took place in the province of Hannover, which "divided the plenary assembly of the lawyers' chamber as well as the executive board into two camps with opposing interests."[39] Applying strictly

when one considers that out of the 384 participants, 300 practiced before superior courts and courts of appeal, 75 only before district courts, and only 9 were simultaneously admitted before district and superior courts; *Simultanzulassung*, 158; Ostler, *Die deutschen Rechtsanwälte*, 74. See also the account of the Hannover Lawyers' Convention in Reidnitz, *Lokalisation*, 129–31. The executive board of the DAV duly informed the Prussian Ministry of Justice of the action taken in Hannover; Executive Board of the DAV to Prussian Minister of Justice, 10 November 1905, G.St.A., I HA Rep. 84a, 10347, 443. A marginal notation states: "Regarding point 1 [simultaneous admission], I have held a discussion with the Minister today. Decisions about the admission of district court lawyers to superior courts will still be made on a case-by-case basis, but admissions will be approved to a greater extent than previously was the case."

37 "Verhandlungen des XVIII. Deutschen Anwaltstages zu Mannheim am 11. und 12. September 1907. Stenographischer Bericht," *JW* 36 (1907): 592, 636–7; see also Ostler, *Die deutschen Rechtsanwälte*, 75, and Schatz, "Bericht," 22.

38 Ostler, *Die deutschen Rechtsanwälte*, 75, where he reports that there were 510 collegial court lawyers at Mannheim as opposed to 130 district court lawyers, and 1,003 from collegial courts at Leipzig as opposed to 189 from district courts.

39 Mundt, *100 Jahre Rechtsanwaltskammer*, 39, 19.

the principle of localization contained in the RAO, the executive board in Celle, dominated at all times by collegial court lawyers, consistently denied applications by district court lawyers for simultaneous admission to the superior court.[40] Because concurring favorable opinions by the court of appeal and the executive board of the lawyers' chamber were necessary to invoke the mandatory provisions of RAO §9, ¶2, this meant that the executive board served as the effective bar to district court lawyers' ambitions. Moreover, the executive board issued a series of advisory opinions and disciplinary rulings that ran contrary to the interests of district court lawyers and eventually provoked their activist response. In 1888 the board condemned the practice of fee splitting between lawyers who acted on behalf of one party in the same case.[41] Beginning in 1899, the board declared jurisdiction by consent and the division of larger claims into multiple ones of less than 300 marks each to be unethical.[42] Moreover, the board refused to endorse proposals to widen the competence of the district courts by increasing the jurisdictional amount.[43]

In 1902, the district court lawyers in the province of Hannover began to assert themselves more. At the plenary meeting that year, lawyers from Harburg brought up for discussion the proposals that no collegial court lawyer should represent parties before other courts (meaning district courts) to which more than one lawyer was admitted and that district court lawyers be represented upon the executive board.[44] Eduard Rose led the Harburg district court lawyers and

---

40　G.St.A. I HA Rep. 84a, 21912, 131 (1886). One admission application involved the lawyer Katzenstein who sought admission to the small superior court in Stade and the district court in the large seaport and commercial center of Harburg. The board explicitly cited the principle of localization, and Katzenstein was admitted only before the district court in Harburg, showing his judgment as to where the more lucrative practice for him lay. The board followed this policy consistently from the early days of the chamber, beginning in 1885, ibid., 116R, including two other denials in 1886, ibid., 130R, 134, and at least one denial in 1888, ibid., 160R, in 1904, ibid., 343R, and in 1909, G.St.A I HA Rep. 84a, 21913, 62. Harburg, the largest district court town in the province of Hannover, remained a hotbed of activism for district court lawyers until after the adoption of simultaneous admission in 1927.

41　G.St.A. I HA Rep. 84a, 21912, 163: "The executive board considers the division of fees in general between lawyers of different courts to be contrary to the interests of the administration of justice and to the interests of the bar in private practice. In particular, it considers general agreements without consideration of the facts of the individual case at hand to be impermissible."

42　G.St.A. I HA Rep 84a, 21912, 279 (1899); G.St.A. I HA Rep. 84a, 21913, 11 (1905); 23 (1906); and 54R (1908).

43　G.St.A. I HA Rep. 84a, 21912, 211 (1893) and I HA Rep. 84a, 21913, 39 (1907).

44　G.St.A. I HA Rep. 84a, 21912, 311R.

proposed that some present members of the executive board resign in order to permit representation of the district court lawyers. The board refused to do so, but in 1904 Rose was elected to the next vacancy on the executive board and served until his death in 1926.[45]

Despite the actions of the Lawyers' Conventions in Hannover in 1905 and in Mannheim in 1907, the lack of progress toward simultaneous admission and the power of the executive boards of lawyers' chambers, dominated by collegial court lawyers, to block their applications for simultaneous admission frustrated district court lawyers. Resolutions by several executive boards in opposition to the increase in jurisdictional amount sharpened their anger. District court lawyers thus began to form special-interest bar associations to represent their interests more effectively than existing bar associations. On 25 January 1907, Rose informed the Prussian Minister of Justice that district court lawyers had formed the Association of German District Court Lawyers and forwarded a copy of the by-laws of the group.[46] The sole purpose of the association was "to promote the interests of district court lawyers" (§1). Rose told the Minister of Justice that even if the proposed increase in jurisdictional amount became law, the association still believed in the need for simultaneous admission. This association set the precedent of a special-interest subgroup of the bar forming its own association to advance its own goals, first within the framework of the DAV, and if necessary, as hints in the writings and speeches of district court lawyers had made clear ever since 1903, outside the framework of the DAV and in direct conflict with it or with other special-interest subgroups of lawyers.[47]

Indeed, the Association of German District Court Lawyers immediately began its campaign for legislative reform, whose aim was to attain simultaneous admission. In 1907 and again in 1910, it petitioned the Reichstag to amend the RAO to provide for mandatory simultaneous admission upon application, presenting the same arguments in its petitions that had aired in 1903–7.[48] Although these petitions lan-

---

45 Mundt, *100 Jahre Rechtsanwaltskammer*, 29; G.St.A. I HA Rep. 84a, 21913, 5.
46 Rose to PMJ, 25 January 1907, G.St.A., I HA Rep. 84a, 10348, 11–18; the bylaws are in ibid., 33–4.
47 See, for example, the New Year's commentary by the editor of the *JW* in 1913, in which he laments the resolution of the district court lawyers' association to "take matters into their own hands" and to make reform proposals directly to the government instead of going through the channels of the DAV; Neumann, "Zum neuen Jahr," *JW* 42 (1913): 1.
48 Petitions to Reichstag, G.St.A., I HA Rep. 84a, 10348, 165–75 (10 February 1907), and ibid., 439–46 (20 April 1910).

guished in inaction after their referral to the Committee on Petitions, the district court lawyers had begun their long resort to institutions *outside* of the profession for redress of their professional grievances.

But the district court lawyers did not abandon their struggle *within* the profession. Since the reforms of 1907–9 had not introduced simultaneous admission, they again placed the topic on the agenda of the twenty-first Lawyers' Convention at Breslau in 1913. Victor Berger, who prepared the position paper published in advance of the convention, assumed that such a measure corresponded to the will of the entire practicing bar, concluded that district court lawyers suffered second-class status, and moved that the DAV reaffirm its support for simultaneous admission.[49] The main speakers at the convention shared this conviction; both treated the matter as settled, citing the resolutions at Hannover and Mannheim, and argued that such a step was necessary to raise the status of district court lawyers.[50] Superior court lawyers in attendance, though, certainly did not consider the issue settled. They argued that simultaneous admission would work economic ruin upon lawyers who practiced before small and medium-sized superior courts. The jurisdictional reforms of 1909 had already enriched district court lawyers at the expense of those at superior courts, and the former should now be satisfied. This was no time to undertake an experiment that would endanger the largest segment of the bar.[51] Explicit now in the arguments of the superior court lawyers was a threat:

Do not believe that you will avoid the impending schism if you adopt simultaneous admission. To be sure, superior court lawyers at small and medium-sized courts have not yet organized; that is their disadvantage against district court lawyers, and it is explicable by the fact that heretofore

49 Victor Berger, "Freizügigkeit und Simultanzulassung. Gutachten, erstattet im Auftrage des Vorstandes des Deutschen Anwaltvereins für den XXI. Deutschen Anwaltstag," *JW* 42 (1913): Zugabe zu Nr. 13, 15: "Localization of district court lawyers degrades the entire bar. 'The district court lawyer is condemned to a life sentence as the lawyer for petty cases.' It cannot be stressed often enough that he is equated with the *Winkelkonsulenten*, even after he has sacrificed many years of his life to study and preparatory legal training. The state denies him the lawyers' monopoly and makes him into a second-class lawyer. That is no mere empty phrase, rather, unfortunately, an only too true saying."

50 "Verhandlungen des XXI. Deutschen Anwaltstages zu Breslau am 12. und 13. September 1913. Stenographischer Bericht," *JW* 42 (1913): Zugabe zu Nr. 20, 16 (Max Friedländer), 27 (Harnier).

51 See the address of Martin Goldschmidt (Ostrowo), ibid., 39–41, as well as idem, "Simultanzulassung," *JW* 42 (1913): 831, 842. Goldschmidt became one of the leading publicists of the superior court lawyers' cause, collecting their chief arguments in *Die Simultanzulassung* (1921).

the question has been addressed only from the standpoint of the district court lawyers.

(Quite right!)

Only he who has organization has power. But I do not know whether it would be a desirable condition if another group, an association of lawyers at small and medium-sized superior courts, appeared alongside the association of district court lawyers.

(Laughter.)

You will not avoid a schism by the endorsement of simultaneous admission, but rather provoke one.

(Quite right!)[52]

After much heated debate, the 1913 Lawyers' Convention removed the question of simultaneous admission from the agenda and referred it to the Committee on Professional Affairs of the DAV for study.[53] That committee met on 31 January 1914, and defeated two motions favorable to simultaneous admission. With the intervention of the First World War, the matter lay dormant until 1919.[54]

District court lawyers, however, had suffered a significant defeat. Whereas their aspirations had found a generally favorable reception within the DAV prior to 1913, their actions had galvanized superior court lawyers into resistance. Especially after the increase in the jurisdictional competence of the district courts in 1909, superior court lawyers who practiced before courts in small and medium-sized towns felt besieged. They exerted their strength as the majority within the DAV at Breslau in 1913, if not to reverse the position of the bar association, at least to exile the issue of simultaneous admission to procedural and parliamentary limbo.

Renewed Conflict, Paralysis, Resolution

After the war, district court lawyers once again raised their demand for simultaneous admission.[55] This renewed call evoked an almost

52   "Verhandlungen des XXI. Deutschen Anwaltstages," Martin Goldschmidt (Ostrowo), 40 (cited in Ostler, *Die deutschen Rechtsanwälte*, 77).
53   Ibid., 41–2; the Committee on Professional Affairs (also referred to as the "4th Committee") was the standing committee of the executive board of the DAV that had jurisdiction over professional matters, changes to the Lawyers' Statute and Fees Statute, etc. For an explanation of the committee structure of the DAV, see Heinrich Dittenberger, "Fünfzig Jahre Deutscher Anwaltverein 1871/1921," *JW* 50 (1921): 969, 1018.
54   Schatz, "Bericht," 23–4; Ostler, *Die deutschen Rechtsanwälte*, 77–8.
55   The exchange began with an article by a district court lawyer, Hawlitzky (Forst), *JW* 48 (1919): 990.

immediate response from superior court lawyers, who contended that simultaneous admission would unavoidably lead to the "annihilation of the economic existence of a very great number of superior court lawyers."[56] Agitation by district court lawyers caused the Reich Justice Ministry to ask the Bavarian and Prussian ministries to consider how they could accommodate the wishes of district court lawyers more than they had in the past.[57] A local association of district court lawyers in Düsseldorf in 1920 petitioned the Reich Ministry of Justice, going over the head of the Prussian ministry. Citing examples of expanding simultaneous admission in other German states since the end of the war, they argued: "What is just for one is equitable for the other."[58] Despite prodding by the Reich ministry, the Prussian Ministry of Justice declined to change its policy of restrictive, case-by-case decision making.[59]

The Association of German District Court Lawyers also sought to revive the question of simultaneous admission within the DAV. In a time of great economic hardship for all lawyers, as well as for the rest of German society, the association in September 1920 petitioned the executive board of the DAV to seek an emergency decree to permit simultaneous admission.[60] At its meeting on 4 and 5 December 1920, the executive board of the DAV affirmed its endorsement of simultaneous admission and referred the matter to the Committee on Professional Affairs to debate draft legislation. The chair of the executive board argued that the existing conflict threat-

---

56 Martin Kanter (Limburg), "Die Zulassung der Amtsgerichtsanwälte bei den Landgerichten," *Abl* 7 (1920): 20–2, 20; see also the further response, Hawlitzky (Forst), "Die Bewegung der Amtsgerichtsanwaltschaft, insbesondere ihre Zulassung zu den Landgerichten," *Abl* 7 (1920): 115–17.

57 RMJ to PMJ, 23 July 1920, G.St.A., I HA Rep. 84a, 71, 125.

58 Verein der Amtsgerichtsanwälte des Oberlandesgerichtsbezirks Düsseldorf to RMJ, 6 July 1920, ibid., 127–8; the association in Düsseldorf had been founded on 28 February 1920, for the purpose of "the improvement of the economic circumstances of district court lawyers and the elimination of the differences between the superior court and district court lawyer (simultaneous admission)"; "Verein der Amtsgerichtsanwälte Düsseldorf," *Abl* 7 (1920): 96.

59 PMJ to RMJ, 7 August 1920, ibid. 131–2.

60 For a description of the economic distress among lawyers toward the end of the war, see Landsberg, "Die Notlage der Anwaltschaft," *JW* 47 (1918): 73. See also Ostler, *Die deutschen Rechtsanwälte*, 152–60, 202–16. It should be noted that the effects of the wartime and postwar inflation were especially harsh for district court lawyers. As prices increased, more and more cases of even a petty nature exceeded the jurisdictional limit of district courts. This "migration of cases" to superior courts seemed to district court lawyers to indicate most sharply the need for simultaneous admission; see *Simultanzulassung*, 44. For the situation during the hyperinflation, see Noest, "Die Lage der Amtsgerichtsanwälte," *JW* 52 (1923): 6, and Hermann Raabe (Barmstedt i. Holstein), "Das Ende der Deutschen Amtsgerichtsanwaltschaft," *JW* 53 (1924): 901.

ened the bar to its very roots and that unity must be restored by adoption of simultaneous admission, despite the possibility of economic harm to superior court lawyers.[61] For the leadership of the DAV, the question was no longer one of the merits of simultaneous admission but rather how to defuse the conflict between district court and superior court lawyers before it destroyed the DAV and the unity of the practicing bar.

The endorsement of simultaneous admission by the executive board of the DAV had precisely the opposite effect. Ninety-seven superior court lawyers from Prussia and Bavaria met at Leipzig on 23 January 1921, and founded the Association of German Superior Court Lawyers.[62] This special-interest bar association held its first meeting at Jena on 22 May 1921 and adopted as its organizational purpose "The safeguarding of the particular professional interests of the German superior court bar."[63] It invited the support of court of appeal lawyers and declared its special task to be opposition to the simultaneous admission sought by district court lawyers, which would damage the interests of the administration of justice and the economic interests of the vast majority of superior court lawyers, especially those who practiced at small and middle-sized courts.[64]

By 1921, then, two special-interest bar associations faced each other with clearly conflicting interests. Each association developed and strengthened its own institutional structure; district court lawyers had had their own monthly newspaper since 1909, and superior court lawyers founded their own monthly in 1925.[65] District court lawyers even held their own separate First German District Court Lawyers' Bar Convention in Frankfurt am Main in September 1921.[66]

---

61 Schatz, "Bericht," 25; see also "Sitzung des Vorstandes des Deutschen Anwaltvereins vom 4. und 5. Dez. 1920," *Abl* 7 (1920): 227–31, 228–9.

62 "Verein deutscher Landgerichtsanwälte, e.V.," *Abl* 8 (1921): 129–30.

63 Carstens (Cottbus), Chair of the Association of German Superior Court Lawyers, to PMJ, 2 June 1921, G.St.A., I HA Rep. 84a, 259–61. As to the organizational purpose of the Association of German Superior Court Lawyers, see also Goldschmidt, *Die Simultanzulassung*, III-V, and Meyerowitz (Magdeburg), "Zur Simultanzulassung," *JW* 50 (1921): 1179, 1181.

64 Carstens to PMJ, 2 June 1921, 259.

65 The district court lawyers' newspaper was called *Mitteilungen für Amtsgerichtsanwälte*; the one for superior court lawyers was *Nachrichtenblatt für die Mitglieder des Vereins Deutscher Landgerichtsanwälte, e.V.*. Copies of these periodicals can be found throughout the records of the Prussian Ministry of Justice, G.St.A., I HA Rep. 84a, 71–80.

66 "I. Deutscher Amtsgerichtsanwaltstag," *Abl* 8 (1921): 201–4; see also Raabe (Barmstedt), Chair of the Association of German District Court Lawyers, to PMJ, 19 September 1921, G.St.A., I HA Rep. 84a, 71, 307, in which he informed the minister of the election of

The very survival of the DAV as the effective voice of the practicing bar was at stake. If the associations of the district and superior court lawyers took it upon themselves to petition for administrative or legislative changes, if they arrogated to themselves the exclusive right to speak for their constituencies on the subject of simultaneous admission, then the unitary expression of the opinion of the bar would be lost. The government, in considering legislative reforms affecting lawyers, could dismiss the positions of the factions as special interest group pressures, contrary to the interests of justice. In the absence of a clear expression from the DAV, the only source of disinterested comment, the government would simply decide the matter in its free discretion. Lawyers would lose all influence in matters of great importance to them if they did not settle their internal dispute internally.[67]

Yet calls for unity did not deter the partisans of the district and superior court lawyers from threatening each other and the DAV. The executive boards of local associations of district court lawyers resolved to use all possible legal means to achieve their goal. First they should seek proportional representation in the executive boards of lawyers' chambers and, failing that, in the last resort create a completely separate organization, complete with its own lawyers' chambers and newspaper.[68] It was up to superior court lawyers to determine whether unity would survive, for drastic measures would certainly become necessary if they continued their stubborn opposition to the legitimate aspirations of district court lawyers.[69] Moreover, if superior court lawyers continued their obstructionism, district court lawyers might resort to an attack upon the principle of mandatory representation by a lawyer, the fundamental basis of collegial court lawyers' market control and monopoly. If the mandatory

association officers at the convention and demanded a promise that the Prussian ministry include the association in all discussions and occasions concerning the administration of justice and jurisprudence. Previously, the Association of German District Court Lawyers had met upon the occasion of a Lawyers' Convention of the DAV, such as in Leipzig in 1920; see the invitation at "Verein der Amtsgerichtsanwälte," *Abl* 7 (1920): 159.

67 Meyerowitz (Königsberg), "Zur Simultanzulassung," *JW* 50 (1921): 1180, 1181.
68 For examples of this strategy in 1921 by the lawyers' chambers in Naumburg and Kiel (both in Prussia), see Hannß (Merseburg), "Zur Frage der Simultanzulassung," *Abl* 8 (1921): 126–9, 126. District court lawyers believed themselves handicapped in attending the annual meetings of the lawyers' chambers. Not only did the law require that such meetings be held in superior court towns, but the best express-train connections favored the lawyers in *other* superior court towns, both to the disadvantage of the attendance of district court lawyers; "I. Deutscher Amtsgerichtsanwaltstag," *Abl* 8 (1921): 201–4.
69 Giese, "Aufhebung des 'örtlichen' Anwaltszwangs," 611.

representation rule disappeared, district court lawyers could practice freely at superior courts, but so could other, nonlawyer competitors. Once again, the choice belonged to the superior court lawyers.[70] Rival local associations of district and superior court lawyers in Schleswig-Holstein boycotted each other for several months in 1922, until finally they reached an agreement to split fees.[71] District court lawyers regularly walked out of meetings of lawyers' chambers after their applications for simultaneous admission had been denied, expressing their contempt for organizations which they accused of being dominated by superior court lawyers.[72]

Superior court lawyers also threatened to escalate the warfare. They argued that the actions of district court lawyers would force them to seek admission to the courts of appeal, increasing tension within the profession and unleashing a war of all against all.[73] They warned the DAV to stay out of the conflict between the special-interest associations. The DAV should not seek to act as arbiter in a case in which neither party wished arbitration and in which neither party would recognize the binding force of the arbitral decision.[74] The struggle would result in total victory for one side and total defeat for the other, and the DAV was irrelevant to the outcome.

But the burden of carrying the struggle forward lay with those who wished to change the status quo, the district court lawyers. They pursued their campaign for change on three fronts: within the DAV, within the lawyers' chambers, and with the state, both the administrative bureaucracies that dealt with legal reform and with the Reichstag.

THE CAMPAIGN WITHIN THE DAV

Once superior court lawyers founded their association, they demanded proportional representation upon the Committee on Professional Affairs of the DAV as it studied the question of how best to implement simultaneous admission. The committee co-opted three leaders of the superior court faction and two from the district court

70 Hawlitzky (Forst), "Zur Simultansulassung," *JW* 50 (1921): 1184, 1185.
71 Raabe, "Das Ende der Deutschen Amtsgerichtsanwaltschaft," 900, n. 1; Hannß, "Zur Frage der Simultanzulassung," 126.
72 Carstens (Cottbus), "Zur Frage der Simultanzulassung der Amtsgerichtsanwälte beim übergeordneten Landgericht," *JW* 50 (1921): 873, 875. For a catalogue of the confrontational tactics of the district court lawyers, see Hannß, "Zur Frage der Simultanzulassung," 126–9.
73 Carstens, "Zur Frage der Simultanzulassung," 875.   74 Ibid.

lawyers, as well as representatives from the regions where simultaneous admission prevailed, and met to discuss the matter on 23 April 1921.[75] The task of the committee was to discuss means of implementing simultaneous admission with as little economic hardship to superior court lawyers as possible, but the representatives of the superior court lawyers insisted that the committee reopen debate on the merits of the matter. Fearing that a decision for or against simultaneous admission by the DAV would sharpen the conflict further, the committee established a subcommittee composed of representatives of the district court and superior court lawyers' associations and chaired by a lawyer who belonged to neither group, to secure an agreement between the groups and to report back to the committee.[76]

The rhetorical battle between the two special interests raged in the professional press.[77] Most contributors lamented the "ugly and wretched" conflict; the practicing bar needed to maintain its unity at all times, and especially in times of economic hardship and hostility from all sides.[78] The practicing bar needed to exercise its right of self-preservation against outside enemies, but it was hampered in doing so by the split within its ranks. Even observers who doubted whether simultaneous admission was in the general interests of the bar or in the special interests of the district court bar believed that the disadvantages that arose from the disunity caused by the dispute outweighed those that would result from its introduction.[79] The only remedy to the continuing damage to the fabric of the practicing bar was for every lawyer to seek a compromise between the factions. Each opposing special-interest organization must find common ground and compromise rather than seek the radical implementation of its maximum program.[80]

The irreconcilable hostility of the two groups of lawyers blocked all efforts of the DAV and its committees to find a compromise solution. The subcommittee of the Committee on Professional Affairs reported

75 *Simultanzulassung*, 44; Schatz, "Bericht," 25.   76 Schatz, "Bericht," 25–6.
77 See Hannß, "Zur Frage der Simultanzulassung," 126–9 (pro-district court lawyers), and Buß (Darmstadt), "Simultanzulassung," *Abl* 8 (1921): 139–42 (pro-superior court lawyers), among many others in the course of 1921.
78 Giese (Mörs a. Rh.), "Aufhebung des 'örtlichen' Anwaltszwangs oder Simultanzulassung," *JW* 50 (1921): 610; Noest, "Zur Simultanzulassung," *JW* 50 (1921): 1179; Marquardt (Rosenberg, Wpr.), "Einigkeit!," *Abl* 8 (1921): 165–6.
79 Werner (Magdeburg), "Zur Simultanzulassung," *JW* 50 (1921): 1182, 1183.
80 Noest, "Zur Simultanzulassung," 1180; Giese, "Aufhebung des 'örtlichen' Anwaltszwangs," 611; Noest, "Die Lage der Amtsgerichtsanwälte," 7.

in March 1922 that its deliberations had collapsed, largely because the two groups insisted upon debating the merits of simultaneous admission instead of discussing the means of implementing it with the greatest protections to the superior court lawyers. Superior court lawyers refused to concede the validity of the endorsement of simultaneous admission by the executive board of the DAV.[81] Both special-interest associations called upon the DAV to withdraw from the discussions and to leave it to them to settle the matter.

The special-interest bar associations also struggled for power *within* the DAV. Focus turned to elections for the DAV representatives' assembly. The first postwar elections in December 1919 had seen a weak turnout, which many believed to have been caused by the difficulties of the territorial settlement in which many lawyers found their former homes now outside of German borders and had to find new places in which to settle. Moreover, local DAV organizations had been weak and the electoral procedure complex.[82] District court lawyers resolved to take better advantage of the next election.

In the representatives' assembly of 30 June 1923, slates of district court lawyers running under the ballot heading "District Court Lawyers" faced slates of superior court lawyers running in each superior court district and on a national list.[83] The Association of German District Court Lawyers implored its members to vote, urging them not to mail their ballots to the local DAV electoral officer but rather to bring them to the local association representative in person or send them by certified mail; the association's representative would then cast the ballots together.[84] While turnout remained low during the dislocation of the hyper-inflation, the result of the election was a remarkable change. District court lawyers rose from one to fifteen representatives in the assembly (out of a total of seventy-three; see Table 4.3); superior court lawyers fell from forty-five to seventeen. The beneficiaries of the sharp mobilization for elections to the representatives' assembly

81 Schatz, "Bericht," 26–8; see the relieved account of the collapse of negotiations given by Schulze (Delitzsch), "Endgültiges Scheitern der Verhandlungen über Simultanzulassung im IV. Ausschuß des deutschen Anwaltsvereins," *Mitteilungen für Amtsgerichtsanwälte* 13 (1922): 19, found in G.St.A., I HA Rep. 84a, 71, 439–50, 449.
82 Heinrich Dittenberger, "Die Vertreterversammlung vom 22. Februar 1920," *Abl* 7 (1920): 59–65, 60.
83 The rubric under which the superior court lawyers ran was *Anwaltszwang*; "Reichswahlvorschläge für die Wahl zur Vertreterversammlung des Deutschen Anwaltvereins," *Abl* 10 (1923): 81–4.
84 Schulze (Delitzsch), "Zur Wahl im Deutschen Anwaltvereins," *Mitteilungen für Amtsgerichtsanwälte* 6 (1923): 15, found in G.St.A., I HA Rep. 84a, 71, 811.

were court of appeal lawyers, whose number rose from twenty-five to forty. But the change in composition of the representatives' assembly brought the DAV no closer to a resolution of the dispute.

In 1924 and 1925, the DAV tried with a tone of increasing despera-tion to effect a compromise between the two factions. After the Association of District Court Lawyers again petitioned the Reichstag to enact simultaneous admission, the executive board of the DAV in November 1924 resolved:

> The executive board declares that it is its duty to settle the conflict between the two groups and to eliminate the causes of conflict. To do this, the Committee on Professional Affairs should work out suitable proposals to bring the interests of the two groups to an equitable compromise (*zum billigen Ausgleich bringen*).[85]

The discussions once again broke down in 1925, as district court lawyers refused to discuss the merits of simultaneous admission, considering that to have been settled in 1905, 1907, and 1920, and superior court lawyers refused to discuss economic safeguards unless the whole question of the merits was reopened.[86] The Association of German District Court Lawyers rejected a resolution that would have limited petitions directly to the government by both groups to the issue of simultaneous admission, in return for the DAV abandon-ing that issue, and the Committee on Professional Affairs had to report to the DAV its inability to reach a result.[87] By July 1925 the DAV was forced to concede its inability to mediate in the dispute and declared that it must "abstain from taking a position, inwardly or outwardly" with regard to the matter.[88]

THE CAMPAIGN WITHIN THE LAWYERS' CHAMBER

At the same time that the special-interest lawyers' groups struggled for control of the DAV, they battled on the more local front of the

---

85 "Aus der Vereinstätigkeit," *Abl* 11 (1924): 167–70, 168; see the plaintive repetition of the call for compromise in "Aus der Vereinstätigkeit," *Abl* 12 (1925): 8–10, 8.
86 The stenographic reports of the debates of the Committee on Professional Affairs in January and February of 1925 are reproduced in *Um die Simultanzulassung I*, 3–20, and Deutscher Anwaltverein, ed., *Um die Simultanzulassung. Bericht über die Ausschußverhand-lungen im Deutschen Anwaltverein (Zweiter Teil)* (Leipzig, 1925), 3–24 (hereafter cited as "*Um die Simultanzulassung II*"). The first session ended upon a hopeful note, but the second collapsed over the implacable opposition of the two factions.
87 *Um die Simultanzulassung II*, 24, with the resolution reprinted as Anlage 4, 27.
88 *Simultanzulassung*, 44–5; see also "Zur Simultanzulassung. Beschlüsse des Vorstandes des Deutschen Anwaltvereins vom 5. Juli 1925," *Abl* 12 (1925): 102.

lawyers' chambers. Their early lack of success in electing their own to membership on the executive boards of the lawyers' chambers had made district court lawyers realize that they were at a disadvantage under the rules of elections for those bodies. For example, in Hannover the elections to the executive board took place at the annual meeting, which was almost invariably held in the city of Hannover. Only those present at the meeting could cast ballots. This procedure favored lawyers who could easily attend the meeting. Not only did this give an advantage to the large bar of the city of Hannover, but rail connections tended to favor superior court lawyers.[89] District court lawyers advanced proportional representation on the executive board of the various segments of the bar and election by written absentee ballot as the just solutions to the problem.[90]

Before Hannoverian district court lawyers could raise the issue, the executive board of the lawyers' chamber, on which Eduard Rose of Harburg remained the only district court member, in 1921 officially rejected the principle of simultaneous admission.[91] As a result, 104 district court lawyers led by Rose and Carl Mosler of Lüchow met in Hannover on 18 December 1921, and founded the Association of District Court Lawyers of the Court of Appeal District Celle, the primary aim of which was to agitate for the introduction of simultaneous admission.[92] At the annual meeting of the lawyers' chamber in Hannover on 2 April 1922, the district court lawyers called for the introduction of generalized simultaneous admission as a matter of right *and* the adoption of a system of proportional representation in elections to the executive board. The particularly well-attended assembly (224 lawyers were present) rejected both motions by a large majority.[93] In an attempt to placate district court lawyers, the plenary

89 For an articulation of the complaints with the electoral process see Verein der Amtsgerichtsanwälte des Oberlandesgerichtsbezirks Celle to RMJ, 9 February 1923, G.St.A., I HA Rep. 84a 71, 738–40.
90 This proposal appeared among several in a discussion at the 22nd Bar Association meeting in Leipzig in September 1920; see "Sind Änderungen in der anwaltlichen Standesauffassung eingetreten und sollen deshalb Bestimmungen der Rechtsanwaltsordnung umgestaltet werden?" *Abl* 7 (1920): 178–80. The speakers opposed introduction of these measures, although one strongly recommended greater inclusion of district court lawyers and younger lawyers. Note that the demand for proportional representation dated back to Bamberger, "Durch welche Mittel?" in 1903.
91 G.St.A., I HA Rep. 84a, 21913, 217.
92 Wolpers (Uelzen), Schriftführer des Vereins der Amtsgerichtsanwälte für den Oberlandesgerichtsbezirk Celle, to PMJ, 16 January 1922, G.St.A., I HA Rep. 84a, 71, 357–8; see also the account in Mundt, *100 Jahre Rechtsanwaltskammer*, 29, 41.
93 District court lawyers published a special summons to their members to attend this meeting; see *Mitteilungen für Amtsgerichtsanwälte* 13 (1922): 20, found in G.St.A., I HA

meeting expanded the size of the executive board to twenty members and elected three district court lawyers to the five new positions, raising their total number to four.[94] This action proved insufficient for the district court activists, who walked out as a body in protest.[95] Although district court lawyers peppered the Prussian and Reich ministries of justice with petitions to introduce proportional representation and absentee balloting, the lawyers' chamber in Hannover never adopted such a reform.[96]

The executive board in Hannover continued stubbornly to oppose the introduction of simultaneous admission, restating its opposition to the court of appeal and Prussian Ministry of Justice in November 1924 and November 1925.[97] Moreover, the executive board also stubbornly continued to deny applications for simultaneous admission; there were two cases in 1920, two in 1921, four in 1924, two in 1925, and two in 1926.[98] Even after the Reichstag had adopted mandatory simultaneous admission in 1927, with an eight-year transitional period, the board denied three applications made under the old version of the RAO.[99] Frustrated in their efforts to gain satisfaction from the lawyers' chambers, district court lawyers had already turned their energies toward a legislative resolution of the dispute.

Rep. 84a, 71, 439–50, 450; for the report of the meeting, see G.St.A., I HA Rep. 84a, 21913, 221R.

94 The reasons advanced for this measure illustrate the assumptions of the lawyer-notables who ran the Celle lawyers' chamber. The increase in number was necessary, they reasoned, because two of the fifteen seats were allocated to lawyers at the court of appeal in Celle as required by the bylaws, four went to the very large superior court bar in the city of Hannover, and one by custom went to a lawyer from each of the remaining superior courts (including Lippe) in order to ensure that the executive board would have firsthand knowledge of conditions in each superior court district. This left only one seat open for a district court lawyer. The solution was not to replace some of the sitting members with district court lawyers but to expand the board in order to create more seats. Vorstand der Anwaltskammer Celle to PMJ, 24 April 1922, G.St.A., I HA Rep. 84a, 71, 495–8.

95 Mundt, *100 Jahre Rechtsanwaltskammer*, 29, 41.

96 Besides the petition to the RMJ of 9 February 1923, see also Verein der Amtsgerichtsanwälte für den Oberlandesgerichtsbezirk Celle to PMJ, 9 February 1923, G.St.A., I HA Rep. 84a, 71, 731–4; Verein der Amtsgerichtsanwälte für den Oberlandesgerichtsbezirk Celle to PMJ, 7 October 1923, G.St.A., I HA Rep. 84a, 72, 121–8; and Mosler (Lüchow), "Verhältniswahl und Anwaltskammervorstand," *Mitteilungen für Amtsgerichtsanwälte* 14 (1923): 16–18, found in G.St.A., I HA Rep. 84a, 71, 811–14.

97 Vorstand der Anwaltskammer Celle to Oberlandesgerichtspräsident Celle, 10 December 1924, N.H.St.A., Hann. 173, Acc. 30/87, 211, 78–90, and Vorstand der Anwaltskammer Celle to Oberlandesgerichtspräsident Celle, 28 November 1925, G.St.A., I HA Rep. 84a, 79, 63–76.

98 G.St.A., I HA Rep. 84a, 21913, 211, 216, 228R, 234, and 241.

99 G.St.A., I Ha Rep. 84a, 21913, 245.

THE CAMPAIGN WITHIN THE GOVERNMENT

At the same time that they agitated for more influence within the
DAV and the lawyers' chambers after the First World War, district
court lawyers resumed their direct efforts to influence both the ministries of justice and the Reichstag. Superior court lawyers responded
in kind. This resort to outside agencies to resolve the internal professional dispute not only threatened to render the official institutions of
the bar irrelevant to the resolution of the battle, but it threatened the
image of the bar as above the fray of interests. It threatened to un-
mask the claim of lawyers to be the general estate.

Again and again after 1921, the Association of German District
Court Lawyers sent submissions to the Prussian and Reich ministries
of justice. They argued to the Reich ministry that the Prussian bureaucracy was biased in favor of superior court lawyers.[100] But the
obdurate opposition of the Prussian ministry blocked any introduction of legislation by the bureaucracy.[101] Accordingly, the association
returned to direct legislative action, sending a bill for simultaneous
admission to the Reichstag.[102] There, a delegate from the German
National People's Party (*Deutschnationale Volkspartei*, DNVP), a district court lawyer from Mecklenburg named Everling, introduced
the bill on 3 March 1925.[103] Although continued efforts by superior
court lawyers to block passage of simultaneous admission, in which
the Prussian Ministry of Justice proved their ally, delayed passage of
the bill, district court lawyers kept up their pressure, with the result
that a bill making simultaneous admission a matter of right passed
the Reichstag on 7 March 1927, and became effective on 1 January
1928.[104]

100 Verein deutscher Amtsgerichtsanwälte to RMJ, 11 March 1922, G.St.A., I HA Rep. 84a,
     71, 437–8; 22 August 1923, ibid., 853–5; 15 July 1926, G.St.A., I HA Rep. 84a, 72, 827–9.
101 See the draft bill sent to the Reich Ministry of Justice by the Association of German
     District Court Lawyers in September 1924, G.St.A., I HA Rep. 84a, 72, 209–15. Al-
     though the subject of much discussion, it was never introduced.
102 Verein deutscher Amtsgerichtsanwälte to Rechtsausschuß des Reichstages, May 1925,
     G.St.A., I HA Rep. 84a, 72, 591–7.
103 *Stenographische Berichte der Verhandlungen des Deutschen Reichstages*, vol. 399, Drucksache
     Nr. 657. Ostler, *Die deutschen Rechtsanwälte*, 186, reports that in the beginning, only the
     Communist Party was interested in the concerns of district court lawyers; neither the
     Reichstag debates nor the archival records of the Prussian Ministry of Justice confirm
     this.
104 The clearest account of the convoluted final months of the effort to enact simultaneous
     admission is at Jarausch, *The Unfree Professions*, 72–3. The law went into effect on 1 January
     1928, and the federal states were allowed to make transitional provisions for a period of
     eight years, in order to ameliorate the negative effects on superior court lawyers.

The DAV had struggled mightily to retain some influence on the legislative process, but its interventions had acquired an increasingly plaintive tone. When the Association of German District Court Lawyers submitted its draft bill directly to the ministries of justice in November 1924, the chair of the DAV executive committee begged the Prussian Ministry of Justice not to "begin inquiries or make decisions about the draft without consulting the DAV."[105] In March 1926, in a memorandum to the ministry outlining its long history of mediation efforts, the DAV ended with the plea that it be consulted about transition provisions if the simultaneous admission bill passed.[106] In the end, despite all of their strivings, the DAV, the lawyers' chambers and the lawyer-notables who led them proved irrelevant to the resolution of the single greatest dispute that divided German lawyers.[107]

Conclusion

The convoluted tale of the struggle for simultaneous admission reveals that by the 1920s the German bar had reached the limits of *Honoratiorenpolitik*. The institutional framework that the RAO provided and that lawyers had fleshed out for themselves depended for its survival upon a complex system of deference to lawyer-notables who led the professional institutions. When older patterns of deference declined, the entire institutional structure came under stress; the outcome of the battle rendered it first the terrain of struggle and then irrelevant to the outcome, destroying the claim, especially of the DAV, to represent the interests either of the bar as a whole or of the "justice-seeking public" or "administration of justice." In other words, the struggle unmasked the emptiness of the claims that the institutions of the bar represented the general interest and thus that the bar constituted the general estate.

But social changes that the RAO unleashed within the bar also helped upset the initial balance. Not only did the new structure call into being a new and distinct district court bar and call into question

105 Vorsitzender des Vorstandes des Deutschen Anwaltvereins to PMJ, 3 December 1924, G.St.A., I HA Rep. 84a, 72, 245.
106 Vorsitzender des Vorstandes des Deutschen Anwaltvereins to PMJ, 15 March 1926, ibid., 785–8.
107 For an account of the feeling of irrelevancy by a member of the DAV executive board, see Max Hachenburg, *Lebenserinnerungen eines Rechtsanwalts und Briefe aus der Emigration*, ed. by Jörg Schadt (Stuttgart, 1978), 163.

the future of the superior court bar in small rural cities, but as the case study of Hannover in Chapter 5 shows it introduced distinctions of social, geographic, and confessional origin as well. District court lawyers ironically tended to be more cosmopolitan and diverse than lawyers who practiced in small superior courts. Specifically, small-town superior court lawyers came from the more traditional recruiting source for lawyers: sons of lawyers or judges, who were Protestant and who grew up in the locality. As scions of the prior generation of the bar, these superior court lawyers expected to assume roles of leadership within the bar and assumed that others would defer to their judgment. District court lawyers, many of whom had experienced social mobility and were proud of it, saw no reason to perpetuate prior patterns of deference. This social tension underpinned the clearer conflict of economic interest between the two segments. Once this social tension combined with economic interest to cause the split, the claim to be the general estate eroded further.

Two characteristics that the German legal profession shared with German liberalism contributed to the sad resolution of the conflict over simultaneous admission. First, the structure of the DAV and the lawyers' chambers as organizations of notables, *Honoratiorenorganisationen*, proved unable to adapt to reform demands advanced by an activist rank and file. Once district court lawyers shed their deference, they adopted tactics that shattered the orderly, traditionally liberal patterns that had previously characterized bar institutions. Superior court lawyers in turn adopted the same tactics. All efforts by traditional leaders to argue that the interests of the whole bar, meaning in the main the interests of the DAV and the lawyers' chambers, should remain paramount failed. Just as the structures of liberal political parties proved ill-adapted to an age of mass politics, the structures of the bar proved incapable of responding to a "mass movement" among lawyers.

Second, the only solutions that bar leaders had to offer were procedural ones. Magnanimous displays of disinterest, offers of mediation, and management of conflict constituted the arsenal of the lawyers who led the bar. But conflict management, reasonable compromise, and appeals to self-sacrifice hold no appeal for groups convinced of both the absolute substantive justice of their position and their economic destruction if they should lose a power struggle. Because the DAV and executive boards of the lawyers' chambers could only offer lawyerly, procedural solutions to the dispute, both organizations found themselves shunted to the side as the parties directly affected resorted to the state to resolve the internal professional crisis. As Chapters 8 and 9 will show, resort to state intervention in two other instances revealed the limits of liberalism and of the bar's posture as the general estate, both to lawyers and to the German public.

8

The Limits of Economic Liberalism:
Freie Advokatur *or* Numerus Clausus?

The internal professional conflict that surrounded the issue of simultaneous admission overlay yet another cleavage that crystallized around calls to reimpose limitations upon admission to the bar, specifically around a movement to reestablish strict limits on the number of lawyers, a *numerus clausus*. The lawyer-notables who controlled the DAV tenaciously defended a strict conception of *freie Advokatur* until December 1932, rejecting a *numerus clausus* out of hand as the road back to state tutelage. Younger, more marginal practitioners in large cities and in small towns increasingly clamored for relief from what they experienced as "proletarianization" during the 1920s and early 1930s, and they came to view the leaders of the bar, who defended *freie Advokatur* so stubbornly, as part of the cause of their misery. Leaders of the provincial lawyers' chambers reflected this conflict but in general defended *freie Advokatur* and opposed the *numerus clausus*. When the representatives' assembly of the DAV endorsed a *numerus clausus* in December 1932, the lawyer-notables finally admitted that the bar had reached the limits of economic liberalism. Professional ideology and structure offered no other solution than to retreat from the *freie Advokatur* that had formed the basis of the bar's identity since the 1860s. The debate about *freie Advokatur* and *numerus clausus* revealed yet again the weakness of professional *Honoratiorenpolitik* and the insufficiency of procedural solutions to respond to structural economic hardship, and in so doing contributed to the unmasking of the bar as a special interest rather than the general estate.

During the nineteenth-century debates about reform of the legal profession, the concept of *freie Advokatur* bore a primarily political meaning. For almost all liberals but especially for Prussians, the term embraced two political goals: to free the practicing bar from state appointment and from state disciplinary supervision. No longer should the ministry of justice or the courts have authority and discretion to appoint lawyers, to determine their place of residence and practice, to control their fees, to vet their politics, or to exercise disciplinary authority over them. The private bar should be established on a free and independent footing, equal in educational selectivity, and hence social status, to the bench. It should be open to persons who met objective, legally prescribed educational and examination standards, who could enter practice at a place and before a court of their own choosing, to the total exclusion of any influence by the state upon the admission process.

For most proponents of *freie Advokatur*, this political conception also included an economic aspect, because the end of the *numerus clausus* necessarily meant the introduction of free-market concepts into the private legal profession.[1] To these observers, *freie Advokatur* meant the right of *every* qualified person to admission to the bar. Most partisans of this concept viewed the economic competition that would result from the opening of the bar as a boon both to the bar and to the public, opening new opportunities for lawyers and giving the skilled and talented a chance to rise to the top. Many of the liberals who campaigned for *freie Advokatur* argued that an economically liberal system would secure the independence of the bar to serve as a politically liberal general estate.

During the debates that led to the Lawyers' Statute (RAO), support for *freie Advokatur* swept all contrary arguments from the field, especially all warnings that it might lead to economic hardship for lawyers. The Imperial Justice Laws installed *freie Advokatur* in its sense of free entry into practice as the central proposition of the legal framework of the private practice of law in Germany.[2] But the RAO passed the Reichstag in the summer of 1878. The Reichstag elections of 30 July 1878, returned a protectionist majority, and with the tariff law of 12 June 1879, the free-market, free-trade era in German economic policy

1 Weißler, *Geschichte der Rechtsanwaltschaft*, 516–22; see also Huffmann, *Kampf um freie Advokatur*, 23–5, 26 ff., 68 ff., 80 ff. The most detailed examinations of the *freie Advokatur-numerus clausus* controversy besides Weißler and Huffmann are two Dr. jur. dissertations, Müller, "Die Freiheit der Advokatur," and Edith Fließ, "Der Kampf um den numerus clausus in der Rechtsanwaltschaft" (Dr. jur. diss., Freiburg i.B., 1933). Fließ, writing at the climax of the debate, favored the adoption of some limitation, emphasizing the claim that because of the principally *political* meaning of *freie Advokatur*, that system was not necessarily inconsistent with the adoption of limitations upon admission. Müller, writing in 1972, analyzed the freedom of the practicing bar *and* the individual lawyer from the state, from the client, from society, and from the profession (*Stand*) itself.
2 Friedländer and Friedländer, *Kommentar zur Rechtsanwaltsordnung*, 3, 27, 79.

and thought was over. Just as the RAO thrust the legal profession into the market economy, the general trend in German thought began to react against and reject economic liberalism and market-determined solutions to social problems.[3] Not surprisingly, the rapid growth that the German bar experienced in the first two decades of *freie Advokatur* gave rise to suggestions that some limitation upon admission, even a return to the *numerus clausus*, might be necessary in order to maintain the economic independence of lawyers. Even before the First World War, but especially during the chaotic years of the Weimar Republic, the profession debated whether it needed some form of limitation upon admission. Increasingly, some argued that the economic concerns of lawyers should now outweigh former fears about political interference from the state; fear of political tutelage faded as fear of economic hardship grew.

Throughout the period 1878 to 1933, the lawyer-notables who directed the German Bar Association (DAV) remained the most consistent proponents of *freie Advokatur* and the staunchest opponents of limitations upon admission. The position of leaders of the lawyers' chambers was more varied according to local circumstances, but in general they too resisted calls for a strict *numerus clausus*. Members of the executive boards of the DAV and the lawyers' chambers lived, or were perceived to live, in more comfortable circumstances than their rank-and-file colleagues. They prospered despite the overcrowding of the bar, yet they imposed and enforced through disciplinary decisions ethical rules that limited acceptable modes of competition. Further, they practiced largely before collegial courts. Thus, a rift emerged between this "upper class" of lawyers, who tenaciously defended the system of *freie Advokatur* contained in the RAO, and the rank and file of the bar, more susceptible to the economic vicissitudes of competition and overcrowding.[4] The struggle between competing visions of *freie Advokatur* and *numerus clausus* coalesced as a struggle

---

3 Later commentators recognized this most clearly: "But 1878 was a watershed year in the internal political development of Germany as scarcely any other single year has been. Bismarck then took the reins of the internal policy of the regime into his own strong hands. The Anti-Socialist law on the one side, the initial social legislation on the other, and further protective tariffs for the 'protection of national labor,' on the whole a much more active state economic policy – these are the milestones that show that the time of economic liberalism and free trade were past, and therewith also the flowering of private law and private autonomy, and that the 'age of social-conservative construction' (Otto Hintze) had begun"; Rumpf, *Anwalt und Anwaltstand*, 21.

4 The German term translated as "upper-class" is *Oberschicht*, which is Rumpf's usage; see ibid., 31.

between these two strata of lawyers. By 1932 the lawyer-notables could no longer withstand the tide, and the DAV endorsed the call for the *numerus clausus.*

Yet despite the long agitation for steps to combat overcrowding in the legal profession, *freie Advokatur* remained the governing principle of the organization of the bar until after the National Socialist seizure of power in 1933. In the face of tensions and often heated debate, the leadership of the private bar successfully resisted calls for reform and held fast to the liberal principle of free entry, a free path for talent, free competition among lawyers in private practice, until 1932. The story of the contest between *freie Advokatur* and *numerus clausus*, then, is a dialectic both of the tenuousness and ambiguity and the tenacity and durability of belief in the power of liberalism to nurture a bar that would be able to serve as the general estate.

Doubts, Debates, and the Meaning of freie Advokatur

During the debates and discussions that surrounded the adoption of the RAO, lawyers clearly recognized that the adoption of a new legal framework to govern the profession might cause economic hardship.

We do not deceive ourselves, for we stand at a turning point in the history of the German bar, and the prediction about the future of lawyers made by the draft [of the RAO] itself is in no way a favorable one, because [it] admits that the German bar goes forth to meet harder times. If the draft ever becomes law, the fate of our profession will be decided for a long time.[5]

Many accepted as true the prediction that the economic circumstances of the practicing bar would worsen with the removal of the *numerus clausus.* Yet the official voice of the DAV, the *Juristische Wochenschrift*, resolutely opposed the limitation in the draft that allowed the executive boards of the lawyers' chambers to exclude applicants upon finding that additional admissions would endanger the successful administration of justice.[6] The position of the *Juristische Wochenschrift* prevailed, and the Reichstag struck the option of the lawyers' chamber to limit admissions. Yet advocacy of a *numerus clausus* (or some other limitation upon admission) persisted. Al-

5 Siegfried Haenle, "Der Entwurf der Rechtsanwaltsordnung," *JW* 7 (1878): 121. Michael John discusses the suspicion with which many Prussian lawyers viewed calls for an end to the *numerus clausus* in John, "Between Estate and Profession," in Blackbourn and Evans, *The German Bourgeoisie*, 162–97, 176–8.
6 Haenle, "Der Entwurf," 122; the German term rendered "successful" is *gedeihlich.*

though the RAO set up a liberal framework for the profession based upon free entry and competition, this liberal victory never went unchallenged by dissenting voices, and the number and shrillness of the dissenters increased over time.

The opening of entry to the practicing bar in 1879 resulted in a great influx of lawyers. Even though it occurred at the time of a rapid increase of population in Germany, it reversed a trend of increasing ratios of population to lawyers. In Prussia the number of lawyers had grown more slowly than the general population, rising from 1,629 in 1851 to 2,100 in 1879, while the ratio of citizens per lawyer had also *risen* from 9,997:1 to 12,218:1.[7] After the reforms the number of lawyers in all of Germany increased (see Table 4.1). The expansion of the bar was most dramatic in large cities, many of which had been severely undersupplied under the *numerus clausus*. In 1879, 98 lawyers practiced in Berlin; in 1880 there were 250; in 1890, 834; by 1905, 1,000.[8] The Prussian *numerus clausus* had very clearly kept the number of lawyers in all of Prussia, and especially Berlin, artificially low. Many commentators recognized this rapid initial growth as a necessary "catch-up," raising the number of lawyers to its "natural" level from the previous "unnatural" low point. They argued that rapid growth expanded the availability of legal representation for "little people," whose cases had formerly been refused by the closed bar and who had thus been forced to rely upon lay practitioners.[9] These observers interpreted the expansion of the bar as a positive phenomenon. The explosive growth in the size of the bar in Berlin, however, also contributed to fear about the creation of a "lawyers' proletariat" and supported those who advocated limitation upon admission. As the case of the province of Hannover shows, the years immediately after 1879 did not bring a dramatic change in the overall number of lawyers in other regions.

7 Julius Magnus, *Die Rechtsanwaltschaft* (Leipzig, 1929), 5, n. 1.
8 Hermann Isay, "Die Anwaltschaft in Berlin," in *Aus dem Berliner Rechtsleben. Festgabe zum 26. Deutschen Juristentag* (Berlin, 1902), 101–12, 111. See also Weißler, *Geschichte der Rechtsanwaltschaft*, 602–3, and Ostler, *Die deutschen Rechtsanwälte*, 59–68. Note for Berlin, however, that the anonymous author in the *Preußische Jahrbücher* in 1864 had predicted that the number of lawyers then needed in Berlin to satisfy the requirements of the public was 800; "Die Advocatur in Preußen," 432. The number of lawyers practicing before the court of appeal in Berlin (*Kammergericht*) rose immediately from seven to twenty on 1 October 1879, and it had risen to eighty-six by 1 October 1903; Holtze, *Geschichte des Kammergerichts*, IV: 295–6, 367.
9 Max Jacobsohn, "Einzug der freien Advokatur in Berlin," in *Festschrift zum deutschen Anwaltstag in Berlin* (Berlin, 1896), 77–108, 108. See also Gneist's comments on commercial reliance upon *Winkelconsulenz* in *Freie Advocatur*, 60–2.

As the number of lawyers rose, complaints began to surface concerning the allegedly low income of lawyers. These complaints were aggravated by the fact that the new fee schedule actually meant a decrease in income for lawyers in many places, even if the number and value of cases handled remained the same.[10] As the complaints mounted, the Prussian Ministry of Justice began to take action, circulating a ministerial rescript to the presidents of each court of appeal in April 1885. The rescript indicated that the annual reports of a number of lawyers' chambers had reported overcrowding, especially in large cities, since the advent of *freie Advokatur*, with a resulting decrease in the incomes of lawyers, and it solicited reports on whether overcrowding existed in each court of appeal district in Prussia.[11] The executive board of the lawyers' chamber in Celle indicated that board members held differing opinions on the issue. Some found no reason to introduce limitations upon admission, citing the "extraordinary importance of the question of the freedom of the bar for the successful effectiveness of the profession." A majority, however, believed that overcrowding had begun in the city of Hannover and endorsed a limitation upon admission when both the court of appeal and the executive board of the chamber agreed that one was necessary.[12] Faced with such contradictory reasoning, the ministry took no further action.

But the Prussian Ministry of Justice remained concerned about the effects of the oversupply of lawyers that it continued to perceive. According to the ministry, the number of lawyers in Prussia had increased from 1,986 in 1882 to 2,679 in 1886, and the number in Berlin from 190 to 362. Despite its concerns, however, the ministry of justice refrained from acting, for it perceived a growing tendency of new lawyers to avoid the overcrowded cities and to seek admission to small district courts, a tendency toward decentralization and amelioration that the ministry encouraged by appointing lawyers in small district court towns to the office of notary sooner than those in big cities.[13]

---

10   "Schlechte Aussichten! Noch ein Beitrag zur Gebührenfrage," *JW* 8 (1879): 36.
11   PMJ to all OLG Präsidenten, 11 April 1885, N.H.St.A., Hann. 173, Acc. 30/87, 312, 1–2 (also found in G.St.A., I HA Rep. 84a, 36, 33–40).
12   Vorsitzender der Anwalts-Kammer Celle to OLG Präsident, 1 July 1885, N.H.St.A., Hann. 173, Acc. 30/87, 312, 6–8.
13   "Der Bericht über die Justizverwaltung und Rechtspflege in Preußen 1882–1887. Seiner Majestät dem Kaiser und König vom Justizminister erstattet am 27. Oktober 1887," *JW* 17 (1888): 5–8, 6–7.

Because of the persistent fear of an oversupply of lawyers, Wilhelm Lexis in 1888 and 1891 produced two versions of a study that investigated what normal number of university students would correspond to Prussian needs for all professions. He concluded that there was at present a fifty percent oversupply of law students to fill *all* legal positions in the bureaucracy, judiciary, and private practice, and he recommended measures to reduce enrollment in the legal faculties.[14] Lexis's study inspired further official action in 1894, when the Prussian Ministry of Justice announced its intention to reimpose a *numerus clausus* upon the practicing bar and invited comment from lawyers in private practice.

The ministry sent a circular to the executive boards of all lawyers' chambers in Prussia, requesting reports about overcrowding in their districts and inviting comment upon the proposed statutory change.[15] As might be expected, several lawyers' chambers replied that overcrowding existed, notably in Berlin; others were very discriminating, indicating that some superior courts in larger cities had oversupplies while other districts, usually rural, suffered no overcrowding. The lawyers' chamber in Celle reported overcrowding in the city of Hannover, even though the ratio of population to lawyers was more favorable than before the RAO (6,700:1 in 1894 as opposed to 5,500:1 in 1878); in the earlier year many of the lawyers had been elderly and less active, while now the bar was substantially younger and more competitive.[16] The response from Celle also reported the widespread feeling that the average level of scholarly and moral qualification among younger lawyers had fallen in recent years. The chamber rejected a statutory *numerus clausus* administered by the government as too rigid, but it repeated its action of 1885 and again endorsed the mandatory rejection of applications for admission before a particular

14 Wilhelm Lexis, *Denkschrift über die dem Bedarf Preußens entsprechende Normalzahl der Studirenden der verschiedenen Fakultäten* (Berlin, 1888; 2nd ed., 1891). The number of persons passing the second bar examination in Prussia peaked in 1887 and declined gradually until 1894; Kolbeck, *Juristenschwemmen*, table 1, p. 10. Hartmut Titze sees the period 1883–98 as one of relative *underproduction* of law graduates, "Die zyklische Überproduktion von Akademikern im 19. und 20. Jahrhundert," 102–3. Both of these measurements show a rational response to a career field that *is* overfilled.

15 PMJ to Vorstand der Anwaltskammer Celle, 19 March 1894, G.St.A., I HA Rep. 84a, 39, 3–7R; see also the printed version of the rescript reproduced in "Der Freizügigkeit der Rechtsanwaltschaft," *JW* 23 (1894): 177.

16 Vorsitzender des Vorstandes der Anwalts-Kammer Celle to OLG Präsident, 1 May 1894, G.St.A., I HA Rep. 84a, 39, 93–102, reprinted in "Die Frage der freien Advokatur. I. Celle," *JW* 23 (1894): 253; the responses of other Prussian lawyers' chambers can also be found in *JW* 23 (1894): 273, 293, 335, 354, and 385.

court when the court of appeals and the executive board of the lawyers' chamber agreed that new admissions would not be in the interests of the administration of justice.[17] Lawyers in Hannover were
unwilling to return to state governance of the size of the practicing bar,
but they endorsed a solution that placed the decision-making power in
the hands of the lawyer-notables who staffed the executive board of
the lawyers' chamber.

Other lawyers' chambers (Posen, Königsberg, Marienwerder, Frankfurt am Main, Kiel, Cologne, Breslau) rejected the *numerus clausus* out
of hand, endorsing free competition among lawyers as the best means
of regulating the size of the profession, while yet others endorsed it
warmly (Naumburg, Hamm). The lawyers' chamber in Berlin rejected
the *numerus clausus* but endorsed another form of limitation, namely a
requirement that a lawyer practice at a district court for a period of years
before admission to a crowded superior court, in effect a return to a
bifurcated profession with a higher and lower branch. Others proposed
a period of additional practical education *after* passing the second bar
examination but before admission to practice (Stettin, Kassel). All of
the chambers insisted that any limitation be so devised that decisions
concerning admission remained free from the discretion of the government bureaucracy.[18]

In response to the 1894 circular from the Prussian Ministry of
Justice, the DAV announced that the topic of the twelfth German
Lawyers' Convention in Stuttgart would be "Whether, and if so to
what extent, a limitation on free entry into the practice of law is
permissible." The association appointed Hermann Pemsel from Munich to lead discussion at the convention. His written report first
considered whether an oversupply was at hand. He allowed for an
expansion from the artificially low number of lawyers in Prussia and
Bavaria before 1879 and for the expansion of the economy in the
fifteen years since the adoption of the reforms, and he concluded that

---

17 G.St.A., I HA Rep. 84a, 39, 98R. The report felt obligated to report that a minority of the
    executive board were of the opinion that "The principles of the freedom of the private
    practice of law and of free movement of lawyers must remain in place for the well-known
    reasons of the administration of justice and of politics, which had led to their introduction
    after a long struggle. . . . [Current conditions] would correct themselves in the long or
    short run"; ibid., 96R–97.
18 Interestingly, the great champion of the *numerus clausus* among Westphalian lawyers, Noest
    from Solingen, who was also an activist in favor of simultaneous admission, somehow got
    hold of the 1894 rescript from the Prussian Ministry of Justice and sent an unsolicited letter
    that proposed that admission to the bar be postponed until a *Referendar* had received a
    permanent offer of employment as a judge; Noest to PMJ, G.St.A., I HA, Rep. 84a, 36,
    111–36, 113.

no oversupply existed except for certain large cities and that even this phenomenon could not be connected conclusively to the introduction of *freie Advokatur*. He soundly rejected calls for a *numerus clausus* and instead suggested that the perceived problems arose not because of an oversupply of lawyers but rather because of an oversupply of young lawyers who entered practice before they had received sufficient supervised practical training. He proposed a new period of practical education that would extend at least two years after the candidate passed the second legal examination.[19]

Pemsel acknowledged the political content of the decision to adopt free entry into the practice of law in 1878, and adopted those concerns as the basis for his continued rejection of the *numerus clausus*. He was, however, less committed to a free-market interpretation of the economic governance of the practice of law:

I am convinced that the organization of the practice of law in Germany is to be seen not as a question of the pursuit of a trade but rather as a question of the constitution of justice. In this realm, there is no room for Manchesterism. The state can never divest itself of responsibility for the health of all organs of justice. When increasing need threatens to reduce the conscientiousness of the legal profession, when the entry of unsuited elements threatens to impair its prestige, the state has the duty with respect to the free entry of the practice of law to come to the aid of the endangered interests of justice.[20]

Pemsel, while dismissing the need for so drastic a remedy to oversupply as a state-imposed *numerus clausus*, largely for political reasons, rejected "economic Manchesterism." He admitted the right, even the duty, of the state to intervene in the affairs of the bar in derogation of the right of free entry, in order to protect the "interests of justice," so long as discretion was limited and political grounds for intervention excluded. The twelfth Lawyers' Convention nearly unanimously rejected any limitation upon free entry, especially through any legislative introduction of a consideration of the question of need.[21] It

19 Hermann Pemsel, "Bericht über die Zulässigkeit von Beschränkungen der freien Advo-
     katur," Beilage zu Nr. 51/52, *JW* 23 (1894), 1 September 1894, 13–16. He relied heavily
     upon the evidence and opinions expressed in the several reports from lawyers' chambers.
     Pemsel argued that the perceived oversupply of lawyers was not based upon factual
     research but rather was the result of personal judgment; ibid., 3.
20 Ibid.
21 The tally is given as "all versus two." The total registration was 172, so the maximum vote
     would have been 170 to 2. Verhandlungen des XII. deutschen Anwaltstages zu Stuttgart,
     JW 23 (1894), Beilage zu Nr. 55, 32. Later proponents of limitation upon admission sought
     to diminish the significance of this rejection of the *numerus clausus* by noting that it oc-
     curred in Stuttgart and that Swabian lawyers had always supported a "*freiere Advokatur*"
     and were predisposed *against* limitations upon admission; Reidnitz, *Freie Advokatur*, 90.

further rejected Pemsel's proposal of a practicum after the second qualifying examination.[22] The Prussian Ministry of Justice withdrew its proposal to enact some form of limitation upon admission to the bar, and *freie Advokatur* as enacted in 1878 remained the rule.

But the 1894 debate over limitation upon admissions revealed a large degree of discomfort among lawyers with the economic consequences of the introduction of *freie Advokatur*. Many were frankly willing to return to a system of government-determined *numerus clausus*, whatever its risk of political oversight or persecution. Others sought a professionally self-administered system of denial of admissions based upon lack of need (such as the proposal from Celle). Pemsel and others raised the issue of inadequate preparation of young lawyers and sought to lengthen the period of practical legal education. This would have two effects: (1) to raise the educational requirements for lawyers *above* those for judges, and (2) by lengthening the period of education, to discourage "unsuited elements" from entering private practice without a real feeling of calling. But a lengthening of the preparatory period would raise the costs of entering the legal profession, tending to limit newcomers to sons of wealthier families.

Proponents of limitation upon admission thus suggested a whole array of possible remedies to oversupply. Opponents tended to obscure this fact and to dismiss all proponents of limitation as advocates of the *numerus clausus*. Pemsel himself was guilty of this when he counted Celle among the lawyers' chambers that backed a *numerus clausus* in its governmental sense.[23] Partisans of *freie Advokatur* argued that divisions among the backers of limitation were just disputes over how to administer the *numerus clausus* (whether by seniority, priority of registration, or free discretion), rather than different proposals. To these paladins of *freie Advokatur*, any divergence from the system of 1879 was a return to the bad old days of governmental appointment and control.

The debate over reintroduction of measures to limit admission persisted into the new century.[24] More and more voices began to rue

---

22 Verhandlungen des XII. deutschen Anwaltstag zu Stuttgart, *JW* 23 (1894), Beilage zu Nr. 55, 32–3.
23 Pemsel, "Bericht über die Zulässigkeit," 9.
24 Around the turn of the century, the rate of growth of the bar slowed somewhat. Critics of the *numerus clausus* and other limitations upon admission raised their voices more boldly. "In relation to the growth in population, the flourishing of industry and commerce, the increase in the number of courts and trials, a corresponding growth of the number of practicing lawyers has never occurred. . . . [With regard to *numerus clausus*, imposition of

what was perceived as too cavalier a treatment of the economic impact of *freie Advokatur* in the debates surrounding the adoption of the RAO. Adolf Weißler in particular lamented the inattention that had accompanied the discussion concerning free entry into the profession, writing that the great transformation of 1878 had been much too much influenced by slogans.[25] According to him, the objective reasons for such a drastic innovation had scarcely been discussed, except for the political considerations.

The issue of limitation upon admissions reappeared at the seventeenth German Lawyers' Convention in Hannover in 1905. Although overshadowed by the discussion of the issue of simultaneous admission of district court lawyers, the second issue under discussion was whether to require two years of practical education after passing the second bar examination before admission to the practicing bar. The convention again adhered to the liberal principles embodied in the doctrine of *freie Advokatur* and rejected the limitation. Part of the membership of the DAV began to be restive, objecting to the policy of refusing to give paramount attention to the economic well-being of lawyers and to the association's resolute refusal to endorse any sort of limitation upon entry into the profession. Led by Hans Soldan, a lawyer from Mainz, some lawyers in 1907 formed the Economic Association of German Lawyers as a complement to the DAV, with the sole purpose of advancing the economic interests of the profession.[26] Much of its time and energy was spent campaigning for some form of limitation upon admission. As the discussion of the limits upon *freie Advokatur* thickened in the professional literature, the DAV announced that the theme of the twentieth German Lawyers' Convention in Würzburg in 1911 would be "Are legislative measures to be recommended against an overcrowding of the practicing bar?"

a practicum after the second bar examination, and differentiation in training between district court and collegial court lawyers], truly these remedies are more dangerous than the ills they seek to cure"; Stranz, "Deutschlands Anwaltschaft an der Schwelle des zwanzigsten Jahrhunderts," *DJZ* 6 (1901): 358, 361.

25 Weißler, *Geschichte der Rechtsanwaltschaft*, 581, 585, 591, 601. He commented: "Blindly, with insane frivolity, was this difficult, difficult question ignored." Weißler was to become a strong adherent of limitations upon admission. Interestingly, this same accusation had been made at the twelfth lawyers' convention by delegate Levy from Berlin: "Gentlemen, that [*freie Advokatur*] is a slogan. As you know, people understand free entry quite differently in the most different states"; "Verhandlungen des XII. deutsche Anwaltstag," 13.

26 Hans Soldan, *Neue Ziele, Neue Wege* (Mainz, 1909), 4. In addition to its activities in agitating for consideration of some form of limitation upon admission, the Economic Association also operated a consumer cooperative for lawyers, offering office supplies and legal publications at reduced prices.

At Würzburg, both proponents and opponents of the *numerus clausus* posed as protectors of *freie Advokatur*, agreeing that admission must remain free from governmental discretion. Opponents emphasized the value of competition as a means of establishing the most trained and diligent bar:

Under free competition, the fittest always come into authority, if special circumstances do not stand in the way. The *numerus clausus* senselessly privileges those who come first and lets the best energies wait and grow old or blocks them out completely in favor of a number of perhaps insufficient and unworthy members of the profession. There cannot be a worse system.[27]

The *numerus clausus* would result in the evil consequences of any economy of privileges. The merits of free competition received repeated praise:

The freedom of competition of all qualified persons is an inestimable good for our profession; it is, as expressed in the opinion of a judge at the Jurists' Convention in Mainz in 1863, the "indispensable life's breath" for our profession. It forces everyone to give his best, and a force that is able to do that in a purely intellectual profession should be retained and not frivolously abandoned.[28]

But even defenders of free competition drew a sharp distinction between the practice of law and a trade. Whereas reduced income for tradesmen would be a mere economic phenomenon, a reduced average income for lawyers would have an impact upon an important, indispensable element in the administration of justice, in whose integrity and welfare the state and people have an extreme, immediate interest.[29]

In his report prepared for debate at the 1911 convention, Max Friedländer conceded that embrace of a *numerus clausus* did not necessarily imply endorsement of the most radical cure proposed for the oversupply, the return to the old Prussian system of appointment in the free discretion of the government. If *numerus clausus* did not mean appointment at government discretion, with all the attendant opportunities for political skullduggery, it did mean a right of admission until a fixed maximum number was reached: "The *numerus clausus* represents no encroachment upon the principle of *freie Advokatur* as

27 Max Friedländer, "Der *numerus clausus*," *JW* 39 (1910): 96–8, 97.
28 Idem, "Empfehlen sich gesetzgeberische Maßnahmen gegen eine Überfüllung des Anwaltstandes?," *JW* 40 (1911), Beilage zu Nr. 11, 17–18.
29 Ibid., 9.

we conceive of it."[30] He nonetheless rejected the *numerus clausus* as impractical and arbitrary, but mostly because:

The *numerus clausus* is in itself no encroachment on the principle of *freie Advokatur*, but it leads of necessity away from *freie Advokatur*, it forms the logical connection to its abolition.[31]

In the final analysis, Friedländer was left with a floodgates argument, a parade of horribles, as his strongest defense against limitation upon admission. Lawyers who advocated limitation upon admission seized upon Friedländer's concession that the *numerus clausus* was not necessarily the antithesis of *freie Advokatur* and exploited it to the maximum.

Proponents of the *numerus clausus* carefully drew a narrow definition of *freie Advokatur*:

The free practice of law means its independence from outside influences; in the narrower and proper sense it means its independence from the influences of the justice ministry.[32]

If a system of *numerus clausus* were erected and administered by the organs of the legal profession itself, no conflict would exist at all between the concepts of *numerus clausus* and *freie Advokatur*. It would not stop free competition but instead ensure that only reasonable competition occurred.[33] Proponents of limitation upon admission went right to the heart of the matter: the result of the material need of countless lawyers, as well as the attendant decline in the social position of lawyers, politically expressed, was the loss of power.

Yet the profession has in its grasp, with one whole measure, with the *numerus clausus*, the ability to win back and to increase its social and economic independence from above and below. The profession must abandon its tendency toward compliance, toward hesitation, and toward submissiveness and instead develop in itself more self-consciousness, pride, distinction

---

30 Ibid., 10–11.
31 Ibid., 16. Not all opponents of the *numerus clausus* shared Friedländer's belief that it was not inconsistent with *freie Advokatur*. Such commentators looked at the prohibition in §13 of the RAO on denial of admission based upon lack of need and argued that *any* consideration of lack of need violated the guarantee of free entry; Max Jacobsohn, "Die Rheinisch-Westfälische Vereinigung von Anwälten," *JW* 42 (1913): 252.
32 Noest, "Der *numerus clausus*. Eine Entgegnung," *JW* 39 (1910): 217–18, 217; see also Kurt Kaßler, "Empfehlen sich gesetzgeberische Maßnahmen gegen eine Überfüllung des Anwaltstandes?" *JW* 40 (1911), Beilage zu Nr. 14, 7. Kaßler's report for discussion at the convention recommended a *numerus clausus* based upon priority of registration, a first-come, first-served system; ibid., 14.
33 Noest, "Der *numerus clausus*," *JW* 39 (1910): 217.

and "Will to Power." Ultimately, only the measure of power that it gains for itself by fighting determines its rank.[34]

Attendance in Würzburg shows the extraordinary interest in the issue of *freie Advokatur*. At a time when the total number of lawyers in Germany was 10,844 and the membership of the DAV was 8,248, 1,049 lawyers registered at the convention (see Table 4.2). After two days of hot debate, the convention again rejected any form of limitation upon free admission, adopting by a vote of 619 to 244 the following resolution:

The 20th German Lawyers' Convention sees in *freie Advokatur* the most certain guarantee for fitness and independence and views all proposed measures that wish to prevent a possible overcrowding of the legal profession by restricting admission in any manner as unjust and harmful to the interests of the administration of justice and of the profession.[35]

Proponents of *numerus clausus* refused to accept the decision of the Würzburg Lawyers' Convention as the final word. They remained increasingly frustrated and restive, and their numbers and organizational base expanded. In the fall of 1912, lawyers from the court of appeals districts of Cologne, Düsseldorf, and Hamm, representing most of the Rhineland and Westphalia, formed the Association of Rhineland-Westphalian Lawyers under the leadership of Noest from Solingen, who was also active in the campaign of district court lawyers for simultaneous admission. The Rhineland-Westphalian Association's primary goal was to overturn the Würzburg decision. These lawyers remained convinced that the 1911 decision did not reflect the

---

34 Kaßler, "Empfehlen sich?," 3, 17.
35 Verhandlungen des XX. deutschen Anwaltstages zu Würzburg, *JW* 40 (1911), Zugabe zu Nr. 20, 50. While the level of participation at the lawyers' convention appeared to have been impressive, as well as the majority in favor of the resolution endorsing *freie Advokatur*, supporters of limitation upon admission belittled the importance of the resolution and the convention: "Whatever reasonable arguments against the *numerus clausus* may be arrived at, the result of the Würzburg vote cannot be counted among them, as has already been explained above. One must observe, not only that less than a thirteenth of the German bar took part in this vote, and further that principally the more well-to-do members of our profession were represented at this convention, who had little understanding of the needs of the poorer and absent members, that the eloquence was unevenly divided between the proponent and opponent of the *numerus clausus* and that the opponent was granted first appearance in the proceeding, while the proponent was in second place and could speak only during the mid-day hours, during which only a small portion of the assembly could follow him, and indeed those in an over-tired condition . . . "; Richard Finger, *Die Kunst des Rechtsanwalts. Eine systematische Darstellung ihrer Grundfragen unter besonderer Berücksichtigung der ehrengerichtlichen Rechtsprechung* (Berlin, 1912), 368–9.

opinion of the overwhelming majority of lawyers in private practice and agitated ceaselessly for its reversal.[36]

A poll conducted in 1911 by Hans Soldan of the Economic Association of German Lawyers regarding the advisability of some form of limitation upon admission harvested 3,618 respondents. Of these, 2,114 supported the introduction of the *numerus clausus*.[37] A second poll by the Association of Rhineland-Westphalian Lawyers in 1913 drew 7,481 responses, 6,447 supporting limitation upon admission and only 1,034 opposing it.[38] Proponents of measures to limit admission claimed that these polls showed that the Würzburg Lawyers' Convention was an aberration and that the majority of lawyers favored some form of limitation. Opponents belittled the methodology of the poll and denied its validity. Many lawyers wished simply for an end to the agitation, believing either that the Würzburg Lawyers' Convention should have settled the issue or that a final vote should be taken at another convention with all parties agreeing to abide by the results.[39] Nevertheless, a majority of German lawyers appeared to support limitation upon admission when the First World War pushed the dispute temporarily into abeyance.

An important shift in the meaning of *freie Advokatur* had surfaced.

36 Noest, "Die Rheinisch-Westfälische Vereinigung von Anwälten," *JW* 42 (1913): 86. See other articles by members of the association throughout 1913: Noest, "Höchstziffer," *JW* 42 (1913): 124; idem, "Numerus clausus," *JW* 42 (1913): 586; idem, "Die Umfrage der Vereinigung Rheinisch-Westfälischer Rechtsanwälte," *JW* 42 (1913): 809; Schenck, "Der Numerus wird weiter spuken," *JW* 42 (1913): 302; and idem, "Die Umfrage der Rheinisch-Westfälischen Vereinigung und ihre Folgen," *JW* 42 (1913): 972 (1913). By 1914 the association had 1,047 members; Schwering (Hamm) to PMJ, 27 March 1914, G.ST.A., I HA, Rep. 84a, 37, 135–6.

37 Wilhelm Kiefe, "Die Überfüllung des Anwaltstandes und ihre Heilmittel," *JW* 40 (1911): 614–15, 614.

38 Arthur Meyerowitz, "Die Umfrage der Vereinigung rheinisch-westfälischer Rechtsanwälte," *Das Recht* 17 (1913): 573–9, 574; for membership statistics, see JW 42 (1913), Zugabe zu Nr. 16, 11. This result came at a time when the total number of lawyers in Germany was 12,324 and the total membership of the DAV was 9,574. Proponents of *freie Advokatur* found much to criticize about this poll, both in the phrasing of the questions like "I believe that limitations upon admission . . . are – necessary – superfluous. (Strike the one that does not apply)" Heinrich Dittenberger, "Umfrage der Vereinigung rheinisch-westfälischer Anwälte betr. Änderung der Zulassungsvorschriften," *JW* 42 (1913): 758, and in the interpretive worth of the results, Max Jacobsohn, "Die Umfrage der Rheinisch-Westfälischen Vereinigung und die Überfüllung," *JW* 42 (1913): 1098. These authors argued that a simple yes-no vote over limitations upon admission obscured more than it revealed. The methodology of the questionnaire does seem questionable, in that the entire membership of the Rhineland-Westphalian Association, 1,048, was counted as a group in favor of limitation upon admission, apparently without counting ballots; Noest, "Die Umfrage der Vereinigung Rheinisch-Westfälischer Rechtsanwälte," *JW* 42 (1913): 809. See also Noest to PMJ, 9 July 1913, G.St.A., I HA, Rep. 84a, 37, 111–12.

39 Hirsch, "Spukt der numerus clausus immer noch?," *JW* 42 (1913): 192; Werner, "Numerus clausus," *JW* 42 (1913): 583.

In the debates that preceded and surrounded the adoption of the RAO, *freie Advokatur* had meant the freedom of the practicing bar from the supervision of the courts or ministries of justice, both in matters of admission and discipline; it had also meant freedom from economic regulation, within the limits suitable to a free profession that was an integral part of the administration of justice. With the growth in the number of practitioners since the inception of the RAO, however, *freie Advokatur* had acquired a third and increasingly influential meaning: freedom of a lawyer from domination by or dependence upon his client. This is the independence "from above and below" to which proponents of the *numerus clausus* referred. Even proponents of *freie Advokatur* voiced concern that economic need might cause a lawyer to temper his professional judgment in order to obtain a client and thus a fee necessary for his livelihood.

> But a lawyer can only be a servant of justice when he does not lower himself to be the slave of the party. He is supposed to be the party's independent helper and advisor, but not his servant. . . . But whoever suffers neediness is more easily exposed than the economically independent to the danger of becoming morally unfree and of forgetting that power, so important for the lawyer, of saying "No!"[40]

Freie Advokatur now had come to include "freedom from economic dependence upon one's clients." The system of free entry worked in opposition to this necessary freedom, it was argued, for:

> The conscientious fulfillment of the requirement not to accept any recognizably unjust cases is in the legal profession the path to economic failure. In our profession, free competition does not bring the fittest to the top, rather the unprincipled, and it works the more corruptingly when it is the more richly endowed.[41]

According to this view, closing the profession, adopting a limitation on admission, by no means represented any retreat from *freie Advokatur* but in reality was the only means of *preserving* it. The structure of the profession that was most likely to preserve the true *freie Advokatur* was the cooperative, united circle of the select who had passed through their examinations, into the practicing bar, and who stood secure, independent from the state and from their clients.

---

40   Friedländer, "Empfehlen sich?" 9; Müller, *Die Freiheit der Advokatur*, 156–61, discussed at length this independence from economic dependence upon clients.
41   Adolf Weißler, "Die Rechtsanwaltschaft am Scheideweg," *JW* 40 (1911): 474–9, 475.

Whoever rejects *Zunftzwang* [guild monopoly] overlooks the fact that the certificate of qualification, the constitution of the lawyers' chambers, and *Anwaltszwang* [mandatory representation by a lawyer], which no one would do away with, already represent a very strong *Zunftzwang* in their combination. But if we form a guild, it is one of the healthiest ideas of guild-thinking: on the one hand to exclude the unfit by the requirement of a stringent certificate of qualification, and on the other hand to secure to the lawyer once admitted an expansive field of activity. The chief idea of free competition, that it produces the selection of the fit, breaks down here, because the selection has already occurred by other means, and the question is no longer that of how the fit can be recognized and the unfit rejected, but rather how the strictness of principles can be maintained among those recognized as fit, without which strictness our profession cannot be properly practiced and which by no means coincides with fitness. . . .

The idea of creating above all a free path for talent and of letting the noncompetitive quietly fail does not suit a cooperative, united circle of the select, especially not for a profession that is supposed to form one of the most essential guarantees of the legal order and whose health is determined in the first place by independence from below. If this cannot be achieved otherwise than by a limitation of the freedom of the individual, then all high esteem for freedom will not prevent us from thinking of the words of Iphegenia:
Dangerous is the freedom that I give,
May the gods avert that which threatens you.[42]

The very guarantees sought by the proponents of *freie Advokatur* in the 1860s and 1870s in order to free the profession from the political interference and arbitrariness of the state, educational and testing qualifications that entitled one to admission to the bar, a system of self-governance through lawyers' chambers, and a requirement that parties be represented by lawyers at the superior court level and above, were now turned about and used to justify the adoption of limitation on admission. With the era of overt political interference by the government in the past, the liberal framework proved suitable to support a protectionist twist of the definition of *freie Advokatur* and to support arguments in favor of the adoption of a *numerus clausus*.[43]

Partisans on both sides of the *freie Advokatur–numerus clausus* debate continued their agitation into 1914, one side arguing that the *numerus*

42 Ibid.
43 Fließ, *Der Kampf um den numerus clausus*, 55, argues that there had arisen a fundamental change in the meaning of *numerus clausus* since the enactment of the RAO. Whereas before it had meant principally an authoritarian measure in the interest of state power, since 1878 it had come to denote a means to cure the economic need of lawyers. No longer was the struggle over a political ideal, but rather against economic suffering.

clausus held no guarantee of accomplishing what its proponents wished, and the other side arguing that the poll taken by the Rhineland–Westphalian Association should be accepted as a plebiscite of the bar in private practice.[44] The DAV felt forced to acknowledge the agitation of the Rhineland–Westphalian Association to the extent of opening the meetings of one of its committees to representatives from the association in order to discuss the problem of oversupply. The DAV representatives blocked any consideration of the *numerus clausus* as such, but they agreed to ask the executive committee of the DAV to prepare pro and con opinions on the matter of whether it would be acceptable to require a period of practical legal education after the second bar examination, and then to poll the membership on the issue. The outbreak of the war interrupted any further discussions of limitation upon admission.[45]

Overcrowding, Chaos, and the Call for numerus clausus

Just as the civil peace that prevailed in Germany after the onset of the First World War brought peace between labor and management, it initially brought a respite in the tumult over limitation upon admission. For most of the first two years of the war, little appeared in the professional literature concerning either the neediness of lawyers or limitation upon admission. As many as half of all German lawyers entered the military, leaving the remainder to handle the business of the courts, together with young judicial candidates and even legal trainees who were left behind as "temporary" substitutes for the lawyers at the front. By 1916, however, the hardships of wartime, especially of inflation, and of emergency measures that reduced the sphere of activity of lawyers, resulted in an outcry against the distress (*Notlage*) of the legal profession. In a speech before the Berlin Bar Association in August 1916, Julius Magnus, one of the editors of the *Juristische Wochenschrift*, claimed that in Berlin, where conditions were not at their worst, the average income of lawyers had decreased by one-third from its prewar level.[46]

---

44 See for example, Wach, "Fragen des Anwaltstandes," *JW* 43 (1914): 180, and the indefatigable Noest, "Plebiszit," *JW* 43 (1914): 183.
45 "Bericht über die Geschäfte des Deutschen Anwaltvereins in den Jahren 1914 bis 1918," *JW* 48 (1919): 531, 534.
46 "Vereine. Berliner Anwaltverein," *JW* 45 (1916): 1112. This must be compared to a decrease in real wages for male workers in all industries of 22.8 percent in September 1916 as compared to March 1914; Bry, *Wages in Germany 1871–1945*, table 53, 211.

The remedies that Magnus called for did not, however, include any limitation upon admission.

By 1917 articles decrying the distress of the bar became much more frequent. In May a committee of the DAV met again with representatives of the Rhineland-Westphalian Association to discuss limitation upon admission. Two measures received consideration at this meeting: (1) the *numerus clausus* (in the form promoted by the association, which they called instead *Höchstziffer*, ["maximum number"]), and (2) a waiting period after the second bar examination. All members of the DAV committee, as well as representatives from the Association of Executive Committees of the Lawyers' Chambers, voted against the maximum number and defeated that proposal. But one member of the DAV committee and two representatives of the lawyers' chambers voted with the delegates from the association on the second proposal, resulting in an eight-to-eight tie. The *Juristische Wochenschrift* laconically reported the result: "The introduction of a waiting period was likewise not endorsed," but in reality the failure to reject a waiting period revealed the tenuousness of opposition to limitation upon admission.[47]

Individual publications also advocated limitation upon admission. August Kneer argued in 1917 that it had been a mistake in 1878 to equate the concept of freedom with the absence of a limitation upon the number of lawyers. He even went so far as to attack the sacred text by Gneist:

But in the long run, the legal profession has come into dependence, by the necessities of life, by numerical freedom into ethical bondage, with the help of this misunderstood conception of freedom. In reality, the saying by Gneist (in his work *Freie Advocatur*): competition is the life's breath for the legal profession, an oversupply in large states will only redound to the advantage of the public, proved to be a theory, and indeed a theory of the most doubtful nature.[48]

Kneer traced the development of the number of lawyers in Germany and the movement for limitation upon admission. He belittled the decision at the Würzburg Lawyers' Convention and endorsed the reliability of the poll by the Rhineland-Westphalian Association.[49] He

47 "Vereine. Deutscher Anwaltverein," *JW* 46 (1917): 582, 583.
48 August Kneer, *Die deutsche Rechtsanwaltschaft* (Mönchen-Gladbach, 1917), 37.
49 "This vote [at Würzburg] concerned a merely happenstantial majority, was merely a victory in a vote, and finally concerned only the opinion of a small fraction of the legal profession, the more well-to-do stratum"; ibid., 38.

defended proponents of the *numerus clausus* from the accusation that they acted out of economic motives by noting that the movement was strongest in the Rhineland and Westphalia, where conditions for lawyers were relatively good. This proved, he argued, that the driving force was the ethical and social interest of the lawyers. Finally, he argued that the current tide flowed ever more strongly in the direction of a well-reasoned limitation upon admission; the question could not remain an open wound.[50]

By 1918 the cries for help had become more desperate, but many commentators remained conflicted. The urgency of the situation demanded immediate measures.

> It can no longer go on this way!
> No one may any more accuse our colleague Soldan of painting a dark picture when he speaks about the irresistible death march of the bar. The looming seriousness of the situation demands strong words, demands trumpet flourishes, so that even the hard of hearing and the sleeping will be roused, the malevolent gotten rid of.[51]

The salvation of the bar from the threatening disaster would require urgent measures, but despite the crisis lawyers still should reject the *numerus clausus*:

> [The *numerus clausus* and similar cures] are to be rejected, despite the rekindled movement in their favor in the last few years, especially from the western part of the Reich. The arguments against them have been strengthened during that period of time. If I were permitted to speak anew for the freedom of the practicing bar and for the open door, as at the Würzburg Convention of 1911, I would gladly do so, with even firmer conviction and redoubled emphasis. I will never forget an encounter that I had while on railway station duty on one of the first nights of the war. A Saxon lawyer, who was travelling through to the Eastern Front with his company, said to me with a serious smile as he departed: "You see, the *numerus clausus* goes now to meet a natural solution!" Can one bring one's self, after all the monstrous experience, in view of so many victims of death, now to close or with blocking measures to impede entry to the profession by the remaining flower of our youth who again seek to pursue civil professions? That would be a denial of the guiding principle "Free path to the diligent;" more than ever the desired economic boom demands the unchecked development of all forces.[52]

Despite the maudlin nature of this argument, it showed that the lawyer-notables who led the DAV, even while admitting the extremity of the need and the urgency of compensatory measures, still

---

50 Ibid., 39.   51 Landsberg, "Die Notlage der Anwaltschaft," *JW* 47 (1918): 73.   52 Ibid.

rejected limitations upon admission, marshalling the war veteran soon to return to practice as a force on the side of *freie Advokatur*. Articles treating the distress of the bar filled the professional journals in 1918, arguing for a widening of the field of professional activity of lawyers, for an increase in fees, and for increased use of freely agreed-upon fees, but seldom endorsing the *numerus clausus* as the cure.

The actual effect of the war was to reduce the number of lawyers in private practice in Germany. The number of candidates who sat for bar examinations shrank greatly, and the number of new admissions fell off sharply. Seven hundred and seventy lawyers actually lost their lives in the military service, and numerous others died in the hardship and straitened living circumstances of the German home front. From 13,135 lawyers in private practice in Germany before the war in 1914, the number fell to 12,011 in October of 1918.[53] The war had indeed imposed a natural *numerus clausus*, but the economic dislocation caused by the war in German society as a whole, and particularly in the administration of justice, prevented lawyers in private practice from seeing any economic benefit from the reduction in the growth of the profession. The number of civil cases of all kinds declined from 3,313,782 in 1913 to 806,727 in 1916 and even further during the last two years of the war.[54] While the divisor had at last shrunk, the dividend had shrunk at a much faster rate.[55]

Peace brought no relief to the economic distress of the bar. The issue of relieving the distress formed the subject of local bar association meetings, of articles in the professional press, and of DAV deliberations. Lawyers proposed myriad remedies such as an increase in

---

53 For the number of candidates who sat for the second state examination (*Assessorprüfung*) in Prussia during the war and for the number of candidates who passed the second examination in the whole empire, see Kolbeck, *Juristenschwemmen*, appendix, 118–19, showing the reduction to as low as one-seventh of the prewar level. "Statistik der im Kriege gefallenen Rechtsanwälte," *JW* 48 (1919): 401, and Paul Burgheim, "Die Wirkungen des Krieges auf den Personenbestand der deutschen Anwaltschaft," *JW* 48 (1919): 433, 440, provide the other figures cited here.

54 Max Oppenheim, "Zur Frage der Kriegsteilnehmer. Abhilfe wirtschaftlicher Not," *JW* 48 (1919): 172, 173. For the decline of caseloads in district and superior courts during the war, see Jarausch, *The Unfree Professions*, tables A.11a and A.11b, 246–7, where his indices reveal sharp dips during the war years with swift recoveries in 1919 and 1920, a sharp dip for district court cases during the inflation years, recovery in 1925–8, and a further dip during the world economic crisis.

55 The imagery of the increasing divisor and the decreasing dividend was widely used by commentators, but most attributed its origin to Julius Magnus, one of the editors of the *JW*. For an example of his use of the image see Magnus, *Die Rechtsanwaltschaft*, 14–15, and idem, *Die Notlage der Anwaltschaft* (Leipzig, 1930).

fees, increased specialization, the reduction of special jurisdictions, and even the bifurcation of the bar into two branches as in England, with a limitation upon the number of lawyers admitted to practice before the courts. Most voices, however, continued to reject the general *numerus clausus*.[56]

Regardless of whatever progress lawyers made in gaining increases in fees and in widening their accepted field of professional activity, the inflation rendered it meaningless. Already in 1920, fees had only one-tenth of their prewar values.[57] During 1923, the title "Distress of the Practicing Bar" became a recurrent theme in the *Juristische Wochenschrift* and the *Anwaltsblatt*. The Reich Ministry of Justice was forced to issue weekly supplements to the fee schedule, setting lawyers' fees as a percentage of the amount in controversy.[58] In such an insane atmosphere, extreme solutions seemed the only road to sanity. One lawyer even proposed that the only means of salvation for the bar was a return to the old Prussian experiment of 1780 and for all lawyers to be appointed state officials and paid set salaries.[59] Such desperate proposals made a self-administered *numerus clausus* seem much less a threat to professional freedom than it had seemed in the comfortable circumstances of the Würzburg Lawyers' Convention in 1911.

In this postwar atmosphere, even opponents of the *numerus clausus* began to admit the necessity of some form of limitation upon admission. In 1922 Sigbert Feuchtwanger conceded that a majority of lawyers favored a maximum number for admissions, but he argued that this would threaten the foundations of the profession and of the

56   Hans Fritz Abraham, "Vereine. Juristische Gesellschaft Berlin, Sitzung vom 10. Mai 1919. Vortrag: 'Wesen und Ziele einer Neuorganisation der deutschen Rechtsanwaltschaft'," *JW* 48 (1919): 427, 430. Levin, *Schutz der freien Rechtsanwaltschaft! Untersuchungen, Folgerungen und Forderungen auf der Grundlage ihrer gerichtsverfassungsmäßigen Stellung* (Leipzig, 1930), and Kurt Ball, *Gebührenlockerung. Welche durch Gesetz oder Verordnung einzuführenden Maßnahmen werden vorgeschlagen, um eine Überfüllung des Anwaltstandes vorzubeugen?* (Leipzig, 1930), both organize their essays around the many proposed forms of limitations upon admissions and expansion of lawyers' field of activity.
57   Landsberg, "Vereine. Berliner Anwaltverein, Sitzung vom 26. Februar 1920. Vortrag: 'Aufgaben, Standeswürde und Nachbarbeziehungen der Anwaltschaft im Zeitenwandel'," *JW* 49 (1920): 484, 485. For an insightful discussion of the economic distress suffered by lawyers during postwar years and the inflation, see Gerald D. Feldman, *The Great Disorder: Politics, Economics, and Society in the German Inflation, 1914–1924* (New York and Oxford, 1993), 527–31.
58   See, for example, the schedules reprinted in *JW* 52 (1923): 811 and 814, for the weeks beginning 29 September and 7 October respectively, with the minimum fees of 15,000,000 marks and 41,000,000 marks.
59   Biermann, "Ein Vorschlag," *JW* 52 (1923): 677.

"democratic-social" state. Absence of a numerical maximum, however, in no way meant unlimited admissions. Admission was already limited by the requirement of two bar examinations. The democratic-social state had the right to enter further into the qualification process, indeed the duty, in order to protect the common welfare of the state, even if its entry had the effect of circumscribing the rights of individuals. Feuchtwanger proposed a tightening of the qualitative selection process, a *numerus clausus* for judicial careers, meaning in practice for legal trainees. This he argued was necessary for the survival of the bar and in no way impinged upon *freie Advokatur*. The freedom of the profession did not extend to free overproduction of lawyers:

Only Nature can allow herself the extravagance of lavishing thousands of seeds so that one can grow while the others may wither. Perhaps the Manchesterite political theory can permit itself to take an analogous position on the question of the overproduction of productive forces, but never the democratic-social policy. The social republic bears the responsibility of finding employment for willing labor forces.[60]

Only this qualitative limit, rather than any quantitative limit, could remedy the problem without decreasing the independence of the profession.

Although the years of stabilization in the Weimar Republic from 1924 to 1927 reduced the urgency of the cries of lawyers for help, the issue of limitation upon admission did not disappear from view. The number of students studying law at university, the number of candidates passing the bar examinations, and the number of practitioners rose at an accelerating rate.[61] Nevertheless, at the twenty-third German Lawyers' Convention in Stuttgart in June 1927 with the theme "The Practicing Bar in Economic and Legal Life," although the speakers loudly lamented the economic plight of German lawyers and readily conceded that a *numerus clausus* was not inconsistent with an independent profession, most speakers remained unwilling to en-

---

60 Sigbert Feuchtwanger, *Die freien Berufe. Im besonderen: Die Anwaltschaft. Versuch einer allgemeinen Kulturwirtschaftslehre* (Munich, 1922), 147, 150, 151.

61 For a useful survey of the perception and reality of overcrowding in the academic professions during the Weimar Republic, see Morris Beatus, "Academic Proletariat: The Problem of Overcrowding in the Learned Professions and Universities during the Weimar Republic 1918–1933" (Ph.D. diss., Madison, Wis., 1975), esp. 155–7 (citing articles from the *Anwaltsblatt* during 1928), and Walter M. Kotschnig, *Unemployment in the Learned Professions: An International Study of Occupational and Educational Planning* (London, 1937), 117–21. See also Table 4.1 in Chapter 4 and Jarausch, *The Unfree Professions*, tables A.5a and A.5b, 238–9.

dorse the *numerus clausus*, arguing that risk and competition were an inherent part of the free professions.[62]

Everyone must be of brave heart and must accept and bear the risk that he can be defeated in the free struggle for existence, if he wishes to enter the ranks of a free profession.[63]

Although the lawyers' convention took no action, circumstances had clearly forced opponents of limitation upon admission to concede the possible future resort to measures that they opposed.

A new element entered into the debate over the introduction of some form of limitation upon admission during the mid-1920s. Proponents of limitation began to argue that opponents came from among the older, more established, and more economically secure segments of the practicing bar. These members of the "lawyers' upper-class" were the champions of the healthiness of economic competition even in such obviously straitened times, the keepers of the flame of true economic liberalism. Through their control of the institutions of the practicing bar, the DAV, the executive boards of the lawyers' chambers, and most especially the disciplinary panels, they imposed their notions of acceptable economic activity for lawyers and acceptable modes of economic competition. In so doing, these lawyer-notables closed avenues of practice that younger lawyers, not yet established in their careers, needed to explore, thereby creating a rift within the bar. In a time of other great cleavages within the legal profession, this class division between lawyer-notables and rank and file over the issue of economic protection further hampered the efforts of the organized bar to alleviate the suffering among its members.[64]

The lawyer-notables who led the DAV remained adamant against any limitation upon admission, but concern within the profession grew. During 1928 no fewer than thirteen articles that called for a *numerus clausus* appeared in the *Anwaltsblatt*. The tide gradually turned. The DAV representatives' assembly in Frankfurt in Novem-

---

62 "Stenographischer Bericht. 23. Deutscher Anwaltstag zu Stuttgart am 11. Juni 1927," *JW* 56 (1927), Beilage zu Nr. 32/33, 13/20 August 1927, 16 (Dr. Rudolf Dix, Berlin).

63 Ibid., 21 (JR Meisner, Würzburg).

64 In addition to Rumpf, *Anwalt und Anwaltstand*, 31–2, and Bauer-Mengelberg, *Standesgefühl*, 58–9, see Rudolf Bauer-Mengelberg, "Die Abgeordneten," *Abl* 18 (1931): 237–40, esp. 238, where he repeats the claim that the leadership was out of touch with the economic concerns of the average lawyer and accuses the leaders of the DAV of being "unrepresentative." Müller, *Die Freiheit der Advokatur*, 55–6, 141–56, discusses the ways in which lawyer-notables who led the bar imposed their own ideas of *standesgemäß* economic competition and behavior upon a rank and file anxious to experiment in order to survive.

ber 1928 defeated a motion to reject all limitations upon admission, accepting for the first time the need for some form of limitation. Yet it also rejected both specific proposed limitations, a waiting period after the second bar examination before entering the bar, and a *numerus clausus* for legal trainees.[65] Although this assembly could not agree positively on what measures should be adopted, an official organ of the DAV had for the first time declined to reject limitations out of hand.

Opponents of *numerus clausus* still sought to defend *freie Advokatur* in its present form as the only means of protecting the independence of the bar. To the list of forces "above and below" from which lawyers needed to be independent were added big business and trade unions, for, if a maximum number for lawyers were adopted those two powerful economic interest groups would be the only ones to benefit, because the ruling economic forces always know how to make their influence felt, even in the selection of lawyers.[66] Such arguments against any limitation remained unheeded, although proponents of limitation could not agree on any single measure.[67] As economic circumstances worsened, the issue of limitation returned again and again for consideration by the representatives' assembly of the DAV. In Leipzig in March 1930, the assembly affirmatively resolved: "The overcrowding of the legal profession must be controlled by limitations upon admission," but adopted no specific limitation.[68] The representatives' assembly,

65 Heinrich Dittenberger, "Vereinigungen. Deutscher Anwaltverein," *JW* 57 (1928): 3094–5. The assembly defeated the rejection of all limitations by a vote of sixty-one to fifty-six; it defeated a call for a waiting period by *Assessoren* by sixty-eight to forty-nine and for a *numerus clausus* for *Referendare* by sixty-four to fifty-two (with one abstention); "Stenographischer Bericht über die 22. Abgeordnetenversammlung vom 3. und 4. November 1928 im Hotel 'Frankfurter Hof' zu Frankfurt a.M.," *Abl* 16 (1929), Beilage zu Heft 2, 115–18.

66 Max Hachenburg, "Juristische Rundschau," *DJZ* 34 (1929): 549, 551–2.

67 Idem, "Juristische Rundschau," *DJZ* 34 (1929): 824, 828, where Hachenburg reports that in a poll of the Berlin Bar Association, 577 lawyers voted against *any* limitation upon admission, while 669 were in favor of some limitation. No single remedy received a majority, however, with the most favored being the *numerus clausus*, but that only drawing support from 328. Hachenburg tried to draw comfort from this disunity, but he could not avoid the fact that the clear majority favored some action.

68 "Beschlüsse der 25. Abgeordneterversammlung des Deutschen Anwaltvereins vom 22. und 23. März 1930 zu Leipzig," *JW* 59 (1930): 1036. The vote to control overcrowding by limitations upon admission was sixty-five to fifty; "Stenographischer Bericht über die 25. Abgeordnetenversammlung vom 22. und 23. März zu Leipzig," *Abl* 17 (1930), Beilage zu Heft 6, 99-102. Max Hachenburg noted with surprise that the chief proponents of the *numerus clausus* came not from the large cities, where the overcrowding was most pronounced, but from medium and smaller districts. He tried to minimize this action, referring to the "very narrow" majority and emphasizing the rejection of a *numerus clausus* for

however, endorsed a *numerus clausus* for legal trainees, the limitation of entry into the period of practical legal training for *all* legal
and judicial careers. This was the solution that found the broadest
support, especially when coupled with a required period of practical education after the second bar examination.[69] The governments
of the Reich and of the states took no action, however, and the
economic situation continued to deteriorate.

By December 1932 the representatives' assembly of the DAV believed that the final crisis had arrived. At its meeting in Berlin on
4 December Freiherr Hodo von Hodenberg, a lawyer from the court
of appeal in Celle, outlined the statistics that proved the extremity of
the situation. He pointed out that the private practice of law was the
only free profession that had not been closed by governmental action,
which had resulted in the acceleration of overcrowding.[70] In the two
and one-half years since the endorsement of the *numerus clausus* for
legal trainees and the waiting period by the assembly at Leipzig, the
economic circumstances of lawyers had only worsened. Those measures would no longer be sufficient, and von Hodenberg called for an
immediate, total, three-year freeze on new admissions, during which
an acceptable *numerus clausus* should be drafted. Von Hodenberg did
not minimize the objections against the *numerus clausus*, but he
advocated it as the only means to avert the impending catastrophe.
Moreover, he argued that the danger of political interference by the
government in the selection process for lawyers posed no greater
threat with a *numerus clausus* for lawyers than with one for legal trainees, which had already been endorsed in 1930. "Gentlemen, we have
progressively and as the result of economic extremity had to disabuse
ourselves of numerous lawyerly objections" to such measures.[71] After
von Hodenberg's address, the assembly voted to petition the govern-

---

lawyers, but he grudgingly had to wish the effort well: "If the measure succeeds, then it is
worthwhile to make the attempt"; Max Hachenburg, "Juristische Rundschau," *DJZ* 35
(1930): 539, 543–4.

69 The vote was sixty-three to fifty-two; "Stenographischer Bericht der 25. Abgeordneten-
versammlung," 102. See the monograph which won the DAV prize for works on the
economic situation of the bar, Levin, *Schutz der freien Rechtsanwaltschaft!*, which recom-
mends exactly these two measures.

70 Freiherr Hodo von Hodenberg, "Lage und Schicksal der deutschen Anwaltschaft. Bericht,
erstattet der 29. Abgeordneten-Versammlung des Deutschen Anwaltvereins in Berlin am
4. Dezember 1932," *JW* 61 (1932), Beilage zu Nr. 51/52, December 1932, 7. Proposals to
apply to the bar the *numerus clausus* system applied to medical doctors in the official health
insurance plans had been made in Franz Bischofswerder, "Die Notstand der Anwaltschaft," *Abl* 16 (1929): 91–3, 93, and criticized in Levin, *Schutz der freien Rechtsanwaltschaft!*, 91–8.

71 Hodenberg, "Lage und Schicksal," 8.

ment to impose an immediate three-year freeze on new admissions to the bar and to use that time to draft a plan for a *numerus clausus* for lawyers.[72] The lawyer-notables of the DAV, the last great champions of *freie Advokatur* in its economic sense, had finally capitulated.[73]

Thus, the ideas about limitation upon admission that had lost at Würzburg in 1911 prevailed in 1932. Defenders of *freie Advokatur* had weakened their case in at least two ways. First, they accepted the argument that *freie Advokatur* included independence *both* from above and below, from political interference by the government but also from economic dependence upon the client. Second, they conceded that some limitation upon admission, even the *numerus clausus*, could be compatible with *freie Advokatur*. Once they conceded that *any* limitation could possibly exist without impinging upon the freedom of lawyers in private practice, they had started down the slippery slope toward von Hodenberg's argument that the final step would concede no more than the intermediate steps already taken. A reserved attitude toward the disorderly nature of free competition, from the "Manchesterism" that it implied, led proponents of *freie Advokatur* down the road toward accepting a *numerus clausus* in a time of great economic hardship. Finally, the very real hardships of life in Germany during the Great Depression, together with the failure of the DAV to widen the scope of lawyers' activity, restrict the activity of competitors such as lay practitioners, or raise the fee schedule, weakened the power of its leadership and again undercut the principles of deference upon which the bar's liberal organizational structure rested.

Conclusion

The long and convoluted history of the conflicts over *freie Advokatur* reveals four reasons why the practicing bar and its institutions reached the limits of economic liberalism. First, economic liberalism had always played a subsidiary role in the doctrine of *freie Advokatur*. The call for free entry emerged in response to the peculiarly German, and most peculiarly Prussian, system of state appointment of lawyers and *numerus clausus*. Recent memories of political persecution from the 1820s to the 1860s made reformers determined to establish the practic-

72 Ibid., 16.
73 The votes on the three-year freeze were 127 to 19 in favor; on the *numerus clausus*, 115 to 31 in favor; "Stenographischer Bericht über die 29. Abgeordnetenversammlung von 4. Dezember 1932 zu Berlin," *Abl* 20 (1933), Beilage zu Heft 3, 70–2.

ing bar on a basis completely independent from the discretionary authority of any state agency. More than any other concern, this political goal of creating a private bar independent, respected, and vigorous in its own right *and* a haven for politically persecuted judges and state officials united the advocates of *freie Advokatur*. Many liberals in the 1860s and 1870s also believed that free-market competition would best regulate the number of lawyers who chose to enter the profession and hence the size of the bar, so that no form of limitation upon admission should replace the *numerus clausus*. This brief blooming of laissez-faire economic liberalism in the 1860s marginalized cautionary warnings so that by 1867 Gneist could fix as dogma the concept that *freie Advokatur* meant free entry to *all* who were qualified, but the principal commitment to free entry remained the political one.

But "free trade" in the private practice of law came at the same time that free trade was abandoned as German national economic policy, and principles of economic liberalism embodied in the RAO became easier to challenge than they had been during the 1870s. As the size of the bar grew and as complaints and concerns arose within and without the bar, leaders of the DAV who opposed limitations on admission found themselves forced again and again to defend their position. In 1894, 1911, and 1928, they encountered recurrent efforts to reinstitute some kind of *numerus clausus*. Given these circumstances, it is more remarkable that free entry remained policy until 1932 than that the leaders of the bar finally abandoned it.

The second reason for the end of economic liberalism within the private legal profession was stratification within the bar itself. The greatest defenders of *freie Advokatur* and opponents of *numerus clausus* were always the lawyer-notables who led the DAV. These lawyers, practicing before higher courts, administered a system of self-government and self-discipline that espoused an ideology of free competition while using the power of the executive boards and disciplinary panels of the lawyers' chambers to create a "code of honor" that strictly limited the acceptable means of competition among lawyers. Under the circumstances of 1880, with a supply of lawyers still insufficient to meet the public demand for legal services and with few competitors to the private bar, all strata within the bar could accept these limitations. By the 1920s, when the number of lawyers had grown dramatically, noncontentious means of dispute settlement had expanded, the field of activity for lawyers had shrunk (for example, labor courts), and competition from nonlawyer competitors such as tax advisors, mediators, and *Syndiken* had increased, this stratification of ethical ideals led to crisis. Rank-and-file lawyers, resentful of the economic comfort of the established, collegial court lawyers who ran their institutions challenged the maintenance of a corporate ideology of practice alongside a free-market ideology of admission.

This stratification is closely entwined with the third reason why the bar reached the limits of economic liberalism. The cleavage between the rank and file of the bar and the lawyer-notables on the issue of *freie Advokatur-numerus clausus* closely tracked that of the dispute over simultaneous admission. Lawyers who felt dissatisfied with the economic policy of the leaders of the bar had a ready example of how to make their point. Proponents of *numerus clausus* sought change within bar institutions, but when thwarted there bypassed the profession to form special-interest associations and to petition governmental authorities. Even individual lawyers such as Noest in Solingen figured prominently in both struggles. The new forms of mobilization pioneered by the district court lawyers, and the emergence of "mass politics" within bar institutions during the 1920s, meant that the liberal *Honoratiorenpolitik* of those institutions again proved inadequate to respond to the needs of the rank and file.

Finally, lawyers reached the limits of economic liberalism because they faced real structural economic problems. The number of lawyers in Germany rose by 50 percent between 1921 and 1932, after 1929 in a time of economic depression. The number of law students and candidates for the bar also increased disproportionately. The market seemed to have failed to provide for any equilibrium, and the orderly procedures followed during the half-century experiment with *freie Advokatur* offered no solution. Decades had been invested in what amounted to a debate without resolution over the best substantive standard to use to administer a *numerus clausus*, and even December 1932 brought no action as to the fairest substantive standard. Procedure had reached the point of exhaustion as outsiders waited in the wings with their own substantive standards for inclusion and exclusion.[74]

74 While Tilmann Krach concludes that anti-Semitism among lawyers did not play a significant role in the decision in December 1932 to endorse a *numerus clausus*, the decision nevertheless "objectively facilitated the National Socialists in their measures against Jewish lawyers"; Krach, *Jüdische Rechtsanwälte*, 75.

9

The Limits of Political Liberalism:
Lawyers and the Weimar State

Beyond the experiences of the internal professional struggles over simultaneous admission and *freie Advokatur*, and the resort to external legislative power to resolve them, German lawyers during the 1920s entered into yet a third set of complex contingent relations with the state that demonstrated the declining power of their liberal professional structure and practice to protect the interests either of individual lawyers or the bar as a whole. Under the Weimar Republic, lawyers encountered for the first time a political system that challenged the comfortable relations that the private bar had established with government bureaucracies, particularly the state and Reich ministries of justice, in the interest of greater substantive justice for other segments of society and for society as a whole. At the same time that bureaucracies became more responsive to other social groups, lawyers experienced a decline in the legislative strength of the liberal parties with which they had traditionally been allied. Through a series of very specific political defeats, the German bar during the Weimar Republic reached the limits of the power of political liberalism to support its self-image as the general estate, reinforcing the conclusion that its liberal professional structure faced only further paralysis and irrelevance in the future.

During the Second Empire (1871–1918), the German bar maintained comfortable relations with the monarchical state. Legislation that affected the profession emerged from the Imperial Office (later Ministry) of Justice, although most of the drafting occurred in the Prussian Ministry of Justice.[1] The bar cultivated close relationships with both bureaucracies, and the important role of lawyers in the

---

1 For a history of the institutional development of the Imperial Justice Ministry, see Hans Hattenhauer, "Vom Reichsjustizamt zum Bundesministerium der Justiz," in Bundesministerium der Justiz, ed., *Vom Reichsjustizamt*, 9–118.

leadership of the liberal parties in the Reichstag ensured them a second line of influence on any legislation in that body.[2] When the empire collapsed in November 1918 and the Weimar Republic came into being in 1919, the upheaval not only swept away the monarchies and the comfortable relationships that had developed between the bar and the ministries of justice but also had profound political consequences for the liberal parties with which lawyers had been most closely identified. The Social Democratic Party of Germany (*Sozialdemokratische Partei Deutschlands*, SPD), whose constituency consisted almost entirely of industrial workers, and the Catholic Center Party (*Zentrum*) constituted the largest parties of the Weimar era, and neither had strong appeal for lawyers. The two liberal parties, the German Democratic Party (*Deutsche Demokratische Partei*, DDP) and the German People's Party (*Deutsche Volkspartei*, DVP) drew significant initial electoral support, especially the DDP in 1919 and the DVP in the mid-1920s, but by 1932 and the economic crisis, the two parties together drew less than 2 percent of the popular vote.[3] During the Weimar Republic, then, German lawyers faced a political situation in which the two largest parties pursued either socialist or organic-corporatist policies in the interests of electoral constituencies alien to lawyers. Moreover, the liberal parties that had provided lawyers both an ideological home and a springboard into public life suffered severe erosion of their electoral and social bases and hence their governmental influence. The story of the travails of the German liberal political parties between 1919 and 1933 is familiar and well told.[4] This chapter will focus instead upon the less-well-known but parallel story of the political travails of lawyers.[5]

2 Lawyers regularly discussed any proposed revisions to procedural law and the lawyers code in their biennial conventions, and the executive board of the DAV made formal submissions to the Imperial or Prussian Ministries of Justice; see, for example, Ostler, *Die deutschen Rechtsanwälte*, 39–46.
3 The definitive work on the liberal parties during Weimar is Larry Eugene Jones, *German Liberalism and the Dissolution of the Weimar Party System 1918–1933* (Chapel Hill, 1988). See also Langewiesche, *Liberalismus*, 240–86, and Tabelle 16: "Reichstagswahlen in der Weimarer Republik," 334.
4 Besides Jones, *German Liberalism*, and Langewiesche, *Liberalismus*, for the period up to 1918 see Sheehan, *German Liberalism*.
5 An earlier discussion of several of the issues discussed in this chapter can be found in Kenneth F. Ledford, "German Lawyers and the State in the Weimar Republic," *Law and History Review* 13 (1995): 317–49; see also idem, "Lawyers and the Limits of Liberalism: The German Bar in the Weimar Republic," in Halliday and Karpik, eds., *Politics Matter* (forthcoming, 1996).

The Challenge of the Social

One issue of social welfare in the early 1920s revealed particularly well the changing nature of lawyers' relations to the German state, to the social and economic upheaval of the era, and of the leadership of the bar to the wishes of the rank and file. The discourse that surrounded the question of a mandatory retirement insurance scheme and the reversal of opinion from initially favorable to ultimately unfavorable show that enthusiasm for such insurance by state bureaucracies with which lawyers were not previously accustomed to dealing triggered suspicion among the bar about the aims of the "democratic-social" republic and concerns for how to maintain the profession's special status and disinterested pose. Moreover, it also revealed the eroding ability of the leadership of the bar to persuade the membership that a given course of action was in the profession's best interests.[6]

Soon after 1871 lawyers had created an "Assistance Fund for German Lawyers" to collect voluntary contributions from individuals, voluntary bar associations, and lawyers' chambers.[7] A number of local charitable and need-based funds also continued to exist.[8] Although the Assistance Fund in 1894–5 had proposed creation of a mandatory "Retirement, Widows', and Orphans' Fund," a lively debate about the feasibility and desirability of such an institution lasted for years.[9] After several considerations of the issue and rejection of a mandatory system, a voluntary fund came into being, but membership remained quite low.[10]

6 For a recent general discussion of the politics of social welfare during the Second Empire, see George Steinmetz, *Regulating the Social: The Welfare State and Local Politics in Imperial Germany* (Princeton, 1993); the classic work remains William Harbutt Dawson, *Social Insurance in Germany 1883–1911. Its History, Operation, Results* (New York, n.d. [1913]).

7 Ostler, *Die deutschen Rechtsanwälte*, 87, 89, 200–1.

8 See the reports of the activities of the local funds in the province of Hannover recorded in the annual reports of the *Anwaltskammer* in Celle, G.St.A., I HA Rep. 84a, 21912 and 21913. Healthy funds in smaller cities fell into extinction after the inflation of 1923.

9 Useful here is the historical outline provided in Hugo Cahn, "Denkschrift des Bayerischen Anwaltsverbandes zur Herbeiführung einer Pensionsversicherung der Deutschen Anwaltschaft," *Abl* 9 (1922): 92–104, 92–6.

10 Proponents of mandatory plans in the 1920s interpreted this rejection as indicative of a certain doctrinaire economic liberalism on the part of lawyers in the two decades around 1900:

Indeed, these bodies [the DAV executive board and the bar conventions] – whose composition and votes were left to chance – normally treated the problem with a certain reserve. This can be explained by the prior character of our profession and the – pardon the expression – plutocratic composition of its congresses. My but we were really inclined

During the First World War, the question of how to care for lawyers wounded in action and for survivors of those killed, combined with the disruptions of professional income and security caused by military service and wartime inflation, led to renewed consideration of mandatory retirement insurance. In March 1918, Adolf Gröber (of the Catholic Center Party, a superior court judge) introduced a resolution in the Reichstag that called for the government to draft a bill to provide for the "social organization of the German bar in private practice" by making membership in the existing two funds mandatory for all lawyers.[11] Although many leaders of the bar greeted this overture as a great opportunity to advance the social security of lawyers, others rejected the proposal, which for the first time extended "mandatory insurance, which has been limited only to workers and employees, to a free profession."[12]

After the turmoil of defeat and revolution, the issue lay dormant until 1922. As inflation continued to erode the value of retirement savings, interest increased among lawyers in some sort of retirement insurance fund that could shelter retirement funds effectively. The DAV again addressed the question of mandatory retirement insurance and in early 1923 created a committee to produce a draft bill. The DAV committee consulted with the executive boards of the various lawyers' chambers, compiled a draft law, and on 2 January 1924 forwarded it to the Reich Ministry of Justice.[13]

The hyperinflation of 1923 had prepared the ground for a generally favorable reception for the DAV's draft, and the executive boards of sixteen lawyers' chambers endorsed the draft. At the March 1924

toward Manchesterism then! A commitment to "*laisser faire laisser aller*" that is incomprehensible today characterized the attitude of the majority.

Ibid., 94.

11 Ibid., 95–6; the resolution is also reprinted in the legislative justification for the draft insurance bill, "Das Versicherungsgesetz für Rechtsanwälte," *Abl* 13 (1926): 31; on the Gröber resolution, see also Ostler, *Die deutsche Rechtsanwälte*, 120–2.

12 Cahn, "Denkschrift," 95–6. Germany had of course since the 1880s developed the most comprehensive system of accident, sickness, and old-age pension insurance in the world, but its coverage had begun with industrial workers and only gradually been extended to other groups, including the "new middle class" of white-collar employees in 1911; see Gerhard A. Ritter, *Social Welfare in Germany and Britain: Origins and Development*, trans. Kim Traynor (Leamington Spa, 1986), 17–130, esp. 91–5.

13 Dr. Strauder, "Pensionsversicherung für Rechtsanwälte," *Abl* 9 (1922): 30–2; Dr. Schweer, "Geldentwertung und Allgemeine Pensionskasse der Rechtsanwaltschaft," *Abl* 9 (1922): 37–8; "Aus der Vereinstätigkeit," *Abl* 10 (1923): 24–6, 25; "Entwurf eines Gesetzes über die Pensionsversicherung der deutschen Rechtsanwälte. Nebst Erläuterungen. Aufgestellt vom Deutschen Anwaltverein Dezember 1923," *Abl* 11 (1924): 15–20.

meeting of the representatives' assembly of the DAV, however, Hamburg lawyers opposed it:

By means of retirement insurance, the bar would fall into a dependence upon the state that is inconsistent with the freedom of the legal profession. Because the national government would permit the bar to pass on the costs of retirement insurance to its clients, the bar would submit itself into a dependent relationship unworthy of itself. It would submit itself voluntarily to the yoke of social insurance, thus into relations that ought to be eliminated, but not extended.[14]

Nevertheless, the representatives' assembly endorsed the draft. Officials in the Reich Ministry of Labor greeted this as an important moment: "The draft before us ventures into new territory, because it represents the first attempt to incorporate a free profession into the social insurance system."[15]

As the draft law ground slowly through the bureaucracies of the Reich Ministry of Justice and the Reich Ministry of Labor, lawyers' attitudes toward mandatory retirement insurance began to change.[16] Private insurance companies bombarded lawyers with advertisements, arguing that higher benefits at lower costs would come by purchasing coverage individually rather than by the profession acting collectively.[17] Continued consultation with the executive boards and annual assemblies of the lawyers' chambers, made possible by the delay, also permitted second thoughts to emerge. For example, the lawyers' chamber in Celle, which had endorsed the mandatory retirement insurance scheme in 1923, rejected it in 1925 (executive committee) and 1926 (plenary assembly), arguing that state intrusion into professional affairs through legislation that mandated retirement insurance would limit the freedom of the legal profession.[18] The representatives' assembly of the DAV met in March

14 "17. Vertreterversammlung des Deutschen Anwaltvereins," *Abl* 11 (1924): 59–64, 62.
15 "Aus der Vereinstätigkeit," *Abl* 12 (1925): 32. The editorial staff of the *Anwaltsblatt* considered this novelty, inclusion of a free profession in a social insurance scheme, to be one of the strengths of the bill; "Die Aufgaben des Jahres 1926," *Abl* 13 (1926): 1–3, 2.
16 For the progress of the bill through the two ministries, see the reports "Aus der Vereinstätigkeit," *Abl* 12 (1925): 10 (Feb.); 17 (March); 32 (April); 97 (June); 145 (Nov.); 167 (Dec.).
17 See the complaints by the editor of the *Anwaltsblatt* and by other supporters of mandatory retirement insurance, arguing that the claims by the insurance companies were false; "Die Pensionsversicherung," *Abl* 12 (1925): 97–8, 97; "Pensionsversicherung," *Abl* 12 (1925): 115–16; Hugo Cahn, "Zwangspensionsgesetz und Lebensversicherungsanstalt," *Abl* 12 (1925): 134–6; "Pensionsversicherung," *Abl* 12 (1925): 163.
18 See the annual reports of the *Anwaltskammer* in Celle, G.St.A., I HA Rep. 84a, 21913, 235 (executive committee, 1925); and ibid., 241 (plenary assembly, 1926, "rejected by an overwhelming majority").

1926 to consider the draft that had by now emerged from the Reich
Ministry of Labor, and it found that the attitude of the bar had
changed fundamentally since the previous year. Out of seventy-five
local associations that had passed resolutions on the subject, thirty-
four supported the draft legislation while forty-one opposed it.[19] At
the conclusion of the debate, the assembly rejected the draft mandatory retirement insurance law by a margin of thirty-eight to forty-
eight, and the issue of mandatory retirement insurance was dead.

The evolution of lawyers' attitudes toward mandatory retirement
insurance reveals the erosion of the ability of the leadership of the
DAV to impress its vision of what was best for the profession on the
rank and file membership. DAV executive board members and the
editorial boards of the two bar newspapers never wavered in their
conviction that mandatory insurance would serve most lawyers best.
They could not, however, withstand the misgivings of the rank and
file. The concept of independence, the crucially important component of professional identity so central to the lawyer-notables who
headed the DAV and lawyers' chambers, ironically became a tool for
the rank and file to thwart their leaders' social schemes. The turning
point came when a new and alien bureaucracy, the Ministry of Labor,
assumed jurisdiction over the matter. This equated lawyers with
other groups subject to social insurance and hence challenged their
special status as the "general estate," guarantors of the *Rechtsstaat*.
Such a derogation of status and independence was a sacrifice German
lawyers were not prepared to make in 1926.[20]

Three Political Defeats

The years between 1919 and 1932 inflicted upon German lawyers
three very specific political defeats that damaged the professional
self-conception by challenging or even denying the unique role of the
bar as the general estate, thus contesting its fundamental assumptions
about itself. Newly enfranchised voices raised claims of substantive
justice that subverted the comfortable proceduralism with which lawyers conceived of their professional sphere and the public political

19 "Die 19. Vertreterversammlung," *Abl* 13 (1926): 118.
20 A nuanced discussion of the status concerns of middle-class groups and the circumstances
    under which they will behave in "solidaristic" ways appears in Peter Baldwin, *The Politics
    of Social Solidarity: Class Bases of the European Welfare State 1875–1975* (Cambridge, 1990),
    esp. 1–54. German lawyers only joined the state-run retirement system in 1957; ibid., 277.

sphere. Lawyers also found that they had to negotiate with different and newly assertive governmental bodies over issues of importance to the profession and to individual practitioners, and those different agencies, which answered to constituencies other than lawyers, listened to lawyers with less deference. Together, these crises unmasked lawyers' pretensions of being the "general estate," representing the common interest, and revealed lawyers to be merely another of the many special-interest groups that struggled to survive in the Weimar political landscape. Lawyers' experience during Weimar, then, mirrored to a remarkable extent the experience of political liberalism itself.

The early 1920s confronted lawyers with a substantive claim of justice that contested their claim to represent the general interest and to serve as guarantors of the *Rechtsstaat*. The Constitution of the Weimar Republic for the first time in German history extended guarantees of equal rights to women (article 109). Article 128 provided further that "All citizens of the State, without distinction, are eligible for public office, as provided by law and in accordance with their qualifications and abilities. All exceptional provisions against women officials are annulled."[21] On its surface, this would seem to have admitted women to all positions in the administration of justice, but lawyers made it clear that they opposed admission of women to their profession. On 13 June 1919, the executive board of the lawyers' chamber in Celle resolved by a vote of ten to one: "As a matter of principle, women ought not to be admitted to the bar." The reasons advanced expressed both economic and ideological-essentialist objections to women's participation in the administration of justice.[22] Similarly, the executive board of the DAV, as well as the representatives' assembly, consistently rejected the admission of women to the private practice of law.[23] At a meeting of the representatives' assembly in January 1922, two papers were delivered, one supporting women's admission, the other rejecting it. Some lawyers questioned whether

---

21 The translation is taken from the text of the Weimar Constitution that can be found in Hucko, ed., *The Democratic Tradition*, 149–90, 177.

22 "Economic reasons were chiefly those mentioned, especially the extraordinarily bad circumstances of judicial officials and lawyers that already now prevail. But the opinion was also voiced that women are ill-suited to these positions and professions"; Mundt, *100 Jahre Rechtsanwaltskammer*, 25–7. See also G.St.A., I HA Rep. 84a, 21913, 207; the lawyers in Hannover were willing to see women serve as lay judges in juvenile and guardians' courts and possibly in divorce actions.

23 Ostler, *Die deutschen Rechtsanwälte*, 169–74; the arguments advanced echoed the essentialist ones voiced by the executive board in Celle.

any action remained to be taken, considering the provision in the Weimar constitution; others argued that women might be suited to be lawyers, but not judges. After a debate that the reporter congratulated those present for conducting with "calm and precision," avoiding the "broad and repetitive conflicts that the nature of the theme might be feared to lead to," the representatives' assembly by a vote of forty-five to twenty rejected the suitability of women to serve either as judges or lawyers.[24]

Not surprisingly, given this opposition, the constitutional provisions that seemed clearly to require the admission of women to bench and bar were not interpreted as self-executing, and the Reichstag had to enact a statute that admitted women to the bar and the judiciary on 11 July 1922.[25] In the course of the Reichstag debate, lawyers found themselves arrayed against a unified group of women members from various parties and the SPD, under the leadership of Gustav Radbruch, a lawyer and briefly in 1922 Reich Minister of Justice. Lawyers thus found their attempts to block the admission of women into the profession thwarted by substantive claims of equal justice championed by women themselves and by socialists. This unpalatable alliance contested lawyers' claim that the professional status quo represented the common good, and lawyers' professional institutions and liberal political allies proved incapable of resisting it under the new political realities of Weimar.

As in the question of the admission of women to the bar, another issue of substantive interest to the SPD conflicted with the symbolic and material interests of the bar. One of the chief items on the legislative agenda of the SPD in the 1920s was the enactment of a comprehensive system of labor law. In pursuing this end, the Social Democrats built upon a legislative foundation that lawyers already hated for both its symbolic and material impact upon their profession. Prior to the enactment of a comprehensive code of labor law, the heavily Roman character of German law provided very little guid-

24 "14. Vetreterversammlung zu Braunschweig am 28. und 29. Januar 1922," *Abl* 9 (1922): 21–5, 23–4.
25 Deutscher Juristinnenbund, ed., *Juristinnen in Deutschland*, 1–16. Following this legislation, the first woman private practitioner in Germany, Dr. Marie Otto, was admitted to practice in Munich on 7 December 1922; the first woman in Prussia was Dr. Maria Munck in 1924; the first woman admitted to the bar in the province of Hannover was Berta Schmidt of Duderstadt, whose father was a lawyer there, who swore her admission oath in September 1927. Three other women effected their admission to the bar in 1931, 2 in the city of Hannover and 1 in Lüneburg, but the total of 4 was only a tiny portion of the total of 820 lawyers in the province. Mundt, *100 Jahre Rechtsanwaltskammer Celle*, 26–7.

ance for an emergent labor law at a time when that field began to assume greatest significance for a majority of the German population. The feeling grew among employees and others that justice in labor law cases was slow and expensive, that courts and judges helped only the wealthy, and that they were hostile to the interests of workers. Not only did the worker have to hire a lawyer and face a lawyer representing the employer, but the losing party, in accord with civil law practice, would have to pay both sets of attorney's fees.[26] Many believed that lawyers only worsened the process and rendered it more expensive. Schooled in dialectical argument, they simply muddied the waters rather than clarifying the state of the facts and the law. Their focus upon legal formalities and procedure obscured the content, substance, and social spirit of labor law.[27] The conviction spread that the exclusion of lawyers from labor law cases would promote speed, economy, simplicity, and "naturalness" of decision making.[28]

After a great wave of strikes in 1889, legislation in 1890 had created industrial courts (*Gewerbegerichte*) with exclusive jurisdiction over employment disputes between masters and journeymen or apprentices, and it excluded lawyers from practice before them.[29] Industrial courts consisted of panels of workers and employers, chaired by an impartial judge. Male workers (and employers) over age twenty-five elected lay judges by direct, secret suffrage. Exclusion primarily hurt the incomes of district court lawyers, but restrictions on appeal also had a negative effect upon superior court lawyers.[30] More important was the blow to the prestige of lawyers, for this was the first deviation from the principle of representation by lawyers. In 1904, despite renewed protest from the bar, the Reichstag created a second court of special jurisdiction, commercial employment courts (*Kaufmannsgerichte*) with exclusive jurisdiction for employment disputes between commercial employers and employees; lawyers were excluded.

26 §87 (later §91) of the ZPO required the losing party to bear all the costs of the successful party, including lawyers' fees.
27 Ludwig Bendix, "Richter, Rechtsanwälte und Arbeitsgerichte," *Die Justiz* 1 (1925–6): 186–93, 187. See also the arguments in Lothar Engelbert Schücking, "Leitwort zur Verabschiedung des Arbeitsgerichtsgesetzes," *Die Justiz* 2 (1926–7): 273–7.
28 Bovensiepsen, "Das Verbot der Zulassung von Rechtsanwälten vor den Gewerbe- und Kaufmannsgerichten," *JW* 42 (1913): 729–30, 729.
29 The most comprehensive work on the history of courts of special jurisdiction for labor disputes is Frieda Wunderlich, *German Labor Courts* (Chapel Hill, 1946). Ostler, *Die deutsche Rechtsanwälte*, 39, discusses the attitude of the private bar toward creation of the industrial courts in 1890.
30 Ostler, *Die deutschen Rechtsanwälte*, 40–1.

Social Democrats and trade unions quite naturally benefited from the political mobilization that surrounded election of lay judges and from the role of union or party officials in representing the interests of their constituents before the industrial and commercial courts. Lawyers just as naturally continued to reject the principle that they could be dispensed with, that they were harmful to the efficient and economic administration of justice. In the Weimar Republic, the SPD and the trade unions as part of the codification of labor law sought to expand the jurisdiction of the special courts to encompass all labor disputes by creating labor courts (*Arbeitsgerichte*).[31] Work began in the Reich Ministry of Labor on a draft of a labor court law. Lawyers responded sharply. On 2 November 1920, the executive committee of the DAV protested to the Reich Ministry of Justice and began to seek support for its position from local bar associations and lawyers' chambers, from state ministries of justice, and from members of the Reichstag.[32] The representatives' assembly of the DAV resolved in 1922 that:

[T]he exclusion of lawyers from the special courts represents a serious blow to the justice-seeking public, employee and employer alike, who would be denied justice by the extension of special jurisdiction to the entire field of labor law. The exclusion of lawyers from the special courts is an unprecedented and unjustified insult [*Kränkung*] to the legal profession.[33]

Proponents of labor courts and the exclusion of lawyers built upon a growing hostility toward lawyers and the entire legal system on the part of the working class, exacerbated by the infamous political justice of the Weimar era.[34] Part of the expression of this suspicion was the fact that the draft labor court law emerged from the Reich Ministry of Labor, with jurisdiction over labor and other social questions, rather

31 See the discussion in Wunderlich, *German Labor Courts*, 40, and Ostler, *Die deutschen Rechtsanwälte*, 179–81. The Weimar Constitution provided that the federal government should adopt a uniform labor code (*Arbeitsrecht*); Art. 157.
32 "Zum Entwurf eines Arbeitsgerichtsgesetzes," Abl 7 (1920): 210–11; see the descriptions of the efforts of the executive committee of the DAV in "Sitzung des Vorstandes des Deutschen Anwaltvereins vom 4. und 5. Dez. 1920," Abl 7 (1920): 227–31, 227; and "Aus der Vereinstätigkeit," Abl 8 (1921): 3–5, 4. See "Aus der Vereinstätigkeit," Abl 9 (1922): 3–5, 3–4, outlining the position of the DAV taken in discussions with the Reich Ministry of Justice.
33 "Entwurf eines Arbeitsgerichtsgesetzes, insbesondere: Die Angliederung der Sondergerichte an die ordentliche Gerichte, Zulassung der Rechtsanwälte," Abl 9 (1922): 19–20, 20; resolution passed at the fourteenth Representatives' Assembly in Braunschweig, 28 January 1922.
34 This attitude is accepted as axiomatic by Hugo Sinzheimer, "Zum Entwurf eines Arbeitsgerichtsgesetzes," *Die Justiz* 1 (1925–6): 6–12, 8. See also the observations on this suspicion and hostility by Hachenburg, *Lebenserinnerungen eines Rechtsanwalts*, 164.

than from the Reich Ministry of Justice, with jurisdiction over courts, lawyers, and legal reform.[35] Indeed, lawyers harshly criticized the fact that the Social-Political Committee of the Reichstag conducted the hearings and debate on the bill rather than the Committee on Law; not only was the former committee less sympathetic to lawyers' interests, but only two or three of its twenty-eight members were themselves legally trained.[36] Lawyers bitterly denounced the draft as "doctrinaire" and "hostile to lawyers," but despite their opposition it passed on 13 December 1926, by a vote of 210 to 140.[37] With a last burst of recrimination against political parties who sought to ingratiate themselves with the bar with claims that they had fought the exclusion, lawyers in private practice had to accommodate themselves to this blow to their dignity and expanded encroachment upon their field of action.[38]

Traditional and comfortable state agencies that had long been familiar negotiating partners, especially the Reich Ministry of Justice, no longer held unrivaled power over issues of importance to lawyers. Other, newer ministries, particularly the Reich Ministry of Labor, with competing if not contradictory policy goals, now entered as actors whose decisions affected lawyers. Parties in the Reichstag, especially the Social Democratic Party, with constituencies and agendas hostile to lawyers, acted in newly assertive and independent ways in the legislature. Under these circumstances of the Weimar Republic that were changed from those of the Empire, lawyers had suffered a humiliating political defeat that reduced their incomes, revealed their lessened political clout, and further eroded their disinterested pose as the "general estate."

The interwar era also saw further state intervention into lawyers' lives through the inclusion of income from legal practice within the scope of the trade tax (*Gewerbesteuer*). Normally used to finance the

35 Wunderlich, *German Labor Courts*, 55–6.
36 Ibid., 121; see the express lament by Heinrich Dittenberger, "1927," *Abl* 14 (1927): 1–3, 1.
37 Out of many examples, see Albert Engel, "Zum Entwurf eines Arbeitsgerichtsgesetzes," *Abl* 12 (1925): 152–6, 152, 153. For a description of the system created by the labor court law, see Horace B. Davis, "The German Labor Courts," *Political Science Quarterly* 44 (1929): 397–420, and esp. his examination of the exclusion of lawyers, 414–16, in which he concludes that their admission would not make much difference as to comparative advantage between capital and labor but does not evaluate the issues of increased expense or delay.
38 See the remarkable exchange between the DAV and the German Democratic Party (DDP), in which the DDP tried to undermine the claim of the German People's Party (DVP) that it supported the interests of lawyers in the whole episode; the DAV rejected the DDP's claims, noting that *both* parties failed to protect the interests of lawyers; "Zum Arbeitsgerichtsgesetz," *Abl* 14 (1927): 57–8.

functioning of local (*Gemeinde*) government, the hard-pressed governments of the early 1920s tried to expand the definition of what constituted a trade in order to offset their diminishing incomes. In 1921 a
proposal by the state government of Saxony to subject income from
all free professions to the trade tax drew the comment and opposition
of the DAV.[39] The DAV argued first that the inclusion of free professions violated federal law, which reserved taxation of income to the
federal government, and second that free professions were not
"trades" within the legal definition of that term and cited limitations
upon competition such as prohibitions upon advertising and upon
combining law practice with other occupations, which they claimed
flowed naturally from "professional morality" (*Standessitte*).[40] Nevertheless, in the course of 1921, Saxony, Baden, and several smaller
states swept professional income into the purview of the trade tax.[41]

    The years of economic stability in the middle 1920s saw a de-
cline in governmental efforts to include the incomes of free professions under the trade tax.[42] Depression again reduced the incomes
of localities and ended the respite for lawyers. By 1929 the battle
raged both on the national level, where draft "framework" legislation for the trade tax expressly *excluded* the incomes of free professions, and on the state level, particularly in Prussia, by far the
largest state in Germany, where the ruling coalition, led by the
Catholic Center Party and the SPD, moved to *include* free professions under the tax.[43] The DAV once again mobilized lawyers'
chambers and local bar associations to oppose the change, and it
also staged a protest assembly and demonstration in Berlin.[44] Although lawyers avoided subjection to the trade tax in 1929, they
were not so lucky in 1930. As economic conditions worsened, the
search for tax revenues became more desperate, and the trade tax
presented itself once again. Tradespeople and their organizations

39 "Aus der Vereinstätigkeit," *Abl* 8 (1921): 3–5, 3–4. The submission by the DAV to the
    Saxon government is reprinted in ibid., 19–21.
40 Wassertrüdinger (Nürnberg), "Gewerbesteuer vom Anwaltseinkommen?," *Abl* 8 (1921):
    182–4, 184.
41 "Aus der Vereinstätigkeit," *Abl* 8 (1921): 104–7, 105–6; the DAV indicated that it would
    rely upon local bar associations to combat introduction of the trade tax on lawyers in their
    states.
42 For the larger political context of governmental fiscal policy during the financial crisis at
    the end of Weimar, see Dietrich Orlow, *Weimar Prussia 1925–1933: The Illusion of Strength*
    (Pittsburgh, 1991), esp. 165–72.
43 "Aus der Vereinstätigkeit," *Abl* 16 (1929): 76–80, 78.
44 "Aus der Vereinstätigkeit," *Abl* 16 (1929): 116–18, 116–17; over 1,500 professionals at-
    tended the Berlin protest.

campaigned to have free professions included in hopes that the effective rates of taxation on their own incomes would be reduced.[45] Despite arguments by lawyers that their profession was not a trade, despite warnings that the revenues would not be significant, and despite warnings that the added burden might crush the already beleaguered profession, the Prussian parliament in March 1930 adopted a new trade tax law that included income from the practice of free professions.[46]

The DAV continued its resistance to the trade tax on two fronts. First, it recommended to the local bar associations that the increased financial burden of the trade tax be passed along to clients through an agreed-upon ten percent surcharge to the statutory attorneys' fees.[47] The local associations declared use of this surcharge to be a "professional duty" (*Standespflicht*), and they imposed the surcharge despite objections by organizations of clients until the government outlawed the practice by decree in 1932.[48] Second, the DAV challenged the legality of the trade tax in two sets of legal cases. One challenge before the national constitutional court (*Staatsgerichtshof*) contested the constitutionality of state taxation of professional income under both the Weimar and Prussian constitutions. The second set of challenges came through resort to appeal of tax assessments through the state finance courts (*Finanzgerichte*).[49] Both challenges wound their way up through the judicial system over the course of 1930 to 1932. In both instances the organized bar met with no success. The constitutional court ruled in 1931 that extending the trade tax to include professional income did not violate the Weimar constitution.[50] After lawyers achieved initial success on the intermediate appellate level, the Prussian Supreme Administrative Court ruled on 5 April 1932, that the Prussian trade tax law could legally be applied to professional

45 "Vereinsnachrichten," *Abl* 17 (1930): 97–100, 99.
46 For lawyers' arguments as to why they should not be included in the tax, see Paul Marcuse, *Die freien Berufe und die Gewerbesteuer* (Leipzig, 1929), and idem, "Die preußische Gewerbesteuer," *Abl* 17 (1930): 116–20.
47 Ostler, *Die deutschen Rechtsanwälte*, 208; see also "Die Abwälzung der Gewerbesteuer," *Abl* 17 (1930): 174–6; by 15 June 1930, fifty-four local bar associations had adopted "pass through" provisions. The device of uniform surcharge tariffs was a reversion to wartime and inflation devices that permitted fees to keep pace with inflation through self-help measures without resort to legislation.
48 See the exchange of letters between the Reichsverband der Deutschen Industrie and the DAV in May 1930, *Abl* 17 (1930): 175–6. As to the outlawing of the policy, see Ostler, *Die deutschen Rechtsanwälte*, 209.
49 "Preußische Gewerbesteuer," *Abl* 17 (1930): 227.
50 "Aus der Vereinstätigkeit," *Abl* 18 (1931): 172–4, 173.

income.[51] With that decision, legal action was at an end and Prussian lawyers, the majority of all German lawyers, continued to operate under the burden of the trade tax.

The financial blow of subjection to the trade tax certainly was important to lawyers, but more important was the blow to their prestige, to their claim to special status. Despite their best efforts in legislature and courts, lawyers found their profession classified as a "trade." The power to make this decision lay in the increasingly polarized legislatures, where the parties of political liberalism, with which lawyers identified, found their numbers and hence their influence sharply reduced. Financial need on the part of localities, whose governing bodies no longer were the exclusive preserve of liberal parties, caused them to seek access to new sources of revenue and to pursue lawyers' incomes in a way that was insulting both to their economic and status security. The organized bar and its liberal allies proved impotent to protect its own interests.

Conclusion

Together with the tales of the struggles over simultaneous admission and *freie Advokatur*, the stories of the political struggles outlined in this chapter show that the German bar followed the same trajectory as a liberalism whose claims to be the "general estate" had long since lost plausibility in the face of an eroding social basis of support.[52] Lawyers who turned to the state for assistance, both leaders of the bar and insurgents, found that their influence in the 1920s and early 1930s did not extend as far as it had before the First World War. Whereas in 1878 lawyers had made up a significant proportion of the delegates in the Reichstag, that dominance had begun to erode by the 1890s, and 1919 changed the entire picture.[53] By 1922 only eleven lawyers in private practice served in the Reichstag, and by 1932 only fourteen.[54] Similarly, city councils, formerly a preserve of liberal

---

51 "Aus der Vereinstätigkeit," *Abl* 19 (1932): 229–30, 229; the opinion is reprinted in *JW* 61 (1932): 2113.

52 The parallel to the analysis of the fate of the liberal parties is striking; see the conclusion in Jones, *German Liberalism*, 476–82.

53 During the Second Empire, 11.2 percent of all delegates to the Reichstag were lawyers; during Weimar, only 5.2 percent; Jarausch, *The Unfree Professions*, 70–1, esp. table 3.2.

54 Julius Curtius, "Anwaltschaft und Parlament," *JW* 51 (1922): 1289–91, 1289. See also complaints about too few lawyers in the Reichstag in "1927," *Abl* 14 (1927): 1–2, 2, and "Aus der Vereinstätigkeit," *Abl* 19 (1932): 188–91, 189–90 (only 14 out of 560 deputies in the just-dissolved Reichstag). For the centrality of political activity and parliamentary

influence and a stronghold of lawyers as members, became more competitive electoral arenas under the reformed suffrage of the republic, and lawyers lost ground.[55] The political voice of lawyers in elective bodies fell with the fortunes of the liberal political parties.[56]

After 1918 lawyers also encountered new, unfamiliar, and less friendly bureaucracies. The Reich Ministry of Justice, previously the principal and usually sympathetic bureaucratic contact, no longer was the sole arena in which lawyers had to contend. Many lawyers cooled in their support of mandatory retirement insurance when the ministry of labor eagerly embraced the idea, and that same ministry steadfastly pursued the Social Democratic program of labor law reform, despite the resistance of the organized bar and its insistence that the justice ministry should have jurisdiction.

Thus, liberal political practice, like liberal professional practice, during the Weimar years reached the limits of its power to further the interests of the German bar. Having reached the limits of *Honoratiorenpolitik* in internal organization in the dispute over simultaneous admission, the limits of economic liberalism in the debate over *freie Advokatur* and *numerus clausus*, and the limits of political liberalism in a series of disappointing legislative defeats, the bar had reached the end of its power to maintain as the center of its professional identity the liberal mission ascribed to it by nineteenth-century reformers.

service to the self-conception of lawyers in France during the late nineteenth and early twentieth centuries, see Karpik, "Lawyers and Politics in France, 1814–1950," 719–20.

55 Hartmut Pogge von Strandmann, "The Liberal Power Monopoly in the Cities of Imperial Germany," in Larry Eugene Jones and James Retallack, eds., *Elections, Mass Politics, and Social Change in Modern Germany: New Perspectives* (Cambridge, 1992), 93–117; Wolfgang Hardtwig, "Großstadt und Bürgerlichkeit in der politischen Ordnung des Kaiserreichs," in Lothar Gall, ed., *Stadt und Bürgertum im 19. Jahrhundert* (Munich, 1990), 19–64; and Jürgen Reulecke, "Bildungsbürgertum und Kommunalpolitik im 19. Jahrhundert," in Kocka, ed., *Bildungsbürgertum im 19. Jahrhundert, Teil IV*, 122–45. For example, whereas lawyers in private practice consistently occupied at least one and often two or three of the twenty-four seats on the Hannover city council before 1918, they held only four of eighty-four in 1920, two of ninety-six in 1921, and one of ninety-four in 1923; figures compiled from *Adreßbuch für die Stadt Hannover*, 1878–1923.

56 For the thesis that a strong expression of working-class interests in the political process diminishes the role of lawyers in politics, see Dietrich Rueschemeyer, "Comparing Legal Professions Cross-nationally: From a Professions-centered to a State-centered Approach," *American Bar Foundation Research Journal* 12 (1986): 415–46, 441.

10

Conclusion: Lawyers and the Limits of Liberalism

On Saturday afternoon, 22 April 1933, members of the lawyers' chamber for the Court of Appeal district of Celle convened at 3:00 P.M. in the city of Hannover for a special meeting to elect a new executive board.[1] This extraordinary and irregular assembly met at the order of the Prussian Ministry of Justice in Berlin, controlled since 30 January by the National Socialist Party.[2] On 3 April the sitting executive board had refused the ministry's demand to resign en masse, and it had further declined to accept the tendered resignation of its single Jewish member, "in consideration of [his] long years of meritorious service."[3] As a result, the ministry of justice had deposed the executive board and appointed a local National Socialist lawyer, Focko Meiborg, as "Commissar" to run the lawyers' chamber until the 22 April meeting could be held to choose a new board that would presumably be more willing to "take its part in the fulfillment of the great tasks that face the administration of justice in the new state."[4]

1 On 1 January 1933, the total membership of the lawyers' chamber was 820 lawyers; 350 attended the meeting, an unusually large number. The summons to the meeting is found in N.H.St.A., Hann. 173, Acc. 30/87, 30, unnumbered loose leaves at front of folder. Accounts of the meeting may be found in the annual report of the lawyers' chamber for 1933, authored by the new National Socialist executive board, ibid., 110–19, 112, and in Mundt, *100 Jahre Rechtsanwaltskammer*, 43–8.

2 The history of the Reich and State Ministries of Justice is beginning to be told in extensive detail. See the massive work, Lothar Gruchmann, *Justiz im "Dritten Reich" 1933–1940. Anpassung und Unterwerfung in der Ära Gürtner*, 2d ed. (Munich, 1990), as well as more focused contributions such as Eli Nathans, *Franz Schlegelberger* (Baden-Baden, 1990). For an overview of National Socialist attitudes toward law and justice, see Dennis L. Anderson, *The Academy for German Law, 1933-1944* (New York and London, 1987); see also Kenneth C. H. Willig, "The Theory and Administration of Justice in the Third Reich" (Ph.D. diss., Philadelphia, 1975), and idem, "The Bar in the Third Reich," *American Journal of Legal History* 20 (1976): 1–14.

3 Vorstand der Anwaltskammer Celle an den Herrn OLGP Celle, 3. April 1933, N.H.St.A., Hann. 173, Acc. 30/87, 30, 91.

4 OLGP Celle an den Herrn Vorsizenden des Vorstandes der Anwaltskammer Celle, ibid., 88, and OLGP Celle an den Herrn PJM in Berlin, ibid., 92; the quotation comes from PJM an den Herrn OLGP, 11. April 1933, ibid., unnumbered loose leaves.

291

At the express order of the justice minister, the assembly was open
to the public, and in the intimidating presence of a large number of
SA brownshirts who lined the back of the room where the meeting
was held, the members of the lawyers' chamber elected a National
Socialist-dominated slate, chaired by Meiborg.[5] Although a conservative lawyer from Hannover protested beforehand that the extraordinary meeting was irregular and illegal, particularly because it would
be open to the public, and a second lawyer from Göttingen soon
afterward published an open letter to Meiborg declaring that the
meeting violated all procedural rules, the new executive board remained in place.[6]

Similarly, the DAV experienced "coordination" (*Gleichschaltung*)
at the hands of the National Socialists. Along with all other segments of German society, in the course of the 1920s some lawyers in
private practice had come to support the National Socialist Party.[7]
The National Socialist Party had formed an auxiliary organization
for legally trained persons in 1928, the League of National Socialist

5   For the order that the meeting be open to the public, see PJM an den Herrn OLGP, 11. April
    1933, ibid., unnumbered loose leaves; see also the invitation to the meeting, ibid., and the
    results of the election reported to Berlin on 24 April ibid., 102–3. A useful account can also
    be found in Mundt, *100 Jahre Rechtsanwaltskammer*, 47–8.
6   Rechtsanwalt Otto Kleinrath an den Herrn PJM, 20. April 1933, N.H.St.A., Hann. 173,
    Acc. 30/87, 30, 97; and Briefwechsel mit dem Kommissar für den Vorstand der Anwalts-
    kammer Celle, Herrn Rechtsanwalt Meiborg in Celle, zur Kenntnis. Rechtsanwalt
    Friedrich-Karl Walbaum, ibid., 104. Kleinrath specifically added that his objection was
    lodged "with the consent of the [local] leadership of the German National People's Party."
    Gripping accounts of coordination of the lawyers' chamber in Berlin, and a summary of
    events elsewhere, can be found in Krach, *Jüdische Rechtsanwälte*, 215–23. For accounts of the
    experience of the courts and judiciary in Hannover during the Third Reich, see Ulrich
    Hamann, "Das Oberlandesgericht Celle im Dritten Reich – Justizverwaltung und Per-
    sonalwesen," in *Festschrift zum 275jährigen Bestehen des Oberlandesgerichts Celle*, 143–231, and
    Volker Kregel, *Die nationalsozialistische Personalpolitik der Justiz im Oberlandesgerichtsbezirk
    Celle* (Hannover, 1989).
7   For example, Walter Luetgebrune of Göttingen had spent much of the 1920s travelling
    around Germany defending right-wing extremists who had been arrested for various of-
    fenses. He made his reputation in his defense of Ludendorff at his trial after the Hitler-*Putsch*
    of 9 November 1923, and after 1932 was the chief legal advisor for the SA and SS; Rudolf
    Heydeloff, "Staranwalt der Rechtsextremisten. Walter Luetgebrune in der Weimarer
    Republik," *Vierteljahrshefte für Zeitgeschichte* 32 (1984): 373–421, based upon idem, "The
    Political-Judicial Career of Dr. jur. Walter Luetgebrune and the Crisis of Weimar and Early
    National Socialist Germany 1918 to 1934," (Ph.D. diss., University of Waterloo, Canada,
    1977). See also Lawrence D. Stokes, "Professionals and National Socialism: The Case
    Histories of a Small-Town Lawyer and Physician, 1918–1945," *German Studies Review* 8
    (1985): 449–80, which traces the involvement of a young lawyer in Eutin, Johann Heinrich
    Böhmcker, in the National Socialist movement both before and after his admission to the
    bar in 1927. Despite these spectacular examples of right-wing activism, Konrad Jarausch's
    research shows that private practitioners were no more inclined to become early members
    of the National Socialist Party than professionals as a whole; *The Unfree Professions*, 102,
    table 4.1 on 101, and table A.16 on 254.

German Jurists (*Bund nationalsozialistischer deutscher Juristen*, BNSDJ), led by Hans Frank, a practicing lawyer in Munich.[8] This group encompassed all kinds of jurists, so private practitioners made up only part of its membership. Prior to 1933, its attractiveness to private practitioners was slight. On 1 January 1931, the BNSDJ had a total of 213 members, of whom 110 were lawyers in private practice; by 1 October 1931, only 253 lawyers had joined, and the best estimate is that fewer than 5 percent of the bar had affiliated before 30 January 1933.[9]

Although the first few meetings of the executive board of the DAV after 30 January seemed to have been little affected by the seizure of power, the Prussian Ministry of Justice was pressuring the DAV to eliminate Jews from its board (eleven of twenty-five members were Jewish).[10] The DAV had refused on 26 March to merge with the BNSDJ because DAV members who were Jewish would be excluded, but by 7 April Jewish members of the DAV executive board responded to requests from the non-Jewish members and resigned. On 6 April the executive board dissolved the representatives' assembly and scheduled new elections for 6 May. On 5 May, however, the Prussian Minister of Justice ordered the DAV to amalgamate with the BNSDJ, and on 6 May the National Socialist Reich Justice Commissar, Hans Frank, appointed another Nazi, Hermann Voß of Berlin, to supervise the DAV. Voß proceeded to appoint the new members of the representatives' assembly rather than permit the election to go forward. Although the DAV continued to exist until 27 December 1933, when it dissolved and was absorbed into the "Specialty Group 'Lawyer' " of the BNSDJ (*Fachgruppe 'Rechtsanwalt'*), its effective independence ended in May.[11]

8   The comprehensive history of the BNSDJ is found in Michael Sunnus, *Der NS-Rechts-wahrerbund (1928–1945). Zur Geschichte der nationalsozialistischen Juristenorganisation* (Frankfurt a.M., 1990), 21–2, which is, however, quite sketchy on the details of the creation of the organization. See also the account in Krach, *Jüdische Rechtsanwälte*, 146–8, and more generally 145–61 for evidence of anti-Semitism within the bar.

9   For the membership as of 1 January 1931, see Krach, *Jüdische Rechtsanwälte*, 147, and Sunnus, *Der NS-Rechtswahrerbund*, 23; for the membership as of 1 October 1931, and the five percent estimate, see Jarausch, *The Unfree Professions*, 102, 109.

10 Ostler, *Die deutschen Rechtsanwälte*, 229.

11 Accounts of the coordination of the DAV can be found in Ostler, *Die deutschen Rechtsanwälte*, 229–35; Krach, *Jüdische Rechtsanwälte*, 223–36, esp. 223–32; Horst Göppinger, *Juristen jüdischer Abstammung im "Dritten Reich." Entrechtung und Verfolgung*, 2d ed. (Munich, 1990), 118–21; and Jarausch, *The Unfree Professions*, 116–19. Jarausch concludes on 119: "In order to preserve their profession, lawyers sacrificed their liberal tradition and vaunted autonomy with astonishing alacrity." The statute of the DAV was altered on 30 September 1933, to exclude lawyers of "non-Aryan extraction"; Ostler, *Die deutschen*

The events of April and May 1933 demonstrate beyond question
the inability of the German bar to withstand the profound illiberalism of the National Socialist movement.[12] The bar in private practice provided no effective barrier to the takeover and the rule of
lawlessness, nor did it serve as an effective educator of successful
resistance to enemies of the legal order.[13] The private bar thereby
"failed" in the great historic task set out for it by the liberal
theorists of the nineteenth century. Why did this sad outcome
occur? For lawyers, who cherished their ascribed role as the general estate and particular bearers and guarantors of the *Rechtsstaat*,
to succumb so easily to the procedural irregularity and illiberalism
of National Socialist coordination, something must have gone pow-
erfully wrong.

Like many aspects of the National Socialist seizure of power, the
easy success of the coordination campaign aimed at German lawyers
in private practice has puzzled historians. Some historians contend
that elimination of Jewish leaders of the bar decapitated the liberal
leadership among practitioners and placed the rudderless bar at the

---

Rechtsanwälte, 233. The assertion in Reifner, "The Bar in the Third Reich," 113, that
"Anti-semitism was the most effective agent in the destruction of the liberal German bar"
must be placed in the context both of generalized National Socialist hostility toward
lawyers and of the weakened state of bar institutions and ideologies.

12 Soon after the seizure of power, the National Socialists took steps to begin to exclude
Jewish lawyers through emergency decrees. On the same day that the regime promulgated
the "Law for the Restoration of the Professional Civil Service" (*Gesetz zur Wieder-
herstellung des Berufsbeamtentums*), 7 April 1933, it also issued the "Law on Admission to the
Practicing Bar" (*Gesetz über die Zulassung zur Rechtsanwaltschaft*), which disbarred Jewish
lawyers who had been admitted since August 1914 and who were neither war veterans nor
the father or son of a soldier killed at the front. The most detailed account of measures
against Jewish lawyers is Krach, *Jüdische Rechtsanwälte*, 165–403; see also Göppinger,
Juristen jüdischer Abstammung, 45–97; and for a selection of primary documents, Ilse Staff,
ed., *Justiz im Dritten Reich. Eine Dokumentation* (Frankfurt, 1964), 40–53, 124–46. Thirty-
four members of the bar in the province of Hannover lost their admission; N.H.St.A.,
Hann. 173, Acc. 30/87, 30, 110R. New admittees had to show proof of their Aryan
descent. A further thirty-three Jewish lawyers lost their admission as a result of the
intensified persecution of Jews in September 1938, when a decree implementing the
Nürnberg Laws of September 1935 extended the prohibition on the practice of law by
Jews even to war veterans. Jewish lawyers also found themselves subject to arbitrary
violence and imprisonment. Horst Berkowitz, a decorated and disabled war veteran who
practiced before the superior court in the city of Hannover had his partnership with a non-
Jewish lawyer dissolved in June 1933. After *Kristallnacht* on 9 November 1938, he was
arrested and sent to the concentration camp at Buchenwald. He was released in December
and returned to Hannover to practice as a *Judenkonsulent*; Beer, *Versehrt, verfolgt, versöhnt*,
55–93.

13 In fact, in many instances, lawyers were especially complicit with the crimes of the Third
Reich; see Gunnar C. Boehnert, "The Jurists in the SS-Führerkorps, 1925–1939," in
Gerald Hirschfeld and Lothar Kettenacker, eds., *Der "Führerstaat": Mythos und Realität.
Studien zur Struktur und Politik des Dritten Reiches* (Stuttgart, 1981), 361–74.

mercy of National Socialist activists.[14] Others lump private practitioners in with the broader class of university-trained jurists, steeped in monarchist and nationalist culture through university life and military training, most of whom were at best only temporarily reconciled to the republic and at worst actively hostile to it.[15] Another recent study of the experience of professionals in general emphasizes that German professions, including the bar, developed along a bureaucratic model very different from the Anglo-American paradigm, but they nevertheless behaved not very differently from professions elsewhere, especially considering the general economic exigencies of the 1920s and early 1930s.[16] Finally, yet another recent work argues that the disruptions and disappointments of 1914–33 made German lawyers, along with other professionals, "repudiate their liberal legacy and openly embrace illiberalism."[17] Lawyers participated in a "corruption of German professionalism"; "abandoning their outmoded ethical moorings," they acted in such a way as to "betray their humanitarian ethics."[18]

Focus upon the drama of the first months of 1933 and upon the economic dislocations of 1929–33 has masked the larger story of the development of the German bar in private practice from the 1830s to 1933, its relationship with German liberalism, and its experience in the generalized crisis of liberal ideologies and institutions from the 1890s to 1933. This book has argued instead that German lawyers did not abandon liberalism so much as they ran out of solutions when their liberal practices failed at every turn to protect their professional interests. Swift coordination occurred because the ideological and institu-

14 Ingo Müller, *Hitler's Justice: The Courts of the Third Reich*, trans. by Deborah Lucas Schneider (Cambridge, Mass., 1991), ch. 8, "Purges at the Bar," 59–67.
15 The focus on the political conservatism of the German judiciary during Weimar dates to contemporary observations; see Ernst Fraenkel, *Zur Soziologie der Klassenjustiz* (Berlin, 1927; repr. ed., Darmstadt, 1968) and Theo Rasehorn, *Justizkritik in der Weimarer Republik. Das Beispiel der Zeitschrift "Der Justiz"* (Frankfurt a. M., 1985). See also Ralph Angermund, *Deutsche Richterschaft 1919–1945. Krisenerfahrung, Illusion, politische Rechtsprechung* (Frankfurt a. M., 1990), and Ralf Dreier and Wolfgang Sellert, eds., *Recht und Justiz im "Dritten Reich"* (Frankfurt a. M., 1989). For radical nationalism and the illiberal milieu of university life, especially in the legal faculties, see Konrad H. Jarausch, *Students, Society and Politics in Imperial Germany*.
16 McClelland, *The German Experience of Professionalization*, 231, 235–7, 239–42.
17 Jarausch, *The Unfree Professions*, 226. Elsewhere he argues that lawyers abandoned liberal practices in their professional governance, embraced neoconservative and even *völkisch* ideas in the general cultural realm, and rejected liberalism in the political realm; idem, "The Decline of Liberal Professionalism: Reflections on the Social Erosion of German Liberalism, 1867–1933," in Jarausch and Jones, eds., *In Search of a Liberal Germany*, 261–86, 284.
18 Jarausch, *The Unfree Professions*, 224–6.

tional structures of the bar proved incapable of accommodating new substantive notions of justice, unfamiliar activism from the democratically reformed state, and paralyzing conflict in internal professional affairs. The procedural approach of lawyers to problem solving and the elite-dominated institutions of the bar, both products and symptoms of liberalism, simply failed to offer effective solutions to the wide array of conflicts that confronted lawyers. This book contends that explanations of the behavior of lawyers in 1933 must move beyond analyses based upon economic exigency, de-professionalization, or moral and ethical failure. Instead, the answer lies in the paralysis of professional institutions and ideology caused by the social diversification of the bar, the exhaustion of the persuasive power of the bar's posture as the general estate, and the procedural conception of the legal profession and of liberalism.

The great legislative reforms of 1877–9 led to increasing and accelerating social diversification within the profession. The most important change that occurred under the new regime was a demographic shift in the composition of the bar. Social groups that had formerly been excluded or had avoided legal study, notably the sons of businessmen, now flocked to the bar. Social change and market pressures steered lawyers into new career paths in new locations, particularly in large cities and in small district court towns. Yet the impact of localization meant that social opening occurred differentially. Not surprisingly, sons of businessmen chose economically thriving cities in which to practice law. Even when the bars of those cities were already large, as in the city of Hannover, these sons of men accustomed to competition were undeterred. Sons of businessmen also ventured into new markets, the small district court towns. Smaller superior court towns, steeped in years of tradition as places of high status in which to practice, proved more attractive to sons of lawyers, higher state officials, and other academically trained persons. Uneven economic and demographic development, then, not only left groups of lawyers practicing in different worlds but combined with free entry to reinforce differences in conditions of practice with differences in social origin.

Especially stressed by the demographic changes were lawyers who practiced before small rural superior courts. These men were privileged under the bylaws of the lawyers' chambers and under the RAO, and often came from families of lawyers long accustomed to having high status conferred automatically by admission before their home courts. Yet their relative proportion in the bar in Hannover declined sharply after 1900 and their hold on institutional power appeared very threatened. They suddenly found that the deference that they had come to expect from lawyers who practiced before lower courts could no longer be assumed. Their superiority in social origin offered small comfort as they faced challenges to the deference that they expected from their traditionally elevated status.

Especially excluded from professional privilege were lawyers who practiced before district courts. Traditionally a small minority of the bar, the combination of free entry and localization caused many lawyers, especially after 1900, to seek their fortunes practicing before these courts. The absence of simultaneous admission now came to be viewed as a crying injustice. These lawyers felt (and were) excluded from power in the DAV and on the executive boards of lawyers' chambers. When they won victories such as the endorsements of simultaneous admission by the DAV, they found the spoils snatched away by superior court lawyers who persisted in repeatedly raising the issue anew. Money was certainly an issue in this conflict between district and superior court lawyers, but more important were status and power. Lawyers who practiced before the small rural superior courts expected deference from district court lawyers and control over the executive boards of the lawyers' chambers, and they clung more fiercely to their status and power in order to compensate for their growing economic and numerical marginalization.

Third, by the tumultuous era of Weimar, younger lawyers had become especially restive. Despite the adoption of liberal, free-market principles regarding admission to the bar, the RAO, through the vague and general terms of §28 defining the duties of a lawyer, permitted the perpetuation of corporate notions of personal private and economic behavior into the twentieth century. Lawyer-notables retained a strict "code of honor," and their position of power in the new institutions of the private bar enabled them to enforce it upon the entire bar. Although few lawyers complained at first, younger lawyers in the twentieth century began to question the utility and modernity of this inheritance. Relatively relaxed in their concern about lawyer-client relations, tolerant of political diversity, and even forgiving with regard to minor transgressions of the criminal law, these men enforced most strictly their opinions about proper personal behavior and the proper means of economic competition among lawyers already admitted to the bar. This system of discipline worked so long as it appeared just and equitable, but when it appeared unjust and inequitable, deference collapsed. By the 1920s, however, these corporate concerns seemed to be relics from a bygone day. Moreover, they seemed especially out of date in view of the stubborn resistance by these same lawyer-notables to proposals for limitation upon admission, insisting instead upon holding steadfastly to the principle of free entry.

All of these disputes and fissures found expression in the struggle for control of the institutions of the profession. Contradictory interests among different groups of lawyers emerged, spawning competing special-interest organizations that challenged existing arrangements within professional institutions and transformed them into a terrain upon which they struggled with each other for hegemony. The reaction of the leaders of the DAV was to attempt to create new procedural avenues through which interests could be expressed. Procedural reforms, such as broader representation for excluded voices, did not resolve substantive claims of justice but only restructured the terms of debate. As the leadership sought to hold liberal institutions together, special interests began to look to outside agencies in order to attain their goals. The inability of the institutions of the bar to mediate those disputes called into question both the legitimacy of bar leaders to represent the interests of the profession *and* the claims of the bar as a whole to special treatment as the "guardians of the law."

Once the professional institutions revealed their inability to respond to the key concerns of the differing strata, they faded in importance. The legal profession, therefore, faced the governmental hostility and economic crises of the 1920s profoundly disunited, wracked and riven with mutually reinforcing factional splits. Far from serving as the general estate, leading and educating the *Bürgertum* toward independence in the liberal state, the practicing bar in Germany could not even maintain itself as a unified profession. Splintered along many lines, the bar in private practice found itself paralyzed. The lawyer-notables who led it were able to retain old forms with remarkable tenacity, but they proved unable to adapt to the new circumstances of the 1920s.

Thus the coordination of the bar was neither a sudden capitulation in the face of Nazi militancy and coercion nor a mysterious abandonment of long-held lawyerly liberalism. Lawyers shared the fate of a liberalism whose claims to be the general estate had long since lost plausibility in the face of an eroding social basis of support.[19] Just as the leaders of German liberal political parties failed to convince the German people that their platforms advanced the general interest, leaders of the bar failed both to make the case to the public that lawyers represented the interests of all of society and to maintain their own claim to be the general estate of private practitioners, representing the interests of all lawyers. Claims of these leaders to represent the interest of all lawyers succumbed to outsiders' conviction, which emerged, especially in the debates surrounding simultaneous admission and limitations upon admission, that they were unrepresentative, a "lawyers' upper class." Moreover, leaders of the bar failed to convince the larger public of the legitimacy of lawyers' claims to special status and special control of their own affairs, as should be the due of the general estate, losing battles to exclude women, to assure lawyers' practice before labor courts, and to avoid the trade tax. Repeated legislative campaigns unmasked the bar's posturing as the general estate and revealed it as one of many competing interest groups.

Lastly, the narrow proceduralism of professional ideology, closely linked with liberal *Rechtsstaat* doctrine, offered no solutions to conflicts within the bar or in German society. Like liberalism, professional ideology fundamentally *denied* the legitimacy of interest groups. It refused to prescribe substantive bases to decide among competing claims, instead focusing upon procedures that avoided addressing the heart of issues. The final refuge of the organized bar was to seek to change the procedural ground rules of entry into the profession by endorsing a *numerus clausus*. They thus prepared the ground for convincing themselves in 1933 that they could remain true to their formal commitment to liberty even while they acquiesced in injustice. Remaining within their framework as the paradigmatic independent, liberal, "free" profession, lawyers demonstrated the limited integrative power of procedural conceptions of liberalism and its inherent weakness in the face of opponents mobilized by substantive ideas of justice.

19 For descriptions of this process of the decay of the *Bürgertum* as a coherent social group, see Hans Mommsen, "Die Auflösung des Bürgertums seit dem späten 19. Jahrhundert," in Kocka, ed., *Bürger und Bürgerlichkeit*, 288–315, and M. Rainer Lepsius, "Zur Soziologie des Bürgertums und der Bürgerlichkeit," in ibid., 79–100.

Methodological Appendix

As discussed in Chapter 5, the fact that lawyers in private practice comprised only one-quarter to one-third of all law graduates means that a study of the social and geographic origins of all law students is an inadequate method of compiling biographical data for those students who later entered private practice. It is possible, however, first to identify private practitioners and then to use data regarding law students in order to secure a reliable source for biographical information about lawyers. This Methodological Appendix is intended to reveal clearly the methods by which the biographies of lawyers on which the analysis in Chapter 5 is based were constructed.

Annual registries of all lawyers in the province of Hannover (as well as all other provinces in Prussia), listed by the court before which they practiced, appear in the Prussian State Handbooks.[1] In addition the yearly reports of the lawyers' chamber in Celle usually contained lists of new admittees, deaths, retirements, changes in residence, and other reasons for lawyers leaving the bar.[2] The registry of members of the lawyers' chamber in Celle, required to be maintained as a roll of practitioners, apparently no longer exists. It was not

1 Königliches Preußisches Statistisches Amt, *Handbuch über den königlichen preußischen Hof und Staat für das Jahr* —— (Berlin), 1878/79 to 1930. These volumes appeared annually from 1878/79 to 1913 (with a closing deadline of 18 December 1913). A volume appeared in 1918, with a closing deadline of 31 March; another was published in 1922, closing deadline January 1922; another was issued in 1925, closing deadline January 1925. Publication resumed on an annual basis from 1926 to 1930. Biennial listings of lawyers are also included in Preußisches Justizministerium, *Jahrbuch der Preußischen Gerichtsverfassung* (Berlin), 1890–1914.
2 G.St.A. I HA Rep. 84a, 21912–21913, N.H.St.A., Hann. 173, Acc. 30/87, 30. The first three annual reports did not contain the lists of new admittees, although the list of initial members of the chamber is found in I HA Rep. 84a, 21912, 23–7. Beginning in 1884/85 and running through 1913–14, the list of new admittees shows up each year. The reports for 1914–15 through 1921, inclusive, do not contain lists of new admittees, although the number of new admissions is noted. The list of new admittees resumes in 1922 and runs through the annual report for 1933.

available at the Niedersächsisches Hauptstaatsarchiv in Hannover, the Geheimes Staatsarchiv in Dahlem, the Oberlandesgericht in Celle, or the Anwaltskammer in Celle.

Nevertheless, the published handbooks and the annual reports of the lawyers' chamber permitted the assembly of a comprehensive list of all lawyers admitted at any time between 1879 and 1933 to any court in the province of Hannover. Careful examination of the published lists permitted a determination of years of admission to and dismissal from the bar; the archival lists provided a double check to guard against oversight. In many cases they also provided an indication of the reasons for lawyers being dismissed from the bar. The result of this effort was the establishment of the universe of Hannoverian lawyers. There were 1,504 separate admissions during this fifty-five year span, representing 1,301 individuals.[3]

Once the universe of all lawyers had been determined, the next task was to secure biographical data for each lawyer. In the cases of some lawyers, archival records simplified the process. Among the personnel records of various court officials (*Personalakten*) are the personnel files for many of the Hannoverian lawyers who were also notaries. Since notaries were state officials appointed by the ministry of justice, the court of appeal maintained records on them. Spanning roughly the entire period of this study, the personnel files concerning 177 lawyer-notaries were found in the Niedersächsisches Hauptstaatsarchiv in Hannover. Most of each file consisted merely of letters seeking approval of a substitute so that the lawyer could leave on holiday, but each file also contained a cover sheet in which certain data concerning that lawyer were recorded. These data included father's occupation, place of birth, places of education, grades on bar examinations (including indications if the lawyer had to repeat the examination), dates of service, and occasionally indicia of confession, marital status, and economic circumstances.[4]

For lawyers who had never become notaries, another method had to be discovered in order to find biographical information. In Prussia the first state bar examination was administered by a commis-

---

3   Each time that a lawyer moved from one court to another and sought a new admission, relinquishing the old one, the lawyers' chamber recorded a new admission. Accordingly, for purposes of admissions, the larger group is used. When discussing the size of the bar at any given time, the smaller group is used.
4   N.H.St.A., Hann. 173, Acc. 84/59, 49/72, 83/76, 67/78, 103/79, and 63/80.

sion appointed at each court of appeal.[5] Because of the localized nature of this important examination and because of the particularities of substantive law at the provincial level, especially pronounced before the effective date of the Civil Law Code in 1900, the research proceeded under the working hypothesis that law students who ultimately practiced in the province of Hannover would have attended the Hannoverian university at some point in their academic careers in order better to prepare themselves for this bar examination. This assumption is rendered more reasonable because of the fact that the legal faculty at the University in Göttingen remained prestigious into the late nineteenth century and was also one of the largest in Germany.[6] Numerous advantages, therefore, attached to the choice of the "home" university as one of the stops on the academic career of a law student who planned to practice later in Hannover.[7]

The Constitution of the Courts (GVG) required that a candidate for the first bar examination first complete at least six semesters' study of law at a university (§2), and it is well known that many law students spent substantially more time at the university.[8] Further, the Prussian regulations for the practical education of candidates for private practice or the judiciary between the first and second bar examinations required a period of four years' practical legal training (*Referendariat*) before a candidate could be admitted to the second examination (*Asses-*

5 Preußisches Gesetz über die juristischen Prüfungen und die Vorbereitung zum höheren Justizdienste vom 6. Mai 1869, Abs. 1, §2, in *Die Vorschriften über die Ausbildung der Juristen in Preußen* (Berlin, 1891), 10.
6 Authors repeatedly comment upon the high prestige and social exclusivity of the Georg-August-University in Göttingen, especially the legal faculty there. See, for example, Huerkamp, *Der Aufstieg der Ärzte*, 69, Erläuterungen zu Tabelle 4. While Göttingen, and especially its legal faculty, was from its very inception by Münchhausen intended to attract sons of nobles, even princes, to be trained for state service, after the annexation of Hannover by Prussia in 1867 its prestige had suffered somewhat. Reduced from a state to a provincial university, and with the seat of government now Berlin rather than the city of Hannover, the university more frequently lost outstanding members of its legal faculty to the University of Berlin; Wilhelm Lexis, *Die Universitäten im Deutschen Reich* (Berlin, 1904), 367.
7 Both Henning and Jarausch comment upon this tendency of students to attend their "home" university during part of their student careers. Henning, *Das westdeutsche Bürgertum*, on 265–6 for state officials and on 417 for free professionals (noting a weakening in the tendency after the 1880s), indicates that Göttingen was at least a stop on the journey, although usually not the only stop. Jarausch found the same pattern at the University of Bonn specifically and in Prussia generally; *Students, Society, and Politics*, 143.
8 Johannes Conrad, *Das Universitätsstudium in Deutschland*, 111–12; Wilhelm Lexis, *Die Universitäten im Deutschen Reich*, 115, 120–1; Friedrich Paulsen indicates that the average length of study for law students in Prussia was 7.47 semesters between 1886 and 1888, idem, *Die deutschen Universitäten und das Universitätsstudium* (Berlin, 1902), 381.

sorenexamen).[9] Usually, therefore, a minimum of eight years must have elapsed between a law student's first matriculation at university and eventual admission to the practicing bar. Since the date of first admission to the bar was known, the *Matrikel* of the Georg-August-University became the source for biographical data concerning that lawyer. The search in this record began ten years before the date of the first admission to the bar. In cases of questionable identity, the assumptions were made that a Hannoverian lawyer would be more likely to have been a Prussian citizen and resident of the province of Hannover.[10] In most cases a law student of the same name as a later lawyer, and often from the same town as the one in which the later practice was established, appeared in the *Matrikel* at the appropriate time. In many instances, however, especially with common names like Meyer, Müller, and Schmidt, ambiguities remained. Data in such cases were not accepted unless there were other indications (such as father's occupation) that a student was in fact the future lawyer. The *Matrikel* for the Georg-August-University in Göttingen has been published in two volumes for the years 1734 to 1900. Unpublished volumes for the years 1900 to approximately 1926 were consulted in the University Archive in Göttingen.[11]

The *Matrikel* revealed the student's indication of father's occupation, the student's hometown and state and province of citizenship, in some instances the kind of secondary school certificate that the student possessed and from what school, the student's faculty of study, other universities attended, and dates of matriculation at Göttingen. If the entry was not the first one, earlier ones had been cross-referenced. These data are much the same as those contained in the

9   Gesetz über die juristischen Prüfungen und die Vorbereitung zum höheren Justizdienste Abs. II, §6. The four-year period clearly was conceived of as a minimum, for the successful candidate had to produce a "convincing evidence" that he had access to sufficient means to afford him an existence worthy of the legal profession (*standesgemäßer Unterhalt*) for five years before he could become a *Referendar*; "Regulative vom 1. Mai 1883, betreffend die juristischen Prüfungen und die Vorbereitung zum höheren Justizdienst, in der durch die Allgemeinen Verfügungen vom 12. März 1888 und vom 3. November 1890 abgeänderten Gestalt," *Vorschriften über die Ausbildung der Juristen*, 24–5.

10 The RAO did not require that lawyers who were citizens of one federal state be admitted either to the bar examination or to the bar of another state. In several cases, the lawyers' chamber rendered advisory opinions in admission cases in which it recommended that the ministry of justice deny admission to lawyers who were citizens of other states.

11 Götz von Selle, ed., *Die Matrikel der Georg-August-Universität zu Göttingen*, Bd. 1:1734–1837 (Hildesheim, 1937); Wilhelm Ebel, ed., Bd. 2:1837–1900 (Hildesheim, 1974). Unpublished *Matrikel* of the Georg-August University in Göttingen, 1900–25, Universitätsarchiv, Göttingen.

Personalakten for lawyers who were notaries, only without the occasional reference to nonprofessional information such as marital status, confession, and economic circumstances. From the universe of 1,301 individual lawyers, biographical data were found for 907.

The biographical information gathered from these sources was then placed in a data base, classified by court and year of admission, and coded for occupation and geographical and career pattern characteristics. From this data base, the annual size and hence rate of growth for the bar as a whole, for each level of court, and for each court could be derived. The annual reports of the lawyers' chamber also contain information concerning the size of the bar but it is too general, both because it only reports the total size of the bar of the court of appeal district and because it includes lawyers in Lippe and the other non-Prussian principalities. Thus, the data derived from this study vary slightly from the totals reported by the lawyers' chamber and from those published in sources such as *Deutsche Justiz-Statistik*, but these variances are accounted for by the exclusion of non-Hannoverian lawyers from this study.

Yet another important methodological problem associated with using information about father's occupation is how to aggregate the accumulated list of occupations into broader social categories that make sense and are useful in explaining changes in social relations.[12] A number of possibilities arise. The Imperial Statistical Office created a classification scheme based upon functional categories for purposes of the Occupational Census, but this system lumped free professionals in with higher state officials and military officers, offering little nuance.[13] Johannes Conrad applied a sixteen-class system in his study of the social origins of university students up to 1881.[14] While such a nuanced scheme is useful in analyzing a universe as large as all university students, it proves too fine for a smaller free profession drawn generally from a narrower social base. Konrad Jarausch has employed a six-class system which appears to be more manageable. He groups

---

12 Jarausch presents a nuanced discussion of these concerns in *Students, Society and Politics in Imperial Germany*, 114–22.

13 *Statistik des Deutschen Reichs*, Bd. 402, "Volks-, Berufs- und Betriebszählung vom 16. Juni 1925" (Berlin, 1931), 7–16, outlines the scheme used for the Occupational Census. Thomas Childers discusses the difficulty of using the broad economic categories of the Occupational Census for an analysis of social structure; *The Nazi Voter: The Social Foundations of Fascism in Germany, 1919–1933* (Chapel Hill, 1983), appendix I, "Methodology," 271–8, esp. 273–8.

14 Johannes Conrad, *Das Universitätsstudium in Deutschland während der letzten 50 Jahre. Statistische Untersuchungen unter besonderer Berücksichtigung Preußens* (Jena, 1884), 51–2.

university students into sons of nobles, of the *Bildungsbürgertum* (including university-educated state officials as well as free professionals), of the *Besitzbürgertum* (including agrarian property owners as well as commercial and industrial ones), of the old *Mittelstand* of peasants, artisans, and traders, of the new *Mittelstand* of nonacademic officials, white-collar workers, and lower-school teachers, and finally sons of the lower classes of skilled and unskilled workers, agricultural laborers, and domestic servants.[15] When applied to lawyers, however, this scheme is both overly broad and overly fine. Based upon the data gathered as to the social origins of lawyers in Hannover, Jarausch's categories could both conceal self-recruitment and produce infinitesimal results concerning the *Mittelstand* and lower classes.

Accordingly, this analysis follows a modified version of Jarausch's system. It employs a nine-part functional system for classifying fathers' occupations. Sons of lawyers constitute category 1. This rubric includes, as always in this study, lawyers in private practice, and it demonstrates the degree of self-recruitment to the legal profession. Category 2 contains sons of academically educated higher state officials, including sons of judicial officials (judges and prosecutors) but excluding most communal and local officials. The *Bildungsbürgertum* outside of government service comprises category 3. Described by Hansjoachim Henning as "independent persons with university education," this group bears a different relation to the marketplace than state officials with university education.[16] Category 4 is the sons of

15 Jarausch, *Students, Society and Politics in Imperial Germany*, 121–2. Roger Chickering uses a four-tiered model of low-, mid-, high-, and top-level status, *We Men Who Feel Most German: A Cultural Study of the Pan-German League 1886–1914* (Boston, 1984), statistical appendix, 306–30, although he also includes a more detailed typology in his tables. Finally, John Craig employs a six-category system similar to Jarausch's in "Higher Education and Social Mobility in Germany," 220.

16 Henning defines the relationship as follows: "Under the category 'independent academic' shall be subsumed occupants of every profession with an academic education, for whom the education for the practice of the profession, like in the career path of higher state officials, is strictly prescribed, but whose income is earned through the independent use of their knowledge. During the time-period of this investigation, this category encompasses medical doctors, architects, and apothecaries; only the professional position of lawyers and notaries does not fit into the sketched framework. These professions had a civil-service-like status, especially . . . after the Law of 9 April 1832 in the Kingdom of Hannover. . . . [T]he RAO, proclaimed in connection with the revision of the Constitution of the Courts, first repealed the quasi-civil-servant status of lawyers in the entire Empire"; *Das westdeutsche Bürgertum*, 415. While Henning overlooks the "free-professional" aspects of the *Advokatur* in Hannover, who were unlimited in number in the seats of superior courts, he is right to distinguish between lawyers and other university-educated free professionals before 1879. After 1879, however, this distinction fell away.

agricultural landlords. Together, these four categories represented the social groups in Germany whose sons traditionally attended university; as a result, one would expect them to constitute the preponderate majority of all lawyers, especially in the early years of the period in question.

Category 5 represents a group whose tendency to attend university had historically been lower, the sons of businessmen. This category is the broadest and most troublesome in the entire scheme. It encompasses sons of industrialists (*Fabrikanten, Fabrikbesitzer, Brauerei-, Ziegelei-,* and *Verlagsbesitzer,* etc.), sons of merchants (*Großkaufmann, Weinkaufmann,* and the omnipresent *Kaufmann*), sons of financiers (*Banquier*), and sons of men who lived from their investment income (*Partikulier, Rentier*). It is impossible to distinguish by any means other than conjecture the economic well-being and status of fathers whose occupations are thus listed in the university *Matrikel,* so the attempt has not been made. The important factor to remember is that *all* business strata historically had been underrepresented at university, and especially so in the legal faculties. After 1880 the number of businessmen in Germany expanded rapidly. Fathers from entrepreneurial groups, moreover, usually possessed the wealth necessary to support a son's classical secondary and university education if they perceived it to be something worth acquiring.

Category 6 includes sons of white-collar-employees, usually in higher levels (*Bankdirektor, Versicherungsagent, Generalagent,* etc.). Category 7 is the traditional *Mittelstand* of artisans (any kind of *Meister*), petty traders (*Lederhändler, Viehhändler,* etc.), innkeepers (*Gastwirt, Wirt,* etc.), and peasants (including *Pächter*).[17] Category 8 is a miscellaneous one, including sons of retired persons (*Rentner*) and instances in which a parent is listed simply as "Widow," with no indication of father's occupation, or as "Parents dead. Of age." Finally, category 9 is lower state officials not requiring university education, mostly employees of the state railways, postal service, and telegraphic service, as well as lower judicial officials such as court executioners (*Gerichtsvollzieher*).

17 Also included in this category is the single instance in which the father's occupation is listed as "Worker."

Bibliography

Archival Sources

Geheimes Staatsarchiv Preußischer Kulturbesitz, Berlin-Dahlem.
I HA Rep. 84a, Justizministerium.
  36, Revision der RAO, 1880–1901.
  37, Revision der RAO, 1902–20.
  38, Revision der RAO, 1885–93.
  39, Revision der RAO, 1894.
  71, Akten betreffend Rechtsanwälte, 1920–3.
  72, Akten betreffend Rechtsanwälte, 1924–6.
  73, Akten betreffend Rechtsanwälte, 1927–9.
  74, Akten betreffend Rechtsanwälte, 1930–2.
  75, Akten betreffend Rechtsanwälte, Jan.–July 1933.
  78, Sammelberichte betreffend Rechtsanwälte, 1909–23.
  79, Sammelberichte betreffend Rechtsanwälte, 1924–30.
  80, Sammelberichte betreffend Rechtsanwälte, 1931–4.
  2398, Die Amtsstellung der Notare, 1899–1907.
  2399, Notare und Notariat, 1908–13.
  3104, Entwurf eines Justiz-Verfassungs-Gesetz für den Norddeutschen Bund, 1870–4.
  3105, Entwurf eines Justiz-Verfassungs-Gesetz für den Norddeutschen Bund, 1874–1910.
  3115, Entwurf eines Justiz-Verfassungs-Gesetz für das Deutsche Reich, in specie: Die Frage der Lokalisierung der Anwaltschaft, 1870–1.
  10344, Gesetzliche Ordnung der Verhältnisse des Anwaltsstandes, 1881–3.
  10345, Gesetzliche Ordnung der Verhältnisse des Anwaltsstandes, 1884–7.
  10346, Gesetzliche Ordnung der Verhältnisse des Anwalts-und Advokatenstandes, 1888–1902.
  10347, Gesetzliche Ordnung der Verhältnisse des Anwalts-und Advokatenstandes, 1903–6.

10348, Rechtsanwälte, 1907–Sept. 1910.
10349, Rechtsanwälte, Oct. 1910–March 1913.
10350, Rechtsanwälte, 1913–16.
10351, Rechtsanwälte, 1917–19.
21912, Jahresberichte, Anwaltskammer Celle, 1878–1904.
21913, Jahresberichte, Anwaltskammer Celle, 1905–28.
Niedersächsisches Hauptstaatsarchiv, Hannover and Pattensen.
  Hann. 173, Oberlandesgericht Celle.
    Personalakten, Acc. 49/72, 83/76, 67/78, 103/79, and 63/80.
    Acc. 30/87, Nr. 210/1, Zulassung zur Rechtsanwaltschaft beim Oberlandesgericht Celle.
    Acc. 30/87, Nr. 211/1, Zulassung zur Rechtsanwaltschaft, Allgemeines, Bd. II.
    Acc. 30/87, Nr. 211/4, Zulassung zur Rechtsanwaltschaft, Allgemeines, Bd. V.
    Acc. 30/87, Nr. 211, Zulassung zur Rechtsanwaltschaft, Allgemeines.
    Acc. 30/87, Nr. 212, Einrichtung von Notarstellen, Allgemeines.
    Acc. 30/87, Nr. 30, Geschäftsberichte der Anwaltskammer Celle.
    Acc. 30/87, Nr. 311, Die Rechtsanwaltsordnung.
    Acc. 30/87, Nr. 312, Die freie Advokatur.
  Hann. 141, Einkommensteuer-Veranlagungskommission.
Universitätsarchiv der Georg-August-Universität zu Göttingen, Göttingen.
  Matrikel der Georg-August-Universität, 1900–30.
Stadtarchiv Hannover.
Stadtarchiv Göttingen.
Archiv und Bibliothek des Oberlandesgerichts Celle, Celle.
Niedersächsische Landes- und Universitätsbibliothek, Göttingen.

Periodicals

Juristische Wochenschrift, 1871–1933.
Deutsche Juristen-Zeitung, 1896–1933.
Nachrichten für Mitglieder des Deutschen Anwaltvereins, 1914–25, continued under the title *Anwaltsblatt*, 1926–33, continued after 1933 under the title *Mitteilungsblatt der Reichsfachgruppe Rechtsanwälte des Bundes nationalsozialistischer deutschen Juristen*.

Published Primary Sources

BOOKS

Adreßbuch der Landeshauptstadt Hannover. Hannover: W. Dorn Verlag, 1878–1923.

Allgemeine deutsche Real-Encyclopädie für die gebildeten Stände. Conversations-Lexikon, 10th ed. Leipzig: F. A. Brockhaus, 1851.

Amtliches Verzeichnis des Personals und der Studirenden der königlichen Georg-August-Universität zu Göttingen. Göttingen: Vandenhoeck & Ruprecht, summer semester 1899–summer semester 1930.

Apfel, Alfred. *Behind the Scenes of German Justice: Reminiscences of a German Barrister, 1882–1933*. London: John Lane, The Bodley Head, 1935.

Bähr, Otto. *Der Rechtsstaat*. Cassel and Göttingen: G. H. Wigand, 1864.

Ball, Kurt. *Gebührenlockerung. Welche durch Gesetz oder Verordnung einzuführenden Maßnahmen werden vorgeschlagen, um eine Überfüllung des Anwaltstandes vorzubeugen?* Leipzig: Oscar Brandstetter, 1930.

Bauer-Mengelberg, R. *Standesgefühl und Solidaritätsgefühl gesehen von der Psychologie des jungen Anwalts*. Leipzig: W. Moeser, 1929.

Benedikt, Edmund. *Die Advokatur unserer Zeit*. Vienna: Manz'sche K. u. K. Hof-Verlags- und Univ.-Buchhandlung, 1903.

Beschorner, J. H. *Aus einer fünfzigjährigen Anwaltspraxis. Erfahrungen und Rathschläge aphoristisch zusammengestellt und seinen Berufgenossen, insbesondere den jüngeren als ein Vermächtnis gewidmet*. Dresden: Wilhelm Baensch Verlagsbuchhandlung, 1885.

Bismarck, Otto. *Die gesammelten Werke*, 15 vols. in 19. Berlin: O. Stollberg, 1924–35.

Bluntschli, Johann Caspar, ed. *Deutsches Staats-Wörterbuch*, 11 vols. Stuttgart and Leipzig: Expedition des Staats-Wörterbuchs, 1851–70.

Brix, Alexander. *Organisation der Advokatur in Preußen, Österreich, Sachsen, Oldenburg, Braunschweig, Baden, Württemberg, Mecklenburg-Schwerin und Strelitz, Schweiz, Frankreich und England, nebst einer Einleitung, quellenmäßig dargestellt*. Vienna: Wilhelm Braumüller, 1868.

Deutscher Anwaltverein, ed. *Stenographischer Bericht über die Reichskonferenz der deutschen Anwaltschaft vom 12. und 13. November 1927 zu Leipzig*. Leipzig: n.p., 1928.

Um die Simultanzulassung. Bericht über die Ausschußverhandlungen im Deutschen Anwaltverein (Erster Teil). Leipzig: Oscar Brandstetter, 1925.

Um die Simultanzulassung. Bericht über die Ausschußverhandlungen im Deutschen Anwaltverein (Zweiter Teil). Leipzig: Oscar Brandstetter, 1925.

Verzeichnis der Rechtsanwälte, Notare und Gerichtsvollzieher, geordnet nach Gerichtsbehörden nebst Mitteilungen über die Organisation der Rechtsanwaltschaft und einem Verzeichnis der Gerichtsorte. Leipzig: W. Moeser, 1928.

Deutscher Anwaltverein. *Richtlinien für die Ausübung des Anwaltsberufs*. Leipzig: Oscar Brandstetter, 1929.

Festschrift für den neunten deutschen Juristentag in Stuttgart. Stuttgart: J. B. Metzler'schen Buchdruckerei, 1871.

Festschrift Herrn Rechtsanwalt und Notar Justizrat Dr. jur. h. c. Albert Pinner zu seinem 75. Geburtstag. Berlin and Leipzig: W. deGruyter & Co., 1932.

Feuchtwanger, Sigbert. *Die Freien Berufe. Im Besonderen: Die Anwaltschaft.* Munich: Duncker & Humblot, 1922.

Finger, Richard. *Die Kunst des Rechtsanwalts. Eine systematische Darstellung ihrer Grundfragen unter besonderer Berücksichtigung der ehrengerichtlichen Rechtsprechung.* Berlin: Struppe & Winckler, 1912.

Freudentheil, Chr. W. E. *Zur Geschichte des Advocatenstandes des Königreichs Hannover bis zum Jahre 1837.* Stade: Pockwitz, 1903.

Friedländer, Adolf, and Max Friedländer. *Kommentar zum Rechtsanwaltsordnung vom 1. Juli 1878*, 3rd ed. Munich, Berlin, and Leipzig: J. Schweitzer, 1930.

Gans, Salomon Phillipp. *Von dem Amte der Fürsprecher vor Gericht, nebst einem Entwurfe einer Advocaten- und Tax-Ordnung.* Celle: G. C. F. Schulzesche Buchhandlung, 1820; 2d ed., 1827.

Gneist, Rudolf. *Das englische Verwaltungsrecht, mit Einschluß des Heeres, der Gerichte und der Kirche, geschichtlich und systematisch*, 2d ed., 2 vols. Berlin: Julius Springer, 1867.

Freie Advocatur. Die erste Forderung aller Justizreform in Preußen. Berlin: Julius Springer, 1867.

Das heutige englische Verfassungs- und Verwaltungsrecht, 2 vols. Berlin: Julius Springer, 1857–60.

Der Rechtsstaat und die Verwaltungsgerichte in Deutschland, 3rd ed. Darmstadt: Wissenschaftliche Buchgesellschaft, 1966 (repr. ed. of 2d ed., 1879).

Selfgovernment. Communalverfassung und Verwaltungsgerichte in England, 3rd ed. Berlin: Julius Springer, 1871.

Goldschmidt, Martin. *Die Simultanzulassung der Amtsgerichtsanwälte beim Landgericht.* Berlin: Carl Heymanns Verlag, 1921.

Haack, A. F. *Ueber Dr. Rudolf Gneist's Freie Advocatur.* Berlin: Haude- und Spener'sche Buchhandlung, 1868.

Hachenburg, Max. *Lebenserinnerungen eines Rechtsanwalts und Briefe aus der Emigration*, ed. by Jörg Schadt. Stuttgart: W. Kohlhammer, 1978 (originally published in 1929).

Haenle, Siegfried. *Referat über die Freigabe der Advocatur erstattet auf dem IX. Anwaltstag, Sonntag, den 6. December 1868 zu Nürnberg.* Nürnberg: Verlag von Sigmund Soldan, 1869.

Hahn, Carl, ed. *Die gesammten Materialien zu den Reichs-justizgesetzen*, 8 vols. in 11, Berlin: R. v. Decker, 1881–98, repr. ed. Aalen: Scientia Verlag, 1983.

Held, Robert. *Die Gebührenteilung. Referat der 3. Abteilung des 4. Ausschußes des Deutschen Anwaltvereins.* Leipzig: Oskar Brandstetter, 1928.

von Hodenberg, Hodo Freiherr. *Lage und Schicksal der deutschen Anwaltschaft*, Bericht, erstattet der 29. Abgeordneten-Versammlung des Deutschen Anwaltvereins in Berlin am 4. Dezember 1932, *JW* 61 (1932), Beilage zu Heft 51/52, Dezember 1932.

Huber, Ernst Rudolf, ed. *Dokumente zur deutschen Verfassungsgeschichte*, 3rd
ed. 4 vols. Stuttgart: Kohlhammer, 1978– .

Hucko, Elmar M., ed. *The Democratic Tradition: Four German Constitutions.*
Oxford: Berg Publishers, 1987.

Jacques, Heinrich. *Die freie Advocatur und ihre legislative Organisation. Eine
Abhandlung zur Reform der deutschen und Österreichischen Gesetzgebung.*
Vienna: Wilhelm Braumüller, 1868.

Kanein, Werner. *Rechtsanwalt und Sachwalter.* Berlin: Julius Springer, 1933.

Kneer, August. *Die deutsche Rechtsanwaltschaft.* Mönchen-Gladbach: Volks-
vereins-Verlag, 1917.

   Der Rechtsanwalt, eine kulturgeschichtliche Studie. Mönchen-Gladbach:
Volksverein-Verlag, 1928.

Kolsen, Hermann. *Das Publikum und der Rechtsanwalt.* Berlin: Verlag von
Paul Moedebeck, 1893.

Königliches Statistisches Amt. *Handbuch über den königlichen preußischen Hof
und Staat für das Jahr* ———. Berlin: R. von Decker's Verlag, 1878/79–
1930.

Leonhardt, Gerhard Adolf Wilhelm. *Betrachtungen über die hannoversche
Justizverwaltung mit Rücksicht auf die Vereinigung des Königreichs Hannover
mit der Preußischen Monarchie.* Hannover: Carl Rümpler, 1866.

   Die bürgerliche Processordnung und deren Nebengesetze, 2d ed. Hannover:
Helwing'sche Hofbuchhandlung, 1853.

Levin, Louis. *Schutz der freien Rechtsanwaltschaft! Untersuchungen, Folgerungen
und Forderungen auf der Grundlage ihrer gerichtsverfassungsmäßigen Stellung.*
Leipzig: Deutscher Anwaltverein, 1930.

Lexis, Wilhelm. *Denkschrift über die dem Bedarf Preußens entsprechende Normalzahl der Studirenden der verschiedenen Fakultäten.* Berlin: n.p., 1888,
2d ed., Berlin: n.p., 1891.

Liebmann, Otto, ed. *Festgabe der deutschen Juristen-Zeitung zum 31. Deutschen
Juristentage in Wien.* Berlin: Verlag von Otto Liebmann, 1912.

Magnus, Julius. *Die Notlage der Anwaltschaft.* Leipzig: Oscar Brandstetter,
1930.

Marcuse, Paul. *Die freien Berufe und die Gewerbesteuer.* Leipzig: Oscar
Brandstetter, 1929.

Die Matrikel der Georg-August-Universität zu Göttingen, Bd. 1: 1734–1837, ed.
by Götz von Selle. Hildesheim: A. Lax, 1937; Bd. 2: 1837–1900, ed. by
Wilhelm Ebel. Hildesheim: A. Lax, 1974.

Olshausen, Thomas, *Der deutsche Juristentag. Sein Werden und Wirken. Eine
Festschrift zum fünfzigjährigen Jubiläum.* Berlin: Guttentag, 1910.

Oncken, Hermann. *Rudolf von Bennigsen, ein deutscher liberaler Politiker*, 2
vols. Stuttgart and Leipzig: Deutscher Verlags-Anstalt, 1910.

Preußisches Justizministerium. *Jahrbuch der Preußischen Gerichtsverfassung.*
Berlin: R. von Decker's Verlag, 1890–1914.

Prischl, F. *Advocatur und Anwaltschaft. Ihr Wesen, ihre Ziele und ihr Verhältnis zu den rationellen Grundlagen des Civilprozesses in vergleichender und geschichtlicher Darstellung.* Berlin: Puttkammer & Mühlbrecht, 1888.

Raabe, Hermann. *Die Simultazulassung der Amtsgerichtsanwälte beim Landgericht. Eine Entgegnung auf die gleichlautende Schrift von Justizrat Goldschmidt-Breslau.* Altona: Hammerich-Lesser-Verlag, 1921.

Ramdohr, Friedrich Wilhelm Basilius von. *Über die Organisation des Advocatenstandes in monarchischen Staaten.* Hannover: Gebrüder Hahn, 1801.

Reichs-Justizamt. *Deutsche Justiz-Statistik.* Berlin: Puttkammer & Mühlbrecht, 1883–1920.

Reidnitz, Georg. *Freie Advokatur und numerus clausus.* Mainz: Verlag der Zentralbuchhandlung Deutscher Rechtsanwälte, 1911.

Juristenbildung, insbesondere die Vorbildung der Rechtsanwälte in ihrer Entwicklung bis heute. Mainz: Verlag der Zentralbuchhandlung Deutscher Rechtsanwälte, 1911.

Lokalisation und Simultanzulassung. Mainz. Verlag der Zentralbuchhandlung Deutscher Rechtsanwälte, 1911.

Riehl, Wilhelm Heinrich. *Die bürgerliche Gesellschaft,* ed. and intr. by Peter Steinbach, originally published 1851; repr. ed., Frankfurt: Ullstein, 1976.

Riezler, Erwin. *Die Abneigung gegen die Juristen.* Munich. Verlag der Hochschulbuchhandlung Max Hueber, 1925.

Rotteck, Carl von, and Carl Welcker. *Staats-Lexikon oder Encyklopädie der Staatswissenschaften,* 15 vols. Altona: Verlag von Johann Friedrich Hammerich, 1834–43.

Rumpf, Max. *Anwalt und Anwaltstand. Eine rechtswissenschaftliche und rechtssoziologische Untersuchung.* Leipzig: Oscar Brandstetter, 1926.

Samter, M. K. *Bedarf die Standesverfassung der deutschen Anwaltschaft einer Änderung?* Berlin: Franz Vahlen, 1911.

Savigny, Friedrich Karl von. *Vom Beruf unsrer Zeit für Gesetzgebung und Rechtswissenschaft.* Heidelberg: Mohr und Zimmer, 1814.

Schramm, Erich. *Vor der Entscheidung. Der deutsche Anwalt und die Forderung der Zeit. Ein Beitrag zur Frage einer Reform der anwaltschaftlichen Standesverfassung.* Hannover: Helwingsche Verlagsbuchhandlung, 1911.

Schubert, Werner, ed. *Die deutsche Gerichtsverfassung (1869–1877). Entstehung und Quellen.* Frankfurt: Klostermann, 1981.

ed. *Entstehung und Quellen der Rechtsanwaltsordnung von 1878.* Frankfurt: Klostermann, 1985.

Siegel, Max, ed. *Die gesammten Materialien zu der Rechtsanwaltsordnung vom 1. Juli 1878.* Leipzig: Verlag der Roßberg'schen Buchhandlung, 1883.

Soldan, Hans. *Neue Ziele, Neue Wege. Ein Vorschlag zur Hebung des deutschen*

Anwaltstandes. Mainz: Verlag des Wirtschaftlichen Verbandes deutscher Rechtsanwälte, 1909.

Spangenberg, Ernst. *Das Oberappellationsgericht in Celle für das Königreich Hannover, nach seiner Verfassung, Zuständigkeit und nach dem bei demselben Statt findenden Geschäftsgange und Proceßverfahren dargestellt.* Celle: E. H. C. Schulze, 1833.

Stahl, Friedrich Julius. *Die Philosophie des Rechts*, 3rd ed., 3 vols. in 2. Heidelberg: J. C. B. Mohr, 1856, vol. 2, *Rechts- und Staatslehre auf der Grundlage christlicher Weltanschauung.*

Statistisches Reichsamt. *Statistik des Deutschen Reichs*, Bd. 402. Berlin: Puttkamer & Mühlbrecht, 1931.

Statistisches Jahrbuch für das Deutsche Reich. Berlin: Puttkamer & Mühlbrecht, 1891, 1901, 1911, 1921/22.

Stern, Jacques ed. *Thibaut und Savigny. Ihre Programmatischen Schriften.* Intr. Hans Hattenhauer. Munich: Vahlen, 1973.

Stintzing, Roderich von, and Ernst Landsberg. *Geschichte der deutschen Rechtswissenschaft.* 3 vols. in 4. Munich and Leipzig: Oldenbourg, 1880–1910.

Sydow, Reinhold. *Die deutsche Gebührenordnung für Rechtsanwälte und das preußische Gebührengesetz*, 10th ed. Berlin: Guttentag, 1911.

ed. *Rechtsanwaltsordnung vom 1. Juli 1878*, 5th ed. Berlin: Guttentag, 1907.

Sydow, Reinhold, and L. Busch, eds. *Gerichtsverfassungsgesetz mit Einführungsgesetz*, 9th ed. Berlin: Guttentag, 1905.

Thomsen, Oberlandesgerichtsrat zu Stettin. *Gesammtbericht über die Thätigkeit des deutschen Juristentags in den 25 Jahren seines Bestehens 1860–1885. Jubiläumsschrift im Auftrage des ständigen Deputations verfaßt.* Berlin: J. Guttentag, 1885.

Verein Deutscher Amtsgerichtsanwälte (e. V.), ed. *Simultanzulassung. Handbuch zum Reichsgesetz vom 7. März 1927.* Berlin: Franz Vahlen, 1931.

Violets Berufswahlführer. Der Jurist: Eine Übersicht über sämtliche auf Grund des juristischen Studiums ergreifbaren Berufe innerhalb und außerhalb des Staatsdienstes. Stuttgart: Violet, 1907.

Die Vorschriften über die Ausbildung der Juristen in Preußen. Berlin: Franz Vahlen, 1891.

Wentzcke, Paul, and Wolfgang Klötzer, eds. *Deutscher Liberalismus im Vormärz. Heinrich von Gagern Briefe und Reden 1815–1848.* Göttingen: Musterschmidt, 1959.

Werner, F. *Die freie Anwaltschaft in Preußen. Ein Vorschlag zur Beschränkung der Niederlassungsfreiheit.* Halle a. d. Saale: C. E. M. Pfeffer, 1890.

Wigand's Conversations-Lexikon. Für alle Stände. Von einer Gesellschaft deutscher Gelehrten bearbeitet., 15 vols. Leipzig: Otto Wigand, 1846–52, vol. 1, "Advocat," 99–100.

ARTICLES

"Erste Berathung der Justiz-Kommission über den neuvorgeschlagenen Titel des Gerichtsverfassungsgesetzes 'Rechtsanwaltschaft'," 7. Januar 1876, in Siegel, *Die gesammten Materialien*, 18–26.

"VII. Schlußberathung und Ablehnung des Titels XI des Gerichtsverfassungsgesetzes 'Rechtsanwaltschaft' im Plenum des Reichstags," 19. Dezember 1876, in Siegel, *Die gesammten Materialien*, 183–91.

Abraham, Hans Fritz. "Vom Beruf des Juristen als Ausdruck seiner Persönlichkeit," in *Festschrift Albert Pinner*, 7–29.

Anon. "Die Advokatur in Preußen." *Preußische Jahrbücher* 14 (1864): 424–39.

"Die freie Konkurrenz in der Advokatur." *Zeitschrift für Gesetgebung und Rechtspflege in Preußen* 1 (1867): 682–97.

Bartolomäus. "Fürst Bismarck und der preußische Richterstand." *Preußischer Jahrbücher* 99 (1900): 177–81.

Beschorner, J. H. "Die Freigebung der Advocatur und die neuesten Ergebnisse der Gesetzgebung und Literatur darüber." *Unsere Zeit. Deutsche Revue der Gegenwart*, New series 6 (1870): 252–62.

"Soll die Zahl der Anwälte und deren Wirkungskreis in einem Staate beschränkt sein oder nicht?" *Archiv für die civilistische Praxis* 31 (1848): 474–93.

Brater, Karl. "Advokatur," in Bluntschli, ed., *Deutsches Staats-Wörterbuch*, I:71–82.

Hellweg, August. "Geschichtlicher Rückblick über die Entstehung der deutschen Civilproceß-Ordnung." *Archiv für die civilistische Praxis* 61 (1878): 78–140.

Isay, Hermann. "Die Anwaltschaft in Berlin," in *Aus dem Berliner Rechtsleben. Festgabe zum 26. Deutschen Juristentag*. Berlin: n.p., 1902, 101–12.

Jacobsohn, Max. "Einzug der freien Advokatur in Berlin," in *Festschrift zum deutschen Anwaltstag in Berlin*. Berlin: n.p., 1896, 77–108.

Lesse, Theodor. "Die preußische Rechtsanwaltschaft während der letzten 50. Jahre," in *Festgabe der Rechtsanwaltschaft des Kammergerichts für den Geheimen Justizrath Dr. Richard Wilke*. Berlin: Franz Vahlen, 1900, 189–206.

List, Friedrich. "Advocat," in von Rotteck and Welcker, eds., *Staats-Lexikon*, I: 363–77.

Meyerowitz, Arthur. "Die Umfrage der Vereinigung rheinisch-westfalischer Rechtsanwälte." *Das Recht* 17: 573–79 (1913).

Mittermaier, Carl Joseph Anton. "Die künftige Stellung des Advokatenstandes." *Archiv für die civilistische Praxis* 15 (1832): 138–50, 277–94, 303–29.

"Ueber die Bestimmungen einer zweckmäßigen Gerichtsverfassung und Proceßordnung." *Archiv für die civilistische Praxis* 14 (1831): 398–420.

Rotteck, Carl von. "Justiz," von Rotteck and Welcker, eds., *Staats-Lexikon*, VIII: 720–56.

Schmoller, Gustav. "Was verstehen wir unter dem Mittelstande? Hat er im 19. Jahrhundert zu- oder abgenommen?" *Verhandlungen des 8. Evangelisch-sozialen Kongresses 1897*, Göttingen, 1897, 132–61.

Statistisches Reichsamt. "Die Einkommensverhältnisse in einigen freien Berufen." *Wirtschaft und Statistik* 12: 242–3 (1932).

Stegemann (Obergerichtsrath zu Göttingen). "Kurze Darstellung der Justiz-verfassung des ehemaligen Königreichs Hannover." *Zeitschrift für Gesetzgebung und Rechtspflege in Preußen* 1 (1867): 255–63.

Secondary Sources

BOOKS

Abel, Richard L. *American Lawyers*. New York and Oxford: Oxford University Press, 1989.

Abel, Richard L., and Philip S. C. Lewis, eds. *Lawyers in Society*, 3 vols. Berkeley and Los Angeles: University of California Press, 1988.

Abel-Smith, Brian, and Robert Stevens. *Lawyers and the Courts: A Sociological Study of the English Legal System 1750–1965*. Cambridge, Mass.: Harvard University Press, 1967.

Albisetti, James C. *Secondary School Reform in Imperial Germany*. Princeton: Princeton University Press, 1983.

Anderson, Dennis, L. *The Academy for German Law, 1933–1944*. New York and London: Garland Publishers, 1987.

Anderson, Eugene N. *The Social and Political Conflict in Prussia 1858–1864*. Lincoln: University of Nebraska Press, 1954.

Anderson, Margaret Lavinia. *Windthorst. A Political Biography*. Oxford: Clarendon Press, 1981.

Angermund, Ralph. *Deutsche Richterschaft 1919–1945. Krisenerfahrung, Illusion, politische Rechtsprechung*. Frankfurt a. M.: Fischer, 1990.

Bader, Karl Siegfried. *Die deutschen Juristen*. Tübingen: J. C. B. Mohr, 1947.

Baldwin, Peter. *The Politics of Social Solidarity: Class Bases of the European Welfare State 1875–1975*. Cambridge University Press, 1990.

Barry, Donald D., ed. *Toward the "Rule of Law" in Russia? Political and Legal Reform in the Transition Period*. Armonk, N.Y., and London: M. E. Sharpe, 1992.

Beer, Ulrich. *Versehrt, verfolgt, versöhnt: Horst Berkowitz, ein jüdisches Anwaltsleben*. Essen: Juristischer Fachbuchverlag, 1979.

Beiser, Frederick C., ed. *The Cambridge Companion to Hegel*. Cambridge University Press, 1993.

Bell, David A. *Lawyers and Citizens: The Making of a Political Elite in Old Regime France.* Oxford: Oxford University Press, 1994.

Benda, Ernst, et al., eds. *Hundert Jahre Rechtsanwaltskammern. Festsprachen bei den Hundertjahrfeiern einiger Rechtsanwaltskammern.* Munich: Beck, 1981.

Bendix, Reinhard. *Von Berlin nach Berkeley. Deutsch-jüdische Identitäten,* Frankfurt: Suhrkamp, 1985.

Berding, Helmut, et al., eds. *Vom Staat des Ancien Regimes zum modernen Parteienstaat. Festschrift für Theodor Schieder.* Munich: R. Oldenbourg, 1978.

Berlanstein, Lenard R. *The Barristers of Toulouse in the Eighteenth Century (1740–1793).* Baltimore: The Johns Hopkins University Press, 1975.

Berneker, Erich, ed. *Die juristische Berufe in Vergangenheit und Gegenwart.* Mainz: Kirchheim & Co., 1948.

Best, Heinrich. *Die Männer von Bildung und Besitz. Struktur und Handeln parlamentarischer Führungsgruppen in Deutschland und Frankreich 1848/49.* Düsseldorf: Droste, 1990.

Beutin, Ludwig. *Gesammelte Schriften zur Wirtschafts- und Sozialgeschichte,* ed. by Hermann Kellenbenz. Cologne and Graz: Böhlau Verlag, 1963.

Black, Antony. *Guilds and Civil Society in European Political Thought from the Twelfth Century to the Present.* Ithaca, New York: Cornell University Press, 1984.

Blackbourn, David, and Geoff Eley. *The Peculiarities of German History: Bourgeois Society and Politics in Nineteenth Century Germany.* Oxford: Oxford University Press, 1984.

Blackbourn, David, and Richard J. Evans, eds. *The German Bourgeoisie. Essays on the Social History of the German Middle Class from the Late Eighteenth to the Early Twentieth Century.* New York: Routledge, Chapman & Hall, 1991.

Blaustein, Albert P., and Charles O. Porter. *The American Lawyer. A Summary of the Survey of the Legal Profession.* Chicago: University of Chicago Press, 1954.

Bleek, Wilhelm. *Von der Kameralausbildung zum Juristenprivileg.* Berlin: Colloquium Verlag, 1972.

Böckenförde, Ernst-Wolfgang. *State, Society and Liberty. Studies in Political Theory and Constitutional Law,* trans. by J. A. Underwood. New York and Oxford: Berg Publishers, 1991.

Bölling, Rainer. *Sozialgeschichte der deutschen Lehrer. Ein Überblick von 1800 bis zur Gegenwart.* Göttingen: Vandenhoeck & Ruprecht, 1983.

Boockmann, Hartmut, et al., eds. *Geschichtswissenschaft und Vereinswesen im 19. Jahrhundert.* Göttingen: Vandenhoeck & Ruprecht, 1972.

Borchard, Edwin M. *Library of Congress Guide to the Law and Legal Literature of Germany.* Washington, D.C.: Government Printing Office, 1912.

Bramsted, Ernest K. *Aristocracy and the Middle Classes in Germany: Social Types in German Literature 1830–1900*. Chicago: University of Chicago Press, 1964.

Brix, Ewald. *Vom Markt zur Metropole. Werden und Wandlung im 7 Jahrhunderten stadthannoverscher Wirtschaftsentwicklung*. Hannover: Schlütersche Verlagsanstalt, 1951.

Brooks, C. W. *Pettyfoggers and Vipers of the Commonwealth. The "Lower Branch" of the Legal Profession in Early Modern England*. Cambridge University Press, 1986.

Brosius, Dieter, and Martin Lust, eds. *Beiträge zur Niedersächsischen Landesgeschichte*. Hildesheim: A. Lax, 1984.

Brüning, Kurt. *Niedersachsen im Rahmen der Neugliederung des Reiches*. vol. 2, *Beispiele über Auswirkingen der Ländergrenzen auf Verwaltung und Wirtschaft*, 2d ed. Bad Pyrmont: Verlagsbuchhandlung Karl Bäkmann, 1931.

Bruford, W. H. *Germany in the Eighteenth Century: The Social Background of the Literary Revival*. Cambridge University Press, 1935.

Brunner, Otto, Werner Conze, and Reinhart Koselleck, eds. *Geschichtliche Grundbegriffe. Historisches Lexikon zur politisch-sozialen Sprache in Deutschland*, 7 vols. Stuttgart: Klett-Cotta, 1972–89.

Bry, Gerhard. *Wages in Germany 1871–1945*. Princeton: Princeton University Press, 1960.

Bundesministerium der Justiz, ed. *Vom Reichsjustizamt zum Bundesministerium der Justiz. Festschrift zum 100jährigen Gründungstag des Reichsjustizamtes am 1. Januar 1877*. Cologne: Bundesanzeiger Verlag G.m.b.H., 1977.

Burdick, William L. *The Bench and Bar of Other Lands*. Brooklyn: Metropolitan Law Book Company, 1939.

Burke, Edmund. *Reflections on the Revolution in France*. Garden City, N.Y.: Anchor Books, 1973.

Burrage, Michael, and Rolf Torstendahl, eds. *Professions in Theory and History. Rethinking the Study of the Professions*. London: SAGE, 1990.

Buschmann, Arno, et al., eds. *Festschrift für Rudolf Gmür zum 70. Geburtstag 18. Juli 1983*. Bielefeld: Ernst und Werner Gieseking, 1983.

Caemmerer, Ernst von, Ernst Friesenhahn, and Richard Lange, eds. *Hundert Jahre deutsches Rechtsleben. Festschrift zum hundertjährigen Bestehen des deutschen Juristentages 1860–1960*, 2 vols. Karlsruhe: C. F. Müller, 1960.

Caenegem, R. C. van. *An Historical Introduction to Private Law*, trans. by D. E. L. Johnston. Cambridge University Press, 1992.

Calhoun, Craig, ed. *Habermas and the Public Sphere*. Cambridge, Mass.: MIT Press, 1992.

Caplan, Jane. *Government without Administration: State and Civil Service in Weimar and Nazi Germany*. Oxford: Oxford University Press, 1988.

Carr-Saunders, A. M., and P. A. Wilson. *The Professions*. Oxford: Clarendon Press, 1933.

Chickering, Roger. *We Men Who Feel Most German: A Cultural Study of the Pan-German League 1886–1914*. Boston: Allen & Unwin, 1984.

Childers, Thomas. *The Nazi Voter: The Social Foundations of Fascism in Germany, 1919–1933*. Chapel-Hill: University of North Carolina Press, 1983.

Cobban, Alfred. *The Social Interpretation of the French Revolution*. Cambridge University Press, 1964.

Cocks, Geoffrey, and Konrad H. Jarausch, eds. *German Professions, 1800–1950*. New York and Oxford: Oxford University Press, 1990.

Cocks, Raymond. *Foundations of the Modern Bar*. London: Sweet & Maxwell, 1983.

Cohen, Jean L., and Andrew Arato. *Civil Society and Political Theory*. Cambridge, Mass.: MIT Press, 1992.

Coing, Helmut, ed. *Handbuch der Quellen und Literatur der neueren europäischen Privatrechtsgeschichte*, 3 vols. in 11. Munich: Beck, 1973–89. *Zur Geschichte des Oberlandesgerichts in Celle*. Celle: Pohl, 1951.

Conrad, Johannes. *Das Universitätsstudium in Deutschland während der letzten 50 Jahre. Statistische Untersuchungen unter besonderer Berücksichtigung Preußens*. Jena: Gustav Fischer, 1884.

Conze, Werner, and Ulrich Engelhardt, eds. *Arbeiterexistenz im 19. Jahrhundert. Lebensstandard und Lebensgestaltung deutscher Arbeiter und Handwerker*. Stuttgart: Klett-Cotta, 1981.

Conze, Werner, and Jürgen Kocka. *Bildungsbürgertum im 19. Jahrhundert. Teil I: Bildungssystem und Professionalisierung im internationalen Vergleich*. Stuttgart: Klett-Cotta, 1985.

Cornell, Drucilla, Michel Rosenfeld, and David Gray Carlson, eds. *Hegel and Legal Theory*. New York: Routledge, 1991.

Dahrendorf, Ralf. *Gesellschaft und Freiheit*. Munich: R. Piper, 1962. *Society and Democracy in Germany*. New York: Norton, 1967.

Dann, Otto, ed. *Vereinswesen und bürgerliche Gesellschaft in Deutschland*. Munich: R. Oldenbourg, 1984.

Dawson, John Philip. *The Oracles of the Law*. Ann Arbor: University of Michigan Law School, 1968.

Dawson, William Harbutt. *Social Insurance in Germany 1883–1911. Its History, Operation, Results*. New York: Charles Scribner's Sons, n.d. (1913).

de Ruggiero, Guido. *The History of European Liberalism*, trans. by R. G. Collingwood. Oxford: Oxford University Press, 1927; repr. ed. Gloucester, Mass.: Peter Smith, 1981.

Deneke, J. F. Volrad. *Die freien Berufe*. Stuttgart: Friedrich Vorwerk Verlag, 1956.

Deutscher Juristinnenbund, ed. *Juristinnen in Deutschland. Eine Dokumentation* (1900–1984). Munich: J. Schweitzer, 1984.

Dicey, Albert Venn. *Introduction to the Study of the Law of the Constitution*, 3rd ed. London: Macmillan, 1889.

Diestelkamp, Bernhard, and Michael Stolleis, eds. *Justizalltag im Dritten Reich*. Frankfurt: Fischer, 1988.

Dingwall, Robert, and Philip Lewis, eds. *The Sociology of the Professions. Lawyers, Doctors and Others*. London: Macmillan, 1983.

Döhring, Erich. *Geschichte der deutschen Rechtspflege seit 1500*. Berlin: Duncker & Humblot, 1953.

Dorwart, Reinhold A. *The Administrative Reforms of Frederick William I of Prussia*. Cambridge, Mass.: Harvard University Press, 1953.

Dreier, Ralf, and Wolfgang Sellert, eds. *Recht und Justiz im "Dritten Reich."* Frankfurt a. M.: Suhrkamp, 1989.

Duman, Daniel. *The English and Colonial Bars in the Nineteenth Century*. London: Croom Helm, 1983.

Eley, Geoff. *Reshaping the German Right: Radical Nationalism and Political Change after Bismarck*. New Haven, Conn.: Yale University Press, 1980.

Elliott, Philip. *The Sociology of the Professions*. London: Macmillan, 1972.

Engelhardt, Ulrich. *Bildungsbürgertum. Begriffs- und Dogmengeschichte eines Etiketts*. Stuttgart: Klett-Cotta, 1986.

Engelmann, Arthur, et al. *A History of Continental Civil Procedure*, trans. and ed. by Robert Wyness Millar. Boston: Little, Brown, & Co., 1927.

Engelmann, Bernt. *Die unsichtbare Tradition. Richter zwischen Recht und Macht. Ein Beitrag zur Geschichte der deutschen Strafjustiz von 1779 bis 1918*, 2 vols. Cologne: Pahl-Rugenstein, 1988–9.

Ensor, Robert Charles Kirkwood. *Courts and Judges in France, Germany, and England*. Oxford: Oxford University Press, 1933.

Evans, Peter B., Dietrich Rueschemeyer, and Theda Skocpol, eds. *Bringing the State Back In*. Cambridge University Press, 1985.

Evans, Richard J., ed. *Society and Politics in Wilhelmine Germany*. New York: Barnes & Noble, 1978.

Eyck, Frank. *The Frankfurt Parliament 1848–1849*. Macmillan: London, 1968.

Fehrenbach, Elisabeth. *Traditionale Gesellschaft und revolutionäres Recht. Die Einführung des Code Napoléon in den Rheinbundstaaten*, 3rd ed. Göttingen: Vandenhoeck & Ruprecht, 1983.

Feldman, Gerald D. *The Great Disorder: Politics, Economics, and Society in the German Inflation, 1914–1924*. New York and Oxford: Oxford University Press, 1993.

Festschrift zum 275jährigen Bestehen des Oberlandesgerichts Celle. Celle: Präsident des Oberlandesgerichts Celle, 1986.

Fitzsimmons, Michael P. *The Parisian Order of Barristers and the French Revolution*. Cambridge, Mass.: Harvard University Press, 1987.

Fließ, Edith. "Der Kampf um den numerus clausus in der Rechtsanwaltschaft." Dr. jur. diss., Freiburg i. B., 1933.

Forsyth, William. *The History of Lawyers, Ancient and Modern.* New York: James Cockcroft & Co., 1875.

Fraenkel, Ernst. *Zur Soziologie der Klassenjustiz.* Berlin, 1927. Repr. ed. Darmstadt: Wissenschaftliche Buchgesellschaft, 1968.

Friedländer, Rudolf. *Der Arbeitspreis bei den freien Berufen, unter besonderer Berücksichtigung der deutschen Rechtsanwaltschaft.* Munich and Leipzig: Duncker & Humblot, 1933.

Gagliardo, John G. *Reich and Nation: The Holy Roman Empire as Idea and Reality 1763–1806.* Bloomington: Indiana University Press, 1980.

Gall, Lothar. *Bürgertum in Deutschland.* Berlin: Siedler, 1989.

——— ed. *Liberalismus,* 3rd ed. Königstein: Athenäum, 1985.

——— ed. *Stadt und Bürgertum im 19. Jahrhundert.* Munich: Oldenbourg, 1990.

Geiger, Theodor. *Die soziale Schichtung des deutschen Volkes. Soziographischer Versuch auf statistischer Grundlage.* Stuttgart: Ferdinand Enke, 1932.

Gellately, Robert. *The Politics of Economic Despair: Shopkeepers and German Politics 1890–1914.* London/Beverly Hills: Sage, 1974.

Gerth, Hans H. *Bürgerliche Intelligenz um 1800. Zur Soziologie des deutschen Frühliberalismus.* Göttingen: Vandenhoeck & Ruprecht, 1976.

Gerth, Hans H., and C. Wright Mills, eds. and trans. *From Max Weber: Essays in Sociology.* Oxford: Oxford University Press, 1946.

Getz, Heinrich. *Die deutsche Rechtseinheit im 19. Jahrhundert als rechtspolitisches Problem.* Bonn: Ludwig Röhrscheid Verlag, 1966.

Gillis, John R. *The Prussian Bureaucracy in Crisis, 1840–1860: Origins of an Administrative Ethos.* Stanford: Stanford University Press, 1971.

Gispen, Kees. *New Profession, Old Order: Engineers and German Society, 1815–1914.* Cambridge University Press, 1989.

Göppinger, Horst. *Juristen jüdischer Abstammung im "Dritten Reich." Entrechtung und Verfolgung,* 2d ed. Munich: Beck, 1990.

Grebing, Helga, ed. *Der "deutsche Sonderweg" in Europa 1806–1945. Eine Kritik.* Stuttgart: W. Kohlhammer, 1986.

Grimm, Dieter. *Recht und Staat der bürgerlichen Gesellschaft.* Frankfurt: Suhrkamp, 1987.

Gruchmann, Lothar. *Justiz im "Dritten Reich" 1933–1940. Anpassung und Unterwerfung in der Ära Gürtner* 2d ed. Munich: R. Oldenbourg, 1988.

Grundmann, Günter, Michael Strich, and Werner Richey, eds. *Rechtssprichwörter.* Hanau (DDR): Verlag Werner Dausien, 1984.

Gunkel, Karl. *200 Jahre Rechtsleben in Hannover. Festschrift zur Erinnerung an die Gründung des Kurhannoverschen Oberappellationsgerichts in Celle am 14.10.1711.* Hannover: Helwingsche Verlagsbuchhandlung, 1911.

Habermas, Jürgen. *Faktizität und Geltung. Beiträge zur Diskurstheorie des Rechts und des demokratischen Rechtsstaats.* Frankfurt: Suhrkamp, 1992.

——— *Strukturwandel der Öffentlichkeit. Untersuchungen zu einer Kategorie der bürgerlichen Gesellschaft.* Darmstadt and Neuwied: Luchterhand, 1962.

Theory of Communicative Action, 2 vols., trans. by Thomas McCarthy. Boston: Beacon Press, 1984.

Hahn, Erich J. C. "Rudolf von Gneist (1816–1895): The Political Ideas and Political Activity of a Prussian Liberal in the Bismarck Period." Ph.D. diss., Yale University, 1971.

Halliday, Terence, and Lucien Karpik, eds. *Politics Matter: Lawyers and the Rise of Western Political Liberalism*. Oxford: Oxford University Press, forthcoming 1996.

Haltern, Utz. *Bürgerliche Gesellschaft. Sozialtheoretische und sozialhistorische Aspekte*. Darmstadt: Wissenschaftliche Buchgesellschaft, 1985.

Hamburger, Ernest. *Juden im öffentlichen Leben Deutschlands*. Tübingen: Mohr [Siebeck], 1968.

Harris, James F. *A Study in the Theory and Practice of German Liberalism. Eduard Lasker, 1829–1884*. Lanham, Maryland: University Press of America, 1984.

Hartmann, Michael. *Juristen in der Wirtschaft. Eine Elite im Wandel*. Munich: Beck, 1990.

Hartstang, Gerhard. *Der deutsche Rechtsanwalt. Rechtsstellung und Funktion in Vergangenheit und Gegenwart*. Heidelberg: C. F. Müller, 1986.

Hartung, Fritz. *Staatsbildenden Kräfte der Neuzeit. Gesammelte Aufsätze von Fritz Hartung*. Berlin: Duncker & Humblot, 1961.

Haskell, Thomas L., ed. *The Authority of Experts*. Bloomington: University of Indiana Press, 1984.

Hattenhauer, Hans. *Geschichte des deutschen Beamtentums*, 2d ed. Cologne: Carl Heymanns Verlag, 1993.

Heffter, Heinrich. *Die deutsche Selbstverwaltung im 19. Jahrhundert. Geschichte der Ideen und Institutionen*. Stuttgart: K. F. Koehler Verlag, 1950.

Hegel, G. W. F. *Elements of the Philosophy of Right*, ed. by Allen W. Wood and trans. by H. B. Nisbet. Cambridge University Press, 1991.

Henning, Hansjoachim. *Die deutsche Beamtenschaft im 19. Jahrhundert. Zwischen Stand und Beruf*. Stuttgart: F. Steiner Verlag Wiesbaden, 1984.

Sozialgeschichtliche Entwicklungen in Deutschland von 1815 bis 1860. Paderborn: Ferdinand Schöningh, 1977.

Das westdeutsche Bürgertum in der Epoche der Hochindustrialisierung 1860–1914. Soziales Verhalten und soziale Strukturen. Teil I: Das Bildungsbürgertum in den preußischen Westprovinzen. Wiesbaden: Franz Steiner, 1972.

Hermann, Heiner. "Die 'Freien Berufe'. Herkunft, Wandlung und heutiger Inhalt des Begriffs." Dr. jur. diss., University of the Saarland, 1973.

Herrmann, Ulrich, ed. *"Die Bildung des Bürgers." Die Formierung der bürgerlichen Gesellschaft und die Gebildeten im 18. Jahrhundert*. Weinheim/Basel: Beltz Verlag, 1982.

Hess, Adalbert. *Das Parlament das Bismarck widerstrebte. Zur Politik und sozialen Zusammensetzung des preußischen Abgeordnetenhauses der Konfliktszeit (1862–1866)*. Cologne and Opladen: Westdeutscher Verlag, 1964.

Heydeloff, Rudolf. "The Political-Judicial Career of Dr. jur. Walter Luetgebrune and the Crisis of Weimar and Early National Socialist Germany 1918 to 1934." Ph.D. diss., University of Waterloo, Canada, 1977.

Hirschfeld, Gerald, and Lothar Kettenacker, eds. *Der "Führerstaat": Mythos und Realität. Studien zur Struktur und Politik des Dritten Reiches*. Stuttgart: Klett-Cotta, 1981.

Hoffmann, Franz. *Der Gewerbebetrieb des Rechtskonsulenten*. Berlin: Carl Heymanns Verlag, 1929.

Hohendahl, P.-U., and P. M. Lützeler, eds. *Legitimationskrisen des deutschen Adels 1200–1900*. Stuttgart: Metzler, 1979.

Holly, Günther. *Geschichte der Ehrengerichtsbarkeit der deutschen Rechtsanwälte*. Frankfurt, Bern, New York, Paris: Peter Lang, 1989 (Dr. jur. diss., University of Gießen, 1989).

Holtze, Friedrich W. *Geschichte des Kammergerichts in Brandenburg-Preußen*, 4 vols. Berlin: Franz Vahlen, 1890–1904.

Hubatsch, Walther, ed. *Grundriß zur deutschen Verwaltungsgeschichte 1815–1945*. Reihe A: Preußen, Bd. 10. Hannover, Marburg: Johann-Gottfried-Herder-Institut, 1981.

Huber, Ernst Rudolf. *Deutsche Verfassungsgeschichte seit 1789*, Bd. 3, *Bismarck und das Reich*. Stuttgart: W. Kohlhammer, 1963.

Huebner, Rudolf, trans. and ed. by Francis S. Philbrick, *A History of Germanic Private Law*. Boston: Little, Brown, & Co., 1918.

Huerkamp, Claudia. *Der Aufstieg der Ärzte im 19. Jahrhundert. Vom gelehrten Stand zum professionellen Experten: Das Beispiel Preußens*. Göttingen: Vandenhoeck & Ruprecht, 1985.

Huffmann, Helga. *Geschichte der rheinischen Rechtsanwaltschaft*. Cologne: Böhlau Verlag, 1969.

  Kampf um freie Advokatur. Essen: Juristischer Verlag W. Ellinghaus & Co., 1967.

Hülle, Werner. *Geschichte der oldenburgischen Anwaltschaft*. Oldenburg: Heinz Holzberg Verlag, 1977.

Hughes, Michael. *Law and Politics in Eighteenth Century Germany: The Imperial Aulic Council in the Reign of Charles VI*. Woodbridge, Suffolk: Royal Historical Society, 1988.

Huskey, Eugene. *Russian Lawyers and the Soviet State: The Origins and Development of the Soviet Bar*. Princeton: Princeton University Press, 1986.

Hutchinson, Allan C., and Patrick Monahan, eds. *The Rule of Law. Ideal or Ideology*. Toronto: Carswell, 1987.

Iggers, Georg, ed. *The Social History of Politics: Critical Perspectives in West German Historical Writing Since 1945.* Leamington Spa: Berg Publishers Ltd., 1985.

Jarausch, Konrad H. *Students, Society and Politics in Imperial Germany: The Rise of Academic Illiberalism.* Princeton: Princeton University Press, 1982.

The Unfree Professions. German Lawyers, Teachers, and Engineers, 1900–1950.* New York and Oxford: Oxford University Press, 1990.

ed. *The Transformation of Higher Learning 1860–1930: Expansion, Diversification, Social Opening, and Professionalization in England, Germany, Russia, and the United States.* Chicago: University of Chicago Press, 1983.

Jarausch, Konrad H., and Larry Eugene Jones, eds. *In Search of a Liberal Germany. Studies in the History of German Liberalism from 1789 to the Present.* New York: Berg Publishers Ltd., 1990.

Joeres, Ruth-Ellen B., and Mary Jo Maynes, eds. *German Women in the Eighteenth and Nineteenth Centuries. A Social and Literary History.* Bloomington: Indiana University Press, 1986.

John, Michael F. "The final unification of Germany: politics and the codification of German civil law in the *Bürgerliches Gesetzbuch* of 1896." Unpublished D. Phil. thesis, Oxford University, 1983.

Politics and the Law in Late Nineteenth-Century Germany: The Origins of the Civil Code.* Oxford: Oxford University Press, 1989.

Johnson, Hubert C. *Frederick the Great and His Officials.* New Haven: Yale University Press, 1975.

Jones, Larry Eugene. *German Liberalism and the Dissolution of the Weimar Party System 1918–1933.* Chapel Hill: University of North Carolina Press, 1988.

Jones, Larry Eugene, and James Retallack, eds. *Elections, Mass Politics, and Social Change in Modern Germany: New Perspectives.* Cambridge University Press, 1992.

Kaelble, Hartmut. *Social Mobility in the 19th and 20th Centuries: Europe and America in Comparative Perspective.* New York: St. Martin's, 1986.

Soziale Mobilität und Chancengleichheit im 19. und 20. Jahrhundert.* Göttingen: Vandenhoeck & Ruprecht, 1983.

Kagan, Richard L. *Lawyers and Litigants in Castile 1500–1700.* Chapel Hill: University of North Carolina Press, 1981.

Kaupen, Wolfgang. *Die Hüter von Recht und Ordnung. Die soziale Herkunft, Erziehung und Ausbildung der deutschen Juristen. Eine Soziologische Analyse.* Neuwied and Berlin: Luchterhand, 1969.

Kehr, Eckart. *Der Primat der Innenpolitik. Gesammelte Aufsätze zur preußisch-deutschen Sozialgeschichte im 19. und 20. Jahrhundert,* ed. by Hans-Ulrich Wehler. Frankfurt, Berlin, Vienna: Ullstein, 1970.

Kern, Eduard. *Gerichtsverfassungsrecht. Ein Studienbuch*, 2d ed. Munich and Berlin: Beck, 1954.

Geschichte des Gerichtsverfassungsrecht. Munich and Berlin: Beck, 1954.

Kirchheimer, Otto, and Franz Neumann. *Social Democracy and the Rule of Law*, trans. by Leena Tanner, trans. and ed. by Keith Tribe. London: Allen & Unwin, 1987.

Knox, T. M., ed. and trans. *Hegel's Philosophy of Right*. Oxford: Oxford University Press, 1952.

Kocka, Jürgen. *Unternehmerverwaltung und Angestelltenschaft am Beispiel Siemens 1847–1914: Zum Verhältnis von Kapitalismus und Bürokratie in der deutschen Industrialisierung*. Stuttgart: Klett-Cotta, 1969.

ed. *Bildungsbürgertum im 19. Jahrhundert. Teil IV. Politischer Einfluß und gesellschaftliche Formation*. Stuttgart: Klett-Cotta, 1989.

ed. *Bürger und Bürgerlichkeit im 19. Jahrhundert*. Göttingen: Vandenhoeck & Ruprecht, 1987.

ed. *Bürgertum im 19. Jahrhundert. Deutschland im europäischen Vergleich*, 3 vols. Munich: Deutscher Taschenbuch Verlag, 1988.

Kocka, Jürgen, and Allan Mitchell, eds. *Bourgeois Society in Nineteenth-Century Europe*. Oxford and Providence: Berg Publishers, 1993.

Kolbeck, Thomas. *Juristenschwemmen. Untersuchungen über den juristischen Arbeitsmarkt im 19. und 20. Jahrhundert*. Frankfurt: Peter Lang, 1978.

König, Stefan. *Vom Dienst am Recht. Rechtsanwälte als Strafverteidiger im Nationalsozialismus*. Berlin and New York: Walter de Gruyter, 1987.

Kötschau, Uwe Lorenz. "Richterdisziplinierung in der preußischen Reaktionszeit. Verfahren gegen Waldeck und Temme." Dr. jur. diss., Kiel, 1976.

Kornmann, Heinrich Wilhelm. "Die Rechtsbeistände." Dr. jur. diss., Freiburg i. B., 1938.

Koselleck, Reinhard. *Preußen zwischen Reform und Revolution. Allgemeines Landrecht, Verwaltung und soziale Bewegung von 1791 bis 1848*. Stuttgart: Ernst Klett Verlag, 1967.

Kotschnig, Walter M. *Unemployment in the Learned Professions: An International Study of Occupational and Educational Planning*. London: Oxford University Press, 1937.

Kovacs, Maria M. *Liberal Professions and Illiberal Politics: Hungary from the Habsburgs to the Holocaust*. Washington, D.C.: Woodrow Wilson Center Press, and Oxford: Oxford University Press, 1994.

Krach, Tillmann. *Jüdische Rechtsanwälte in Preußen. Bedeutung und Zerstörung der freien Advokatur*. Munich: Beck, 1991.

Kregel, Volker. *Die nationalsozialistische Personalpolitik der Justiz im Oberlandesgerichtsbezirk Celle*. Hannover: Niedersächsische Landeszentrale für politische Bildung, 1989.

"Die Personalpolitik der Justiz im 3. Reich – dargestellt am Beispiel der

Personalbewirtschaftung für den höheren Dienst im Oberlandes-gerichtsbezirk Celle." Dr. jur. diss., Göttingen, 1986.

Kremer, Willy. *Der soziale Aufbau der Parteien des Deutschen Reichstages von 1871–1918.* Emsdetten: Heinr. & J. Lechte, 1934 (Dr. phil. diss., University of Cologne, 1934).

Krieger, Leonard. *The German Idea of Freedom: History of a Political Tradition.* Chicago: University of Chicago Press, 1957.

Krieger, Leonard, and Fritz Stern. eds. *The Responsibility of Power. Historical Essays in Honor of Hajo Holborn.* Garden City, N.Y.: Doubleday, 1967.

Kroeschell, Karl. *Deutsche Rechtsgeschichte 3 (seit 1650).* Opladen: Westdeutscher Verlag, 1989.

    ed. *Festschrift für Hans Thieme zu seinem 80. Geburtstag.* Sigmaringen: Jan Thorbecke Verlag, 1986.

Kronman, Anthony T. *Max Weber.* Stanford: Stanford University Press, 1983.

Kübl, Friedrich. *Geschichte der österreichischen Advokatur,* 2d ed. Vienna: Verlag Notring der wissenschaftlichen Verbände Österreichs, 1967 (1st ed., 1925, manuscript completed 1917).

Kulemann, Wilhelm. *Die Berufsvereine: Erste Abteilung: Geschichtliche Entwicklung der Berufsorganisationen der Arbeitnehmer und Arbeitgeber aller Länder,* Erster Band: Deutschland I. Einleitung – Organisation der Arbeitnehmer I (Öffentliche Beamte – Freie Berufe – Privatangestellte). Jena: Verlag von Gustav Fischer, 1908 ("Zweite, völlig neu bearbeitete Auflage der 'Gewerkschaftsbewegung' ").

Kunz, Andreas. *Civil Servants and the Politics of Inflation in Germany, 1914–1924.* Berlin and New York: deGruyter, 1986.

Langewiesche, Dieter. *Liberalismus in Deutschland.* Frankfurt: Suhrkamp, 1988.

Larson, Magali Sarfatti. *The Rise of Professionalism: A Sociological Analysis.* Berkeley and Los Angeles: University of California Press, 1977.

La Vopa, Anthony J. *Grace, Talent, and Merit: Poor Students, Clerical Careers, and Professional Ideology in Eighteenth-Century Germany.* Cambridge University Press, 1988.

    Prussian Schoolteachers: Profession and Office, 1763–1848. Chapel Hill: University of North Carolina Press, 1980.

Learned, William Setchel. *The Oberlehrer. A Study of the Social and Professional Evolution of the German Schoolmaster.* Cambridge, Mass.: Harvard University Press, 1914.

Lexis, Wilhelm. *Die Universitäten im Deutschen Reich.* Berlin: A. Ascher & Co., 1904.

    ed. *Die Deutschen Universitäten,* 2 vols. Berlin: A. Ascher & Co., 1893.

Ludewig, G., et al. *Wirtschaftliche und kulturelle Zustände in Alt-Hannover,* 2nd ed. Hannover: Johannes Rathje, 1929.

Luhmann, Niklas. *Legitimation durch Verfahren*. Luchterhand: Neuwied, 1969.

Lundgreen, Peter. *Sozialgeschichte der deutschen Schule im Überblick: Teil I: 1770–1918*. Göttingen: Vandenhoeck & Ruprecht, 1980.

Magnus, Julius, ed. *Die Rechtsanwaltschaft*. Leipzig: W. Moeser, 1929.

Mayer, Arno J. *The Persistence of the Old Regime: Europe to the Great War*. New York: Pantheon, 1981.

McClelland, Charles E. *The German Experience of Professionalization. Modern Learned Professions and their Organizations from the Early Nineteenth Century to the Hitler Era*. Cambridge University Press, 1991.

The German Historians and England: A Study in Nineteenth-Century Views. Cambridge University Press, 1971.

State, Society, and University in Germany, 1700–1914. Cambridge University Press, 1980.

Marx, Karl. *Early Writings*, intr. by Lucio Colletti and trans. by Rodney Livingstone and Gregor Benton. Harmondsworth: Penguin, 1992.

Merryman, John Henry. *The Civil Law Tradition*, 2d ed. Stanford: Stanford University Press, 1985.

Mikat, Paul, ed. *Festschrift der Rechts- und Staatswissenschaftlichen Fakultät der Julius-Maximilians-Universität Würzburg zum 75. Geburtstag von Hermann Nottarp*. Karlsruhe: C. F. Müller, 1961.

Morazé, Charles. *The Triumph of the Middle Classes. A Study of European Values in the Nineteenth Century*. Cleveland and New York: World Publishing Co., 1967.

Mosse, George L. *The Crisis of German Ideology: Intellectual Origins of the Third Reich*. New York: Grosset & Dunlap, 1964.

Müller, Ingo. *Furchtbare Juristen. Die unbewältigte Vergangenheit unserer Justiz*. Munich: Knaur, 1989. In English as *Hitler's Justice: The Courts of the Third Reich*, trans. Deborah Lucas Schneider. Cambridge, Mass.: Harvard University Press, 1991.

Müller, Lothar. "Die Freiheit der Advokatur. Ihre geschichtliche Entwicklung in Deutschland während der Neuzeit und ihre rechtliche Bedeutung in der Bundesrepublik Deutschland." Dr. jur. diss., Würzburg, 1972.

Mundt, Hermann. *100 Jahre Rechtsanwaltskammer für den Oberlandesgerichtsbezirk Celle*. Hannover: n.p., 1979.

Nathans, Eli. *Franz Schlegelberger*. Baden-Baden: Nomos, 1990.

Neumann, Franz L. *The Rule of Law: Political Theory and the Legal System in Modern Society*. Leamington Spa: Berg Publishers, 1986.

Nipperdey, Thomas. *Deutsche Geschichte 1800–1866. Bürgerwelt und starker Staat*. Munich: Beck, 1983.

Deutsche Geschichte 1866–1918, 2 vols. Munich: Beck, 1990–2.

Die Organisation der deutschen Parteien vor 1918. Düsseldorf: Droste, 1961.

Noakes, Jeremy. *The Nazi Party in Lower Saxony, 1921–1933*. London: Oxford University Press, 1971.

Oncken, Hermann. *Rudolf von Bennigsen. Ein deutscher liberaler Politiker*, 2 vols. Stuttgart and Leipzig: Deutsche Verlag-Anstat, 1910.

Orlow, Dietrich. *Weimar Prussia 1925–1933: The Illusion of Strength*. Pittsburgh: University of Pittsburgh Press, 1991.

Ostler, Fritz. *Der deutsche Rechtsanwalt. Das Werden des Standes seit der Reichsgründung*. Karlsruhe: C. F. Müller, 1963.

Die deutschen Rechtsanwälte 1871–1971, 2d ed. Essen: Juristischer Fachbuchverlag, 1982.

Parsons, Talcott. *Essays in Sociological Theory*, rev. ed. New York: Free Press, 1954.

Paulsen, Friedrich. *Die deutschen Universitäten und das Universitätsstudium*. Berlin: A. Ascher & Co., 1902. English ed. *The German Universities and University Study*, trans. by Frank Thilly and William W. Elwang. New York: C. Scribner, 1906.

The German Universities: Their Character and Historical Development. New York: Macmillan, 1895.

Geschichte des gelehrten Unterrichts auf den deutschen Schule und Universitäten vom Ausgang des Mittelalters bis zur Gegenwart, 2 vols. Berlin and Leipzig: Vereinigung wissenschaftlicher Verleger, Walter deGruyter & Co., 1919–21.

Pflanze, Otto. *Bismarck and the Development of Germany*, 3 vols. Princeton: Princeton University Press, 1990.

Plathner, Günther. *Der Kampf um die richterliche Unabhängigkeit bis zum Jahre 1848 unter besonderer Berücksichtigung Preußens. Eine dogmengeschichtliche Untersuchung*. Breslau: M. & H. Marcus, 1935.

Prest, Wilfrid R. *The Rise of the Barristers. A Social History of the English Bar 1590–1640*. Oxford: Clarendon Press, 1986.

ed. *Lawyers in Early Modern Europe and America*. New York: Holmes & Meier, 1981.

ed. *The Professions in Early Modern England*: London: Croom Helm, 1987.

Puhle, Hans-Jürgen. *Von der Agrarkrise zum Präfaschismus. Thesen zum Stellenwert der agrarischen Interessenvebände in der deutschen Politik am Ende des 19. Jahrhunderts*. Hannover: Verlag Fur Literatur und Zeitgeschehen, 1972.

Rasehorn, Theo. *Justizkritik in der Weimarer Republik. Das Beispiel der Zeitschrift "Der Justiz."* Frankfurt a. M.: Campus, 1985.

Rawls, John. *A Theory of Justice*. Oxford: Oxford University Press, 1971.

Rechtsanwaltsverein Hannover, ed. *Festschrift zur 150-Jahr-Feier des Rechtsanwaltsvereins Hannover e.V. (1831–1981)*. Hannover: G. Jahnke, 1981.

Reader, W. J. *Professional Men: The Rise of the Professional Classes in Nineteenth Century England*. London: Weidenfeld & Nicolson, 1966.

Rejewski, Harro-Jürgen. *Die Pflicht zur politischen Treue im preußischen Beamtenrecht (1850–1918). Eine rechtshistorische Untersuchung anhand von Ministerialakten aus dem Geheimen Staatsarchiv der Stiftung Preußischer Kulturbesitz.* Berlin: Duncker & Humblot, 1973.

Rheinstein, Max, and Edward Shils, eds. and trans. *Max Weber on Law in Economy and Society.* Cambridge, Mass.: Harvard University Press, 1954.

Riehl, Wilhelm Heinrich. *Die bürgerliche Gesellschaft,* ed. and intr. by Peter Steinbach, 1851, reprint ed. Frankfurt, Berlin, Vienna: Ullstein, 1976.

Riezler, Erwin. *Die Abneigung gegen die Juristen.* Munich: Max Hueber, 1925.

Ritter, Gerhard A. *Social Welfare in Germany and Britain: Origins and Development.* Trans. by Kim Traynor. Leamington Spa: Berg Publishers, 1986.

Ritter, Gerhard A., and Merith Niehuss, eds. *Wahlgeschichtliches Arbeitsbuch. Materialien zur Statistik des Kaiserreichs 1871–1918.* Munich: Beck, 1980.

Robson, Robert, *The Attorney in Eighteenth Century England.* Cambridge University Press, 1959.

Rosenbaum, Louis. *Beruf und Herkunft der Abgeordneten zu den deutschen und preußischen Parlamenten 1847 bis 1919. Ein Beitrag zur Geschichte des deutschen Parlaments.* Frankfurt: Frankfurter Sozietäts-Druckerei, 1923.

Rosenberg, Hans. *Bureaucracy, Aristocracy and Autocracy: The Prussian Experience 1660–1815.* Cambridge, Mass.: Beacon Press, 1958.

——— *Große Depression und Bismarkzeit. Wirtschafsablauf, Gesellschaft und Politik in Mitteleuropa.* Berlin: de Gruyter, 1967.

Rosendahl, Erich. *Geschichte Niedersachsens im Spiegel der Reichsgeschichte,* 2 vols. Hannover: Helwing'sche Verlagsbuchhandlung, 1927.

Ruppert, Wolfgang. *Bürgerlicher Wandel. Die Geburt der modernen deutschen Gesellschaft im 18. Jahrhundert.* Frankfurt a. M.: Fischer, 1983.

Rueschemeyer, Dietrich. *Lawyers and their Society: A Comparative Study of the Legal Profession in Germany and the United States.* Cambridge, Mass.: Harvard University Press, 1973.

Sandel, Michael J. *Liberalism and the Limits of Justice.* Cambridge University Press, 1982.

——— ed. *Liberalism and Its Critics.* New York: New York University Press, 1984.

Schaer, Friedrich-Wilhelm. *Die Stadt Aurich und ihre Beamtenschaft im 19. Jahrhundert, unter besonderer Berücksichtigung der hannoverschen Zeit (1815–1866).* Göttingen: Vandenhoeck & Ruprecht, 1963.

Schairer, Reinhold. *Die akademische Berufsnot. Tatsachen und Auswege.* Jena: Eugen Diederichs Verlag, 1933.

Schieder, Wolfgang, ed. *Liberalismus in der Gesellschaft des deutschen Vormärz.* Göttingen: Vandenhoeck & Ruprecht, 1983.

Schioppa, Antonio Padoa, ed. *The Trial Jury in England, France, Germany 1700–1900.* Berlin: Duncker & Humblot, 1987.

Schnabel, Franz. *Deutsche Geschichte im neunzehnten Jahrhundert*, 4 vols. Freiburg i. B.: Herder & Co., 1928–51. Repr. ed. Frankfurt a. M.: Deutscher Verlagsanstalt, 1988.

Schnath, Georg, et al. *Geschichte des Landes Niedersachsens*. Würzburg: Ploetz, 1973.

Schwarz, Max. *MdR: Biographisches Handbuch der Reichstage*. Hannover: Verlag für Literatur und Zeitgeschehen, 1965.

Sheehan, James J. *German Liberalism in the Nineteenth Century*. Chicago: University of Chicago Press, 1978.

Siegrist, Hannes, ed. *Bürgerliche Berufe. Zur Sozialgeschichte der freien und akademischen Berufe im internationalen Vergleich*. Göttingen: Vandenhoeck & Riprecht, 1988.

Siemann, Wolfram. *Die Frankfurter Nationalversammlung 1848/49 zwischen demokratischem Liberalismus und konservativer Reform. Die Bedeutung der Juristendominanz in den Verfassungsverhandlungen des Paulskirchenparlaments*. Bern and Frankfurt: Peter Lang, 1976.

Smith, Steven B. *Hegel's Critique of Liberalism. Rights in Context*. Chicago: University of Chicago Press, 1989.

Staff, Ilse, ed. *Justiz im Dritten Reich. Eine Dokumentation*. Frankfurt: Fischer, 1964.

Stark, Gary D. *Entrepreneurs of Ideology: Neoconservative Publishers in Germany, 1890–1933*. Chapel Hill: University of North Carolina Press, 1981.

Stehlin, Stewart A. *Bismarck and the Guelph Problem 1866–1890. A Study in Particularist Opposition to National Unity*. The Hague: Martinus Nijhoff, 1973.

Steinmetz, George. *Regulating the Social: The Welfare State and Local Politics in Imperial Germany*. Princeton: Princeton University Press, 1993.

Stern, Karl. *Anwaltschaft und Verfassungsstaat. Festrede bei der Feier "100 Jahre Freie Advokatur" in der Frankfurter Paulskirche*. Munich: Beck, 1980.

Stintzing, Roderich von, and Ernst Landsberg. *Geschichte der deutschen Rechtswissenschaft*, 4 vols. Munich and Berlin: R. Oldenbourg, 1880–1910.

Stölzel, Adolf. *Brandenburg-Preußens Rechtsverwaltung und Rechtsverfassung, dargestellt im Wirken seiner Landesfürsten und obersten Justizbeamten*, 2 vols. Berlin, 1888; repr. ed., Vaduz: Topos, 1989.

Strauss, Gerald. *Law, Resistance, and the State: The Opposition to Roman Law in Reformation Germany*. Princeton: Princeton University Press, 1986.

Sunnus, Michael. *Der NS-Rechtswahrerbund (1928–1945). Zur Geschichte der nationalsozialistischen Juristenorganisation*. Frankfurt: Peter Lang, 1990.

Suval, Stanley. *Electoral Politics in Wilhelmine Germany*. Chapel Hill: University of North Carolina Press, 1985.

Tecklenburg, August, and K. Dageförde. *Geschichte der Provinz Hannover*. Hannover: Verlag von Carl Meyer, 1921.

Treue, Wilhelm. *Niedersachsens Wirtschaft seit 1760. Von der Agrar- zur Industriegesellschaft.* Hannover: H. Hofmann, 1964.

Uelschen, Gustav. *Die Bevölkerung in Niedersachsen 1821–1961.* Hannover: Gebrüder Jänecke Verlag, 1966.

Underdown, E. M. *The French Judiciary and Bar.* London: Printed by Order of the Masters of the Bench of the Honourable Society of the Inner Temple, 1911.

Unger, Roberto Mangabeira. *Law in Modern Society: Toward a Criticism of Social Theory.* New York: The Free Press, 1976.

Various European Authors. *A General Survey of Events, Sources, Persons, and Movements in Continental Legal History.* Boston: Little, Brown, & Co., 1912.

Vehrenberg, Hans. "Geschichte der deutschen Rechtsanwaltsordnung vom 1. Juli 1878." Dr. jur. diss., Freiburg i. Br., 1935.

Verein für Sozialpolitik, ed. *Die Zukunft der Sozialpolitik. Die Not der geistigen Arbeiter. Jubiläumstagung des Vereins für Sozialpolitik in Eisenach 1922.* Munich und Leipzig: Duncker & Humblot, 1923.

Vondung, Klaus, ed. *Das wilhelminische Bildungsbürgertum: Zur Sozialgeschichte seiner Ideen.* Göttingen: Vandenhoeck & Ruprecht, 1976.

Wagner, Albrecht. *Der Kampf der Justiz gegen die Verwaltung in Preußen. Dargelegt an der rechtsgeschichtlichen Entwicklung der Konfliktsgesetzes von 1854.* Hamburg: Hanseatische Verlagsanstalt, 1936.

Walker, Mack. *German Home Towns: Community, State, and General Estate, 1648–1871.* Ithaca, N. Y.: Cornell University Press, 1971.

——— *Johann Jakob Moser and the Holy Roman Empire of the German Nation.* Chapel Hill: University of North Carolina Press, 1981.

Watson, Alan. *The Making of the Civil Law.* Cambridge, Mass.: Harvard University Press, 1981.

Weber, Max. *Economy and Society An Outline of Interpretive Sociology,* ed. by Günther Roth and Claus Wittich, 2 vols. Berkeley and Los Angeles: University of California Press, 1978.

——— *Gesammelte Politische Schriften,* 4th ed., ed. by Johannes Winckelmann. Tübingen: J. C. B. Mohr (Paul Siebeck), 1980.

Wehler, Hans-Ulrich. *Deutsche Gesellschaftsgeschichte,* 4 vols. Munich: Beck, 1989- .

——— *Das deutsche Kaiserreich 1871–1918.* Göttingen: Vandenhoeck & Ruprecht, 1973.

——— *Preußen ist wieder chic . . . : Politik und Polemik in zwanzig Essays.* Frankfurt: Suhrkamp, 1983.

——— ed. *Sozialgeschichte Heute. Festschrift für Hans Rosenberg zum 70. Geburtstag.* Göttingen: Vandenhoeck & Ruprecht, 1974.

Weißler, Adolf. *Geschichte der Rechtsanwaltschaft.* Leipzig: Pfeffer, 1905.

Wentzcke, Peter, and Wolfgang Klötzer. *Deutscher Liberalismus im Vormärz.*

Heinrich von Gagern, Briefe und Reden 1815–1848 (ed. by Bundesarchiv and the Hessian Historical Commission in Darmstadt). Göttingen, Berlin and Frankfurt: Musterschmidt Verlag, 1959.

Weyrauch, Walter O. *The Personality of Lawyers.* New Haven, Conn., and London: Yale University Press, 1964.

White, Dan S. *The Splintered Party: National Liberalism in Hessen and the Reich, 1867–1918.* Cambridge, Mass.: Harvard University Press, 1976.

Whitman, James Q. *The Legacy of Roman Law in the German Romantic Era.* Princeton: Princeton University Press, 1990.

Wieacker, Franz. *Privatrechtsgeschichte der Neuzeit*, 2d ed. Göttingen: Vandenhoeck & Ruprecht, 1967.

Willig, Kenneth C. H. "The Theory and Administration of Justice in the Third Reich." Ph.D. diss., University of Pennsylvania, 1975.

Wunder, Bernd. *Geschichte der Bürokratie in Deutschland.* Frankfurt: Suhrkamp, 1986.

Wunderlich, Frieda. *German Labor Courts.* Chapel Hill: University of North Carolina Press, 1946.

Ziolkowsky, Theodore. *German Romanticism and Its Institutions.* Princeton: Princeton University Press, 1990.

250 Jahre Oberlandesgericht Celle 1711–1961. Celle: Pohl, 1961.

ARTICLES

Abelshauser, Werner. "The First Post-Liberal Nation: Stages in the Development of Modern Corporatism in Germany." *European History Quarterly* 14 (1984): 295–6.

Albisetti, James C. "Women and the Professions in Imperial Germany," in Joeres and Maynes, eds., *German Women in the Eighteenth and Nineteenth Centuries*, 94–109.

Anderson, Margaret Lavinia. "Voter, Junker, *Landrat*, Priest: The Old Authorities and the New Franchise in Imperial Germany." *American Historical Review* 98 (1993): 1448–74.

Anderson, Margaret L., and Kenneth Barkin. "The Myth of the Puttkamer Purge and the Reality of the *Kulturkampf:* Some Reflections on the Historiography of Imperial Germany." *Journal of Modern History* 54 (1982): 647–86.

Arato, Andrew, "A Reconstruction of Hegel's Theory of Civil Society," in Cornell, et al., eds., *Hegel and Legal Theory*, 301–20.

Baldwin, Simeon E. "A German Law-Suit." *Yale Law Journal* 19 (1909–10): 69–79.

"The German Law-Suit without Lawyers," *Michigan Law Review* 8 (1909–10): 30–8.

Bell, David A. "Barristers, Politics, and the Failure of Civil Society in Old Régime France," in Halliday and Karpik, eds., *Politics Matter*.

Berman, Harold J. "The Rule of Law and the Law-Based State with Special Reference to the Soviet Union," in Barry, ed., *Toward the "Rule of Law" in Russia?*, 43–60.

Best, Heinrich. "Soziale Morphologie und politische Orientierungen bildungsbürgerliche Abgeordneter in der Frankfurter Nationalversammlung und in der Pariser Assemblée nationale constituante 1848/49," in Kocka, ed., *Bildungsbürgertum im 19. Jahrhundert. Teil IV*, 53–94.

Beutin, Ludwig. "Das Bürgertum als Gesellschaftsstand im 19. Jahrhundert (Ein Entwurf)," in idem, *Gesammelte Schriften*, 284–319; originally in *Blätter für deutsche Landesgeschichte* 90:132–65 (1953).

Blackbourn, David. "The German Bourgeoisie: An Introduction," in Blackbourn and Evans, eds., *The German Bourgeoisie*, 1–45.

"The *Mittelstand* in German Society and Politics, 1871–1914." *Social History*, No. 4 (January 1977): 409–34.

Blankenburg, Erhard, and Ulrike Schultz. "German Advocates: A Highly Regulated Profession," in Abel and Lewis, eds., *Lawyers in Society*. Vol. 2: *The Civil Law World*, 124–59.

Blasius, Dirk. "Bürgerliches Recht und bürgerliche Identität. Zu einem Problemzusammenhang in der deutschen Geschichte des 19. Jahrhunderts," in Berding, et al., eds., *Vom Staat des Ancien Regimes*, 213–24.

"Der Kampf um die Geschworenengerichte im Vormärz," in Wehler, ed., *Sozialgeschichte Heute*, 148–61.

Böckenförde, Ernst-Wolfgang. "The Origin and Development of the Concept of the *Rechtsstaat*," in idem, *State, Society and Liberty*, 47–70.

Boehnert, Gunnar C. "The Jurists in the SS-Führerkorps, 1925–1939," in Hirschfeld and Kettenacker, eds., *Der "Führerstaat*," 361–74.

Boigeol, Anne. "The French Bar: The Difficulties of Unifying a Divided Profession," in Abel and Lewis, eds., *Lawyers in Society*. Vol. 2: *The Civil Law World*, 258–94.

Bouwsma, William J. "Lawyers and Early Modern Culture." *American Historical Review* 78 (1973): 303–27.

Breuilly, John. "State-Building, Modernization and Liberalism from the Late Eighteenth Century to Unification: German Peculiarities." *European History Quarterly* 22 (1992): 257–84.

Caplan, Jane. "Profession as Vocation: The German Civil Service," in Cocks and Jarausch, eds., *German Professions, 1800–1950*, 163–82.

Charlé, Christophe. "Professionen und Intellektuelle. Die liberalen Berufe in Frankreich zwischen Politik und Wirtschaft (1830–1900)," in Siegrist, ed., *Bürgerliche Berufe*, 127–44.

Childers, Thomas. "The Social Language of Politics in Germany: The Sociology of Political Discourse in the Weimar Republic." *American Historical Review* 95 (1990): 331–58.

Conrad, Hermann. "Der deutsche Juristentag 1860–1960," in Ernst von Caemmerer, et al., eds., *Hundert Jahre deutsches Rechtsleben*, I: 1–36.

Conrad, Johannes. "Allgemeine Statistik der Deutschen Universitäten," in Wilhelm Lexis, ed., *Die Deutschen Universitäten*, I: 115–68.

Conze, Werner, and Jürgen Kocka. "Einleitung," in idem, *Bildungsbürgertum im 19. Jahrhundert*, 9–26.

Cook, J. J. "The Judicial System of Germany." *The Juridical Review. A Journal of Legal and Political Science* 1 (1889): 70–80, 184–92, 298–306.

Craig, John E. "Higher Education and Social Mobility in Germany," in Jarausch, ed., *The Transformation of Higher Learning*, 219–44.

Dahrendorf, Ralf. "Die Ausbildung einer Elite. Die deutsche Oberschicht und die juristischen Fakultäten." *Der Monat* 14 (1962): 15–26.

"Deutsche Richter. Ein Beitrag zur Soziologie der Oberschicht," in idem, *Gesellschaft und Freiheit*, 176–96.

Davis, Horace B. "The German Labor Courts," *Political Science Quarterly* 44 (1929): 397–420.

Dawson, Philip. "The Bourgeoisie de Robe in 1789." *French Historical Studies* 4 (1965): 1–21.

Demeter, Karl. "Die soziale Schichtung des deutschen Parlaments seit 1848." *Vierteljahrschrift für Sozial- und Wirtschaftsgeschichte* 39 (1952): 1–29.

Dilcher, Gerhard. "Das Gesellschaftsbild der Rechtswissenschaft und die soziale Frage," in Vondung, ed., *Das wilhelminische Bildungsbürgertum*, 53–66.

"Die preußischen Juristen und die Staatsprüfungen. Zur Entwicklung der juristischen Professionalisierung im 18. Jahrhundert," in Kroeschell, ed., *Festschrift für Hans Thieme*, 295–305.

Dorn, Walter L. "The Prussian Bureaucracy in the Eighteenth Century." *Political Science Quarterly*, Part I, 46 (1931): 403–23; Part II, 47 (1932): 75–94; Part IV, 47 (1932): 259–73.

Eggert, Wolfgang. "Jüdische Rechtsanwälte und Richter im Deutschland des 19. und 20. Jahrhunderts." *Historische Mitteilungen* 2 (1989): 79–115.

Eley, Geoff. "Nations, Politics, and Political Cultures: Placing Habermas in the Nineteenth Century," in Calhoun, ed., *Habermas and the Public Sphere*, 289–339.

"Notable Politics, the Crisis of German Liberalism, and the Electoral Transition of the 1890s," in Jarausch and Jones, eds., *In Search of a Liberal Germany*, 187–216.

Erffa, Margarethe Freiin von, and Ingeborg Richarz-Simons, "Der weibliche Rechtsanwalt," in Julius Magnus, ed., *Die Rechtsanwaltschaft*, 471–85.

Ernst, C. W. "Law Reforms in Germany." *American Law Review* 18 (1884): 801–13.

Evans, Richard J. "Introduction: Wilhelm II's Germany and the Historians," in idem, ed., *Society and Politics*, 11–39.

"The Myth of Germany's Missing Revolution." *New Left Review* 149 (1985): 67–94.

Ewing, Sally. "Formal Justice and the Spirit of Capitalism: Max Weber's Sociology of Law." *Law and Social Inquiry* 21 (1987): 487–512.

Fletcher, Roger. "Recent Developments in West German Historiography: The Bielefeld School and Its Critics." *German Studies Review* 7 (1984): 451–80.

Freidson, Elliot. "Are Professions Necessary?," in Haskell, ed., *The Authority of Experts*, 4–27.

Friedrich, Carl J. "The Continental Tradition of Training Administrators in Law and Jurisprudence." *Journal of Modern History* 11 (1939): 133–42.

Führ, Christoph. "Gelehrter Schulmann – Oberlehrer – Studienrat. Zum sozialen Aufstieg der Philologen," in Conze and Kocka, eds., *Bildungsbürgertum im 19. Jahrhundert*, 417–57.

Fuller, Paul. "The French Bar." *Yale Law Journal* 16 (1907): 457–70.

Gale, Susan Gaylord. "A Very German Legal Science: Savigny and the Historical School." *Stanford Journal of International Law* 18 (1982): 123–46.

Gall, Lothar. "Liberalismus und 'bürgerliche Gesellschaft'. Zu Charakter und Entwicklung der liberalen Bewegung in Deutschland," in idem, ed., *Liberalismus*, 162–86.

Gerber, David J. "Idea-Systems in Law: Images of Nineteenth-Century Germany." *Law and History Review* 10 (1992): 153–67.

Gispen, C. W. R. "German Engineers and American Social Theory: Historical Perspectives on Professionalization." *Comparative Studies in Society and History* 30 (1988): 550–74.

Göhmann, Rudolf. "150 Jahre Advokaten- und Rechtsanwaltsverein Hannover (1831–1981) – Ein Bericht zum 150. Gründungstag am 1.7. 1981," in Rechtsanwaltsverein Hannover, ed., *Festschrift zur 150-Jahr-Feier*, 1–41.

Gordon, Robert W. "Critical Legal Histories." *Stanford Law Review* 36 (1984): 57–125.

Grimm, Dieter. "Bürgerlichkeit im Recht," in Kocka, ed., *Bürgertum im 19. Jahrhundert*, I:149–88, and in Grimm, *Recht und Staat der bürgerlichen Gesellschaft*, 11–50.

"Bürgerlichkeit im Recht," in Kocka, ed., *Bürger und Bürgerlichkeit*, 149–88.

H. "The Continental Bar – State of the Profession in France, Germany, Spain, and Italy." *The Law Magazine or, Quarterly Review of Jurisprudence* 13 (1835): 287–309.

Hagan, William W. "Descent of the *Sonderweg*: Hans Rosenberg's History of Old-Regime Prussia." *Central European History* 24 (1991): 24–50.

Hahn, Erich J. C. "Rudolf Gneist and the Prussian Rechtsstaat: 1862–1878." *Journal of Modern History* 49 (1977): D1361–81.

Hamann, Manfred. "Politische Kräfte in der Provinz Hannover am Vorabend des Ersten Weltkrieges," in Brosius and Lust, eds., *Beiträge zur Niedersächsischen Landesgeschichte*, 421–53.

"Politische Kräfte und Spannungen in der Provinz Hannover um 1880." *Niedersächsisches Jahrbuch für Landesgeschichte* 53 (1981): 1–40.

Hamerow, Theodore S. "Guilt, Redemption, and Writing German History." *American Historical Review* 88 (1983): 53–72.

Hardtwig, Wolfgang. "Großstadt und Bürgerlichkeit in der politischen Ordnungdes Kaiserreichs," in Gall, ed. *Stadt und Burgertum*, 19–64.

"Strukturmerkmale und Entwicklungstendenzen des Vereinswesens in Deutschland 1789–1848," in Dann, ed., *Vereinswesen und bürgerliche Gesellschaft*, 11–50.

Harris, James F. "Eduard Lasker and Compromise Liberalism." *Journal of Modern History* 42 (1970): 342–60.

Hattenhauer, Hans. "Richterleitbilder im 19. und 20. Jahrhundert," in Dreier and Sellert, eds., *Recht und Justiz*, 9–33.

"Vom Reichsjustizamt zum Bundesministerium der Justiz," in Bundesministerium der Justiz, ed., *Vom Reichsjustizamt*, 9–118.

Heile, Bernhard. "Die Zeit von 1733 bis 1866," in *Festschrift zum 275jährigen Bestehen des Oberlandesgerichts Celle*, 63–111.

Heydeloff, Rudolf. "Staranwalt der Rechtsextremisten. Walter Luetgebrune in der Weimarer Republik." *Vierteljahrshefte für Zeitgeschichte* 32 (1984): 373–421.

Hueber, Alfons. "Das Vereinsrecht im Deutschland des 19. Jahrhunderts," in Dann, ed., *Vereinswesen und bürgerliche Gesellschaft*, 115–32.

Huerkamp, Claudia. "Frauen, Universitäten und Bildungsbürgertum. Zur Lage studierender Frauen 1900–1930," in Siegrist, *Bürgerlich Berufe*, 200–22.

Hüttenberger, Peter. "Interessenvertretung und Lobbyismus im Dritten Reich," in Hirschfeld and Kettenacker, eds., *Der "Führerstaat,"* 429–57.

Iggers, Georg. "Introduction," in idem, ed., *The Social History of Politics*, 1–48.

Izenberg, Gerald, N. "Die 'Aristokratisierung' der bürgerlichen Kultur im 19. Jahrhundert," in Hohendahl and Lützeler, eds., *Legitimationskrisen*, 233–44.

Jarausch, Konrad H. "The Crisis of German Professions 1918–33," *Journal of Contemporary History* 20 (1985): 379–98.

"The Decline of Liberal Professionalism: Reflections on the Social Erosion of German Liberalism, 1867–1933," in Jarausch and Jones, eds., *In Search of a Liberal Germany*, 261–86.

"Illiberalism and Beyond: German History in Search of a Paradigm." *Journal of Modern History* 55 (1983): 268–84.

"Jewish Lawyers in Germany, 1848–1938 – The Disintegration of a Profession." *Yearbook Leo Baeck Institute* 36 (1991): 171–90.

"Die Krise des deutschen Bildungsbürgertums im ersten Drittel des 20. Jahrhunderts," in Kocka, ed., *Bildungsbürgertum im 19. Jahrhundert. Teil IV*, 180–205.

"The Perils of Professionalism: Lawyers, Teachers, and Engineers in Nazi Germany," *German Studies Review* 9 (1986): 107–37.

"Die unfreien Professionen. Überlegungen zu den Wandlungsprozessen im deutschen Bildungsbürgertum 1900–1950," in Kocka, ed. *Bürgertum im 19. Jahrhundert*, II:124–46.

Jarausch, Konrad H., and Larry Eugene Jones. "German Liberalism Reconsidered: Inevitable Decline, Bourgeois Hegemony, or Partial Achievement?" in Jarausch and Jones, eds., *In Search of a Liberal Germany*, 1–23.

Jessen, Peter. "Die Gründung des Oberappellationsgerichts und sein Wirken in der ersten Zeit," in *Festschrift zum 275jährigen Bestehen des Oberlandesgerichts Celle*, 21–59.

John, Michael. "Associational Life and the Development of Liberalism in Hanover, 1848–66," in Jarausch and Jones, eds., *In Search of a Liberal Germany*, 161–85.

"Between Estate and Profession: Lawyers and the Development of the Legal Profession in Nineteenth-Century Germany," in Blackbourn and Evans, eds., *The German Bourgeoisie*, 162–97.

"The Peculiarities of the German State: Bourgeois Law and Society in the Imperial Era." *Past and Present* 119 (May 1988): 105–31.

"The Politics of Legal Unity in Germany, 1870–1897." *Historical Journal* 28 (1985): 341–55.

Kagan, Richard L. "Law Students and Legal Careers in Eighteenth-Century France." *Past and Present* 68 (1975): 38–72.

Kantorowicz, Hermann, "Savigny and the Historical School of Law," *The Law Quarterly Review* 53 (1937): 326–43.

Karpik, Lucien. "Lawyers and Politics in France, 1814–1950: The State, the Market, and the Public." *Law and Social Inquiry* 13 (1988): 707–36.

Kater, Michael H. "Professionalization and Socialization of Physicians in Wilhelmine and Weimar Germany." *Journal of Contemporary History* 20 (1985): 677–701.

Kehr, Eckart. "Das soziale System der Reaktion in Preußen unter dem Ministerium Puttkamer," in idem, *Der Primat der Innenpolitik*, 64–86.

Kocka, Jürgen. "Bildungsbürgertum – Gesellschaftliche Formation oder Historikerkonstrukt?," in idem, ed., *Bildungsbürgertum im 19. Jahrhundert. Teil IV*, 9–20.

"'Bürgertum' and Professions in the Nineteenth Century: Two Alternative Approaches," in Burrage and Torstendahl, eds., *Professions in Theory and History*, 62–74.

"Bürgertum und bürgerliche Gesellschaft im 19. Jahrhundert. Europäische Entwicklungen und deutsche Eigenarten," in idem, ed., *Bürgertum im 19. Jahrhundert*, I:11–76.

"Bürgertum und Bürgerlichkeit als Probleme der deutschen Geschichte vom späten 18. zum frühen 20. Jahrhundert," in idem, ed., *Bürger und Bürgerlichkeit*, 21–63.

"Der 'deutsche Sonderweg' in der Diskussion," *German Studies Review* 5 (1982): 365–79.

"German History before Hitler: The Debate about the German *Sonderweg*." *Journal of Contemporary History* 23 (1988): 3–16.

Kraehe, Enno E. "Practical Politics in the German Confederation: Bismarck and the Commercial Code." *Journal of Modern History* 25 (1953): 13–24.

Kregel, Volker. "Die Personalpolitik der Justiz im 'Dritten Reich' am Beispiel des Oberlandesgerichts Celle," in Dreier and Sellert, eds., *Recht und Justiz*, 226–40.

Kroeschell, Karl. "Geschichte der Advokatur in welfischen Landen," in Ernst Benda, et al., eds., *Hundert Jahre Rechtsanwaltskammer*, 1–24.

Landau, Peter. "Die Reichsjustizgesetze von 1879 und die deutsche Rechtseinheit," in Bundesministerium der Justiz, ed., *Vom Reichsjustizamt zum Bundesministerium der Justiz*, 161–211.

"Schwurgerichte und Schöffengerichte in Deutschland im 19. Jahrhundert bis 1870," in Schioppa, ed., *The Trial Jury*, 241–304.

Langewiesche, Dieter. "Bildungsbürgertum und Liberalismus im 19. Jahrhundert," in Kocka, ed., *Bildungsbürgertum im 19. Jahrhundert. Teil IV*, 95–121.

Laufke, Franz. "Der deutsche Bund und die Zivilgesetzgebung," in Mikat, ed., *Festschrift Herbert Nottarp*, 1–57.

La Vopa, Anthony J. "Conceiving a Public: Ideas and Society in Eighteenth-Century Europe." *Journal of Modern History* 64 (1992): 79–116.

Ledford, Kenneth F. "Conflict within the Legal Profession: Simultaneous Admission and the German Bar 1903–1927," in Cocks and Jarausch, eds., *German Professions, 1800–1950*, 252–69.

"German Lawyers and the State in the Weimar Republic," *Law and History Review* 13 (1995): 317–49.

"Lawyers and the Limits of Liberalism: The German Bar in the Weimar Republic," in Halliday and Karpik, eds., *Politics Matter*.

"Lawyers, Liberalism, and Procedure: The Imperial Justice Laws of 1877–79." *Central European History* 26 (1993): 165–93.

Lenthe, Gerhard von. "Die Rechtsanwaltschaft am Oberlandesgericht Celle," in *250 Jahre Oberlandesgericht Celle*, 179–208.

Lepsius, M. Rainer. "Zur Soziologie des Bürgertums und der Bürgerlich-keit," in Kocka, ed., *Bürger und Bürgerlichkeit*, 79–100.

Linde, Hans. "Das Königreich Hannover an der Schwelle des Industrie-zeitalters." *Neues Archiv für Niedersachsen*, Heft 24 (1951) 413–43. Bremen-Horn: Walter Dorn Verlag.

Lühr, Karl. "Die ersten zweihundert Jahre," in *250 Jahre Oberlandesgericht Celle 1711–1961*, 1–61.

Lundgreen, Peter. "Wissen und Bürgertum. Skizze eines historischen Ver-gleichs zwischen Preußen/Deutschland, Frankreich, England und den USA, 18.–20. Jahrhundert," in Siegrist, ed., *Bürgerliche Berufe*, 106–24.

"Zur Konstituierung des 'Bildungsbürgertums': Berufs- und Bildungsaus-lese der Akademiker in Preußen," in Conze and Kocka, eds., *Bildungsbürgertum im 19. Jahrhundert*, 79–108.

Mayer, Arno J. "The Lower Middle Class as Historical Problem." *Journal of Modern History* 47 (1975): 409–36.

McClelland, Charles E. "Zur Professionalisierung der akademischen Berufe im Deutschland," in Conze and Kocka, eds., *Bildungsbürgertum im 19. Jahrhundert*, 233–47.

Moeller, Robert G. "The Kaiserreich Recast? Continuity and Change in Modern German Historiography." *Journal of Social History* 17 (1984): 655–83.

Mok, Albert L. "Alte und neue Professionen." *Kölner Zeitschrift für Sozio-logie und Sozialpsychologie* 21 (1969): 770–82.

Mommsen, Hans. "Die Auflösung des Bürgertums seit dem späten 19. Jahrhunderts," in Jürgen Kocka, ed., *Bürger und Bürgerlichkeit*, 288–315.

Mosse, Werner E. "Albert Mosse: A Jewish Judge in Imperial Germany." *Leo Baeck Institute Year Book* 28 (1983): 169–84.

Nipperdey, Thomas. "Verein als soziale Struktur im späten 18. und frühen 19. Jahrhundert," in Boockmann, et al., eds., *Geschichtswissenschaft und Vereinswesen*, 1–44.

O'Boyle, Lenore. "The Democratic Left in Germany, 1848." *Journal of Mod-ern History* 33 (1961): 374–83.

"The Middle Classes in Western Europe, 1815–1848." *American Historical Review* 71 (1966): 826–45.

Parsons, Talcott. "The Professions and Social Structure," in idem, *Essays in Sociological Theory*, 34–49.

"A Sociologist Looks at the Legal Profession," in idem, *Essays in Sociologi-cal Theory*, 370–85.

Pfeiffer, Gerd. "Die freie Anwaltschaft im Rechtsstaat," in Benda, et al., eds., *Hundert Jahre Rechtsanwaltskammern*, 57–78.

Pflanze, Otto. "Juridical and Political Responsibility in Nineteenth-Century Germany," in Krieger and Stern, eds., *The Responsibility of Power*, 162–82.

Prud'hon, Pierre, and Jean Appleton. "Frankreich," in Julius Magnus, ed., *Die Anwaltschaft*. Leipzig: W. Moeser, 1929, 92–100.

Pulzer, Peter. "Religion and Judicial Appointments in Germany, 1869–1918." *Yearbook of the Leo Baeck Institute* 28 (1983): 185–204.

Ranieri, Filippo. "From Status to Profession: The Professionalisation of Lawyers as a Research Field in Modern European Legal History." *Journal of Legal History* 10 (1989): 180–90.

"Vom Stand zum Beruf. Die Professionalisierung des Juristenstandes als Forschungsaufgabe der europäischen Rechtsgeschichte der Neuzeit." *Ius Commune* 13 (1985): 83–105.

Reifner, Udo. "The Bar in the Third Reich: Anti-Semitism and the Decline of Liberal Advocacy." *McGill Law Journal* 32 (1986): 96–124.

Reimann, Mathias. "Nineteenth-Century German Legal Science." *Boston College Law Review* 31 (1990): 837–97.

Retallack, James N. "Social History with a Vengeance? Some Reactions to H.-U. Wehler's 'Das Deutsche Kaiserreich." *German Studies Review* 7 (1984): 423–50.

Reulecke, Jürgen. "Bildungsbürgertum und Kommunalpolitik im 19. Jahrhundert,'" in Kocka, ed., *Bildungsbürgertum im 19. Jahrhundert, Teil IV*, 122–45.

Rheinstein, Max. Review of Weyrauch, Walter O. *The Personality of Lawyers*. *Yale Law Journal* 74 (1965): 1331–4.

Riedel, Manfred. "Bürger, Staatsbürger, Bürgertum," in Brunner, et al., eds., *Geschichtliche Grundbegriffe*, I: 672–725.

Roscher, Theodor. "Gerichtsverfassung und Anwaltschaft im einstmaligen Kurstaat und Königreich Hannover," in *Festschrift zum siebzehnten Deutschen Anwaltstage. Hannover 1905*. Hannover: Göhmannschen Buchdruckerei, 1905.

Rottleuthner, Hubert. "Die gebrochene Bürgerlichkeit einer Scheinprofession. Zur Situation der deutschen Richterschaft zu Beginn des 20. Jahrhunderts," in Siegrist, ed., *Bürgerliche Berufe*, 145–73.

Rueschemeyer, Dietrich. "Bourgeoisie, Staat und Bildungsbürgertum. Idealtypische Modelle für die vergleichende Erforschung von Bürgertum und Bürgerlichkeit," in Kocka, ed., *Bürger und Bürgerlichkeit*, 101–20.

"Comparing Legal Professions Cross-nationally: from a Professions-centered to a State-centered Approach." *American Bar Foundation Research Journal* 12 (1986): 415–46.

"Doctors and Lawyers: A Comment on the Theory of the Professions." *Canadian Review of Sociology and Anthropology* 1 (1964): 17–30.

"Professional Autonomy and the Social Control of Expertise," in Dingwall and Lewis, *Sociology of the Professions*, 38–58.

"Professionalisierung. Theoretische Probleme für die vergleichende Geschichtsforschung." *Geschichte und Gesellschaft* 6 (1980): 311–325.

Sachße, Wieland. "Lebensverhältnisse und Lebensgestaltung der Unterschicht in Göttingen bis 1860. Ein Projektsbericht," in Conze and Engelhardt, eds., *Arbeiterexistenz im 19. Jahrhundert*, 19–45.

Sandel, Michael J. "The Procedural Republic and the Unencumbered Self." *Political Theory* 12 (1984): 81–96; reprinted in Shlomo Avineri and Avner de-Shalit, eds. *Communitarianism and Individualism*. Oxford: Oxford University Press, 1992, 12–28.

Schack, Haimo. "Private Lawyers in Contemporary Society: Germany." *Case Western Reserve Journal of International Law* 25 (1993): 187–205.

Schmid, Peter. "Oberappellationsgericht, Appellationsgericht und Oberlandesgericht in der Zeit von 1866 bis 1933," in *Festschrift zum 275jährigen Bestehen des Oberlandesgerichts Celle*, 113–142.

Schmitt, Hans S. "From Sovereign States to Prussian Provinces: Hanover and Hesse-Nassau, 1866–1871." *Journal of Modern History* 57 (1985): 24–56.

Schröder, Rainer. "Die Richterschaft am Ende des zweiten Kaiserreiches unter dem Druck polarer sozialer und politischer Anforderungen," in Buschmann, et al., eds., *Festschrift für Rudolf Gmür*, 201–53.

"Der zivilrechtliche Alltag des Volksgenossen. Beispiele aus der Praxis des Oberlandesgerichts Celle im Dritten Reich," in Diestelkamp and Stolleis, eds., *Justizalltag*, 39–62.

Schubert, Werner. "Der Ausbau der Rechtseinheit unter dem Norddeutschen Bund. Zur Entstehung des Strafgesetzbuchs von 1870 unter besonderer Berücksichtigung des Strafensystems," in Buschmann, *Festschrift für Rudolf Gmür*, 149–89.

"Preußens Pläne zur Vereinheitlichung des Zivilrechts nach der Reichsgründung." *Zeitschrift der Savigny-Stiftung für Rechtsgeschichte, Germanistische Abteilung* 96 (1979): 243–56.

"Die unveröffentlichten Quellen zu den Reichsjustizgesetzen." *Juristenzeitung* 33 (1978): 98–102.

Sellert, Wolfgang. "Die Reichsjustizgesetze von 1877 – Ein gedenkwürdiges Ereignis?" *Juristische Schulung. Zeitschrift für Studium und Ausbildung* 17 (1977): 781–9.

Shaw, Gisela. "East German 'Rechtsanwälte' and German Unification." *German Life and Letters* 47 (1994): 211–31.

Shklar, Judith. "Political Theory and the Rule of Law," in Hutchinson and Monahan, eds., *The Rule of Law*, 1–16.

Siegrist, Hannes. "Bürgerliche Berufe. Die Professionen und das Bürgertum," in idem, ed., *Bürgerliche Berufe*, 11–48.

"Gebremste Professionalisierung – Das Beispiel der Schweizer Rechtsanwaltschaft im Vergleich zu Frankreich und Deutschland im 19. und frühen 20. Jahrhundert," in Conze and Kocka, *Bildungsbürgertum im 19. Jahrhundert*, 301–31.

"Professionalization with the Brakes On: The Legal Profession in Switzerland, France and Germany in the Nineteenth and Early Twentieth Centuries." *Comparative Social Research* 9 (1986): 267–98.

"Public Office or Free Profession? German Attorneys in the Nineteenth and Early Twentieth Centuries," in Cocks and Jarausch, eds., *German Professions, 1800–1950*, 46–65.

"Die Rechtsanwälte und das Bürgertum. Deutschland, die Schweiz und Italien im 19. Jahrhundert," in Kocka, ed., *Bürgertum im 19. Jahrhundert*, II:92–123.

Stephenson, Jill. "Women and the Professions in Germany, 1900–1945," in Cocks and Jarausch, eds., *German Professions, 1800–1950*, 270–88.

Stokes, Lawrence D. "Professionals and National Socialism: The Case Histories of a Small-Town Lawyer and Physician, 1918–1945." *German Studies Review* 8 (1985): 449–80.

Strandmann, Hartmut Pogge von. "The Liberal Power Monopoly in the Cities of Imperial Germany," in Jones and Retallack, eds., *Elections, Mass Politics, and Social Change*, 93–117.

Summers, Robert S. "A Formal Theory of the Rule of Law." *Ratio Juris* 6 (1993): 127–42.

Tenfelde, Klaus. "Die Entfaltung des Vereinswesens während der Industriellen Revolution in Deutschland (1850–1873)," in Dann, ed., *Vereinswesen und bürgerliche Gesellschaft*, 55–114.

Titze, Hartmut. "Enrollment Expansion and Academic Overcrowding in Germany," in Jarausch, ed., *The Transformation of Higher Learning*, 57–88.

"Die zyklische Überproduktion von Akademikern im 19. und 20. Jahrhundert." *Geschichte und Gesellschaft* 10 (1984): 92–121.

Trubek, David M. "Max Weber on Law and the Rise of Capitalism." *Wisconsin Law Review* 1972: 720–53.

"Reconstructing Max Weber's Sociology of Law." *Stanford Law Review* 37 (1985): 919–36.

Turner, R. S. "The *Bildungsbürgertum* and the Learned Professions in Prussia, 1770–1830." *Histoire sociale – Social History* 13 (1980): 105–35.

Vondung, Klaus. "Zur Lage der Gebildeten in der wilhelminischen Zeit," in idem, *Das wilhelminische Bildungsbürgertum*, 20–33.

Wadle, Elmar. "Der Zollverein und die deutsche Rechtseinheit." *Zeitschrift der Savigny-Stiftung für Rechtsgeschichte, Germanistische Abteilung* 102 (1985): 99–129.

Waldron, Jeremy. "The Rule of Law in Contemporary Liberal Theory." *Ratio Juris* 2 (1989): 79–96.

Weber, Max. "Class, Status, and Party," in Gerth and Mills, eds., *From Max Weber*, 180–95.

"Politics as a Vocation," in Gerth and Mills, eds., *From Max Weber*, 77–128.

"Politik als Beruf," in *Gesammelte Politische Schriften*, 505–60.

Wehler, Hans-Ulrich. "'Deutscher Sonderweg' oder allgemeine Probleme der westlichen Kapitalismus?," in idem, *Preußen ist wieder chic . . . ,* 19–32.

"Deutsches Bildungsbürgertum in vergleichender Perspektive – Elemente eines 'Sonderwegs'?," in Kocka, ed., *Bildungsbürgertum im 19. Jahrhundert. Teil IV,* 215–37.

"Wie bürgerlich war das Deutsche Kaiserreich?," in Jürgen Kocka, ed., *Bürger und Bürgerlichkeit,* 243–80.

Wesenberg, Gerhard. "Die Paulskirche und die Kodifikationsfrage (Zu §64 der Paulskirchenverfassung)." *Zeitschrift der Savigny-Stiftung für Rechtsgeschichte, Germanistische Abteilung* 72 (1955): 359–65.

Westphal, Kenneth. "The basic context and structure of Hegel's *Philosophy of Right,*" in Beiser, ed., *Cambridge Companion to Hegel,* 234–69.

Willig, Kenneth C. H. "The Bar in the Third Reich." *American Journal of Legal History* 20 (1976): 1–14.

Woloch, Isser. "The Fall and Resurrection of the Civil Bar, 1789–1820s." *French Historical Studies* 15 (1987):241–62.

Index